THE
BOOK OF THE
HORSE

THE
BOOK OF THE
HORSE

G P PUTNAM'S SONS, NEW YORK

Consultant Editor
Pamela Macgregor-Morris
Technical Consultant
Jane Starkey

Contributing Editors
Peter Churchill · W.S. Crook · Jane Kidd · Dr Bruce Macfadden B.S. PhD.
Pamela Macgregor-Morris · Jonathan Powell · Fiona Scott
Colin Vogel · Toni Webber

A QED BOOK

Published by G. P. Putnam's Sons
200 Madison Avenue
New York, New York 10016
LCC: 79–84551
SBN: 399–12424–1

Filmset in Britain by Vantage Photosetting Co. Ltd.
Colour origination in Italy by Starf Photolito SRL., Rome
Printed in Hong Kong by Lee Fung Asco Ltd.

80-460

This book was designed and produced by
QED Publishing Limited
32 Kingly Court, London W1
Editorial Director Jeremy Harwood
Art Director Alastair Campbell
Production Director Edward Kinsey
Art Editor David Mallott
Editors Jenny Barling, Marion Casey, Alastair Dougall,
David MacFadyen
Art and editorial co-ordinator Heather Jackson
Designer Marnie Searchwell
Illustrators Kai Choi, Harry Clow, Christopher Forsey,
Tony Graham, Rory Kee, Elaine Keenan, Edwina Keene,
·Abdul Aziz Khan, Kathleen McDougall, John Woodcock,
Clive Haybal, Martin Woodford, Kathy Wyatt, Jim Marks
Photographers Mike Busselle, Mike Fear, Colin Maher,
Jay Swallow, Jon Wyand
Picture Research Maggie Colbeck, Linda Proud
Paste up Jean Kelly

QED would like to thank the many individuals and organisations who have helped in the preparation of this book. Invaluable assistance was given by: Mr H. J. Cooper F.W.C.F.; Gill Ennis; Melanie Gee; Diana James; Mr Martin Kiley of the Santa Sleigh Stud; Mr A. S. Laing, Hon. Sec. of the Vale of Aylesbury Hunt; Leslie Lane; Mr Lanigan of the Coolmore Stud; Sheana MacFadyean; Marcia McCloud; Patricia Monaham; Bill Nicholls; Sue Peach; Carol Rodwell; Warner Shepherd, Leicester; Miss Pauline Voss and Mrs G. M. Taylor of the Huntersfield Farm Riding Centre, Sutton, Surrey; The British Horse Society; The British Show Jumping Association; The Department of Palaeontology at the Natural History Museum, London; The Diamond Centre for the Handicapped, Carshalton, Surrey; The National Equestrian Centre, Kenilworth, Warks.; Spillers Ltd.; The Riding Department of Austin Reed, Regent St. London W1; The Royal College Veterinary Library; The Worshipful Company of Farriers; Rosalind Billingham.

Contents

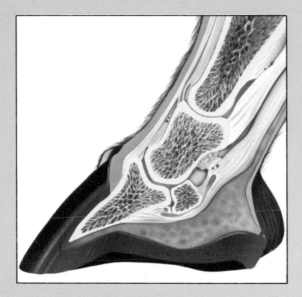

Foreword

by Lucinda Prior-Palmer

Lucinda Prior-Palmer, with her horse 'Be Fair', after winning the 1975 European Individual Three Day Event Championship. She is one of the most distinguished and successful event riders in the world.

It is with genuine appreciation that I write the foreword to this book. The Book of the Horse is, I believe, revolutionary of its kind. It is the first time that I have read an encyclopedia of the horse which lays out in such a modern and captivating formula all the various subjects connected with this, the greatest of all animals.

A great deal of magic is attached to the horse. If you like him, you love him. There is an obsessive attraction in his personality, his adroitness and courage and in his ability to reciprocate human communication. Such qualities go unremarked by non-believers. They may acknowledge that one end bites and the other kicks, but it seems as if they do not wish to understand more than that. More the pity for them; they will never know what a wealth of fascination and happiness they are missing.

The Book of the Horse serves a dual purpose. I personally find it intriguing, as it gives a wealth of vital information, precisely and imaginatively presented. Many fascinating pictures and illustrations take the place of the cumbersome mass of text normally associated with instructional literature. Following the modern trend of thought that the mind retains visual images better than verbal ones, the practical sections contain many lessons and rules of equitation in accurate and appealing diagrams. Anyone wishing to learn about horses from the beginning would be well advised to start their pursuit of knowledge here.

One question remains to be answered. Books on horses exist in abundance and have done so for many years. Why? Why do people read so much about horses, especially when many have very little connection with them?

The answer is anyone's guess, but I would like to believe that it represents a tribute to the animal that has featured through the ages with such vital importance. From the earliest days of recorded history, the horse took part in sport and war; for thousands of years he was the everyday means of transport. Later, with the advent of mechanization, a stronger emphasis was placed on sport and leisure.

There is no animal in the world as versatile. Horses are involved in many different spheres – polo, jousting, steeplechasing, flat racing and hunting in many different forms being but a few. The horse takes part in no less than four separate Olympic contests – show jumping, dressage, pentathlon and horse trials. Such extensive involvement, even though his use as a means of transport has declined, surely explains at least a part of the reason why so many people are interested in reading about the horse.

Many spectators must watch in awe and envy the top-class exponents of equestrian sport. Among them Lester Piggott and Eddie Macken are two artists who spring immediately to mind. They have come as near to perfection as nature will permit. Such heights seem unattainable. To some, it may seem barely worth learning or continuing to ride. The maestros have obviously been born with something that normal people do not possess. That, however, I do not believe. As the introduction to the chapter on Basic Riding states: 'The key to learning to ride is basically one of confidence.' The rider needs faith in his or her ability to communicate with the horse. Equally, the horse needs such confidence in the rider.

Confidence and communication. This forms the basis of success with horses from the beginning right through to the star of the show. It may be many years before such confidence takes sufficient root. Work, perseverance and patience are the secret of the search. Luck, of course, is a transient quantity important to everyone in anything they undertake.

Every step is worth it, even though it is frequently two steps forward and one step back. It is an education in life as well as in horses, and the learning lasts forever.

Horses carry the history of mankind on their backs. If you should find one is carrying you as well, acknowledge your good fortune and indeed your honour. When trust and respect, the foundation rock of any satisfactory partnership, is formed between you and your horse, an unexpected dimension will be added to your life.

Chapter One

The origins of the horse

Man's partnership with the horse dates back some 5,000 years or so to the time when the animal was first domesticated in Asia. However, the history of horses themselves goes much further back than that – to the remote prehistoric past. The present-day horse species – these include the domestic horse and its close relatives, the zebras, asses, kiang and Przewalski's horse – are only the remains of a once much bigger collection belonging to the group, or genus, *Equus* that lived during the Ice Age, or Pleistocene Epoch. Many of these species became extinct at the end of the Pleistocene some 12,000 to 15,000 years ago.

But even the Pleistocene is not the starting point for horse history. In fact, *Equus* was preceded by a spectacular history of numerous kinds of fossil horses spanning some 55 million years of geological time. The story of this evolutionary process, leading up to the present-day *Equus*, is the theme of this chapter.

Palaeontologists and horses

The major source of knowledge as far as the evolution of the horse is concerned is based on the very rich fossil deposits of western North America. However, the story begins during the first half of the nineteenth century in England. There, in 1840, the great British palaeontologist Sir Richard Owen was the first to describe a genus of fossil horse, to which he gave the name *Hyracotherium*. This horse had been collected the previous year from the Eocene clay deposits that surround London; these are about 55 million years old.

In the latter half of the nineteenth century, the focus of the science switched to North America, with the foundation of many of the now prominent natural history museums there. The establishment of these museums increased public interest in palaeontology and numerous expeditions were sent out by them to explore and collect the rich fossil deposits in the west. As a result, numerous fossil horses were collected and sent back to the museums for study by some of the founders of North American palaeontology. Such early studies were very influential; for example, they had a profound influence on the acceptance of Darwin's Theory of Evolution, because of the palaeontological support they provided for it.

One of the most prominent students of horse evolution during the second half of the nineteenth century was O. C. Marsh, the Professor of Palaeontology at Yale University. The Yale expeditions to western North America were frequently both exciting and successful, and, as a result, one of the largest collections of fossil horses was amassed there.

In these studies, Marsh was aided by fellow scientists such as Oscar Harger, Max Schlos-

The British palaeontologist Sir Richard Owen. In 1840, he discovered and described the first genus of fossil horse.

ser, George Baur and Samuel Wendell Williston – all of whom worked under him at Yale. He also was aided by the vast private fortune of his uncle, George Peabody; part of this was used to establish the Peabody Museum of Natural History at Yale and part of it financed the various collecting expeditions.

In 1876, Marsh named a new genus of

fossil horse, *Eohippus*, or the 'dawn horse'. During Marsh's time, this was the earliest-known horse collected in North America, and it still is today. It is known from late Paleocene and early Eocene deposits in western North America, which are about 55 million years old – roughly the same age as the Eocene London Clay deposits. During the twentieth century, prominent British and American palaeontologists compared the collections of *Hyracotherium* from England and Europe with those of *Eohippus*, from North America and concluded that these two different names actually represented only one form. Based on the accepted scientific rules, Owen's genus *Hyracotherium*, named in 1840, has priority over Marsh's *Eohippus*, named in 1876. But the name 'eohippus' or the 'dawn horse' is still in general use as the vernacular for *Hyracotherium*.

After the early flowering of studies of horse evolution by Marsh and others, it became apparent that the North American deposits contained the principal links in the history of the subject. As a result, the North American palaeontologists have contributed greatly to the understanding of the group. These major figures include Henry Fairfield Osborn of the American Museum of Natural

Fossil horses, particularly Eohippus or 'dawn horse' (below), played an important part in confirming Charles Darwin's revolutionary theory of evolution, contained in his monumental treatise 'On the Origin of Species' published in 1859. A quarter of a century later in 1876 the great British naturalist Thomas Huxley (near right), a prominent supporter of Darwin's theory, came to the USA and studied the major palaeontological collections of the time.

He was particularly impressed by the collection of fossil horses that O. C. Marsh (far right), Professor of Palaeontology at Yale University, had amassed as a result of his expeditions into western North America. Huxley felt that this collection gave considerable support to Darwin's views.

During a discussion between the two men, Huxley began sketching his idea of the then hypothetical ancestral horse, Eohippus, and then added a rider, which Marsh christened Eohomo ('dawn man'). Later that year, Marsh was able to scientifically describe the horse, if not its rider.

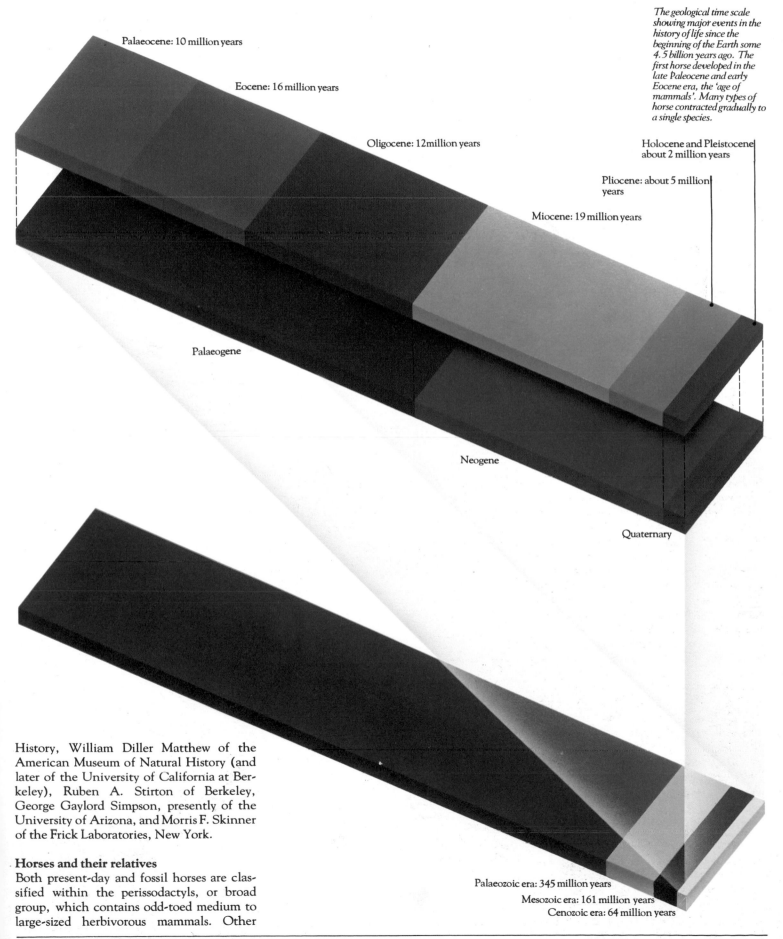

Palaeocene: 10 million years

Eocene: 16 million years

Oligocene: 12million years

The geological time scale showing major events in the history of life since the beginning of the Earth some 4.5 billion years ago. The first horse developed in the late Paleocene and early Eocene era, the 'age of mammals'. Many types of horse contracted gradually to a single species.

Holocene and Pleistocene about 2 million years

Pliocene: about 5 million years

Miocene: 19 million years

Palaeogene

Neogene

Quaternary

Palaeozoic era: 345 million years

Mesozoic era: 161 million years

Cenozoic era: 64 million years

History, William Diller Matthew of the American Museum of Natural History (and later of the University of California at Berkeley), Ruben A. Stirton of Berkeley, George Gaylord Simpson, presently of the University of Arizona, and Morris F. Skinner of the Frick Laboratories, New York.

Horses and their relatives
Both present-day and fossil horses are classified within the perissodactyls, or broad group, which contains odd-toed medium to large-sized herbivorous mammals. Other

odd-toed ungulates (hoofed animals) include the tapirs and rhinoceroses, as well as some extinct groups which include the largest land mammals that ever lived, the brontotheres. These ungulates derive their name from the fact that there are an odd number of digits – five, three or one – on each limb. In contrast, the artiodactyls, or even-toed ungulates, such as cows and sheep, generally have two digits, plus, in many cases, the reduced remains of two additional side toes.

The ancestry of the perissodactyls appears to have been within a wholly extinct group of primitive ungulates called the condylarths. The relatively well-known condylarth *Phenacodus* lived at the same time as *Hyracotherium*, and certain species of *Phenacodus* showed perissodactyl-like trends. However, the actual direct perissodactyl ancestor is not known from older Paleocene deposits.

For a long time, *Hyracotherium* was in fact considered to be the basic stock from which all the major groups of perissodactyls were ultimately descended. In a sense, therefore, *Hyracotherium* was thought to be as much a tapir or rhinoceros as it was a horse. Recent work, based on the structure of *Hyracotherium*'s skull, however, shows that it is indeed a horse.

Four-toed horses

Throughout the history of horse evolution,

Below *The present-day tapir (**left**) and rhinoceros (**right**). Both these animals are close perissodactyl relatives of the horse.*

several general trends can be seen related to the progressive adaptations of different types of horses to their own environment. Most of these have concerned their feeding and locomotion.

As has been seen, the earliest, or 'four-toed', horses, including *Hyracotherium*, first appear in late Paleocene deposits some 55 million years ago and range throughout the Eocene epoch until about 38 million years ago. These horses were already relatively advanced over their condylarth ancestors in many of their skull and skeletal adaptations. They had four digits (meaning both fingers and toes) in their fore foot – hence the name of this group – and three toes in their hind foot. The presence of four digits on the fore

feet of these early horses represented a transitional perissodactyl stage in the reduction from five to three toes – not a trend towards an even number of digits as seen in artiodactyls. Condylarths and many other mammals have five digits on each limb.

Besides a reduction in the number of digits, the four-toed (and later) horses also showed a trend towards elongation of the limbs, allowing for a longer stride while running; this, of course, would be especially important in evading predators. Their skull showed that trends were developing toward specialization for feeding on leafy material, or for browsing. Evidence for this includes the elongation of the molar grinding series of teeth and their deepening, along with a

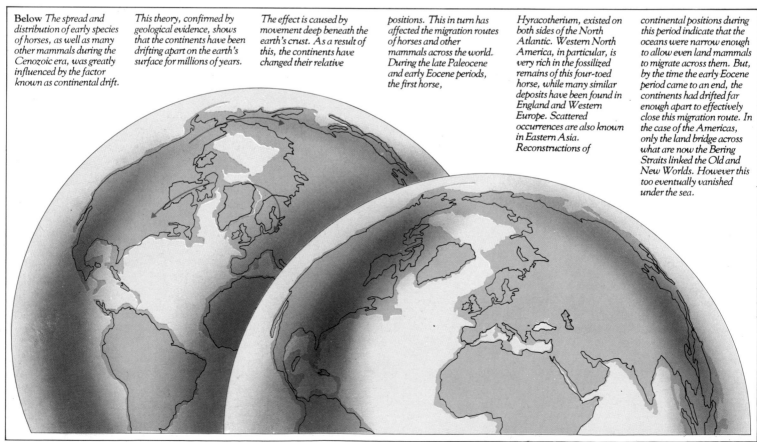

Below *The spread and distribution of early species of horses, as well as many other mammals during the Cenozoic era, was greatly influenced by the factor known as continental drift.*

This theory, confirmed by geological evidence, shows that the continents have been drifting apart on the earth's surface for millions of years.

The effect is caused by movement deep beneath the earth's crust. As a result of this, the continents have changed their relative

positions. This in turn has affected the migration routes of horses and other mammals across the world. During the late Paleocene and early Eocene periods, the first horse,

Hyracotherium, existed on both sides of the North Atlantic. Western North America, in particular, is very rich in the fossilized remains of this four-toed horse, while many similar deposits have been found in England and Western Europe. Scattered occurrences are also known in Eastern Asia. Reconstructions of

continental positions during this period indicate that the oceans were narrow enough to allow even land mammals to migrate across them. But, by the time the early Eocene period came to an end, the continents had drifted far enough apart to effectively close this migration route. In the case of the Americas, only the land bridge across what are now the Bering Straits linked the Old and New Worlds. However this too eventually vanished under the sea.

Above *The Condylarth Phenacodus and* (**right**) *the one-toed horse Dinohippus, from late Miocene deposits of North America.*

deepening of the skull and jaws. In addition, recent and very interesting work on fossil brain endocasts (internal mud fillings) of *Hyracotherium* and other horses has shown that even the earliest horses were progressive in their brain evolution relative to more primitive mammals like condylarths.

The four-toed horses were of very small stature in contrast to *Equus*: for example, *Hyracotherium* was about the size of a fox terrier. Geographically, they were widespread. Though their best-known remains are from North America, they are also well represented in early Eocene deposits in England and western Europe.

This geographical dispersion, together with the great similarity in *Hyracotherium* in the Old and New Worlds, also shared by many other mammals that lived at the same time, implies that it was possible to migrate between these areas before the middle Eocene (about 49 million years ago). One probable migration route at that time was across the then much narrower Atlantic Ocean. After early Eocene times, however, the North Atlantic migration route seems to have been inactive, due to the ever-increasing width of the ocean as a result of continental drift. Furthermore, after about 49 million years ago, it appears that horses and other land mammals could only have crossed between the Old and New Worlds via the land bridge over what are now the Bering Straits.

With the exception of one little-known genus from the western USA, found in early Oligocene sediments, the four-toed horses became extinct some 38 million years ago, at the end of the Eocene period. At this time, one kind of four-toed horse seems to have given rise to primitive three-toed horses.

Three-toed horses
The three-toed horses flourished during the middle portion of the Cenozoic Era. This group consisted of the primitive browsers, feeding on leafy vegetation, and the advanced grazers, feeding on grassy vegetation.

The three-toed browsers, represented by *Mesohippus*, appeared at the beginning of the Oligocene Epoch some 38 million years ago. When contrasted with four-toed horses, these animals show a general increase in size. Obviously, as their name implies, they had three digits on each limb. The fourth digit on the forelimbs had gradually become reduced in the four-toed horses until it was a vestigial splint, or completely lost, as in the three-toed horse. There was also a relative elongation of the limbs.

All of these features, as well as other ones, were indications that the horses were further adapting to a diet of leafy material and a more efficient way of running. During the Oligocene, they were confined to North America; however, during the early Miocene (some 20 million years ago), the anchithere three-toed browsers, represented by *Anchitherium*, also spread to the Old World. The browsers ultimately became extinct about 12 million years ago.

It is the development of three-toed grazers, as well as browsers, that makes the Miocene an important time in the history of horse evolution, for this division represents an important diversification of feeding habits. Both at this time and later during their fossil record, the most important evidence for this change comes from developments in the three-toed grazers' skull and teeth. Grazing generally implies the eating of grasses as opposed to leafy material, and this means that a grazer's dental structure will experience a significant amount of wear, as grasses have a high content of very abrasive minerals. Thus, the early three-toed grazers show an increased trend towards a deepening of their grinding molars, jaws and skulls, which apparently was a response to this then newly-acquired source of food.

The history of the three-toed grazers is located principally in North America, though one very successful member of this group, the hipparions, migrated from the New World to the Old World during the late Miocene. This was some 10 to 11 million years ago. Hipparions were relatively diverse

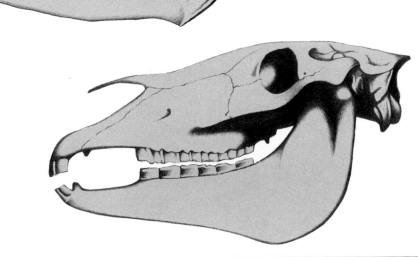

The skull of the fossil horse Hippidion (**above**) *compared with that of present day Equus* (**below**). *The bizarre one-toed Hippidion is chiefly known from Pleistocene deposits in South America. Its chief characteristic was the elongated nasal 'notch' covered with soft tissues and hide, in the top and front of the skull.*

in kinds and very abundant at most late Miocene localities on both sides of the Atlantic. They became extinct during the early Pleistocene.

One-toed horses
One-toed horses first appeared during the middle Miocene, about 15 million years ago. These grazing horses apparently descended from one type of three-toed grazer in North America.

The transition from three toes to one was the result of a gradual reduction in the size of the side digits during the course of evolution, until only the central digit on each limb played any role in running. Advanced one-toed horses, like those of the present day, have small splints on each limb that represent the vestiges of the side toes. The dental structure of the one-toed horses was also advanced over that of their predecessors, with further deepening of the molars, jaw and skull. With some exceptions, there was a general trend towards increased body size relative to most earlier horses.

Most of the fossil groups of one-toed horses were confined to North and Central America, where the horse originated. However, one bizarre group, represented by such forms as *Hippidion*, did migrate into South America during the Pleistocene some two to three million years ago.

It was the one-toed horse *Dinohippus* that was apparently ancestral to the Pleistocene representatives of the present-day genus, *Equus*; these first appear in middle Pliocene deposits in North America between three

and four million years ago. There followed a surprising evolution of different species during both the Pliocene and the Pleistocene, resulting in the ancestors of many of the types of horses that we know today.

Pleistocene representatives of *Equus* were the most geographically widespread of all fossil horses. It appears that about three million years ago they were very abundant in North America and that they also migrated into Central and South America, Asia, Europe and Africa. But, by the end of the last

Ice Age, about 12,000 to 15,000 years ago, many of the fossil species of *Equus* had become extinct and only a few survive today.

The reasons for the extinction of late Pleistocene *Equus* are as enigmatic as for all the other large mammals, including the mammoth, mastodon and sabre-toothed cat, that became extinct at the same time. Some have suggested the reason lay in the change of climate, the influence of man, or perhaps a combination of these and other factors. Whatever the cause, the process was ex-

Above *Early Equus. After many million years of development, this is the ancestor of all present-day horses.*

Right *Przewalski's horse, or the wild horse of Mongolia. The ancestors of this animal were among the first horses to be domesticated in Southern Russia about 3000 BC.*

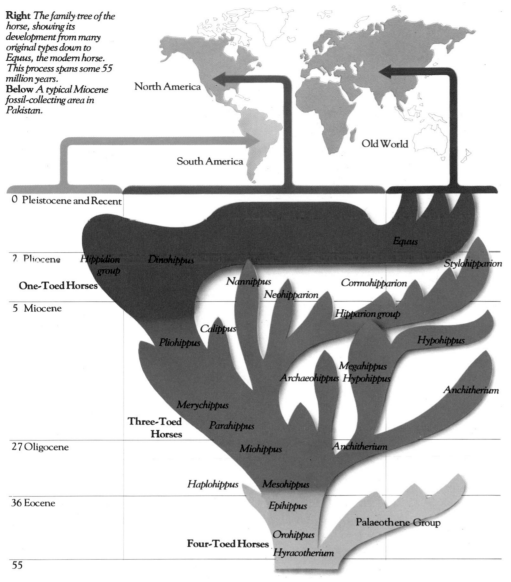

Right *The family tree of the horse, showing its development from many original types down to Equus, the modern horse. This process spans some 55 million years.*
Below *A typical Miocene fossil-collecting area in Pakistan.*

North America

South America

Old World

0 Pleistocene and Recent

Equus

2 Pliocene

Hippidion group

Dinohippus

Stylohipparion

One-Toed Horses

Nannippus

Cormohipparion

Neohipparion

5 Miocene

Hipparion group

Calippus

Hypohippus

Pliohippus

Megahippus

Archaeohippus Hypohippus

Anchitherium

Merychippus

Three-Toed Horses

Parahippus

27 Oligocene

Miohippus

Anchitherium

Haplohippus

Mesohippus

36 Eocene

Epihippus

Palaeothene Group

Orohippus

Four-Toed Horses

Hyracotherium

55

treme, particularly in the New World. There, horses became totally extinct until their subsequent re-introduction to the region by the Spanish *conquistadores*.

Changes through time

As the fossil record of horses is reviewed, several changes or evolutionary trends are apparent, as the process of natural selection led to the development of forms better able to survive in a given environment. One of the most striking changes is a general increase in size from the earliest *Hyracotherium* to the present-day *Equus*, though there were some exceptions to this during the Miocene and Pliocene, when some horses remained the same size or even became smaller. Other changes seen during the course of horse evolution specifically relate to feeding and locomotion. Particularly in the grazers there was a deepening of the skull and jaws along with the evolution of the higher crowned molars needed to grind abrasive grass. As far as locomotion is concerned, horses show a trend toward relative elongation of the limbs and reduction or loss of the side toes. The most advanced form of this is the present-day one-toed horse *Equus*.

Domestication of the horse

The evidence for domestication of the horse comes principally from archaeological sites in the Old World. It includes skeletal remains of horses themselves, as well as cultural artifacts that depict horses, such as sculptures, carvings and coins. However, there is by no means universal agreement as to the origins of the domesticated horse.

For a long time, archaeologists have asked two interrelated questions: Were horses originally domesticated in one, or more than one, general region of the Old World? Was one, or more than one, kind of horse originally domesticated? In answer to the first question, there seems to be some agreement that the horse was first domesticated in Asiatic Russia around 3,000 BC, and that the process spread rapidly. By about 1500 BC there is evidence that the domestic horse was part of cultures throughout the Old World. It was found in cultures as far apart as those of Greece, Egypt, India and the Far East. The second question has proved harder to answer. Firstly, there is no general agreement as to what constitutes a distinct horse breed, variety, race, or even species. Some scientists feel that two different kinds – Przewalski's horse and the extinct tarpan – were involved in the original Russian domestication event. Others argue that the tarpan is merely an extinct form of Przewalski's horse, and therefore only one kind of horse was involved in the process.

Chapter Two

The horse and man

The first horse peoples

It has been suggested that among the first animals to be domesticated was the reindeer, which in North-east Asia was both ridden and used to draw sleds, as well as to provide milk, meat and leather. In this area, the habitats of both horse and reindeer overlapped to some extent, and it may be that, at some distant date, the horse first became domesticated as a kind of reindeer substitute. The theory does have possibilities, because even at a primitive level of technology, it would not have been too difficult for a reindeer-keeping people to begin taming wild horses. In poor weather conditions, such as heavy snow, the wild horse would not be able to attain, or sustain its usual speed of flight, so enabling a man driving a light reindeer sledge to come within roping range. During the summer, however, the only animals likely to be caught uninjured would be unweaned foals which, though deprived of their mothers, could be fostered instead by reindeer, whose milk is perfectly digestible by young horses. That of the cow, curiously enough, is not.

But probably it will never be known who the first true horsemen were. Some authorities suggest the ancient Chinese, others the Brahmins of India. In Brahmin mythology, Manu, the first human, is given a horse to ride, making it clear that the tradition of equitation in the sub-continent is a very ancient one indeed. On the other hand, Chinese ceramics of 3500 BC show horses both ridden and harnessed; perhaps, therefore, they were the first people to master both riding and driving.

To whichever nation the honour of first domesticating the horse properly belongs, it is certain that by the third millennium BC, similar skills of horsemanship were being developed by many different peoples in Asia, Europe and North Africa – in fact, in almost any area where the wild horse occurred. Persians, Assyrians and Sumerians had all learned to master the horse at a very early period, or so it would seem from the scanty written and archaeological evidence available at the present time.

The early horse peoples

The first literary mention of the animal occurs in a text of the Third Dynasty of Ur, dating from about 2100 BC, in which it is described as having 'a flowing tail', so distinguishing it from the onager or the ass. Mention is also made of it 'at the caravan route' – a colloquial phrase apparently meaning that the creature had been tamed. But for the next thousand years or so, pictorial or written records of the horse that have survived are rare indeed.

The first people to domesticate the horse in Europe may have been a hardy, resourceful and aggressive group of Aryan tribes who lived in the Great Steppes to the north of the mountains that border the Black and Caspian Seas. About 2000 BC, bands of these Steppe people began to migrate east, west, and south, taking with them great herds of cattle and horses. Seeking new homes was for them a necessity, since their native pastures and ranges had become virtually barren – probably through overgrazing. Recent discoveries of settlements in different parts of northern and western Europe, all containing horses' bones and all dating back to about 1700 BC, help lend weight to the theory.

Oddly enough, in some parts of the world, it would seem that harnessing and driving the horse actually preceded riding. The chariot seems to have been the usual way of going to the hunt, or to war, for the Hittites, for example, whose war-chariots were the scourge of the ancient world, and for the Egyptians, to whom the notion of riding a horse does not appear to have occurred.

A prehistoric cave painting from Lascaux in southern France. Primitive man hunted the horse for food, and such paintings were probably a plea to the gods to bring him fortune and success in the hunt.

Perhaps the chariot was a development from a domestic cart, though there is no evidence for this. Certainly, once it was invented, no army could afford to be without it, and by 2000 BC, the chariot was standard equipment throughout the Mediterranean and even as far as India.

On some peoples, of course, especially to wandering hunters and herdsmen, the idea of riding dawned at a very early period. Neolithic cave-paintings depict men riding four-legged equines, but unfortunately not in sufficient detail to positively identify the animals – they may in fact be onagers, which were domesticated before horses. But the original wild horses were small animals, no bigger than 12 or 13 hands high, and it is at least feasible that they could have been controlled by a man with a rope halter. After all, the American Indians required no further tack when they re-domesticated the feral

mustang, which they rode with neither saddle nor bit right up to the present day.

The earliest written reference to horse-riding is a rather disparaging one. It occurs in a letter written by King Zimm-Linn of Mari – a vassal state of Babylon – to his son: 'My lord should not ride upon a horse. Let my lord ride on a chariot or even on a mule, and let him know his royal status'. Presumably at this time – about 1800 BC – the mule and the chariot were considered more *de rigueur* than the horse.

Certainly, during the Bronze Age the use and ownership of the horse drawn chariot was the prerogative of rank and seemed to be almost a badge of aristocracy among the ancient nations of the Near East.

Somewhere in the region, unknown genius devised the light mobile vehicle which superceded the heavy solid-wheeled Sumerian onager drawn chariot. Extraordinary skill and balance were required to drive the new, light, one, two or three man chariots, in which the charioteer looped the reins around his waist, leaving his hands and arms free to work with bow, spear or sword.

Probably the greatest of the charioteers were the Hittites, whose empire, in the fourteenth century BC, reached across Kurdistan, Armenia and Syria. Surviving Hittite writings show a surprisingly modern approach to the training, breeding, feeding, exercising, grooming and veterinary care of horses. What appears to be the foundations of an indoor riding school have been discovered near the ancient city of Ugarit. There, skeletal remains and the dimensions of the stables seem to indicate that Hittite horses were probably about the size of a modern pony. Somewhat endearingly, according to the texts, their stallions were given names like 'Foxy', 'Starry', 'White' and 'Piebald'. White horses were especially prized in the ancient Near East, where it was believed that after death, they drew the chariots of the gods.

Incidentally, it was also in Assyria that something approaching modern tack seems to have been first invented – at least, so far as the Near East is concerned. Though they chiefly preferred the chariot both for riding and for hunting, relief sculptures depict Assyrian noblemen at the hunt riding horses fully equipped with saddle, bridle and even a martingale to prevent the horse from raising its head too high. They did not, however, possess stirrups, which were probably invented by nomadic Huns on the Chinese border in about 500 AD; their use did not penetrate into Europe for at least another three centuries.

Throughout early history, Chinese horsemanship was generally far in advance of that

A relief of an early horse-man, dressed for war, from the palace of Guzana in west Asia.

in the West. As long ago as 1000 BC, the Chinese were using horses for almost every modern purpose – as battle chargers, as mounts for herdsmen, as draught and pack animals, and in all manner of farm work. Even at this early period, they had mastered the principles of selective breeding and raised different types of horse for particular purposes. Many of their skills had been learned, and then improved upon, from those practised by the Mongols, who had raided over the Chinese borders since time immemorial.

Horses had been domesticated in Egypt since about 1650 BC, the breed being later

Top left *King Ashurbanipal of Assyria leading his horses and* **below** *grooming and feeding in the royal stables. Assyrian horses were among the first to be equipped with saddles and bridles, though their riders had no stirrups. The horse, too, had its role in Assyrian religion as well as on the battlefield.*

A tax collector's wagon, laden with corn collected from Egyptian peasants. The horse soon made its mark in transport as well as war.

much improved by Libyan stock captured by the great Rameses, one of the most accomplished generals of antiquity – himself a brilliant charioteer, if his portraits are to be believed. In these, he is depicted driving an open-fronted chariot balancing with one foot on the chariot pole.

As Egypt declined, so the Persian Empire rose, to become supreme military power of the western world in about 600 BC. Much of Persian success was due to their horses, specially bred to carry heavy arms and armour. Despite their efficiency, they were not, however, elegant animals, and their gen-

erally unrefined appearance suggests a certain admixture of Przewalski blood.

The writings of Xenophon
Though the ancient Greeks were excellent horsemen, they were never as successful with cavalry as were the Persians. All the same, out of Greece came Xenophon, one of the most original writers on horses and horsemanship who ever lived. Xenophon was born of a wealthy family in Athens in 430 BC. Famous as a soldier and poet while still a young man, he also wrote the first known book on equitation. One of his main points

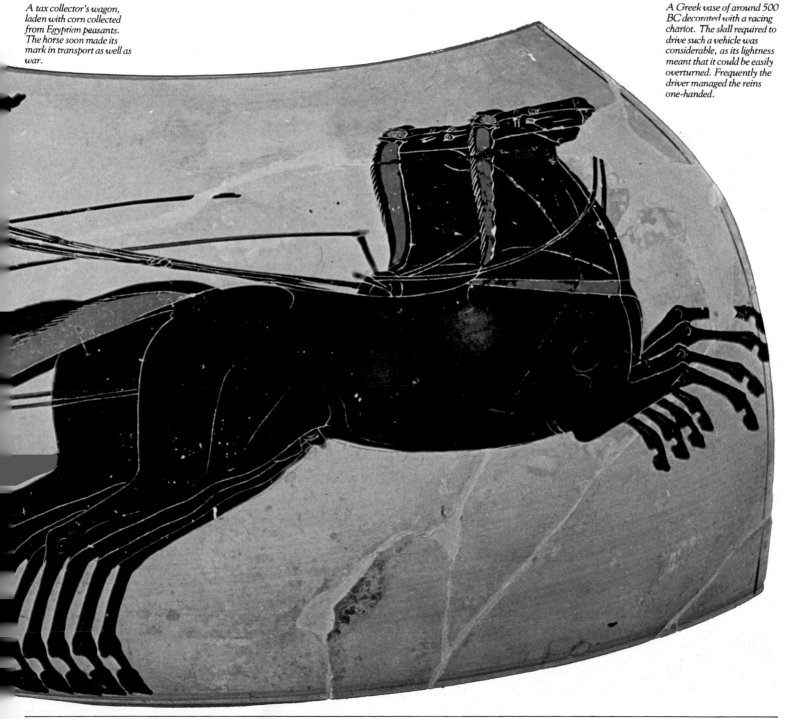

A Greek vase of around 500 BC decorated with a racing chariot. The skill required to drive such a vehicle was considerable, as its lightness meant that it could be easily overturned. Frequently the driver managed the reins one-handed.

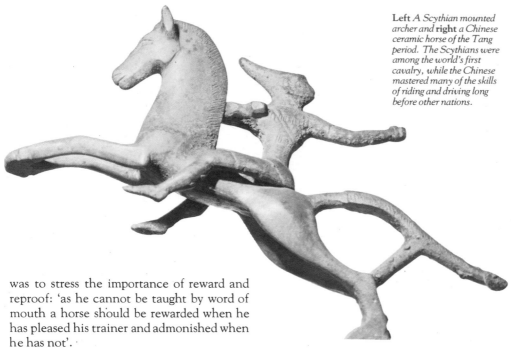

Left *A Scythian mounted archer and* **right** *a Chinese ceramic horse of the Tang period. The Scythians were among the world's first cavalry, while the Chinese mastered many of the skills of riding and driving long before other nations.*

was to stress the importance of reward and reproof: 'as he cannot be taught by word of mouth a horse should be rewarded when he has pleased his trainer and admonished when he has not'.

Horsemen of today are unlikely to agree with Xenophon's views on head-carriage: 'The horse's neck should rise straight to the poll and thus the crest will then be in front of the rider.' Although he also wrote that the neck should bend at the poll, most Greek horses are depicted with virtually no bend at all. Nevertheless, he had a certain amount of reason on his side, for as he said: 'A horse with this type of conformation would be least able to bolt even if he was very spirited. For it is not by flexing the neck but by stretching it out that horses endeavour to bolt.'

In Xenophon's day, a roughened snaffle style of bit was used for training the young horse, and when sufficiently schooled, it progressed to a smooth, less severe type of snaffle. Concerning the rider's seat on the horse, Xenophon advised: 'I do not approve

A relief of a four-horse chariot from Cyprus. One of the main uses of horses was in war and, in it, chariots were the backbone of many armies.

of the seat as in a chair, but that which is like a man standing upright with his legs apart. For the thighs in this way have a better grip of the horse, and with the body erect one can with more force hold the javelin and strike from horseback if necessary.' Until the twentieth century, this was to remain the orthodox seat in Europe and remains so in the Western riding style of the United States. At this time, saddles with trees did not exist and although saddle cloths were sometimes used, they were considered to be suitable only for 'soft-bottomed' Persians, who, Xenophon observed, 'lay more coverlets upon the backs of their horses than upon their bodies, for they think of sitting softly rather than securely'.

Xenophon wrote that one must never lose one's temper when dealing with horses. 'When a courageous horse is unwilling to approach some object, it must be explained to him that it is not so awful, and if this fails, you must lead him gently to it and touch it yourself. Those who compel a horse with blows, make him more frightened than ever, for horses believe whenever they receive harsh treatment in such circumstances, that the feared objects are responsible for their discomfort.'

When or how the horse first arrived in Italy is uncertain; the earliest known record is a painted vase of the seventh century BC which depicts an Etruscan army on the march accompanied by horses. Although the Romans of the Republic and early Empire followed the Greek style of equitation, they were not really great horsemen. The Roman army consisted almost entirely of heavy infantry, and such cavalry as it possessed were largely ancillaries recruited from different parts of the Empire.

From Xenophon to Alexander the Great, the quality of riding did not develop to any large extent. On the other hand, the quality of horses was improved by crossing the Bactrian horse with the Macedon Tarpan-type of local stock.

In the ancient world, mares were kept mainly for breeding and soldiers almost always rode stallions. Although the practice of gelding slaves was considered acceptable and even necessary, it was thought to be too painful and dangerous for stallions. For hundreds of years the Scythians were the only people who denied this rule. Living on the plains north of the Danube, they used both mares and geldings in war. The reasoning behind this is very sound, as a stallion in war can become quite unmanageable if he detects the presence of a mare in season.

Celts and Arabs

It was probably the Scythians who chased the Celts out of the Danube valley and set in motion the migration which was to lead them eventually to the Atlantic coast and to Britain. On the way, through raiding and barter, they acquired many horses, the most important of which were the large, heavy horses from the Alpine foothills. These they crossed with their own Tarpan type chariot ponies, and the resulting stock was crossed yet again with the aboriginal ponies of Britain to produce what has become known as the 'ancient British horse'.

Despite Xenophon's brilliance, it was actually the Celts who developed a painless method of compelling the horse to bend its neck at the poll. They invented the curb-bit which enabled them to control their mounts not by force, but through gentle pressure on the reins. Nevertheless, the remainder of the ancient world stuck to their original bits.

At the beginning of the Christian era, horses were very rare animals among the Arabs. Camels were used for war and transport and donkeys for domestic work. The Bedouin had begun to breed horses before the days of the Prophet, but it was he, realizing the necessity of cavalry in the expansion of the Muslim world, who gave the first great impetus to Arab horsebreeding. Breeders were promised 'The horse shall be for a man a source of happiness and wealth; its back shall be the seat of honour and its belly riches, and every grain of barley given to it shall purchase the indulgence of a sinner and be entered in the register of good works'. Out of such splendid promises was born 'the drinker of the wind', the Arab horse that is arguably the finest, the most intelligent and courageous animal ever created.

The horse at war

'In dreary, doubtful waiting hours
Before the brazen frenzy starts
The horses show him nobler powers:
O patient eyes, courageous hearts'

Thus wrote the British poet Julian Grenfell of the feelings of many an apprehensive cavalry soldier, standing beside his horse in the anxious moments before the crash of action. The emotions he describes must have been felt by almost all horse warriors.

Probably the world's first cavalry were the Mongolians, who, in about 5000 BC, began to break and train the little red, brown and dun wild horses of the steppes, descendants of those which had crossed the land bridge from North America. These horses were about 13 hands high, with upright manes and dorsal stripes. By all accounts, the Mongolians were incredibly skilful horsemen – their mounted archers, standing on the saddle, could split an apple at twenty paces while riding at full gallop. Hordes of Mongolian cavalry repeatedly invaded China, to which they incidentally introduced the horse, and, from there, the knowledge and use of horses

spread along the trade routes further into Asia, Europe and Africa.

Charioteers and bowmen
Though the Chinese were quick to appreciate the advantages of the horse in war, they chose at first to harness the animals to chariots, rather than to ride them. Chinese war lords were doing battle in chariots in 2300 BC; by 1200 BC, the custom had spread westwards to Egypt. There, the ruling Pharaohs – notably Rameses II in his campaigns against the Hittites – frequently fought in this way.

The Chinese, however, had learned many other lessons in fighting horsemastership from their ferocious Mongol neighbours, which were to take another twenty centuries to reach the Middle East and Europe. They learned to live close to their horses, to drink

Top right *The Norman cavalry go into action at the Battle of Hastings, from the Bayeux Tapestry.* **Right** *Uccello's depiction of the Battle of S. Romano and* **below** *a Japanese screen painting of the rival generals at the Battle of the Uji river in 1184. The medieval* *period was the great age of the horse at war, when the armoured knight and his charger dominated the battlefield. This dominance lasted until first archery and then gunpowder came to challenge their invincibility. A whole mystique grew up around the age.*

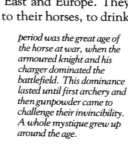

mare's milk and to make a strong liquor–*kummis*–from it. From them they copied the saddle and the stirrup–devices that were almost unkown in Europe until AD 400. They also adopted the Mongols' rigid horse collar. This was probably the first harness to take the weight of the load off the horse's windpipe and jugular vein. The innovation had an immense impact on the logistics of war, since it more than doubled the horse's draught potential.

In the Middle East, the chariot took its place in Egyptian and Persian battle lines as the first form of mobile fire-power. The lumbering carts of earliest times were soon replaced by lighter vehicles, drawn by powerful purpose-bred armour-clad horses. These horses, perhaps the ancestors of the purebred Arabian, gave the chariots a speed and momentum that had a devastating effect on enemy foot soldiers. The armoured drivers stood in turrets of strong timber, from which they fired fusillades of arrows, while threefoot scythes on the axle trees wrought fearful execution as they crashed into the infantry.

The first cavalry outside Mongolia were the mounted bowmen of the Assyrians and Scythians who took to the field in about 1200 BC. Later, mounted spearmen or lancers were incorporated into the armies as well. Most interestingly, their horses–Arab types with fine, slightly-dished faces and clean well-boned legs–were being bred even as early as this for their speed and boldness in battle, while baggage train animals ·were stockier, more workmanlike and commoner. Selective breeding at this time already included gelding; grain feeding, too, for better performance, was the rule.

Much military horse lore was passed to the

Greeks by the Egyptians but, despite Xenophon and his remarkably perceptive treatises on horsemanship, their most persistent enemies, the Persians, had by far the greater cavalry strength. In 500 BC Xerxes had under his command 80,000 chariot and ridden horses in all, an almost unbelievable equine army for the time. The best horses were those of the Niceans, which came from Media and Armenia. These were the biggest horses then known, standing between 14 and 15 hands high.

Tales of the awesome ferocity in battle of these early war horses may not be all fable. The animals ridden in action were invariably stallions, and they were often schooled to use their natural foreleg 'boxing' action to batter at the infantry before them.

Greeks, Persians, Romans and Chinese

However Greek horsemanship should not be underestimated, largely because of Xenophon. His treatises on cavalry training and horsemanship written in 360 BC were designed to produce a horse useful in battle, and contained advice on how to judge and buy a horse. Xenophon advocated precision of pace, balance, proper carriage, acceptance of the bit, flexion and considerate application of the aids. These precepts and preoccupations are still fundamental to the art of horsemanship today, even after twenty three centuries.

At about this time – the 3rd century BC – the Chinese, too, were perfecting an 8,000-strong cavalry force to confront the Huns along the Great Wall of China. At first this force was mounted on shaggy little Mongolian ponies, but gradually these were re-

Above *A gaily-caprisoned officer of Napoleon's Imperial Guard and* below *the charge of the Scots Greys at the battle of Waterloo in 1815. With the introduction of firearms and artillery, the role of the horse on the battlefield changed, as cavalry became more of a fast-moving blitzkrieg weapon. Hussars, Dragoons and Lancers all had their respective roles to play, and in all the European armies of the day, the cavalry became regarded as the élite striking force, its membership being largely aristocratic. Nowhere was this more true than in the British army during the*

Napoleonic Wars. Then, the cavalry tended to treat the order to charge as though starting a fox-hunt. This was certainly the case in the Greys' charge at Waterloo, when, their blood being up, they pursued their fleeing foes into the heart of the French position heedless of loss. In contrast, Napoleon's cavalry were usually more professional.

The horse had its other uses too. Far right *A romantic view of the 'Remnants of an Army,' as the sole survivor of a British disaster on the Indian north-west frontier is saved by the courage, speed and stamina of his horse.*

placed by bigger and stronger animals, bred from Niceans imported from what is now Samarkand. This war horse breeding programme reached a major climax in AD 1040. Until then the Chinese armies had relied on ponies from the Mongolian plateau to the north, where they were, and are, still, massed in great herds. In a drive to end dependence for such essential war material on a potential enemy-controlled region, the authorities instituted a Horse Breeding Law, which decreed that every rural family had to keep at least one horse. This was such a success that it realized 30,000 cavalry remounts in just five years.

The cavalry of the early Romans was thin on the ground – for example, they fielded only 3,000 against Hannibal's 8,000 swift Barbs (ridden without bridle or rein, being guided by a short whip), and they were never a great success. Only after the defeat of Carthage did the Roman cavalry achieve high standards and effectiveness, although, according to Caesar's account of his Gallic wars, most of his 10,000 mounted soldiers were German, Spanish and Numidian mercenaries. The cavalry, however, was still no match for the 40,000 Parthians on their fast, nimble Nicaean horses, ridden with the noseband and single rein of five centuries before. These were the first fully armoured horses in the world, though the amount of metal they carried was not yet heavy enough to necessitate special breeding for extra strength.

By this time, the principal nations were producing two main types of horse in their military horse-breeding programmes, each for its own particular qualities. The

'warmblood' was the more volatile, spirited, finer-made horse and the 'coldblood' was more placid, phlegmatic, and thus suitable for draught and load-carrying. Although the Romans appeared to appreciate the importance of this, their cavalry was allowed to become decadent, and the army depended more and more on mounted mercenary auxiliaries. As a result, Alaric the Goth's cavalry sacked Rome with the same ease that Attila's Huns, on their medium-sized, hardy Steppes ponies, were able to invade Italy. The roots of this Roman decline, however, dated back much further. The failure of Caesar's first assault across the Channel was largely due to the speed and flexibility of the Celtic mounted archers and charioteers. The credit for his success in 54 BC belongs almost entirely to his 2,000 Gaulish cavalry, mounted on their heavy, 15-hand horses.

The age of chivalry
From the fall of the Roman Empire to the Norman conquest of England, little is known of the war horse. In Saxon Britain, for example, though the English kings Alfred and Athelstane imported stallions and imposed export restrictions on good horses, no developments of military significance took place.

In the Arab world, however, the picture was very different. The Prophet Mohammed instilled his people with his own respect for the influence of the horse on war. In consequence, the Arab cavalry horse developed in step with the burgeoning Saracen Empire; Saracen cavalry swept across Arabia, North Africa and up into Spain, and not until they encountered Charles Martel's powerful, mail-clad Frankish cavalry at Poitiers in AD 732 was their advance halted.

The tenth century saw the opening of the great age of chivalry in Europe. This was to culminate in the breeding of huge battle horses, capable of carrying up to 400 lb of armoured knight. The Norman invasion of 1066 introduced the forerunners of the massive Percheron and Shire to a cavalryless English army. William of Normandy's warriors were mostly mounted, they knew how to fight on horseback, and in their thundering waves they broke and routed the gallant Saxon infantry. The Norman horses were not yet massive, being about 14 hands high, but under William's imaginative command at Hastings, their shock effect was more than enough to win the day.

The Crusades for the first time contrasted the battle qualities of fleet Arabs and Barbs with those of the European knights on their heavier horses. Here, considerations of mobility, protection and striking power had to be weighed against each other with infinite

care and thought. This too—the twelfth century—was the age of the largest cavalry force in history—Ogtai Khan's one and a half million superbly organized and disciplined Mongol cavalry who, on their tough 13-hand Mongol ponies, swept through Asia and eastern Europe until they were eventually stopped by heavily armoured cavalry on the borders of Poland.

By the end of the fifteenth century, the massive European *destrier,* or charger, had to carry in tournament and battle nearly 500 lb of armour, as well as its noble knight. But with the spread of firearms, most armour became obsolete. The sixteenth and seventeenth centuries heralded the beginnings of a new kind of cavalry—fast, manoeuvrable and lightly armoured—the kind of formations typified by Cromwell's Ironsides in the English Civil War. Thus, firearms by no means heralded the end of cavalry, but they changed its role from battering ram to swift, shock attack and reconnaissance.

Dragoons, Lancers and Hussars
The development of the English Thoroughbred which began during the reign of Charles II (1660–85) infused the blood of the existing English horse with that of the Arab. This had a considerable influence not only on the British cavalry, but on that of most of the Western world. In Russia, for instance, the Cossacks were remounted and trained on Arab and Throughbred-influenced stock from the breeding farms of the great Steppes; by the eighteenth century, Peter the Great was commanding a mounted force of 84,000 men.

New horse-breeds, too, led to the development of three very distinct kinds of cavalry throughout the armies of Europe: the Dragoon, primarily a foot soldier, but mounted for movement on solid, cobby horses; the Lancer, riding a much finer animal suited for fast flanking movements and sudden charges; and the galloping, sabre-wielding Hussar, the *Blitzkrieg*-weapon of battlefield and campaign.

The Napoleonic Wars furnish the first

authentic records of the difficulties of sustaining horses through a major campaign. The Emperor took 30,000 cavalry, and probably as many pack and draught horses, into Russia in 1812. But through cold, starvation and the savage attacks of the Cossacks, he re-crossed the River Niemen after the terrible retreat from Moscow with fewer than 2,000 animals. Thereafter his cavalry was almost always inferior to that of his enemies, and it was indeed the charge of Blücher's Prussians that finally swung the day against him at Waterloo.

From Waterloo to World War
After Waterloo canister, shrapnel and the advent of automatic weapons began to force the massed cavalry charge into obsolescence. But the golden age of cavalry was far from over, and until the end of the nineteenth century at least the fast, flexible and efficient horse artillery batteries, whose drivers rode as postillions on the nearside horses, played a highly important part in battle.

In the British Indian campaigns of the nineteenth and early twentieth centuries, the English hunter type was soon replaced by tough little Arabs from Persia, and by the big Australian Arab and Thoroughbred cross from New South Wales. These Walers, as they were called, made excellent troop and artillery horses, and eventually more than 120,000 of them served with British and Empire forces in the First World War.

To this period, too, belongs one of the most catastrophic cavalry charges in all history. The Charge of the Light Brigade at Balaclava in the Crimea in 1854 was the nadir of British horse campaigning and management. The entire campaign was a chapter of dreadful privation for both horse and man, which came to a climax that October day, when of the 673 horses which, on a misunderstood order, charged 2,000 yards into the muzzles of the Russian artillery, only 260 survived. The remainder, those that were not killed outright, still struggled on in their parade places until they fell. One charger, dreadfully lanced, carried its badly wounded rider a full mile to safety before collapsing.

In the USA, the great Indian Comanche and Kiowa tribes, who had learned to break and ride the feral descendants of the horses of the Conquistadores (the 16th-century Spanish invaders of America), had become as skilled as the Mongols in mounted archery, though they never compared with them in respect of other aspects of horsemastership. By the 1860s, however, the white settlers had begun to push westwards, and the stage was set for the great cavalry campaigns of the Indian wars. In these, the Indians found worthy opponents in the US cavalry, but, in the end, it was overwhelming technological superiority, rather than particular tactical brilliance, that won the day for the expanding white man.

Technological development, too, was one of the factors behind the revolution in cavalry tactics that took place in the US Civil War; the barrel superceded the blade, and much of the actual fighting took place dismounted. As far as the mounted man was concerned, it was a war of long hard marches and sudden shock actions—'Git thar fustest with the mostest.' It was a sudden and intense metamorphosis from tradition to pragmatism, and, once again, the equine suffering at least equalled the human. In one veterinary hospital alone, in a period of five months, no more than a half of the 7,000 horses could be saved, and in the last year of the war 180,000 Northern cavalry horses alone died of starvation.

World War and after

As weaponry grew ever more complex, so the horse's battlefield privations increased – often as a result of outdated tactical dogma and die-hard worship of brilliant mounted reviews and drills. In the South African War of 1899–1902 the carbine-armed Boers on their hardy ponies ran rings round the British regulars. In the last phase of the war, one regiment of Dragoons could muster, of their original complement of 775 horses, a mere 27–the losses being due almost entirely to privation and disease. In the war as a whole, out of more than half a million horses, 350,000 died.

Even after 1900, the cavalry horses of most European nations were still expected to carry some 300 lb, which included rider and weapons—sabre or lance, rifle, ammunition – and campaign kit. During the First World War millions of horses were employed on all the many fronts at any given time—draught and pack animals as well as cavalry mounts. Again, losses were appalling, those from privation and exposure being five times greater than those incurred in battle itself. Seven thousand horses were killed in one day alone

Left *The Charge of the Light Brigade at Balaclava during the Crimean War;* below *and* right *two views of Custer's legendary last stand at the Little Big Horn by an Indian and American artist respectively. Both these actions were disasters for both the horses and the men concerned. At Balaclava, the bravery of the Light Brigade in charging straight in to the face of the massed Russian artillery in blind obedience to a mistaken, or misunderstood, order inspired one of Tennyson's finest poems. It also prompted a French general to comment 'It is magnificent, but it is not war.' Similarly, Custer's cavalry, surrounded by their Indian foes fought to the last man.*

during the Battle of Verdun (1916) – and not one single major cavalry action was fought in four years on the Western Front.

On the Eastern Front, until 1917, Cossacks, German and Austro-Hungarian cavalry engaged in corps-strength battles reminiscent of wars a century earlier, while in the Middle East General Allenby's 20,000-strong Desert Mounted Corps of Australian, New Zealand, British and Indian cavalry made forced marches of up to 60 miles a day, often without water or forage. In one action, 172 Yeomanry charged and routed four Turkish infantry battalions and three batteries of artillery. This action is still held as an example of the capabilities of determined cavalrymen.

The story of the horse in war does not end in climax. After the armistice in 1918, mechanization gradually replaced the operational cavalry, artillery and draught horse. But even as late as 1939, Poland fielded almost 90,00 horses on active service, the Germans – supposedly the most mechanized army in the world – 800,000 (including five SS cavalry divisions), while the Russians had a million and a quarter animals available for battle.

What was probably the last full-scale cavalry charge was made by the Russians in November 1941, near Moscow. Squadron after squadron of horsemen charged the astounded German 106th Infantry Division, 'stirrup touching stirrup, riders low on their horses' necks, drawn sabres over their shoulders' – straight into a storm of modern small arms and artillery fire. Thirty reached the German ranks, and were there machine-gunned. All 2,000 horses and men of the 44th Mongolian Cavalry Division lay fallen in the snow. There were no German casualties.

However, draught and pack animals were critically important in Second World War campaigns that took place in mountainous or forested areas – in Italy, for example, and in the jungles of Burma. The British and Americans regularly air-lifted pack horses and mules, many 'muted' by painless operation to preserve secrecy on clandestine missions, and the Japanese too relied heavily on animal transport.

Today, other than in China, which still maintains four full cavalry divisions, only a few operational horsed formations still remain – notably in the USSR, India, South America and South Africa.

The story of the horse in war is a brave one. Paradoxically, now that its day is past, many soldiers feel mankind has lost, in this age of mechanized combat, a valuable dimension of feeling and of sacrifice inspired by the selflessness, loyalty and affection of man's oldest military ally.

Scenes from modern war.
Left cavalry pick their way
around a mine crater on the
Western Front in 1917,
while **below** an ammunition
wagon moving up to the
front at the Battle of the
Somme (1916); German
First World War transport,
with horses and drivers both
in gasmasks; loading a
packhorse; and a scene from
the Eastern Front in 1943,
as Soviet horse artillery
pursues the fleeing
Germans, with air support.
The twentieth century saw
the final disappearance of the
horse from an active role on
the battlefield, with the
advent of machine guns,
barbed wire and tanks.
Below right a legacy from
the past, as Soviet cavalry
emerge from concealment to
attack the advancing
German panzers in
September 1941.

The horse at work

Speed, sure-footedness and spiritedness, rather than horse-power, were the qualities demanded by the men who first broke horses to harness. Heavy work, especially ploughing, was accomplished by oxen. Their steady, plodding gait and sheer brute strength were particularly suited to the heavy beam ploughs that hardly changed from the Middle Ages to the eighteenth century. Where speed did not matter, ox-power was paramount, and indeed, teams of oxen—six to a plough—were fairly commonplace in many parts of Europe until the Second World War. Another advantage of the ox was that after hauling a plough for four years, it could be fattened during the ensuing summer and then slaughtered for meat, so providing a double return for the farmer.

Through more than a thousand years of European farming, probably until the seventeeth century, most of the horses available to agriculture were far too light to attempt much more than carting and harrowing, though in the latter task especially they excelled. They did not object to the skittering of the harrow over broken ground that would have driven oxen, used to the steady drag of the plough, into hysteria; but being little more than ponies, the heavy work of the farm was beyond their strength.

Yet the ideal horse for this work did exist, and had done so since the Normans swept across Europe in the eleventh century. A principal factor in their spectacular military success was the *destrier,* the great war horse, that could carry an armoured knight through opposing infantry like a reaper through grain. Of Andalusian and northern European descent, the 'Great Horses' became the ancestors of every modern breed of draught horse—the Percherons and the Brabants, the Shires, Clydesdales and many others. Later, an Arab strain was introduced into some of these to give them lightness and speed·

For centuries, it would have seemed sacrilege to have put such animals to any employment other than that of war; they were the knight's proudest, and most expensive, possession, and there were other factors too that limited their wider distribution and use. One was the shortage of sufficiently good grassland to support such enormous beasts in any great number, while another was the slow development of suitable harness. The hard collar, for example, was not introduced into western Europe until the late Middle Ages; until then, horses hauled from a breastband that constricted their breathing and prevented them from throwing their full strength into their work.

But it was the invention of gunpowder and finally, the cavalry pistol that released

heavy horses from war. A pistol ball could penetrate any armour; in consequence, it became obsolete and speed and manoeuvrability replaced weight-carrying as the most desirable qualities in cavalry mounts.

Carts and waggons

Curiously, it was not in agriculture that the demobilised heavy horses first made their mark, but as draught animals for royalty. In 1564, Queen Elizabeth I ordered a travelling wagon—to be drawn by six great horses. In this, she journeyed from London to Warwick, but, so it was reported, was unable to sit down for a week afterwards. Nevertheless, she persisted, and on her famous progresses became accustomed to moving about the country in wagon trains drawn by 400 heavy horses. Only these, with their great strength, were capable of hauling over, or rather through, the abominable road surfaces of the period.

Encouraged by royal example, both in England and Europe, the first public stage wagons, each dragged along by eight massive draught horses, were carrying passengers and freight between cities before the close of the sixteenth century. But it was to be many a long year before road surfaces improved sufficiently to allow such vehicles to compete on equal terms with the ridden horse, the pack horse and the pack horse trains.

Not until the eighteenth century did the draught breeds make their first real impact on agriculture. Better land drainage, improved grazing and selective breeding methods greatly increased the number and strength of draught horses available. At the same time, the revolution in farm machinery necessitated the use of an animal more intelligent and more adaptable than the ox.

The hey-day of the agricultural draught horse, and of the specialized craftsmen who served it was from the end of the eighteenth century until the outbreak of the First World War in 1914.

Prince of these was the wheelwright, who

Left A horse and plough in a medieval illuminated manuscript and below an Etruscan urn of about 150 to 100 BC, depicting a couple taking their last journey to the underworld in a horse-drawn wagon. It was in transport and agriculture that the horse proved its indispensibility, though it did not become a major force in European farming until the invention of a suitable collar in the Middle Ages. Until then, too, the horse's value in war was too great to allow its use for civilian labour on a large scale.

combined the crafts of blacksmith, joiner and woodsman in creating not only wheels, but entire farm carts and wagons which, by the end of the period, had developed into masterpieces of rural engineering. In Australia, Europe and the New World, wheelwrights built carts and wagons great and small superbly adapted to the soil, work and conditions of the particular area. Probably the most glorious glimpse of the draught horse is that afforded by a matched team of Shires or Percherons hauling a Suffolk wagon, with its 8ft-dished wheels and blazing colours. But like the clipper captains who flourished at the very end of the era of sail, so

perhaps the greatest of working horsemen evolved almost as the tractors moved in. These were the mule-skinners of Australia and the western plains of the USA and Canada who drove combine harvesters powered by 30-strong teams of horses or mules. It was said of the drivers that they could remove a fly from the ear of the lead horse with a 40 ft whip; it may even have been true.

Carriages and coaches

The earliest vehicle extant that might be described as a carriage is the State Chariot of King Tutankhamen. This dates back to the fourteenth century BC, but so far as our own

era is concerned, the ancestry of both carriages and coaches reaches no further back than the massive public stage wagons of the sixteenth century. One such vehicle of the period was named after the town of Kotze in Hungary where it was built, and this in turn may have lent its name to the whole breed of coaches that followed. However, coaches and carriages as we think of them – light, well-strung vehicles with independently turning front axles and drawn by teams of speedy horses – were an impossible dream before the great road engineering schemes of the eighteenth century. Nevertheless, once these had been accomplished, coach design

improved almost overnight and the great draught horses were relegated to the farm. Their places between the shafts were usurped by lighter, faster breeds such as the Cleveland Bay, the Kladruber, the Oldenburg and the Fredricksborg.

As early as 1784, the British post office made transport history by setting up staging posts every ten miles or so between London and Bath. Changing horses at each stage, the mail coach accomplished the journey – about a hundred miles – in the then incredible time of 15 hours at an average speed of 6⅔ mph. Within a very few years, a complex system of coaching inns and staging posts was established throughout Britain and Europe. Some idea of the size of the operation may be gathered from Hounslow, the first staging post on the Great West Road out of London; at its peak, just before the coming of the railways, 2000 horses were stabled there.

In the new countries, most notably in Australia with its vast distances of virgin territory, the stagecoach remained a major means of transport for much longer than in Europe. The most famous Australian coachmen were Cobb & Co., who in the 1880s controlled a coaching network covering some 6000 miles of road. They bred their own type of hardy 'coacher' horses to pull their 14-passenger vehicles that continued to drive through the night by the light of powerful acetylene lamps.

The improvement of roads in Europe also led to a proliferation of private coaches and carriages until, by the end of the first quarter of the nineteenth century, there were almost as many types on the road as there are makes of car today. Heavier vehicles were driven by a coachman and drawn by four or six horses – in the latter case, one of the lead horses was often ridden and guided by a postillion. Lighter carriages, such as the two-wheeled gig, the high-cocking cart, with a box beneath the seat for fighting cocks, and the crane-necked phaeton, the 'high-flyer', whose high sprung seat towered over the two or four horses between the shafts, were owner-driven. These were the sports cars of the age, the property of young bloods with a taste for speed and thoroughbred, matched horses. For the more sober-minded, there were enclosed broughams and landaus, and open victorias for those who wished to see and be seen; for moving children from one place to another, there were governess carts

and dog carts.

Each country evolved light carriages according to its needs. Some of the most famous were those developed in the USA, such as the four-wheeled buggy with a fixed or folding roof, fringe-top surreys for well-turned out families and buckboards for the rough trails of the West.

Cities and industry

Like mankind, horses first became ac-quainted with industry on a large scale in about the middle of the eighteenth century. Since Biblical times they had been used to operate wine and olive presses and to grind corn, while for hundreds of years they had powered windlasses at mine pitheads and worked ore-crushing machinery. Pit ponies, however, were not used until the nineteenth century, when the first horizontal drifts or galleries were constructed in coal mines; the last pit ponies working in a major coal mine in the UK went into honourable retirement in 1972.

Probably the first major equine contribution to the Industrial Revolution was in canal transport, which for 50 years before the coming of the railways was the fastest possible means of moving raw materials and finished goods between market, port and factory. Barges worked most efficiently at high speeds, with their noses lifted on to their own bow waves; to achieve this, relays of draught

Top left *Perils of the city are vividly shown in this* Punch *version of a nineteenth-century traffic jam.* Top right *A highwayman, one of the perils of the road, and* inset *US stage coaches meet in the wilds of the west. In both the Australian outback and the wild west there was a constant threat of highway robbery from bush rangers or outlaws; in the UK, however, the highwayman was a vanishing breed.*

horses were stationed along towpaths. The horses moved at a fast trot between one stage and the next, never pausing, except at locks.

The advent of the railways and the growth of industry actually raised the demand for workhorses to an unprecedented peak. As coaching companies went gradually out of business and the canals silted up, more and more horses were drafted into the cities, where, indeed, the railway companies were among their biggest employers. Teams of two or four hauled heavy wagons between factory, dock and railhead; well within living memory, it was possible to see apparently endless queues of patient Shires and Clydesdales waiting outside dock gates in the rain, their drivers muffled in sacking and tarpaulins against the weather.

For short-haul shifting of heavy loads in cities, draught horses were sufficiently economical to carry their supremacy well into the age of the internal combustion engine.

Only after a long struggle did the city draught horse finally yield to the falling price of petrol. To prove the point, in 1935, two Shires employed by Liverpool Corporation in the UK turned and moved with ease a load of 16½ tons over sleet-slippery granite setts.

Most of the lighter horses had gone long before, not entirely to the regret of many city-dwellers. Exhaust fumes and motorised jams are bad enough, but manure-filled streets and a tangle of irascible horses and

iron-shod wheels was probably infinitely worse. All the same, the dashing hansom cabs and the four-wheeled growlers, the fiacres of Paris, the smart equipages of the rich parading in the parks, the racing, bell-ringing fire engines, the beautifully matched horses of the brewers' drays and even the humble milk float, possessed a romance with which–at least in retrospect–no motorised vehicle could possibly compete.

Work horses and the future

A very few years ago most people would have said that the draught horse had no future at all; that apart from a few retained by en-thusiasts for old times' sake, it was doomed to vanish from the Earth. This process started at the beginning of the century with the de-velopment of the internal combustion engine and the oil price wars that dramatically re-

duced the cost of petrol. It continued at the close of the First World War, when the tens of thousands of American, Australian and British horses that had hauled guns and sup-plies up to the lines, were left to celebrate Armistice Day in the knacker's yard. It accel-erated between the wars as farms became steadily more mechanised. There was a brief hiatus during the Second World War, at least in Europe where horses resumed their old roles in agriculture, city haulage and barge towing. Then, as petrol became plentiful and cheap once more, the steady march of mechanisation resumed.

It was during the oil crisis of the early 1970s that it began to occur to some people that perhaps the draught horse had a place in our economy after all. Farmers wondered if they were over-mechanised, if perhaps their tractors and combines were over-adequate to

the acreage they worked, and it was dis-covered that in certain jobs and on certain soils, especially heavy clays, the horse was actually more efficient. Oddly enough, one of these is harrowing, one of the earliest tasks that the first farmers to use the horse ever put the animal to. Tractors compact wet, heavy soil while horses, though slow, harrow as cleanly as ever their forebears did.

In the cities too, horses are making some-thing of a comeback. British brewers, who cut down on their superbly matched teams only with infinite reluctance, are now reopening their stables. As the price of petrol rises, it becomes ever more economical to make city deliveries involving long halts by dray, rather than by truck.

Such ventures have led to the resumption of draught horse breeding, not out of senti-ment but in the belief that these creatures

Above *Horse power was still essential in the new steam age, as this picture of 'Old Nig' on the US North Pacific railroad shows. Such massive engineering feats would have been impossible without the horse as a hauler of men, machinery and materials.*

Above right *A fire engine races through the New York streets; in the cities, too, the horse for long remained the sole source of motive power. Gradually, however, mechanisation took over;* **far right** *UK pit ponies leave their mine for the last time in 1971.*

have a real part to play in the modern world. It is doubtful if the ploughman, walking a perfectly straight furrow behind his team of two great horses controlled by a single rein, will ever gain much more than the applause of crowds at agricultural shows. But all lovers of nature will rejoice that such skills are kept alive.

The saddle-horse
The working saddle-horse's role as a means of

Below *A horse at work on a Brazilian peasant farm,* **bottom** *a prize-winning team of Clydesdales hauling a brewer's wagon in the USA,* **right** *clearing trees in an Australian forest and* **below right** *pony transport for seaweed on the Patagonian coast.* **Far right** *A hay-making scene in Norfolk, UK;* **inset** *, a Norwegian Fjord pony at work and a horse-drawn plough toiling over a field.*

The horse has never lost its importance to poorer societies, where it is still one of many farmers' most valuable assets. Their entire living can well depend on it. Now, even in the industrialised nations of the west, the rising cost of oil and petrol has led to its reappearance on the scene. Farmers, for example, have realised that the horse is actually more efficient at certain tasks, such as harrowing, than the tractor. In both Canada and Australia, lumberjacks frequently prefer to use horses for hauling fallen timber, because of their greater ability to cope with heavy ground and confined spaces.

In cities, too, the horse is reappearing on the streets — and in a working role, not solely for purposes of display. Brewers, in particular, have always favoured horses as the ideal traction for their drays; even in the days of cheap diesel fuel, many of them kept on their carefully-matched teams, though in many cases, their main role was in the showing arena rather than actually at work, Now, however, the horse-drawn wagon, according to enthusiasts, is proving its superior versatility over the truck that once brought it close to extinction; horses, for instance, do not eat fuel in traffic jams.

It is unlikely, however, that the working horse will ever again play the same essential role as it did only half a century ago, though some speculative writers have predicted the opposite.

everyday conveyance for ladies, gentlemen and soldiers is now largely a nostalgic memory. So too, in many parts of the world, is its role as a pack animal; as roads improved, the best pack horses were promoted to carriage work where their special qualities of apparent tirelessness and endurance continue to be valued to this day. One of the finest breeds to undergo the transformation in the UK was the Chapman's horse, which during the seventeenth and eighteenth centuries travelled between fairs and markets all over Britain, carrying the wares of the Chapmen, the travelling salesmen of the day. Moving at the pace that suited them best, 'walk five miles in the hour and trot sixteen', Chapman horses could carry up to 700 lb over 60 miles in 24 hours. This ability that was to stand them in good stead when they were bred into Cleveland Bays, and became one of the most sought after of carriage horse breeds.

Better roads and the spread of the railways also put an end to the saddle horse's centuries-old service as a speedy carrier of mails and despatches. In Europe, one of the earliest of such services was in the hands of the Praetorian Guard who, at the height of the Roman Empire and using relays of riders and horses, carried messages from London to Rome in five days, a record that was scarcely improved upon for the best part of two thousand years. But the most celebrated of all mail-riding epics was surely that of the Pony Express in 19th-century America. So famous has this become, that it is hard to believe that it lasted for little more than 18 months between 1860 and 1862. The service ran from St Joseph, Missouri, through Kansas, Nebraska, Colorado, Wyoming, Utah and Nevada, to Sacramento, California – a distance of 1,966 miles which the company guaranteed to cover in ten days. Four hundred horses–or rather, ponies, since none were more than 14 hands–stood ready in the relay stations established along the route, saddled and waiting for the mails to be slung across their backs and to gallop on to the next staging post. The riders too, were small and wiry, but heavily armed with pistols and carbines against bandit and Indian attack. Like their ponies, they were a special breed, and almost before Wells Fargo had taken over most of their route, their exploits had become legend.

Ranching and cowboys

Only in one task does the working saddle horse still reign supreme–that of helping to guard and control livestock in remote plains and great grasslands. In the Camargue, for example, the salt-marsh delta of the Rhône in France, the *guardiens*, or cowboys, ride a local breed of horses–virtually unchanged since Roman times–in pursuit of the wild black bulls that are exported to the bull-rings of Spain. In Australia, despite such recent innovations as the light aeroplane, the cattle truck and the jeep, the bulk of ranch work is still accomplished by the stockman on horseback. Generally, he rides a Waler, a tough, hardy crossbreed first developed in New South Wales as a remount for the British cavalry in India.

But the most famous of all working horsemen was, and probably still is, the cowboy of the south-western United States. As with the Pony Express rider, film and fable have combined to give the notion that he dominated a very large portion of American history. In fact, the 'Golden Age' of the cowboy lasted little more than 25 years, from the end of the Civil War in 1865, to the arrival of the railroads in Texas in about 1890.

Conversely, his antecedents are considerably more ancient than most film fans suspect, for they reach back to the cattle ranches of medieval Spain and Portugal. In the sixteenth century, Cortes and his Conquistadores brought this style of farming to Mexico, from which it spread to what would later become the south-western states of the USA. The language, equipment and dress of the modern cowboy are all traceable to those early beginnings. Even the deep, comfortable Western saddle, rising fore and aft, is only a slight adaption from the war-saddle of the Conquistadores. When roping a steer, the rider takes a turn of the lariat (*reata*–leather thong) round the horn of the saddle, which is secured by cinches (*cincha*–girth). The cowhand's broad-brimmed hat and jingling, rowelled, spurs are adapted from the dress of the Mexican *vaquero,* whose very name has been anglicised to 'buckaroo'.

Oddly enough, it is only the cowboy's horse, the renowned Quarter horse, that comes from the eastern USA. Its name and ancestry stemmed from Virginia, where in the eighteenth century, racehorses capable of phenomenal speeds over a quarter of a mile were bred. Short bursts of speed, hardiness, good bone and muscle, was exactly what was required in cattle country, and the Quarter horse was moved west, to breed there in thousands.

Until the Civil War, there was no demand for, or at least no means of transporting, western beef to the markets of the east. The cattle's only value lay in their hides and tallow; the meat, as often as not, was left to rot. But as the railroads drove ever farther west, to Missouri, Kansas and Colerado, it became feasible and highly profitable to drive Texas cattle north on the hoof. Each Longhorn that reached the railheads at Kansas City, Abilene, Dodge, or Denver fetched an

Far left *A mounted policeman in New York,* below *Magyar riders at a Hungarian horse festival and* left *the first US Pony Express rider leaves for the west in 1860. The saddle horse, too, has its role as a working horse. Even today, it is still used on the cattle ranches of the USA, South America and Australia.*

average of $10; and they arrived in millions. It was out of these drives, over trails 1,500 miles and more long, with names such as Chisholm and Shawnee, Western and Goodnight-Loving, that the legend of the cowboy was born.

'Take 'em to Missouri!'

During this period, it is estimated there were about 40,000 men engaged in the business of moving beef from the scrublands of Texas to the railheads, not counting those who were working to the north in Wyoming, Montana and Oregon. They were paid $30 a month, and were expected to supply their own clothing, bedding, boots and saddles; on the last two items, beautifully stitched and ornamented, they would cheerfully spend two years' pay. Food and horses were provided by the rancher or the trail boss; generally, it was reckoned that each cowhand required about ten horses to see him through a drive. This might last six months or more and during it both horse and rider might easily work eighteen hours a day. Breaking and training this vast number of horses was considered an inferior trade to that of cowhand; a horse-breaker was paid $25 a month, or $3 a horse.

Tough though trail work was, moving at a snail's pace during the day with occasional wild dashes after strays, and riding herd over the bedded-down cattle for half the night, it did at least have the compensation of an occasional visit to a town along the route. There were few such compensations for the ranch hand, who for weeks on end might ride round the boundaries of the range digging fence post holes, repairing barbed wire, branding, castrating and dehorning calves, with only a horse for company. However, it was on such expeditions that both horse and rider learned their trades – cutting out a single calf from a herd, hauling fences taut, or roping a runaway steer.

Modern conditions have changed much of this vigorous and demanding way of life. Today, for instance, cowhands' horses, ready-saddled, are transported to the more distant ranges by trailer. Glamorous, blond maned palominos, and dappled Appaloosas, descended, so it is said, from the horses of Cortes, now work alongside the great-grandchildren of the Quarter horses that blazed the cattle trails. But the standard of horsemanship, and of rapport between horse and rider, remains as high as ever.

The horse in human imagination

For thousands of years, up to the present day, man has credited the horse with wisdom, courage, loyalty, strength, dignity and mystery. For us, with a dozen means of fast communication at our disposal, it is easy to forget that until a relatively short time ago, and for millenia before that, the greatest speed at which even the most vital message could be delivered was limited to that of the galloping horse. Or that the fate of nations and entire civilizations were decided by the presence on the battlefield of a number of herbivorous quadrupeds.

By easy transference, the horse became more than the mere bearer of messengers and warriors. It became instead a partisan, an active arbiter in the destinies of men. From there it was but a short step to divine status, though in Western mythology there is only one horse god, or rather goddess, as such – Epona of the Celts, whose representation is probably carved into the chalk hillsides of southern England. But as lesser divinities, and as the favoured means of transport of the gods, horses have an unrivalled role. The Greeks believed that the sun was a horse-drawn chariot, driven daily across the sky by the god Helios, while the Hindus assigned a similar role to Surya; virtually the same legend appears in the mythologies of almost every early civilization.

Divine tidings and death

Horses brought divine tidings to men, both good news and bad. The Norse spring began as Freya rode across the world, scattering flowers. This story is echoed in British folklore in the tale of Lady Godiva who lifted the burden of taxation imposed on the people of Coventry by riding naked through the streets. As with Freya, to look upon her on her mission brought heavenly retribution, instant and terrible.

Horses carried the messengers of Death and often conveyed the dead themselves to their ultimate destination. The Valkyries, the 'choosers of the slain', rode across Norse battlefields selecting the bravest of the brave for inclusion among the immortals of Valhalla. Later, the Four Horsemen of the Apocalypse of St John – War, Famine, Pestilence and Death – haunted the imagination, and the art, of the Middle Ages.

Satan, or the Devil, on the other hand, was always thought of as riding a black horse, a convention followed by super-villains all the way through history down to the early days of Western movies. The Devil's horse breathed fire, however, and was covered with scales, spikes or other unusual accoutrements. In this it resembled the mount of Woden, the northern god who led his Wild Hunt across Europe on nights of wind and storm, snatching up any mortal who dared to raise his face from the earth. According to legend, he rides still through the forests of Windsor Great Park that surround Queen Elizabeth II's principal residence. There he is known as Herne the Hunter; to glimpse him or his horse, both with antlers sprouting from their brows, means death within the year.

Similar penalties are incurred by those who have the misfortune to encounter any one of a whole range of phantom horses and horsemen, indicating perhaps, that the legend of the Wild Hunt is more deeply entrenched in our collective subconscious than we would like to think. Sometimes, horse and rider are invisible, as in the case of the Wicked Lady Ferrers, England's only highwaywoman, whose horse's hoof-beats are still reputedly heard in the quiet lanes of Hertfordshire. In other instances they are only too visible; Ghost Riders in the Sky, a popular song of a few years ago, recounts the legend, firmly believed in by many old-time cowhands, that evildoers in their profession are condemned to ride some spectral range for ever, in desperate pursuit of a herd they can never catch. But audible or visible, the fate of those who meet the phantom riders is the same; death or some great misfortune within the year.

Horses and heroes

Otherworld denizens apart, there are a large number of horses whose deeds – or those of their riders – have brought them an immortality that hovers somewhere between legend and history. The Duke of Wellington's Copenhagen, whose imperturbability in battle was equalled only by that of his master, is one example, and Napoleon's Marengo, the

The Amazons – the mythical warrior women of ancient Greek history – were superb riders, as this gold tracing on a silver panel shows. Depiction of combat between Amazons and Classical heroes, such as Theseus, was a favourite subject for Greek artists.

Carried off in a chariot, Persephone faces rape at the hands of Pinax. Winged horses – the most celebrated being Pegasus – were a major force in Greek mythology, being credited with many magic properties.

Emperor's inseparable companion in victory and defeat, is another. Deeper into the realms of legend was Bayard, on which Sir Roland and his three brothers fled the anger of the great Emperor Charlemagne, and Bucephalus, favourite charger of Alexander the Great who after the animal's death, built the city of Bucephala, in present-day Pakistan, over his grave. A different immortality was awarded to the horse of Emiliano Zapata, the Mexican patriot. When his master was shot down in ambush, the horse escaped and, so it is said, still wanders the hills awaiting Zapata's return.

All in all, heroes are much improved by the presence of a horse; as status symbols and supporting players in ballad and legend they

can hardly be improved upon. King Arthur, his knights and their chargers sleep an entranced sleep in a cave, save for one night in the year – May Day Eve – when they ride proudly together over the hills of Somerset and Wales. The life of Cuchulainn, the Celtic folk-hero, was saved by the prescience of the Gray of Macha, who anticipating disaster, refused to be yoked for battle. Young Lochinvar galloped into the sunset, safe from outraged parents and bridegroom, with Fair Ellen mounted on his saddlebow.

Creation myths
Such wondrous beasts, our ancestors felt, could have sprung from no ordinary beginnings. According to the ancient Greeks, they

were created by Poseidon, God of the Sea, and first appeared to men out of the ocean. Perhaps this belief arose out of some long ago invasion, when horses and warriors swam ashore together; if so, it would go far to explain the origins of the Centaur, half-man, half-horse, whose lustful kidnapping of women was offset, to some extent, by its wisdom. Mistaking horse and rider for a single creature was an error made much later by the Aztecs of Mexico, who appalled by the mounted Conquistadores, allowed them to achieve their bridgehead unmolested. A similar invasion may also account for the Ting-ling, centaur-like beings which, according to Chinese legend, once inhabited the island of Formosa. Like the Greek varie-

Left *The familiar myth of St George and the dragon is captured by an African artist in an Ethiopian setting.* **Above right** *the dominant figure of Napoleon crossing the Alps, captured by J. L. David, the apostle of Romanticism in art, and* **far right** *a myth is translated into music. Amalie Materna poses as Brunnhilde in the Bayreuth premiere of Richard Wagner's opera Die Walküre ('The Valkyrie'), one of whose most famous scenes is the 'Ride of the Valkyries.' In this, Wagner tried to capture the rhythm of galloping horses in his music.*
Horses have always been closely linked with heroes and heroines of the past. Knightly figures, such as St George, always had a faithful charger, while Marengo, Napoleon's fiery steed, inspired almost as many legends as his master. Wagner's Brunnhilde had Grane as her companion. In the last act of Gotterdämerung ('The Twilight of the Gods'), she rides him into the flames of Siegfried's blazing funeral pyre to join her beloved in death.

ty, these too were renowned for their wisdom.

Not content with the speed of mortal horses – or the sagacity of the centaur – Greek myth also created Pegasus, the winged horse sent by Poseidon to reveal the source of fresh water to Man. It was tamed by the warrior Bellerophon, with the aid of Athene, Goddess of Wisdom, who gave him a golden bridle for the purpose. Thus Bellerophon became the first horseman and, indeed, the first cavalryman, since mounted on Pegasus, he fought and overcame both Medusa and the Gorgons.

It is not surprising that the Arabs, among the greatest horsemen in the world, should have their own version of how their superb breed of horses originated. The first horse, they believe, was created out of a handful of the south wind by Allah, who declared: 'Thy name shall be Arabian, and virtue bound into the hair of thy forelock and plunder on thy back. I have preferred thee above all beasts of burden inasmuch as I have made thy master thy friend. I have given thee the power of flight without wings, be it in onslaught or in retreat. I will set man on thy back that shall honour and praise Me and sing Halleujah to My Name.'

Never was a promise more brightly fulfilled; and its first rider was Ishmael, son of Abraham and first ancestor of the Bedouin.

One of the most widely known but least observed horses of antiquity was the unicorn. The Greeks believed that it lived in India, while the Hindus were convinced that it was native to Ceylon, or perhaps somewhere else.

Everyone, however, was aware of its beauty and of its proud and imperious nature which made it very difficult to tame. The only means of doing so was to induce a virgin to sit alone and naked under a tree. The unicorn would then approach, and overcome by the girl's loveliness and purity, would lay its head peacefully in her lap. It could then be seized and bridled without further trouble.

Capturing or killing a unicorn was well worth while, since its horn, if dipped into cup or food, had the effect of neutralising any poison. This made it much in demand by royalty. Queen Elizabeth I bought such a horn, and exhibited it at Windsor Castle during the later years of her reign. It was valued at £100,000, despite the comments of some of her more well-travelled subjects who thought it might have been the horn of a narwhal.

Smiths, magic and ritual

Some of the magic of horses has settled upon those who handle them – especially blacksmiths, whose dealings with fire and iron gave them invulnerability against all forms of enchantment and witchcraft. This belief persisted well into the Christian era, as can be seen from the story of St Dunstan, who as well as being a great and good man, gave us the protection of the horseshoe against evil.

Sometime in the 16th century, or perhaps even earlier, a secret society was formed in England, Scotland and other parts of Europe.

Variously known as the Horse Whisperers or the Horseman's Word, its members were ploughmen and head horsemen, the most valued of skilled farm-workers. Membership gave a power over horses that amounted almost to witchcraft; it was believed by outsiders that the members of the society had the power to tame the most savage horse by a whisper, or that they could induce one to stand stock-still.

The society flourished until well within living memory, and in districts where the horse continues to play a part in the economy, may flourish still.

Such secret societies, it is thought, could be among the last manifestations of the Celtic horse cult that existed in Europe up to, and well into, the Roman occupation. On the great Celtic festivals of Samain (November 1), Imbolc (February 1), Beltane (May 1) and Lugnasad (August 1), which were based on key dates in the agricultural and pastoral year, with Samain as New Year's Day, horse-races were run in honour of the horse-goddess Epona or Rhiannon. Traces of this preoccupation with horses, perhaps mingled with memories of Woden and the Wild Hunt, may still linger on in the mumming plays that are performed in many villages of Europe on November 1, known now as All Saints' Day. A central character in a number of these is the Obby Oss, a grotesque creature, half man, half horse, with a grin-

Left *Eclipse by the eighteenth-century artist George Stubbs, probably Britain's most celebrated horse painter,* **right** *'Bronco Buster', captured in action by the US artist Frederic Remington (1861–1909) and* **below** *Eadweard Muybridge's sequential galloping horse. For many centuries, artists found it impossible to depict a moving horse at speeds greater than a walk. Even Stubbs, whose* interest in horses was such that it led him to make detailed anatomical studies of them, was unable to reveal the true rhythm of a galloping horse. Like all artists of the period, his studies are formalised.*

It was the pioneer photographic work of Muybridge that made realism possible. Taken at high speed to achieve clarity, his studies had a profound influence on Remington.

ning wooden head and gaping jaws.

The horse and the arts

There is little doubt that one of the chief roles of the horse in art – painting, literature, films – as in life, is that of servant, companion and prop to the ego of Man. We can have very little idea of how a horse feels in its natural state, but left to itself, it is unlikely that it would pull a plough, bear a knight or cavalryman into a situation that would almost certainly lead to death or dismemberment for horse or rider, prance picturesquely under the guiding hand of an emperor, or do most of the other things that have attracted painters and writers to the animal since the dawn of history. The horse has been broken – an apt term – to the will and wishes of man. Consequently, by an odd transference, we ascribe to it the virtues and qualities we most admire in ourselves – courage, loyalty, intelligence and diligence – and it is as the embodiment of these that it has been so often praised by painters and poets. To these qualities are added the horse's own beauty, speed and strength, so that what we are frequently moved by in both art and literature, is actually a centaur-like being that combines all the advantages of both man and beast. An outstanding example of this is provided by the 'Mounted Emperor' school of sculpture and painting, in which the dignity, authority and personality of the man is magnified by his being mounted on a horse. The earliest of such portraits surviving is that of Marcus Aurelius, the second century Roman emperor, whose colossal equestrian statue dominates the Capitoline Hill in Rome.

This statue, or the symbolism it represented, so influenced sculptors and portrait

painters that until our own time, it was almost impossible to envisage a 'Great Man' in any situation other than on horseback. Titian's Charles V, Van Dyck's Charles I, and Falconet's bronze of Peter the Great, all enhance royal dignity astride a horse. Napoleon, not surprisingly, preferred something more spirited. His favourite painter was J. L. David, a founder of the Romantic movement, who depicted his patron in a number of epic situations in which the Emperor is shown directing operations from the back of a rearing horse. The most dramatic, perhaps, is *Napoleon crossing the Alps.* The horse's hooves plunge against a darkening sky crisscrossed by lightning. Its eyes start and its nostrils flare; but the fact that Napoleon is in charge of both horse and the situation is made apparent by his firm seat, his stern visage and his outstretched arm.

Horses at war, or in swift movement have challenged artists since the earliest times.

The wild, springing creatures drawn on the cave walls at Lascaux are probably a prayer of our ancestors of 20,000 years ago that the swift horse might stay within range of their spears; by painting a picture of the animal, they captured its spirit and so gained ascendancy over it.

The artists made their living by hunting; exact observation of animal behaviour and movement was of vital importance to them. Consequently, though executed in swift, simple strokes, the horses that graze, gallop and wheel across the cave walls precisely mirror the living creatures. This was an ability that was to escape many artists for thousands of years to come.

The challenge of movement

In the magnificent Assyrian stone relief *The lion hunt of King Assurnasipal,* the sculptor depicted all the horses of the royal chariot lifting their forefeet at the same time, a convention that appealed to a great many artists and sculptors among the ancients. Even the Greeks, superb horsemen and strivers after realism in art though they were, could not quite capture the movement of a galloping horse – as can be seen from the otherwise glorious Parthenon frieze. Despite the anatomical drawings of the horse by Leonardo da Vinci, artists of the Renaissance and after continued to be blind to any equine movement more rapid than a sedate walk. The famous English sporting paintings and prints of the eighteenth and early nineteenth centuries persisted in portraying galloping hunters and racehorses with all four legs outstretched – an anatomical and mechanical impossibility. It was the American pioneer cinematographer, Eadweard Muybridge, who by means of freeze-action photographs, was able to prove that at canter and gallop, the horse draws its feet together, and at one point of the action, all four feet leave

Two views of horses seen by artists from different times and cultures. **Left** *A Chinese handscroll on silk of polo players, painted by Lin-Lin in about 1635 and* **right** *Le Petit Cheval Bleu (The Little Blue Horse) by the German expressionist painter Franz Marc (1880–1916). In their different ways, both artists reveal their sympathy with their subject – Lin-Lin in his vivid appreciation of one of China's oldest games and Marc in his warmth and depth of colour.*

Marc's sympathy with horses lasted until his death. One of his diary entries before he was killed near Verdun in 1916 expressed sympathy for the sufferings of the artillery horses.

the ground at once. George Stubbs, doyen of horse-painters, had begun to appreciate this in the eighteenth century, and 100 years later, Toulouse-Lautrec seized upon the point in paintings such as *Jockeys* and *Mail Coach to Nice.* But the realism of the horse portraits of Sir Alfred Munnings, and the true appreciation shown in the work of Frederic Remington, pioneer recorder of the life of the US cowboy, was only made possible through the observations of Muybridge.

Portraits and sporting paintings apart, the role of the horse in the art of the machine age has been largely symbolistic. Innocence is the theme of the red and blue horses of Franz Marc, and happiness is inherent in the quickly glimpsed race meetings of Raoul Dufy. But in his massive *Guernica,* Picasso assigns the animal to a different twentieth-century role. At the focus of the painting, a horse struggles among the ruins of the bombed town, screaming in uncomprehending terror at the

The horse in literature

'On your imaginary forces, work. . . .' suggests Chorus in Shakespeare's *Henry V*, 'Think, when we talk of horses, that you see them, printing their proud hooves i' the receiving earth. . . .' As so often in his work, Shakespeare in this play uses the horse as an image to convey a sense of urgency, of great deeds a-stirring, of their culmination in triumph or tragedy. On the sleepless, uneasy night before Agincourt, the opposing armies stir restlessly as across no-man's land 'steed threatens steed with high and boastful neigh', while the Dauphin of France bores his companions with praises of his horse, which he likens to a mistress. 'Methought your mistress shrewdly shook your back yesterday', comments the Constable sarcastically, and resumes his brooding on the morrow.

Richard III's oft-quoted cry of 'My Kingdom for a horse!', if taken within the context of the play, sums up the king's final self-realisation and sense of bitter betrayal. It is also the moment when the audience, having followed Richard through his innumerable

aircraft raining death from the jagged sky.

villainies, begins to sympathise with his plight and has a reluctant admiration for his courage. Again, in *Richard II*, a king's downfall is emphasised by a horse – 'a jade hath eat bread from my royal hand' – Richard's own beloved charger, that, without a thought for his old master, carries his supplanter to his coronation.

Throughout the ages the horse has been a favourite subject for writers from almost all over the world. The horses of fiction are legion, from Don Quixote's steed which in fact he loved much better than his lady, Dulcinea, to Black Beauty, whose anthropomorphous musings did much to reveal the condition of horses in the cities of nineteenth-century England; and to The Pie, the horse that Velvet Brown, heroine of *National Velvet* rode to victory in the Grand National. Human vision is inspired by the horse, like that of the little boy who could 'see' the winners of future races whenever he rode his rocking-horse in D. H. Lawrence's story *The Rocking-horse Winner*. In his fable, *Animal Farm*, George Orwell presents two cart horses as epitomising working-class virtues, but whose labour and loyalty do them little good in the end. Curiously enough, David Low, the British political cartoonist of the same epoch, also used a cart horse image, but to personify what he saw as the plodding Trades Union movement of his time.

The great horse writers of the nineteenth century, such as Surtees, creator of Jorrocks, were actually more concerned with horsemen than with animals. To them, the horse was a means of transport and a beast of burden, which was referred to, if at all, in words of casual insult. It is left to us, in the jet era, to restore to the animal some of the awe felt for it by our farther-off ancestors. This is expressed in Peter Shaeffer's play, *Equus*, in which a lonely, disturbed boy blinds the horse that has become to him part god and part keeper of his conscience.

The horse, it seems, exercises its magic still, even if many of us seldom see one except on cinema or television screens. There at least, in a line of John Ford's cavalrymen against the sky, or in the slow, menacing advance of the French knights in Olivier's *Henry V*, we can feel again the stir in our blood that must surely be ancestral.

Above *A Belgian child's wall drawings of a horse and* **left** *the young Elizabeth Taylor, playing the heroine of 'National Velvet', mounts The Pie. This film, the story of a young girl and her horse winning the British Grand National, is one of the most popular of all time in countries all over the world.*

Left *Cervantes's tragi-comic Don Quixote and his elderly steed Rosinante prepare to tilt at the windmill in this poster by the Beggarstaffs.* **Below** *Robert Bevan captures the earthy realism of a horse sale in his 'Horse Dealers'.*

Chapter Three

The points of the horse

The most striking feature of the horse is that it can perform the many tasks asked of it by man, though its physical make-up is in many ways unsuited to such demands. In its main period of evolution, the horse developed from a four or even five-toed marsh dweller to take the basic form it has today at a relatively early date; and even though it has somewhat changed its shape and improved its performance, the basic working mechanism remains the same.

Such basic physical facts should always colour the rider's attitude to the horse, and what he or she expects of it. With a basic understanding of the so-called points of the horse, it should be possible, for example, to go some way towards lessening the risk of muscular strains. These are all too common and, in extreme cases, can lead to a horse having to rest for weeks, if not months. More important still, knowledge of these points acts as a valuable guide in deciding what is a suitable or unsuitable horse for the prospective rider. The most vital attribute of any riding horse is depth of girth, which denotes toughness and strength. Tall, leggy horses invariably lack stamina. Short legs and a deep body, with plenty of heart room, are the signs to look for.

The most important points of the horse are its limbs and feet. Both in the wild and in domesticity, the horse depends on its means of locomotion for survival.

Feet and legs require therefore to be as correctly conformed as possible, if the horse is to remain sound and mobile. Correct conformation is, indeed, the most valuable asset any horse can possess.

The hind leg

Experts differ as to whether the most important single asset is a good hind leg or a good foreleg. As the hind leg is the propelling force, it is usually given priority. At the point

Body colours of horses vary. The principal ones are black, brown, bay and chestnut, though Thoroughbreds can be bay/brown, grey and roan as well. Non-Thoroughbred horses and ponies can also be dun, cream, piebald, skewbald, odd-coloured, whole coloured, palomino and Appaloosian. Within all these colours there are variations of shade. If there is any doubt about the colour of a horse, the deciding factor is the colour of its points – that is, the muzzle, tips of the ears, mane, tail and the lower parts of all four legs. Some body colours, correctly pointed, are shown (below).

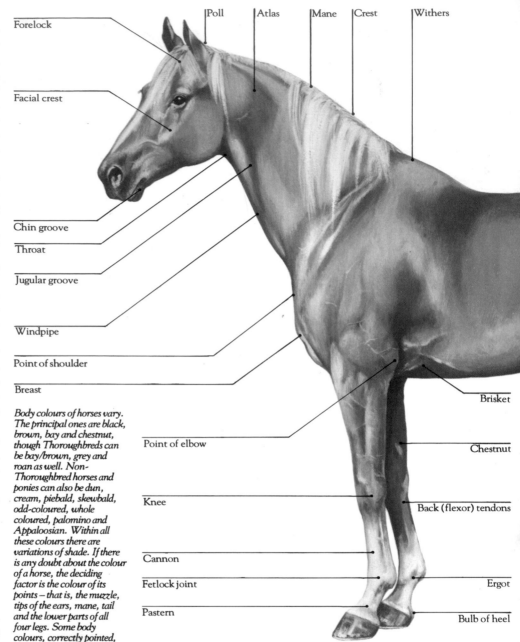

Forelock · Facial crest · Poll · Atlas · Mane · Crest · Withers · Chin groove · Throat · Jugular groove · Windpipe · Point of shoulder · Breast · Brisket · Point of elbow · Chestnut · Knee · Back (flexor) tendons · Cannon · Fetlock joint · Ergot · Pastern · Bulb of heel

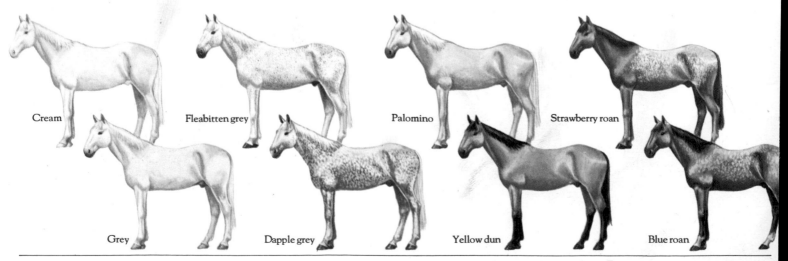

Cream · Fleabitten grey · Palomino · Strawberry roan · Grey · Dapple grey · Yellow dun · Blue roan

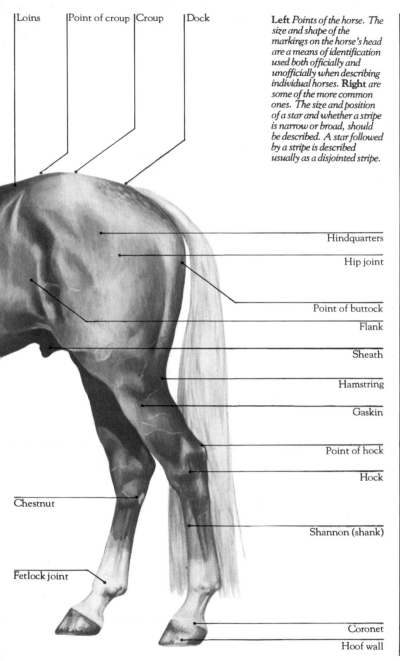

Loins | Point of croup | Croup | Dock

Hindquarters

Hip joint

Point of buttock

Flank

Sheath

Hamstring

Gaskin

Point of hock

Hock

Chestnut

Shannon (shank)

Fetlock joint

Coronet

Hoof wall

Left *Points of the horse. The size and shape of the markings on the horse's head are a means of identification used both officially and unofficially when describing individual horses.* **Right** *are some of the more common ones. The size and position of a star and whether a stripe is narrow or broad, should be described. A star followed by a stripe is described usually as a disjointed stripe.*

White face

Stripe

Blaze

Snip

Star

Right *White leg markings are an important means of identification. A sock covers the fetlock and part of the cannon, while a stocking extends to the knee or hock. Other marks take the name of their site.*

Chestnut

Bay

Piebald

Odd coloured

Liver chestnut

Brown

Skewbald

Black

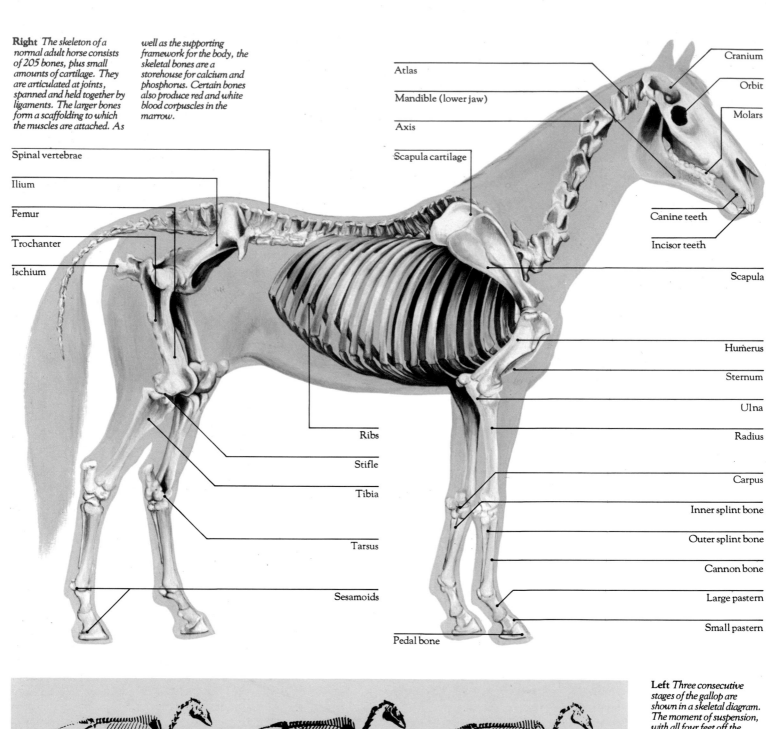

Right *The skeleton of a normal adult horse consists of 205 bones, plus small amounts of cartilage. They are articulated at joints, spanned and held together by ligaments. The larger bones form a scaffolding to which the muscles are attached. As well as the supporting framework for the body, the skeletal bones are a storehouse for calcium and phosphorus. Certain bones also produce red and white blood corpuscles in the marrow.*

Spinal vertebrae

Ilium

Femur

Trochanter

Ischium

Ribs

Stifle

Tibia

Tarsus

Sesamoids

Pedal bone

Atlas

Mandible (lower jaw)

Axis

Scapula cartilage

Cranium

Orbit

Molars

Canine teeth

Incisor teeth

Scapula

Humerus

Sternum

Ulna

Radius

Carpus

Inner splint bone

Outer splint bone

Cannon bone

Large pastern

Small pastern

Left *Three consecutive stages of the gallop are shown in a skeletal diagram. The moment of suspension, with all four feet off the ground, reveals how the hindlegs are gathered in through the action of the hock and stifle joints, which are the main propelling force.*

Below Left *Three phases of a jump – take off, flight and landing – show hock and stifle joints in action again, powering the spring and gathering up the hindlegs to clear the obstacle. The unique structure of the foreleg, which is attached to the upper body solely by muscles and ligaments, cushions the spine from the concussive shock of the landing.*

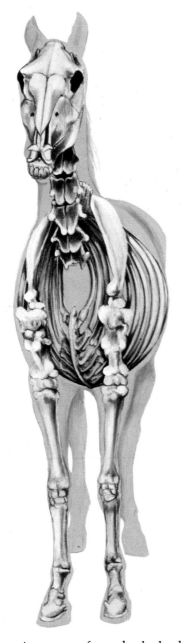

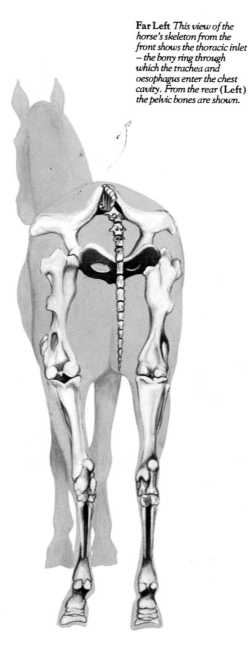

Far Left *This view of the horse's skeleton from the front shows the thoracic inlet – the bony ring through which the trachea and oesophagus enter the chest cavity. From the rear (**Left**) the pelvic bones are shown.*

able ride, they, too, are a sign of weakness that could lead to future trouble.

The foot

The size of foot varies with the type of horse. Thoroughbreds usually have small, rounded feet and, often, low heels. Heavy breeds, such as Clydesdales, Shires and Percherons, have larger, flatter feet.

The foot should be wide and open, not narrow, 'boxy' and contracted. The horn should look healthy and be free from unsightly cracks or ridges. Under it lies the sensitive laminae.

When the foot is lifted up, a well-developed frog should be visible on the underside. Starting at the bulbs of the heel and running upwards to end in a point near the toe, the frog acts as an anti-slip device and also helps to absorb concussion.

Each hoof is surmounted by the coronary band, which lies between the foot and the pastern.

Proper care of the feet is vital. In jumping, for instance, one forefoot has to take the whole weight of both horse and rider at the moment of landing. Good shoeing is therefore essential, or lameness will result. A young horse, too, can develop a form of lameness called pedal ostitis, caused by an excess of pressure on the sensitive sole of the foot by the os pedis – the terminal bone. This comes about largely through overwork, particularly in jumping.

The foreleg

The unique feature of the horse's foreleg is that it is attached to the upper part of the body by nothing more than muscle and ligamentous tissue. The horse has no equivalent to the human clavicle, or collar bone. The chief advantage of this is that the muscle is able to absorb a great deal of the concussion that would otherwise be transmitted to the spine. However, if undue strain is placed on the muscle, the horse can easily break down. This is particularly the case in race horses – often because the horse is what is known as 'back at the knee' (the shape is concave rather than convex).

The foreleg extends from the body below the point of the shoulder. The forearm runs down into the knee, which, like the hock, should be big, flat and prominent. Then the cannon bone, with tendons standing out clear and hard, runs down into the fetlock. The pastern separates this from the foot.

The legs have one final individual feature – the horny growths inside the legs above the knees. These are called chestnuts, and are, like fingerprints, completely individual. They are thought to be the remains of a digit.

where it emerges from the body the stifle joint is situated. This corresponds to the human knee and is similarly equipped with a patella, or kneecap. This acts like a pulley block to give added strength to the muscles extending the stifle.

The stifle itself is synchronized in its movements with the hock, as it is controlled by the same muscles and ligaments. As one flexes, so does the other.

Then comes the gaskin, or second thigh. This should be muscular and well-developed enough to stand up to the work and strain demanded of it. This runs down into the hock – probably the most important part of the leg as the main propelling agent which enables the horse to gallop and jump.

The hock is made up of a whole series of joints, tightly bound together by ligaments. It articulates directly with the tibia (another

vital bone) only through one bone – the astralagus. The feature as a whole should be big, flat and free from unsightly lumps, bumps or swellings. These can be indications of various types of unsoundness, such as curbs, spavins or thoroughpins.

The hock should also be near to the ground; short cannon bones from hock to fetlock and from knee to fetlock are a sign of strength. The tendons should stand out sharply and there should be no thickening of the lower leg.

The fetlock joint should also be well-defined and not puffy – a puffy fetlock resembles a human swollen ankle. This leads on to the pastern, which should be of medium length and slope. Very short pasterns cannot fulfill one of their main tasks – absorbing the concussion produced by movement. Though over-long pasterns give a springy, comfort-

The body

The shoulder runs from the withers – the bony prominence dividing the neck from the back and the highest part of the dorsal spine – down to the point of the shoulder. The shoulder itself should be long and sloping, especially at the upper end. An upright shoulder reduces endurance, as the horse has to do more work to cover the ground, and it cannot help to reduce concussion, which instead is passed on to the rider, making the horse uncomfortable to ride. This is particularly the case if the horse is ridden downhill.

The breast lies to the front of the shoulder, between the forelegs. It should be broad and muscular; narrow-breasted horses are weak and lack stamina. The underside of the neck should be concave and not unduly muscular.

The jaws run down to the muzzle. Well-defined, slightly distended nostrils and a large, generous eye are a sign of quality and good breeding. So are alert, well-pricked ears, which should not be too large. Between them lies the poll, leading to the top of neck, the crest, which runs down to the withers and back. The back consists of about eleven of the eighteen dorsal vertebrae, as well as the arches of the corresponding ribs. Behind it lie the loins, which should be strong and well-muscled. These extend to the croup, or rump, which runs down to the tail and its underside, the dock.

Standing behind the horse, the points of the hip can be seen projecting outwards on either side of the backbone, above the flanks. This outwards projection means that they can easily be injured.

Just below the loins, a triangular depression, known as the 'hollow of the flank', is located. This is the highest point of the flank, which stretches downwards from the lumbar spine. The condition of the flank often acts as a guide to the health of the horse; if the horse is sick, it may well be 'tucked up' or distended.

Teeth and age

Age in the horse is determined by examining the six incisors (grinding teeth). The two central incisors are cut when a foal is ten days old and are followed within a month or six weeks by the lateral incisors. The corner incisors follow between six and nine months, to complete the horse's full set of milk teeth.

The trot (below) is an active, two-time pace, the legs moving in diagonal pairs with a moment of suspension. The rider rises in the saddle for one stride, then sits again.

The walk (right) is the slowest pace of the horse. The animal moves one leg after another in the sequence, left fore, right hind, right fore, left hind, in a regular four-time rhythm.

Trot

Canter

Gallop

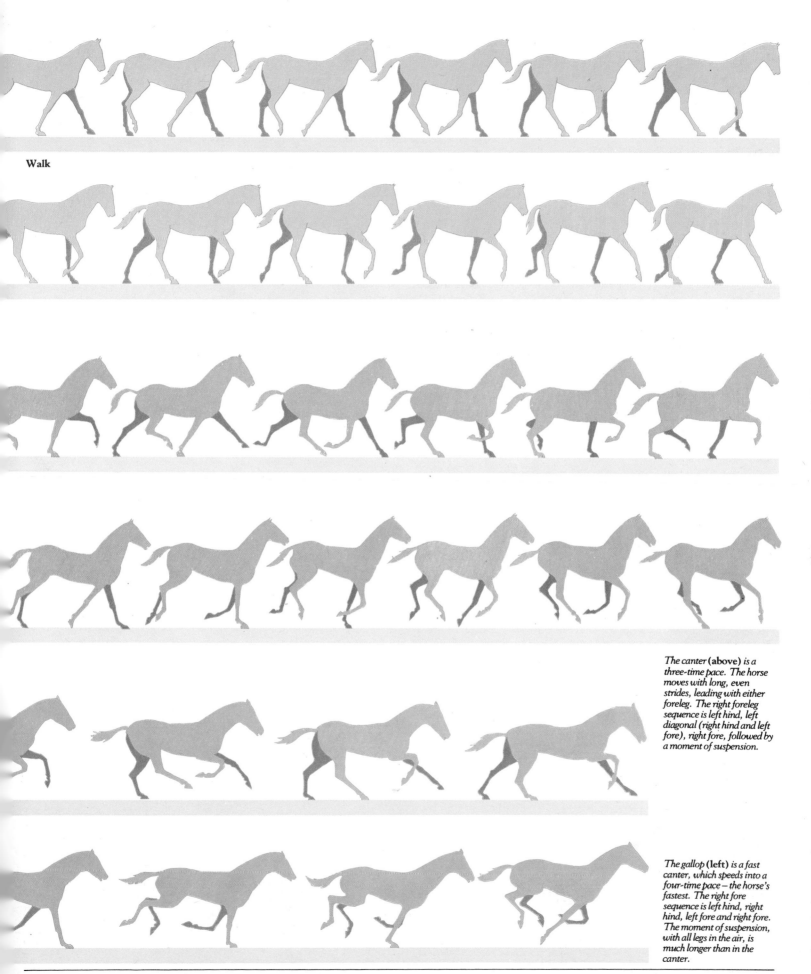

Walk

The canter (**above**) is a three-time pace. The horse moves with long, even strides, leading with either foreleg. The right foreleg sequence is left hind, left diagonal (right hind and left fore), right fore, followed by a moment of suspension.

The gallop (**left**) is a fast canter, which speeds into a four-time pace – the horse's fastest. The right fore sequence is left hind, right hind, left fore and right fore. The moment of suspension, with all legs in the air, is much longer than in the canter.

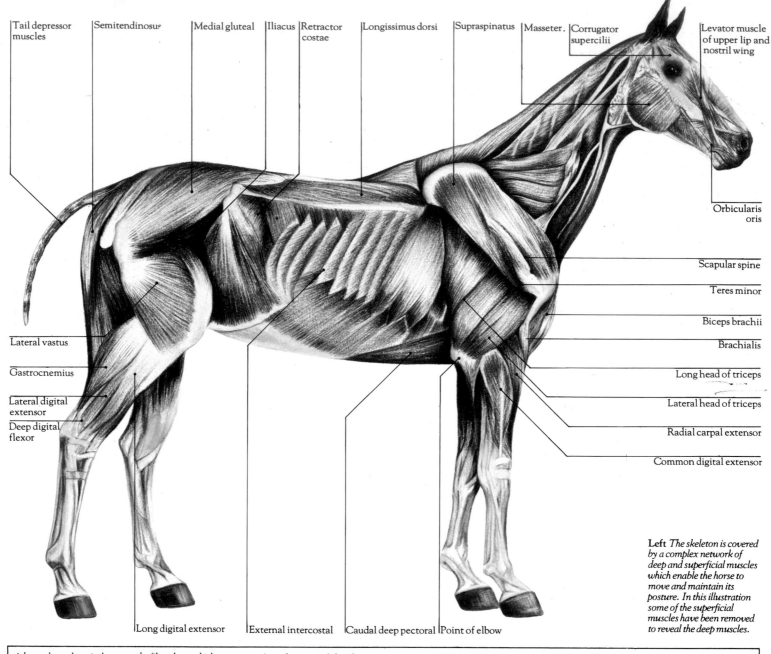

Tail depressor muscles

Semitendinosus

Medial gluteal

Iliacus

Retractor costae

Longissimus dorsi

Supraspinatus

Masseter.

Corrugator supercilii

Levator muscle of upper lip and nostril wing

Orbicularis oris

Scapular spine

Teres minor

Biceps brachii

Brachialis

Long head of triceps

Lateral head of triceps

Radial carpal extensor

Common digital extensor

Lateral vastus

Gastrocnemius

Lateral digital extensor

Deep digital flexor

Long digital extensor

External intercostal

Caudal deep pectoral

Point of elbow

Left *The skeleton is covered by a complex network of deep and superficial muscles which enable the horse to move and maintain its posture. In this illustration some of the superficial muscles have been removed to reveal the deep muscles.*

A horse depends on its legs for survival, but unfortunately, the system which it has evolved for moving legs is not ideal. All the muscles are grouped together at the top of the leg, and the force from their contractions is transferred by tendons to the appropriate bone or joint. These stretched lines of communication are very prone to injury.

Tendons consist of thousands of collagen fibres lying in a groundwork of connective tissue. These fibres lie in the approximate direction of the force which is transmitted along the tendon. The connective tissue consists of an inert matrix with a network of blood vessels, elastic fibres and various individual cells. Chief among these cells are

the fibroplasts which are responsible for forming the collagen fibres.

Each tendon is surrounded by a smooth membrane, the peritendineum, and enclosed in a tendon sheath which also has a smooth lining. Movement of the tendon within its tendon sheath is further facilitated by the presence of tenosynovial fluid as a sort of lubricant.

If a tendon is strained the collagen fibres slip and rupture. There is also haemorrhage and tissue fluids collect at the site of the damage. New collagen has to be formed to repair the damage, and the orientation of these new collagen fibres is vitally important. If scar tissue is formed, then the materials and cells involved arrive at the site by migration

from the synovial sheath around the tendon and so consist of Collagen Type 3. If, instead of scar tissue, the existing collagen is regenerated, then this consists of Collagen Type 1 – a stronger type.
The extra fluid which is released at the site of the tendon injury is important for three reasons. Firstly, if it contains a great deal of fibrin it may clot rather like blood and form adhesions which will affect future movement. Secondly, the pressure which the fluid causes, both between the fibrous bundles and in the tendon sheath, is a major cause of pain. Finally, if the 'filling' of the leg becomes chronic it is an unsightly blemish. Regeneration always takes time, during which the horse should be completely rested.

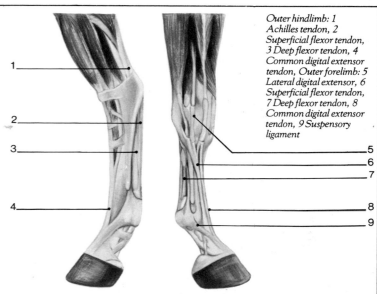

Outer hindlimb: 1 Achilles tendon, 2 Superficial flexor tendon, 3 Deep flexor tendon, 4 Common digital extensor tendon, Outer forelimb: 5 Lateral digital extensor, 6 Superficial flexor tendon, 7 Deep flexor tendon, 8 Common digital extensor tendon, 9 Suspensory ligament

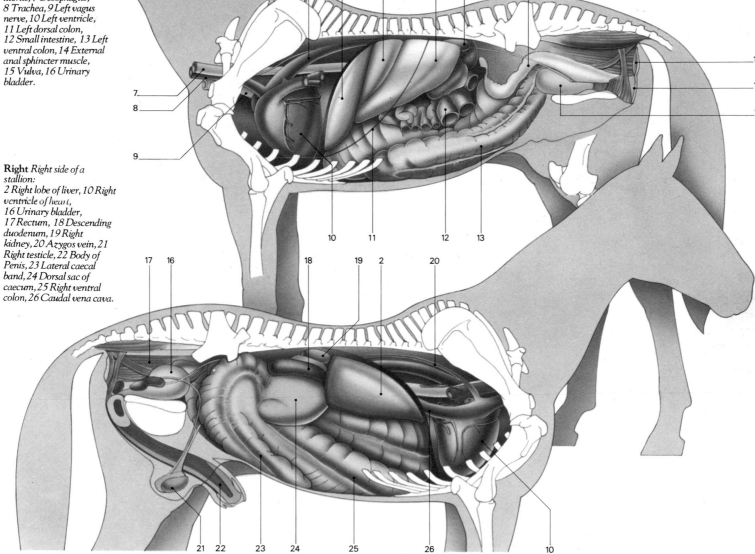

These are white in colour, in contrast to the yellow of the permanent teeth, and taper to a point at the base.

These last the horse until the age of three, when the central incisors are replaced by permanent teeth. At four, the lateral incisors are similarly replaced, and male horses also grow a tush, or canine tooth. At five the last milk teeth, the corner incisors, give way to permanent teeth.

At six, the corner incisors have worn level, while by the age of seven they will have developed a hook shape. At nine a dark line is visible on the biting edge and Galvayne's groove, a longitudinal furrow, appears on the corner teeth, near the gum. At ten, the slope of the teeth increases and at fifteen this becomes even more pronounced; this process reaches its climax between the ages of twenty and twenty-five. At twenty, too, Galvayne's groove reaches the lower edge of the teeth,

though, from that time, it starts to disappear at the same rate it first appeared.

All these factors – length, slope and the increasingly triangular shape – make it possible to estimate a horse's age reasonably accurately. After the age of eight, however, when the horse is said to be aged, it is not possible to be exact.

Measuring height
The horse's height is measured from the highest point of the withers to the ground. On the European continent, it is measured in centimetres, while in the UK, Ireland, North America and Australasia, it is measured in hands. A hand is officially defined as 4 in (10.16 cm) – the distance across a man's knuckles; 14 hands 3 inches, or 14.3 hands, is the accepted breakdown for fractionalised measurement. The common abbreviation 'hh' stands for 'hands high'.

Markings and colours
Markings on the head of the horse are described as a star (a small white patch of hair on the forehead); a stripe (a white line running down the face); a blaze (a broad white mark); a white face (like a Hereford cow); and a snip (a white line running into the nostril or around it). White markings on the legs are either socks (short) or stockings (long). These definitions have been established by the various breeding authorities.

Colours of the horse vary. They range from bay (the colour of a horse chestnut, with a black mane, tail and, usually, black lower legs, described as black points); black; brown; chestnut (varying shades of red, from bright to liver chestnut); dun (cream-coloured, shading to yellow, with black points, dorsal stripe, mane and tail); cream (with light mane and tail); palomino (varying shades of gold, with flaxen mane and tail); blue or red

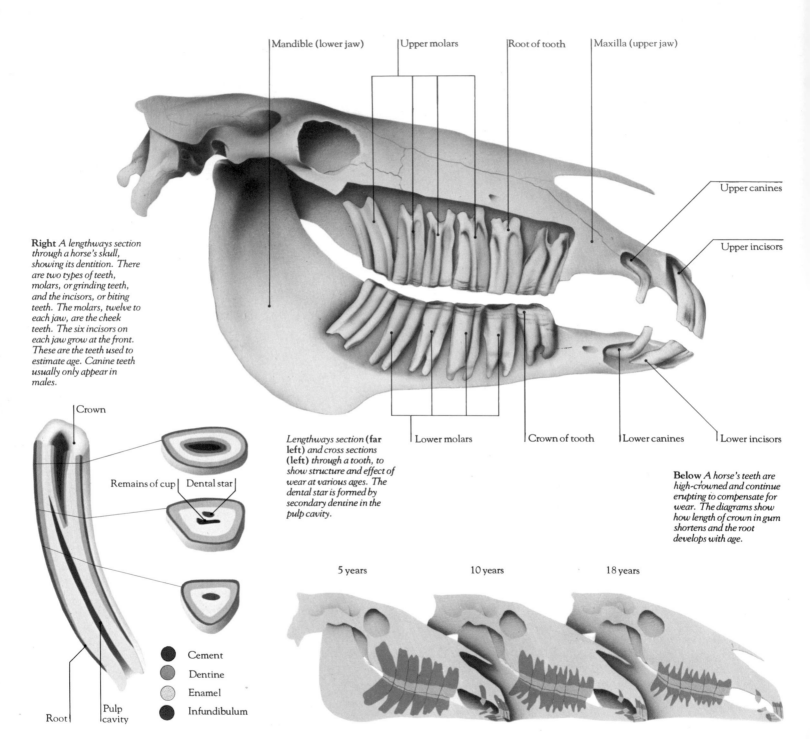

Mandible (lower jaw) Upper molars Root of tooth Maxilla (upper jaw)

Upper canines

Upper incisors

Right *A lengthways section through a horse's skull, showing its dentition. There are two types of teeth, molars, or grinding teeth, and the incisors, or biting teeth. The molars, twelve to each jaw, are the cheek teeth. The six incisors on each jaw grow at the front. These are the teeth used to estimate age. Canine teeth usually only appear in males.*

Crown

Remains of cup Dental star

Lengthways section (far left) and cross sections (left) through a tooth, to show structure and effect of wear at various ages. The dental star is formed by secondary dentine in the pulp cavity.

Lower molars Crown of tooth Lower canines Lower incisors

Below *A horse's teeth are high-crowned and continue erupting to compensate for wear. The diagrams show how length of crown in gum shortens and the root develops with age.*

Cement
Dentine
Enamel
Infundibulum

Root Pulp cavity

5 years   10 years   18 years

roan (grey or chestnut, with a white fleck throughout); piebald (black and white); skewbald (red or chestnut or bay and white); to pinto (piebald, skewbald, or odd-coloured, grey or roan and white, for example).

Gaits of the horse

The four basic gaits of the horse are the walk, the trot, the canter and the gallop. In addition, US saddle horses can have four extra gaits – the pace, the stepping pace, the slow gait and the rack.

The walk is a marching pace in which the four legs follow one another in the following sequence – left hind, left fore, right hind, right fore, left fore, right hind, right fore and left hind. When the four beats cease to be well accented, even and regular, the walk is termed disunited or broken. The gait itself is further sub-divided into ordinary walk, collected walk, extended walk and free walk.

The trot is a two-time pace on alternate diagonals (near fore and off hind and vice versa), separated by a moment of suspension. The gait can be ordinary, collected or extended, as can the canter.

The canter is a three-time pace. Leading with the off fore, or right foreleg, the horse follows this sequence: near hind, left diagonal (right hind and left fore), right fore, fol-

lowed by a period of suspension with all four legs in the air before it takes the next stride forwards.

The gallop is the horse's fastest pace, during which it never has more than two feet on the ground, and, more often than not, one. During a forward leap, all the feet leave the ground and the horse is, literally, flying. The legs can be lifted in one of two sequences – either left fore, right fore, left hind and right hind, or right fore, left fore, right hind and left hind.

Common faults

With the exception of obvious faults of con-

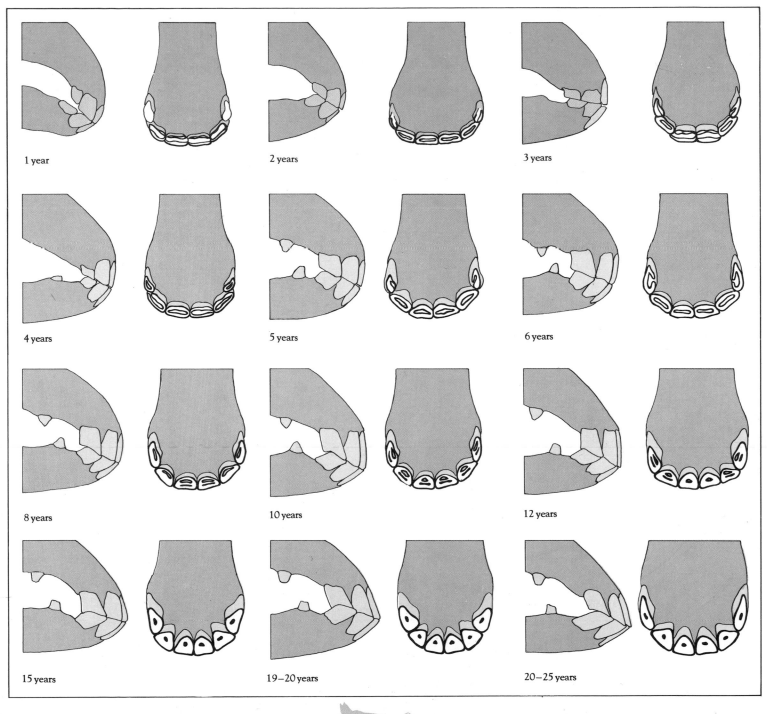

1 year

2 years

3 years

4 years

5 years

6 years

8 years

10 years

12 years

15 years

19–20 years

20–25 years

formation, which should be discovered on initial examination, few horses are bad – if they are, they have generally been made so by faulty handling and training. It is important to realize that a horse's brain is small compared to its body size, that it cannot reason, and that it should not be given credit for a human-type intelligence. Weaknesses such as brushing (striking one foot with the shoes of the opposite foot) and forging (striking the forefoot with the toe of the hind) are usually caused by faulty action or general unfitness. A fit, well-fed and carefully exercised horse will seldom have to face such problems.

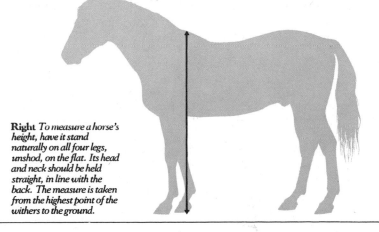

Right *To measure a horse's height, have it stand naturally on all four legs, unshod, on the flat. Its head and neck should be held straight, in line with the back. The measure is taken from the highest point of the withers to the ground.*

Above *Changes in dentition, signs of wear and marks of age are used to estimate the age of a horse. The replacement of temporary incisors with permanent ones is an accurate gauge up to five years. From then until eight, wear on cups and corner teeth is a useful indicator. After this, the growth of Galvayne's groove on the upper corner incisor, the appearance of dental stars, wearing away of cups and the increasing forward slope of incisors are the best guides.*

Chapter Four

Types and breeds

In this chapter, a breed is defined as one that has a stud book. There are two main types. Many stud books are open, that is, stock is registered in the breed stud book on condition that the parents are approved by the relevant breed society and are of pedigree stock themselves. The stallion and mare concerned need not necessarily be both of the same breed. The Hanoverian, for example, often has Arab, Thoroughbred or Trakehner ancestors. However, most of the older breeds – Arab and Thoroughbred, for instance – have closed stud books. This means that stock is only registered if both parents are registered members of that breed.

In addition, there are horses that are not registered in any stud book; most of these are defined as types. Hunters, hacks and cobs all come under this category, though it is possible to have a registered Thoroughbred hunter or hack.

There are also horses that are difficult to place within this system. The Australian Brumby, for instance, is the feral descendant of horses which escaped from captivity when the first European settlers came to Australia in the late eighteenth century. Thus, it is not a true breed, nor is it really a type. Nevertheless, it is cross-bred with domestic horses to produce very sturdy off-spring.

In the subsequent pages, each breed is discussed under its place of origin.

North America

America is now thought to be where the modern horse (*Equus caballos*) evolved. Before the land bridge linking North America and Asia was submerged to become the Bering Straits, horses probably migrated across it, to spread through Asia and, eventually, Europe. Some almost certainly stayed in America, but what happened to them is uncertain. No equine remains have been found dateable to any period after the Ice Age, so it seems that for 7000 years there were no horses in America. They re-entered the continent in 1511, when the Spanish adventurer Hernan Cortes landed in Mexico with a small force of conquistadores and 16 Andalusians.

The North American Indians were poor breeders of horses, taking no pains to breed selectively. The one exception was the Nez Percé tribe. By the end of the eighteenth century, they had developed high-quality, spotted horses which they christened Appaloosas. The other horses used by the Indians were the Mustangs, which escaped from the early settlers to run wild.

The colonists of the Atlantic coast also brought horses with them. The first distinct native breed to emerge from these imports was the Narrangansett Pacer, which was developed on Rhode Island mainly from Nor-

folk Trotter stock. However, losses through export and cross-breeding led to the pure-bred Narrangansett dying out.

In the mid-nineteenth century, cross-breeding produced one of the greatest of the US breeds, the Standardbred. The name comes from the standards set for horses to achieve during the selective breeding process. Today the Standardbred is the basis of the major sport of trotting, and has played a crucial part in improving foreign breeds.

The Quarter-horse is the oldest surviving American breed. It is also the most numerous in the USA; 800,000 are registered worldwide. The horse was developed by the seventeenth century settlers in Virginia and the Carolinas as an all-purpose animal. Its ability was tested by racing it over a quarter of a mile, and from this comes its name. As the Americans expanded westwards, the Quarter-horse proved to be an excellent cow pony.

Galiceno

Garranos → Galiceno

Pony
Height: 12.2 hands.
Colour: bay, black or dun.
Physique: short-coupled, narrow frame.
Features: versatile, natural running walk.
Use: ranch work and transportation.

Standardbred

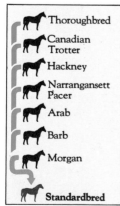
Thoroughbred
Canadian Trotter
Hackney
Narrangansett Pacer
Arab
Barb
Morgan
→ Standardbred

Warmblood
Height: 15.2 hands.
Colour: solid colours.
Physique: varies as it is bred for speed; usually muscular Thoroughbred type with longer back, short legs and powerful shoulders.
Features: stamina, speed.
Use: driving and racing.

Pinto
Warmblood
Height: varies.
Colour:: black with white or white with any colour

but black.
Physique: varies.
Use: ranch work, riding or showing.

Quarter-Horse

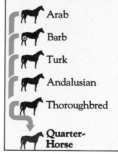
Arab
Barb
Turk
Andalusian
Thoroughbred
→ Quarter-Horse

Warmblood
Height: 15.3 hands.
Colour: solid colours, usually chestnut.
Physique: short head,

powerful, short-coupled body, large round hindquarters and fine legs.
Features: fast and versatile.
Use: riding, racing, ranch work and rodeos.

Appaloosa

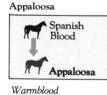
Spanish Blood → Appaloosa

Warmblood
Origin: Western States.
Height: 15 hands.
Colour: six basic patterns of spots usually on roan or white, white sclera around eye.
Physique: short-coupled, thin mane and tail, hard feet which are often

The Morgan is another of the old-established American breeds. It was the product of a single foundation sire – either a Welsh Cob or a Thoroughbred, foaled in 1793. The horse was the property of an innkeeper called Justin Morgan, hence the name.

With the Thoroughbred and the Narrangansett Pacer, it was also the foundation stock for the Saddlebred. This breed was developed by the nineteenth century plantation owners of the South, who wanted showy animals that were comfortable to ride. The result was the Saddlebred, a spectacular horse with three or five gaits. It is very popular in the show ring, where it is ridden or shown in harness. Then in Tennessee a horse was developed with an even smoother gait than that of the Saddlebred – the Tennessee Walking Horse. It was officially recognized as a breed in 1935.

striped.
Use: as a cow pony, a pleasure and parade horse and in the circus.

Mustang

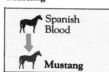
Spanish Blood → Mustang

Warmblood
Origin: Western States and Mexico.
Height: 14.2 hands.
Colour: most colours.
Physique: sturdy, tough lightweight frame, good bone and tough feet.
Features: hardy and frugal.
Use: riding, showing, trail riding, endurance trials, competitions and stock work.

Quarter-Horse

Appaloosa

Canadian Cutting Horse

Galiceno

Pinto

Standardbred

The USA also has registers for horses that are defined according to colour, but do not yet breed true to type. Of these, the most attractive is the Palomino, the glamorous Hollywood cowboy pony. The Pinto was the Indians' favoured horse; its two colours were supposed to aid camouflage. The Albino, however, is a more recent development. Its genes appear to be prepotent.

As far as imported stock is concerned, the Thoroughbred is the most numerous, racing being a major industry in the USA. Second in number is the Shetland. This is used in halter and fine harness classes, as well as in trotting races. Other imported breeds with their own stud books are the Welsh, Hackney, Cleveland Bay, Percheron, Belgian, Trakehner, Clydesdale and Arab.

The only native American pony is of recent origin. It is the Pony of the Americas, which was developed in the 1960s, using an Appaloosa sire (with Arab and Quarter-horse ancestors) and Shetlands.

Canada has no native breed of horse, the Canadian Cutting Horse being classed only as a type. Horse-breeding, however, has flourished, ever since the first horses were brought across the Atlantic by French settlers in 1665. Some of the descendants of these horses are to be found in the Sable Islands where they have roamed semi-wild since the eighteenth century.

Palomino

Saddlebred

Tennessee Walking Horse

Morgan

Tennessee Walking Horse

- Narrangansett Pacer
- Standardbred
- Canadian Pacer
- Saddlebred
- Morgan
- **Tennessee Walking Horse**

Warmblood
Origin: Tennessee.
Height: 15.2 hands.
Colour: solid colours.
Physique: common head, crested neck, strong, sloping shoulder, powerful loins and hindquarters, clean legs and full mane and tail, carried artificially high.
Features: kind temperament; has a running walk with the forefeet raised high and the hind legs moving with long strides.
Use: showing and riding.

Canadian Cutting Horse
Warmblood
Height: 15.2 – 16.1 hands.
Colour: almost any colour.
Physique: like the American Quarter Horse. Long body, short legs, powerful hindquarters.
Features: intelligent, fast and agile.
Use: competition and stock work.

Albino

- Arab
- Morgan
- **Albino**

Warmblood
Height: any.
Colour: white with pink skin, pale blue or dark brown eyes.
Physique: lightweight frame, otherwise varies.
Use: riding.

Palomino
Warmblood
Origin: California.
Height: 14 hands.
Colour: golden, with no markings other than white on face or below the knees. Mane and tail white, silver or ivory; dark eyes.
Physique: varies; registered for colour, so does not yet breed true to type.
Use: riding, driving and stock work.

Pony of the Americas

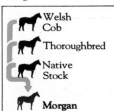

- Shetland Pony
- Appaloosa
- **Pony of the Americas**

Pony
Height: 12.1 hands.
Colour: Appaloosa patterns.
Physique: Arab-like head, short back and round body.
Use: trail riding, competitions and as a children's pony.

Missouri Foxtrotting Horse
Warmblood
Origin: Tennessee.
Height: 15.2 hands.
Colour: sorrel.
Physique: compact, strong body, long neck and intelligent head tapering to muzzle.
Features: broken gait called 'foxtrot', walking with forelegs and trotting with hindlegs at speeds of 10 to 15 mph
Use: riding and stock work.

Morgan

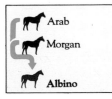

- Welsh Cob
- Thoroughbred
- Native Stock
- **Morgan**

Warmblood
Origin: Massachusetts.
Height: 15 hands.
Colour: bay, brown, black or chestnut.
Physique: short, broad head, thick neck, strong shoulders, back and hindquarters, good bone and full mane and tail.
Features: versatile, tough and good-tempered with a high action.

Saddlebred

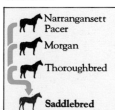

- Narrangansett Pacer
- Morgan
- Thoroughbred
- **Saddlebred**

Warmblood
Height: 15.2 hands.
Colour: black, brown, bay, grey or chestnut.
Physique: small head with straight profile.
Features: five-gaited.
Use: showing and riding.

Scandinavia

Denmark's equine history revolves around the Fredericksborg. This was popular in the late sixteenth and seventeenth centuries as a High School horse, and in the eighteenth century as an improver of other breeds. However, today there are only a few of the animals left. They were named after Frederick II, who originated the breed at the Royal Fredericksborg Stud, founded in 1562.

The most popular Danish breed today is the Fjord Pony, followed by the Jutland, which has been bred in the peninsula for hundreds of years.

From the 1960s, the Danes, too, have had a stud book for a national riding horse – the Danish Sports Horse – based on imported pedigree stallions from Germany, Sweden, France and the UK, and local mares.

Sweden has been meeting the demand for riding horses with pedigree blood for over one hundred years. A stud book was started as early as 1874 for the Swedish Halfbred, which excells in dressage and eventing. Hanoverian, Trakehner, French, British and Arab blood has also been used, with the proviso that it is truly pedigree and that the stallions involved all pass performance tests.

For working the land and hauling timber, the Swedes use the Swedish Ardennes. This breed was established a century ago, when the Belgian Ardennes and the North Swedish were cross-bred. The Gotland is Sweden's pony. It is thought to be a direct descendant of the Tarpan, having run wild on Gotland Island since the Stone Age.

Norway, too, has a primitive pony type – the Norwegian Fjord – which has been bred for centuries. It was used by the Vikings, and now is popular all over the world. Its strength, toughness and good temperament make it suitable for all types of work, in addition to riding and driving.

The other Norwegian breed – the Døle – is not as internationally popular as the Fjord, but is more numerous in its homeland. Its offshoot, the Døle Trotter, was developed in the nineteenth century, to meet the demand for a fast carrying horse. It is now used in trotting races.

In Finland, the Finnish Horse (formed by the amalgamation of the Finnish Universal and Finnish Draught) is declining in numbers, largely due to the mechanization of agriculture, transport and timber hauling. However, imported warmbloods, used for riding, competitions and trotting, are on the increase.

Horses were introduced into Iceland over a thousand years ago, and the Icelandic Pony still breeds there freely. Even today, it still has a major role to play in the country's economy.

SWEDEN

Swedish Halfbred

- Oriental
- Spanish
- Friesian
- Trakehner
- Hanoverian
- Thoroughbred
- Arab
- **Swedish Halfbred**

Warmblood
Height: 16.1 hands.
Colour: Any solid colour.
Physique: smallish, intelligent head, large, bold eye, longish neck, deep girth and straightish back.
Features: intelligent, with an extravagant, straight action.
Use: general riding and competitions.

Gotland

- Tarpan
- Little Oriental
- **Gotland**

Pony
Origin: Gotland Is.
Height: 12.1 hands.
Colour: dun, black, brown or chestnut.
Physique: light frame, small straight head, long back and low set tail.
Features: hardy, active, sometimes obstinate.
Use: light agricultural work, trotting races, and as a children's pony.

Swedish Ardennes

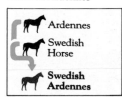

- Ardennes
- Swedish Horse
- **Swedish Ardennes**

Coldblood
Height: 15.3 hands.
Colour: black, brown, bay or chestnut.
Physique: similar to but smaller than the Belgian Ardennes.
Features: active, good-tempered.
Use: agricultural work and timber hauling.

DENMARK

Fredericksborg

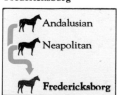

- Andalusian
- Neapolitan
- **Fredericksborg**

Warmblood
Height: 15.3 hands.
Colour: chestnut.
Physique: strong, plain harness horse, big chest, strong back.

Features: good-
tempered, active.
Use: light draught, riding.

Jutland

Ancient
Stock

Yorkshire
Coach Horse

Cleveland
Bay

Suffolk
Punch

Jutland

Coldblood
Origin: Jutland Is.
Height: 15.3 hands.
Colour: chestnut or roan.
Physique: massive,
compact horse; plain head
and short, feathered legs.
Features: good-tempered.
Use: draught.

Danish Sport Horse

Hanoverian

Native
Halfbred

Thoroughbred

Trakehner

Polish

Anglo-
Norman

**Danish
Sports Horse**

Warmblood
Origin: Denmark –
developed by crossing
various breeds from
Northern Europe with
locally bred mares
Height: 16.1 hands
Colour: all colours
Physique: varies,
middleweight build
Use: general riding

Knabstrup

Flaebehoppen

Fredericksborg

Knabstrup

Warmblood
Height: 15.3 hands.
Colour: spotted,
Appaloosa patterns on
roan base.
Physique: similar to but
lighter than the
Fredericksborg.
Use: circus.

NORWAY

Fjord

Asiatic
Wild Horse

**Norwegian
Fjord Pony**

Pony
Height: 14 hands.
Colour: dun, cream or
yellow with dorsal stripe
and upright black and
silver mane.
Physique: small head,
strong, short neck and
powerful, compact body.
Use: work in the
mountains; agriculture,
transport, riding and
driving.

Døle

Danish
Cold Blood

Thoroughbred

Trotter

Døle

Warmblood
Height: 15 hands.
Colour: black, brown or
bay.
Physique: two types; heavy
draught – similar to the
Dale; pony type – upright
shoulder, deep girth, short
legs with good bone and
little feather.
Features: tough, versatile.
Use: agricultural work,
riding and driving.

Døle Trotter

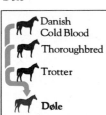

Trotter

Døle

**Døle
Trotter**

Warmblood
Height: 15 hands.
Colour: black, brown or
bay.
Physique: lighter version
of Døle with no feather.
Use: trotting races.

FINLAND

Finnish

Indigenous
Forest pony

Finnish
Draught

Finnish

Finnish
Universal

Coldblood
Height: 15.2 hands.
Colour: chestnut, bay and
brown.
Physique: short neck,
upright shoulder, deep,
strong legs, light feather.
Features: tough, long-
lived, even-tempered and
fast.
Use: timber hauling,
agriculture and trotting
races.

ICELAND

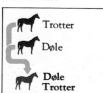

Iceland Pony

Pony

Irish
Blood

**Iceland
Pony**

Pony
Height: 12.2 hands.
Colour: grey, dun.
Physique: stocky, compact
body, full mane and tail.
Features: independent,
tough and able to amble.
Use: mining, pack and
communications.

Fjord

Iceland Pony

Finnish

Knabstrup

Fredericksborg

Døle

Swedish Halfbred

The Middle East and Africa

The world's oldest and most influential pure bred is the Arab, descended, it is believed, from Asiatic wild stock that ran wild in the desert lands of the Middle East as long ago as 5000 BC. Some experts claim that this original desert home was in either Persia, Syria or Egypt, but the majority hold that it was in the Yemen in the Arabian peninsula. From these origins, the Arab's special features – speed, endurance, fine coat and toughness – developed.

The main reason for the Arab's vast influence is because its equine virtues proved to be prepotent, that is they have been transmitted from one generation on to the next.

Today, Arabs are found all over the world, and their breeding is a flourishing industry. In the Arab's homeland, the Middle East, the most celebrated is the Persian – the oldest domesticated Arab – and the Egyptian, which, like the Polish Arab, is in heavy demand for export. This prepotency developed through the selective in-breeding pursued for centuries by the Bedouin tribesmen.

In Iran, too, there are other breeds of horse, which the recently formed Royal Horse Society is doing much to promote. Vast sums are being invested in both Thoroughbreds (mostly imported) and Turkomans for racing. The Turkoman itself has very early origins, which, in the adjacent USSR, played a part in the development of the Akhal Teké and Iomud. Most of the other strains of the Persian horse have now been amalgamated into one stud book for the Plateau Persian.

Under the Ottomans, Turkey produced many fine Arab strains from the sixteenth to twentieth centuries. The Byerley Turk played its part as a foundation sire for the Thoroughbred (see p. 84), but, during this century, the native stock deteriorated. This has led to the importation of the Nonius from Hungary to improve it and breed the Karacabey.

The other foundation stock for the Thoroughbred – the Barb – has its home in North Africa. It is often confused with the Arab, but experts claim that its origins lie with European, rather than with Asiatic, wild stock. It is distinguished from the Arab by its ram-like head, a lower-set tail, and its wilder temperament, but frequent crossing since the Arabs conquered North Africa has meant that there are few pure breeds surviving.

The rest of Africa, with one exception, has no native horses. The only native horse in South Africa – the Basuto Pony – developed from Barbs and Arabs imported in the mid-seventeenth century.

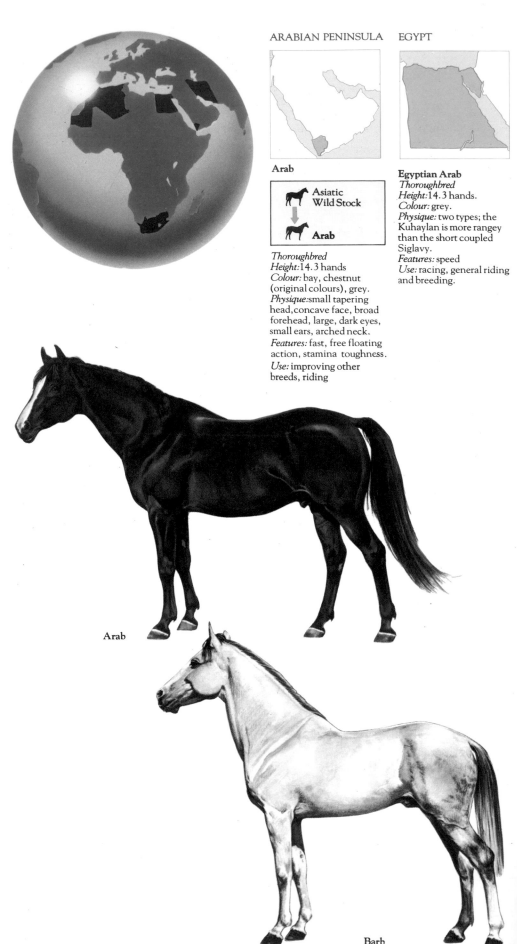

ARABIAN PENINSULA   EGYPT

Arab

Asiatic Wild Stock → Arab

Thoroughbred
Height: 14.3 hands
Colour: bay, chestnut (original colours), grey.
Physique: small tapering head, concave face, broad forehead, large, dark eyes, small ears, arched neck.
Features: fast, free floating action, stamina toughness.
Use: improving other breeds, riding

Egyptian Arab
Thoroughbred
Height: 14.3 hands.
Colour: grey.
Physique: two types; the Kuhaylan is more rangey than the short coupled Siglavy.
Features: speed
Use: racing, general riding and breeding.

Arab

Barb

IRAN

Caspian Pony
Pony
Origin: Iran
Height: 10–11.2 hands
Colour: grey, brown, bay, chestnut
Physique: Arab-type head, fine boned
Features: sure footed
Use: transport, riding

Pahlavan
Warmblood
Origin: Iran
Height: 15.2–16 hands
Colour: solid colours
Physique: strong, elegant
Features: developed by crossing Plateau Persian

with Arab and Thoroughbred
Use: riding

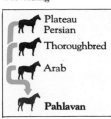

Plateau Persian
Thoroughbred
Arab
Pahlavan

Persian Arab

Tarpan
Persian Arab

Thoroughbred
Height: 15 hands
Colour: grey or bay.
Physique: elegant, compact body, otherwise as Arab.
Features: possibly older than the desert Arab.
Use: similar to the Arab.

Plateau Persian

Arab
Shiragazi
Quashquai
Darashouri
Basseri
Bahhtiari
Jaf
Plateau Persian

Warmblood
Origin: Central Persian Plateau.
Height: 15 hands.
Colour: grey, bay or chestnut.
Physique: Arab features, but this varies as this breed is an amalgamation.
Features: good action, strong and sure-footed.
Use: riding.

Turkoman (Turkmen)

Mongols' Horse
Scythians' Horse
Turkoman

Warmblood
Height: 15.2 hands.
Colour: solid colours.
Physique: narrow chest, light but tough frame.
Features: floating action, speed and endurance.
Use: foundation stock for other breeds, riding, cavalry and racing.

ALGERIA & MOROCCO

Barb

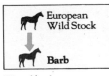

European Wild Stock
Barb

Warmblood
Height: 14.2 hands.
Colour: bay, brown, chestnut, black and grey.
Physique: long head, straight profile, sloping quarters, low set tail and long strong legs.
Features: frugal and tough.
Use: improving other breeds, riding and transport.

SOUTH AFRICA

Basuto

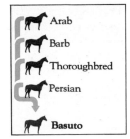

Arab
Barb
Thoroughbred
Persian
Basuto

Pony
Height: 14.2 hands
Colour: chestnut, bay, brown and grey.
Physique: quality head, longish neck and back, strong, straightish shoulder, short legs and hard hooves.
Features: sure-footed, tough with great stamina.
Use: racing, polo and riding.

Persian Arab

Basuto

Caspian

East Asia and Australia

India's native stock is mostly 'country bred' (not selectively bred), but there are several distinct types. Of these, the Manipur has the best claim to fame, for it was the original polo pony. In the 1850s, English planters discovered this native game in Assam, which they then took up and spread around the world.

China is the home of the oldest surviving breed of horse – the Mongolian Wild Horse – originally bred by the Tartars, and rediscovered by Colonel Przewalski in 1881.

The working, and most numerous, pony in China is the Mongolian. It is similar to the Japanese native breed, the Hokaido.

Poor communications on the 3000 islands that make up Indonesia mean that ponies are vital for transport and agriculture. As they make such an important contribution to the economy, the government supports their breeding – the Batak being most supported. In Sumatra the best of the Batak mares are put to Arab stallions to improve quality.

Another of the Indonesian ponies which has a more unusual, romantic use is the Sumba, bred as a dancing pony. Bells are tied to its knees and it 'dances' to tom-tom rhythms.

Australia has no native horse of its own, and the first horses there were imported by the early British settlers some 200 years ago. The horses came first from South Africa and South America, and later from Europe and the USA. The country proved to be an excellent one for rearing horses, as did New Zealand later. Today, from originally having been importers, both nations are major exporters.

The first major Australian breed was the Waler. This was developed by crossing Arab, Thoroughbred and Anglo-Arab stallions with local mares and cobs, but, until fairly recently, the breed was still defined as 'country bred'. A stud book was not formed until 1971, when the Waler was given the new title of the Australian Stock Horse. In contrast, the Australian Pony's stud book was started as early as 1929, for stock which could be traced back to the Welsh Mountain stallion Grey Light.

The breeding of Thoroughbreds too, has flourished in Australasia. The descendants of the stock which originally came from France, the UK and the USA now underpin one of the most prosperous racing industries in the world. Trotting is also popular; Standardbreds have been imported from the USA since 1869.

Riding breeds are overseen by the Light Horse Breeders Association, which holds an annual all-breeds show. Since 1957, the Arabian Horse Society of Australasia has encouraged Arab breeding.

Burma Pony

Manipur

INDIA

Spiti and Bhutia

Mongolian Pony

Spiti Bhutia

Height: Spiti, 12 hands; Bhutia, 13.1 hands.
Colour: grey.
Physique: thickset and short-coupled.
Features: sure-footed and tough.
Use: transportation in mountains.

Manipur

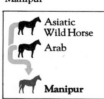

Asiatic Wild Horse

Arab

Manipur

Pony
Height: 12 hands.
Colour: most colours.
Physique: thickset with high-set tail.
Features: quick and manoeuvrable.
Use: riding and polo.

Kathiawari and Marwari
Pony
Origin: Kathiawar and Marwar provinces.
Height: 14.2 hands.
Colour: most colours.
Physique: light, and narrow with some Arab features.

Features: frugal and tough with great stamina.
Use: pack, transport and riding.

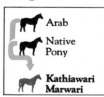

Arab

Native Pony

Kathiawari Marwari

CHINA

Mongolian Wild Horse (Asiatic Wild Horse), *equus przewalskii poliakov)*
Pony
Origin: Mongolia.
Height: 13.1 hands.
Colour: black, brown, bay

Mongolian Wild Horse

Australian Stock Horse

or dun.
Physique: thickset, short-coupled, good bone.
Features: tough, frugal, with great stamina; fast over short distances.
Use: work pony of nomadic tribes; mares provide milk for cheese, which if fomented provides a national drink, called kumiss.

Foreign Stock
Asiatic Wild Horse
Mongolian

JAPAN

Hokaido (Hocaido)

Mongolian
Hokaido

Pony
Similar to Mongolian.

BURMA

Burma

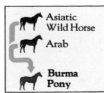

Asiatic Wild Horse
Arab
Burma Pony

Pony
Height: 13 hands.
Colours: all colours.
Physique: larger version of Manipur.
Use: polo and general work.

TIBET

Native Tibetan (Nanfan)

Mongolian Pony
Native Tibetan

Pony
Height: 12.2 hands.
Colour: all colours.
Physique: sturdy frame.
Features: energetic and tough.

Use: riding and general work.

AUSTRALIA

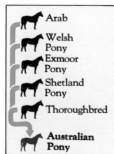

Australian Pony

Arab
Welsh Pony
Exmoor Pony
Shetland Pony
Thoroughbred
Australian Pony

Height: 13 hands.

Colour: most colours.
Physique: Arab head, longish neck, sloping shoulder, deep girth, round hindquarters.
Use: riding.

Australian Stock Horse

Arab
Spanish
Thoroughbred
Australian Stock Horse

Warmblood
Origin: New South Wales
Height: 16 hands.
Colour: all colours.
Physique: varies; usually alert head, deep girth, strong back.
Features: hardy, with a strong constitution.
Use: herding and cavalry.

INDONESIA

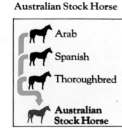

Timor

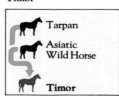

Tarpan
Asiatic Wild Horse
Timor

Pony
Origin: Timor.
Height: 11.1 hands.
Colour: dark colours.
Physique: fine but sturdy frame.
Features: agile, good-tempered.
Use: agricultural work and transportation.

Java

Sumba

South America

It was on the vast, fertile plains of Argentina that the Criollo – the horse of the *gaucho* (cowboy) – developed from horses imported by the Spanish settlers in the sixteenth century. The basic stock is supposed to have come from a shipload of 100 Andalusians and some light draught horses that arrived in 1535, and escaped to run wild on the pampas after Buenos Aires was sacked by the Indians. Through their adaptation to the rough native conditions, the Criollo was born.

Various attempts to improve the Criollo with outcrosses have proved failures, and the Argentinians now breed them selectively. One of the tests used for potential breeding stock is an annual 470-mile ride, during which the horses must carry 17 stone and may not be fed.

The world-famous Argentine polo pony is an off-shoot of the Criollo, being a cross between it and the Thoroughbred. The former provided the toughness and stamina, the latter the speed.

Argentina is also one of the world's largest producers of Thoroughbreds. However, the home demand is so great that relatively few are exported.

Brazil has 9 million horses, one of the largest equine populations in the world. Its native horse is the Crioulo, a smaller version of the Criollo·

Much of this vast work force is used by the army, which finds the horse invaluable in the rough, mountainous areas of the country. Stallions are made available by the army either at its own remount centres, or horses are lent to large breeders. Arabs and Thoroughbreds are used to produce riding horses and Bretons for draught horses.

Some of the Crioulo stock has been improved with outcrosses from Spanish and Portuguese horses, and, in the last century, this foreign blood was used to found the larger Mangalarga. This breed, in turn, was selectively bred by Cassiano Campolino in the 1840s to produce the Campolino.

Peru was the main Spanish base in South America and therefore few horses were allowed to escape and run wild. The most famous Peruvian horse is the Stepping Horse, developed from Barb and Arab stock 300 years ago. It has a unique lateral gait, which it can maintain at up to 14 mph.

Peruvian Stepping Horses were exported to Puerto Rico, where they acted as foundation stock for the Paso Fino. This is now found in large numbers in the USA.

Venezuela, like most South American countries, has its own Criollo type, derived from adapting imported Spanish and Portuguese stock to the hot, rough local conditions. This is known as the Llanero.

Sandalwood

Arab
Native Pony
Sandalwood

Pony
Height: 13 hands.
Colour: dun with dorsal stripe, dark mane and tail.
Physique: lighter frame, finer coat and more elegant than other Indonesian ponies.
Features: fast.
Use: bareback racing and general work.

Sumba

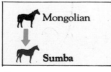

Mongolian
Sumba

Pony
Height: 12.2 hands.

Colour: dun with dorsal stripe, dark mane and tail.
Physique: primitive type.
Use: dancing pony, general work.

Bali

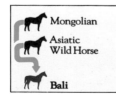

Mongolian
Asiatic Wild Horse
Bali

Pony
Origin: Indonesia/Bali
Height: 12.2 hands
Colour: dun with dorsal stripe and dark points
Physique: sturdy frame
Features: frugal and strong
Use: riding and general pack work

Java

Pony
Origin: Java.
Height: 12.2 hands.
Colour: most colours.

Tarpan
Asiatic Wild Horse
Java

Physique: strong frame.
Use: pulling 'sados' (two-wheeled taxis).

Batak

Native Pony
Arab
Batak

Pony
Origin: Indonesia Sumatra.
Height: 12.2 hands
Colour: most colours
Physique: comparatively refined, good conformation
Features: frugal, good temper
Use: agriculture, transport.

Paso Fino

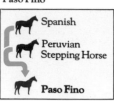

Spanish
Peruvian Stepping Horse
Paso Fino

Warmblood
Height: 14.3 hands.
Colour: most colours.
Physique: Arab-like head, strong back, loins and quarters and hard legs which are light of bone.
Features: spirited; extra four beat gaits, of which the slowest is the paso fino, then the paso corto and the paso largo.

BRAZIL

Crioulo

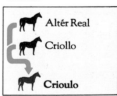

Altér Real
Criollo
Crioulo

Warmblood
Height: 15 hands.
Colour: lighter Criollo colours.
Physique: prominent withers, high set tail and longish neck.
Features: frugal and tough.
Use: riding and herding.

Mangalarga

Altér Real
Andalusian
Criollo
Mangalarga

Warmblood
Origin: Meiras Gerais.
Height: 15 hands.
Colour: grey, sorrel, roan

Peruvian Stepping Horse

Falabella

or bay.
Physique: longish head, short back, powerful hind-quarters, low set tail and long legs; lighter frame than the Criollo.
Features: hardy; gait called 'marcha', between a canter and a trot.
Use: riding and ranch work.

Campolino

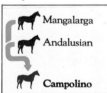

Warmblood
Height: 14.3–15.4 hands
Physique: similar to the Mangalarga but with a heavier frame and more bone.
Use: riding and light draught.

PERU

Peruvian Stepping Horse

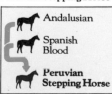

Warmblood
Height: 15 hands.
Colour: bay or chestnut.
Physique: broad chest,

short-coupled, and strong, round hindquarters.
Features: endurance and a special extended gait similar to an amble.
Use: riding and stock work.

ARGENTINA

Falabella

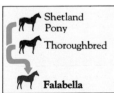

Pony
Height: 7 hands.
Colour: all colours.
Use: harness pony and pet.

Criollo

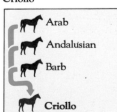

Warmblood
Height: 14.2 hands.
Colour: dun with dark points, dorsal stripe with dark snippets; red and blue roan, sorrel and skewbald.
Physique: short head

tapering to muzzle, short-coupled, sturdy frame, strong, sloping shoulder, short legs, good bone and small, hard feet.
Features: tough and manoeuvrable.
Use: long distance riding and ranch work.

VENEZUELA

Llanero

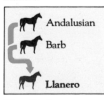

Warmblood
Height: 14 hands.
Colour: dun, yellow with dark mane and tail, white and yellow cream or pinto.
Physique: lighter frame than the Criollo; head similar to the Barb.
Feature: tough.
Use: ranch work and transport.

Criollo

Mangalarga

The USSR

Within the boundaries of the present-day USSR is thought to lie the region in which the horse was first domesticated in about 3000 BC. Russian horse-breeding therefore has an exceptionally long history. Different foundation stock has been important in varying parts of the country, the Arab having most influence in the west and the Mongolian Wild Horse further to the east. Striking variations of geography and climate have also led to the emergence of many different types of horse, and it is therefore no surprise that 40 breeds and breed groups are officially recognized. Currently, the Soviet government stipulates that each region should produce two or three breeds,

This development has largely taken place since the last war. During this time, the USSR has tried to establish its horse-breeding on a more rational, scientific basis – a task undertaken by the All-Union Research Institute of Horse Breeding. Some breeds have been selected for improvement with outside crosses. Those needing some refining influences have had Thoroughbred and Arab blood added – these include the Cossack Steppe horse, the Don, and the Kabardin, a tough mountain horse. When toughening-up was needed, the Russians then used Don blood.

New breeds have been developed, and, at the same time, some of the famous nineteenth-century breeds have been allowed to die out – but not before they were used as foundation stock for the replacement breeds. Thus the Strelets (a large Arab) was used as a basis for the Tersky (established 1948); and the Klepper (a tough, preponent pony) for the Toric and Viatka.

The most important influence on the Russian ponies has been the Asiatic Wild Horse, though some have had Arab blood added as a refining influence. This use continues the traditional Arab involvement in Russian horse-breeding.

More recently, too, the Thoroughbred has also played its part in refining other breeds, but its chief role has been in the establishment of the Russian racehorse. The best of these have headed westwards and Anilin was good enough to come second in the 1966 Washington D.C. International.

Trotting is an equally popular equestrian sport, with 42 studs producing Orlov and Russian Trotters. This began a century ago, when, in 1877, Count Orlov crossed an Arab stallion with a Dutch/Danish mare to found the breed that bears his name. However, the Orlov did not prove as fast as its foreign competitors, and American Standardbreds were therefore crossed with Orlovs to creat the speedier Russian Trotter.

Karabakh

Warmblood
Origin: Karabakh mountains.
Height: 14.2 hands.
Colour: dun, bay or chestnut with metallic sheen.
Physique: tough mountain horse with a small, fine head, low set tail and good feet.
Features: energetic and good-tempered.
Use: riding, equestrian games and racing.

Russian Trotter

Warmblood
Height: 15.3 hands.
Colour: black, bay or chestnut.
Physique: the breed resulted from crossing Orlovs and Standard breeds.
Features: faster than the Orlov.
Use: trotting races.

Orlov Trotter
Warmblood
Height: 16 hands.
Colour: grey, bay or black.
Physique: thickset, upright shoulder, broad chest, deep girth and long straight back.
Features: active and fast.
Use: trotting races, riding, harness.

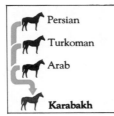

Zemaituka (Pechora)

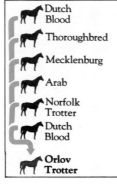

Pony
Origin: Baltic States.
Height: 13.2 hands.
Colour: brown, palomino or dun with dorsal stripe.
Physique: straight face, smallish ears, short neck and straight back.
Features: hardy, good-tempered and frugal.
Use: riding and work.

Akhal Teké

Warmblood
Origin: Steppes.
Height: 15 hands.
Colour: bay, chestnut, grey or black, usually with metallic sheen.
Physique: elegant, long head, straight profile, long, thin neck, long back, low set tail, long legs with light, strong bone and silky tail.
Features: hardy,

temperamental, fast and versatile; some pace.
Use: riding.

Kabardin

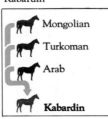

Warmblood
Origin: Northern Caucasus.
Height: 15 hands.
Colour: bay or black.
Physique: sturdy frame, short legs and long, straight back.
Features: good-tempered, sure-footed, tough and long-lived.
Use: mountain work as pack or riding horse, local equestrian games and racing.

Don

Warmblood
Origin: Central Asia (steppes)
Height: 15.2 hands.
Colour: chestnut, bay or grey.
Physique: deep body, long, straight neck and back and long legs.
Features: versatile, frugal

with great stamina.
Use: the original Cossack horse; now driving, riding and long distance racing.

Viatka

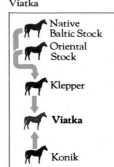

Pony
Origin: Viatsky territory – Baltic States.
Height: 13.2 hands.
Colour: dark, sometimes with dorsal stripe.
Physique: plain head, sturdy frame, broad, straight back, short legs with good bone.
Features: frugal, tough and fast.
Use: all-purpose pony.

Budyonny (Budenny)

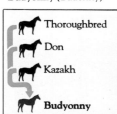

Warmblood
Height: 15.3 hands.
Colour: chestnut or bay with golden sheen.
Physique: strong frame, crested neck, close-coupled and deep-bodied.
Features: good tempered, fast and enduring.
Use: riding, competitions and steeplechasing.

Karabakh

Orlov Trotter

Akhal Teké

Don

Budyonny (Budenny)

Tersky

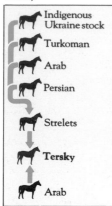

- Indigenous Ukraine stock
- Turkoman
- Arab
- Persian
- Strelets
- **Tersky**
- Arab

Warmblood
Origin: Stavropol region.
Height: 15 hands.
Colour: grey.
Physique: Arab features.
Use: racing, competitions and the circus.

Russian Heavy Draught

- Swedish Ardennes
- Percheron
- Orlov Trotter
- Indigenous Ukraine stock
- **Russian Heavy Draught**

Coldblood
Origin: Ukraine.
Height: 14.2 hands.
Colour: chestnut, bay and roan.

Physique: smallest coldblood; thickset, massive neck, broad back and sloping croup.
Features: strong, active and fast.
Use: agricultural work.

Novokirghiz

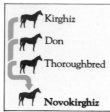

- Kirghiz
- Don
- Thoroughbred
- **Novokirghiz**

Warmblood
Origin: Kirghiz and Kazakhstan.
Height: 15 hands.
Colour: bay, grey, or chestnut.
Physique: long neck, long, straight back, sloping croup, short legs.
Features: tough, surefooted and frugal.
Use: mountain work – harness and saddle.

Lithuanian and Latvian Heavy Draught

- Zemaituka
- Oldenburg
- Finnish Draught
- Swedish Ardennes
- **Lithuanian and Latvian**

Coldblood
Origin: Lithuania and Latvia – Baltic States.
Height: 15.3 hands.
Colour: bay, black, or chestnut with flaxen mane and tail.
Physique: large head, strong, long neck, sloping, bifurcated croup and little feather.
Features: good-tempered.
Use: draught.

Iomud

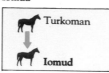

- Turkoman
- **Iomud**

Warmblood
Origin: Central Asia
Height: 14 hands.
Colour: grey, chestnut, or bay.
Physique: similar to but more compact than the Akhal Teké.
Features: great stamina, although not as fast as the Akhal Teké.
Use: riding, racing.

Lokai

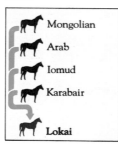

- Mongolian
- Arab
- Iomud
- Karabair
- **Lokai**

Warmblood

Origin: Uzbekistan.
Height: 14.3 hands.
Colour: grey, bay or chestnut often with golden tint.
Physique: varies, but usually sturdy frame with tough hooves; hair may be curly.
Features: a strong, surefooted mountain horse.
Use: riding, pack, and racing.

Bashkirky

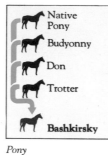

- Native Pony
- Budyonny
- Don
- Trotter
- **Bashkirsky**

Pony
Origin: Bashkiria.
Height: 13.2 hands.
Colour: bay, dun or chestnut.
Physique: thickset, prominent wither, longish back, low set tail and short legs.
Features: tough.
Use: riding and pulling sleighs; mares are milked for kumiss, a medicinal and alcoholic drink.

Vladimir Heavy Draught
Coldblood
Origin: Vladimir district.
Height: 16 hands.
Colour: any solid colour.
Physique: long, muscular

Physique: strong frame, good conformation, with feather on legs.
Features: active, good-tempered and powerful.

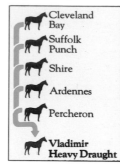

- Cleveland Bay
- Suffolk Punch
- Shire
- Ardennes
- Percheron
- **Vladimir Heavy Draught**

Toric

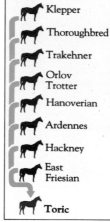

- Klepper
- Thoroughbred
- Trakehner
- Orlov Trotter
- Hanoverian
- Ardennes
- Hackney
- East Friesian
- **Toric**

Warmblood
Origin: Estonia.
Height: 15.1 hands.
Colour: chestnut or bay.
Physique: long, muscular

---

body, short strong legs with light feather.
Features: strong, good-tempered, with great stamina.
Use: light draught.

Karabair

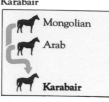

- Mongolian
- Arab
- **Karabair**

Warmblood
Origin: Uzbekistan.
Height: 15.2 hands.
Colour: bay, chestnut, or grey.
Physique: similar to the Arab but stouter. Two types – the Saddle and Harness.
Features: versatile
Use: agriculture, riding and driving, mounted sports.

Kazakh

- Mongolian Wild Horse
- Don
- **Kazakh**

Pony
Origin: Kazakh.
Height: 13 hands.
Colour: bay, chestnut or grey.
Physique: Mongolian.
Features: tough.
Use: riding and herding, milk and meat.

Vladimir Heavy Draught

Tersky

Eastern Europe

Systematic breeding in Bulgaria began when Turkish rule ended in 1878. Arabs and Thoroughbreds were imported from Hungary and Russia to improve the local stock, and, by the beginning of the twentieth century, three halfbreds had been established. These were the Pleven – the most Arab-like – the Danubian, which had Nonius features, and the East Bulgarian, which was closest to the Thoroughbred. Apart from these halfbreds, the Russian Heavy Draught and the Arab are also bred at the state studs.

Hungary's horse-breeding history dates back to the coming of the Magyars in the 9th century AD. Their tough horses later benefited from cross-breeding with Arabs, brought into this country during the Turkish invasions of the Middle Ages, and the Arab has remained a major influence ever since. So, too, has British blood.

Horses have also been imported from the UK. Thoroughbreds arrived as racing increased in popularity and one of Hungary's two important warmblood strains – the Furioso – also originated there. The other major warmblood breed is the Nonius.

The work horse of Hungary – the Murakosi – is a borderline warmblood/coldblood. It was developed in the 1920s to meet the demand for a fast, strong horse, so Oriental, as well as coldblood, foundation stock was used.

Czechoslovakia is the home of the oldest operational stud in the world, Kladruby, near Pardubice, where the original stud was founded by Emperor Maximillian II in the mid-sixteenth century. The Spanish horses he imported were the ancestors of today's white Kladrubers. Czechoslovakia also breeds Thoroughbreds, Furiosos, Noniuses and Arabs. The last-named now have a large centre on the 2,323-acre stud at Topolcianka in Slovakia. It is mainly stocked with Shagya and Polish Arabs, many of which are exported.

Poland has been a horse-breeding country for many centuries. Today, there are 42 major studs, each housing between 50 and 200 stallions. As a result, the country has the largest horse population in Europe – about 3 million.

As in other East European countries, the government controls the state studs. Horses for riding and sport (mainly of Trakehner origins) are bred in the largest quantities, followed by the Arab.

Poland is also the home of the Tarpan, a pony whose origins date back to the Ice Age and is the ancestor of most warmbloods. Herds of Tarpan roam wild in the forests of Popielno, but they are not thought to be pure-bred, the last true Tarpan having died in captivity in 1887. The modern Tarpan of

Poland today is an act of skilled recreation by the Polish government in a selective breeding programme.

Naturally, the Tarpan has greatly influenced the other Polish pony breeds. The Huçul, which roamed wild in the Carpathians for centuries, has its primitive features, as does the larger and more manageable Konik, the foundation stock for many East European breeds.

In the highland areas of Yugoslavia, the work horse still has an important role to play on the land and in transport. The state promotes its breeding at national studs, where Noniuses, Belgians, Norics, Arabs and Lipizzaners are all produced. It is, however, the Bosnian Pony – a descendant of the Tarpan – that makes up a third of the horse population; it is selectively bred by the state studs.

Shagya Arab

Murakosi

POLAND

Tarpan

Equus Celticus
Tarpan

Pony
Height: 13 hands.
Colour: brown or dun with dorsal stripe, dark mane and tail, and stripes on the forelegs and inner thighs. Coat may change to white in winter.
Physique: long head, longish ears, short neck, longish back and fine legs.
Features: tough and fertile.
Use: exhibited in zoos and also roams wild.

Konik

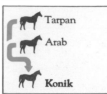

Tarpan
Arab
Konik

Pony
Height: 13.1 hands.
Colour: yellow, grey or blue dun, usually with dorsal stripe.
Physique: similar to the Huzul.
Features: long-lived, frugal, hardy and good-tempered; the foundation stock for many Polish and Russian breeds.
Use: agricultural work for lowland farmers.

Huzul

Pony
Origin: Carpathian mountains.
Height: 13.2 hands.
Colour: dun or bay.
Physique: Tarpan head and robust body.
Features: good tempered, tough and frugal.
Use: pack and agricultural.

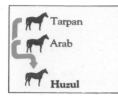

Tarpan
Arab
Huzul

Sokolsky

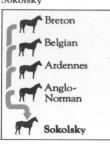

Breton
Belgian
Ardennes
Anglo-Norman
Sokolsky

Warmblood
Height: 15.2 hands.
Colour: chestnut, brown or grey.
Physique: large head, sturdy frame, short, straight back, short legs and large round feet with little feather.
Features: good tempered, frugal.
Use: agricultural work.

Wielkopolski

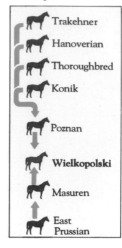

Trakehner
Hanoverian
Thoroughbred
Konik
Poznan
Wielkopolski
Masuren
East Prussian

Warmblood
Height: 16 hands.
Colour: chestnut or bay.
Physique: a compact, well-proportion horse.
Features: good-tempered; formed by amalgamating the Masuren and Poznan.
Use: riding competitions and light draught.

Polish Arab
Warmblood
Height: 14.3 hands.
Colour: grey, chestnut and bay.
Physique: similar to the Arab, but with more sloping quarters and with tail carried lower.
Use: racing, breeding and riding.

HUNGARY

Shagya Arab

Syrian Arab
Shagya Arab

Warmblood
Height: 15 hands.
Colour: grey.
Physique: Arab features, small head.
Features: hardy, frugal and active.
Use: cavalry, general riding and driving..

Murakosi

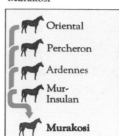

Oriental
Percheron
Ardennes
Mur-Insulan
Murakosi

Coldblood
Height: 16 hands.
Colour: chestnut with flaxen mane and tail.
Physique: strong frame, little wither, dip in back, round hindquarters and little feather.
Features: strong and active.
Use: general draught and agricultural work.

Nonius
Warmblood
Height: Large Nonius,

Tarpan

Konik

Kladruber

over 15.3 hands; small Nonius, under 15.3 Hands.
Physique: elegant head, long neck, strong back.
Features: versatile, long-lived and active.
Use: riding and agricultural work.

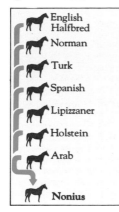

Furioso

Warmblood
Height: 16 hands.
Colour: dark colours.
Physique: muscular body, straightish back, sloping hindquarters and low set

tail.
Features: robust.

CZECHOSLOVAKIA

Kladruber

Warmblood
Origin: Kladruby, Bohemia.
Height: 16.2 hands.
Colour: grey.
Physique: larger Andalusian.
Use: agriculture and harness.

BULGARIA

Danubian

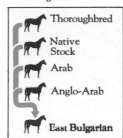

Warmblood
Height: 15.2 hands.
Colour: black or dark chestnut.
Physique: short-coupled, deep girth, high set tail and fine strong legs.
Features: strength.
Use: light draught, riding and competitions.

Warmblood
Height: 15.3 hands.
Colour: chestnut or black.
Physique: smallish head, straight profile, deep girth and longish straight back.
Features: energetic, hardy, fast and versatile.
Use: riding, agriculture, competitions and steeplechasing.

Pleven

Warmblood
Height: 15.2 hands.
Colour: chestnut.
Physique: sturdier version of the Arab.
Features: robust.
Use: an all-purpose horse.

YUGOSLAVIA

Bosnian

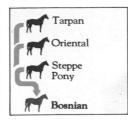

Pony
Height: 12.2 hands.
Colour: dun, brown chestnut, grey, black.
Physique: compact mountain pony, similar to the Huzul.
Features: endurance.
Use: agricultural work.

Bosnian

Wielkopolski

Furioso

France

The French government is more actively involved with horse-breeding than the governments of all other Western countries. Its involvement dates back to the days of Louis XIV, who created a government department responsible for providing officially-approved stallions for French breeders. This department developed into the Service des Haras, today a part of the Ministry of Agriculture and responsible for the French horse industry.

The Service runs 23 stallion depots, which are scattered throughout France. In the best breeding areas, such as Normandy, the depots house as many as 200 stallions. Each depot keeps a selection of stallions, ensuring that suitable sires are available to breed for racing, competitions, pleasure, work – and even for meat. Each one is strictly selected according to its conformation, athletic ability, pedigree and the success of its progeny.

The main competition horse in France is the Selle Français. The stud book for this breed was started only in 1965, when it took over from 45 different breed groups. Previously, there were many different warmbloods in France, although the Anglo-Norman (the French carriage horse, refined with Norfolk Trotter and Thoroughbred blood during the last century) and the Anglo-Arab (bred by crossing Thoroughbreds, Arabs and Oriental stock from south-west France) were the most numerous and successful.

The Arab has played an important part in French breeding since the conquering Moors brought them into the country 1200 years ago. They are the ancestors of all current French breeds, and are still extensively used for cross-breeding.

The French Thoroughbred has its origins in stock imported from the UK, but, since Gladiateur crossed the English Channel to win the Derby in 1865, French home-breds have challenged the best in the world. French trotters have also been internationally successful. Their home country is Normandy, where they were developed at the turn of the nineteenth century by crossing Norfolk Trotters with Thoroughbreds and Norman mares. Today, they are used both for trotting and for cross-breeding.

Of the French heavy horses, the Percheron is the most numerous nationally and internationally. The best-known pony is the Camargue, which roams wild in the marshlands of that district in southern France. The shape of its head implies that the Oriental influence was of Barb origin. The little Basque pony is also found running wild in the Pyrenees and Atlantic cantons. The most domesticated of these native breeds is the Landais, while the Shetland is the most popular imported pony.

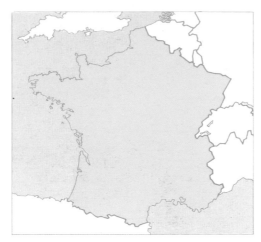

Landais

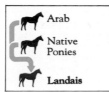

Pony
Origin: The Landes region.
Height: 13.2 hands.
Colour: dark colours.
Physique: varies – usually fine frame with an Arab-like head.
Features: frugal.
Use: riding and driving.

Anglo-Arab

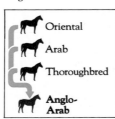

Warmblood
Height: 16 hands.
Colour: solid colours.
Physique: good shoulder and well-proportioned, powerful hindquarters.
Features: stamina and good movement.
Use: riding, competitions and racing.

Comtois

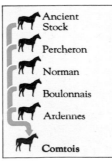

Coldblood
Origin: Franche-Comté.

Height: 15.1 hands.
Colour: bay or chestnut.
Physique: largish head, straight neck, long, straight back and little feather.
Features: active and sure-footed.
Use: agriculture.

Breton

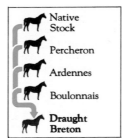

Coldblood
Height: 16.1 hands.
Colour: grey, chestnut or bay.
Physique: the Postier Breton – close-coupled, elegant head and short legs with little feather. The Draught Breton – larger, more elongated body.
Features: strong and active, although the Draught is less energetic.
Use: agricultural work.

Boulonnias

Coldblood:
Origin: Northern France.
Height: 16.1 hands.
Colour: grey, chestnut or bay.
Physique: similar conformation to the Percheron; silky coat.
Features: active and good-tempered.
Use: draught.

Basque

Pony
Origin: Basque region.
Height: 13 hands.
Colour: most.
Physique: primitive, with head slightly concave, small ears, short neck and long back.
Features: stamina and toughness.
Use: mining, riding; also runs wild.

Camargue (Camarguais)

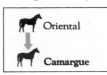

Pony:
Origin: The Camargue, Rhone delta.
Height: 14 hands.
Colour: grey.
Physique: Oriental-type head, straightish shoulder, short body, fine legs with hard bone.
Features: hardy.
Use: herding, trekking; also roams wild.

French Trotter

Warmblood
Origin: Calvados.
Height: 16.1 hands.
Colour: any solid colour.
Physique: tall, light-framed horse with a fine head, prominent wither, strong back and sloping hindquarters.
Features: athletic and fast.
Use: trotting, riding and cross-breeding.

Selle Francais

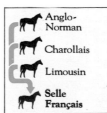

Warmblood
Origin: Northern France.
Height: 16 hands.

Colour: solid colours.
Physique: robust frame, powerful shoulder, strong, longish back, deep girth and powerful hindquarters.
Features: good-tempered and athletic.
Use: riding and competitions.

Poitevin

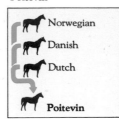

Coldblood
Origin: Poitiers.
Height: 16.3 hands.
Colour: dun.
Physique: plain conformation, large head, long body, big feet with heavy feather.
Features: docile.
Use: mares put to Baudet Poitevin (jackasses of about 16 hands) to breed large mules.

Percheron

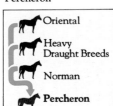

Coldblood
Height: 16.1 hands.
Colour: grey or black.
Physique: Oriental-type head, strong, well-proportioned body, full mane and tail and clean, hard legs without feather.
Features: a good action and great presence.
Use: draught.

Ardennais

Coldblood
Origin: France – Lorraine, Champagne, foothills of Vosges
Height: 15.3 – 16 hands
Colour: bay and roan
Physique: short, more thick set than any other carthorse, stocky, compact, heavyweight, very muscular with a large bone structure, strong head and broad face
Features: docile, gentle, hardy
Use: agriculture – 'the carthorse of the north'

Breton

Camargue (Camarguais)

French Trotter

Ardennais

Percheron

Anglo-Arab

Western Europe

Belgium was the home of one of the most celebrated horses of medieval times – the Flanders Horse – a coldblood which is the ancestor of many modern heavy horses. Its direct descendant is the Belgian, a breed now found throughout the world. The country's other heavy horse, the Ardennes, is shared, like the area in which it is bred, with France. It is thought to be a descendant of the medieval Great Horse. The Belgian Warmblood is a more recent innovation.

In Holland, stud book societies exist for Arabs, Hackneys, five pony breeds, Trotters, Racehorses, Dutch Warmbloods, and for the three native breeds. These are the Gelderland, a popular carriage horse, the increasingly rare Gronigen, and the Friesland, which is one of the oldest breeds in Europe.

Austria's most celebrated horse is the Lipizzaner, famous as the mount of the internationally-known Spanish Riding School in Vienna. The horse's name comes from its original home – Lipizza, near Trieste – but it is now bred at Piber, in southern Austria. Its origins date back to 1580, when the Hapsburg Archduke Charles imported Spanish horses (with Arab, Barb, and Andalusian forebears) from the Pyrenees. Italian, German and Danish blood was added to improve the stock in the eighteenth century, and Arab in the nineteenth. Today, there is no such out-breeding, but some in-breeding is practised.

Home-produced halfbreds, Hanoverians and Trakehners, are used to breed the Austrian riding horse. State aid is also given to support the breeding of the other famous Austrian horse, the Halflinger, bred originally in the district of Halfling, near Merano.

The Noriker takes its name from the Roman province of Noricum, where it was originally bred by the Romans. It is now used in both Austria and Germany.

Switzerland's state-financed national stud has produced work horses for agriculture and the army since the nineteenth century. The two main types were the Einsielder, originally bred by the monks of Einsiedeln Abbey in the eleventh century, and the Freiberger, a light draught horse from the Jura Mountains. With the fall in demand for these work horses, the stud started to breed a Swiss Halfbred in the 1960s. Stallions and mares were imported from Germany, France, Sweden and the UK; all breeding stock was put through rigorous performance tests, and stud books were started. This development had the desired effect of cutting down the previously high number of imported riding horses, and the breed is proving itself capable of holding its own with other European warmbloods.

AUSTRIA

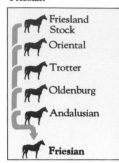

Noriker (South German Coldblood)

Coldblood
Height: 16.1 hands.
Colour: chestnut, bay, sometimes spotted.
Physique: largish head, short thick neck, straight shoulder, broad back and short legs.
Features: sure-footed.
Use: agricultural and mountain work.

Lipizzaner

Warmblood
Height: 15.1 hands.
Colour: grey.
Physique: largish head, small ears, crested neck, compact body, short, strong legs and full fine mane and tail.

Features: intelligent, athletic
Use: high school equitation and driving.

Halflinger

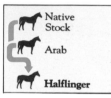

Pony
Origin: The Tirol.
Height: 14 hands.
Colour: chestnut with flaxen mane and tail.
Physique: head tapers to muzzle, broad chest, deep girth, long, broad back and short legs.
Features: kind temperament, frugal, tough, sure-footed.
Use: mountain work.

BELGIUM

Ardennes (Ardennais)

Coldblood
Origin: The Ardennes.
Height: 15.3 hands.
Colour: bay, chestnut or roan.
Physique: muscular, short-coupled body, crested neck, broad chest and

short, feathered legs.
Features: strong, active and good tempered.
Use: agricultural work.

Belgian Heavy Draught (Brabant)

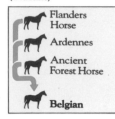

Coldblood
Origin: Brabant.
Height: 16.2 hands.
Colour: red roan with black points or chestnut.
Physique: heavy, large frame, shortish back, short legs with feather on fetlocks.
Features: strength, presence and good action.
Use: draught.

HOLLAND

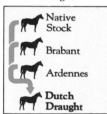

Gelderland

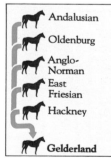

Warmblood
Origin: Gelderland.
Height: 15.1 hands.
Colour: chestnut, or grey.
Physique: plain head, crested neck, short-coupled with a high set tail.
Features: extravagant action and great presence.
Use: carriage work, riding.

Groningen

Warmblood
Origin: Groningen.

Height: 15.3 hands.
Colour: dark colours.
Physique: straight profile, long ears, deep, powerful body and high set tail.
Features: frugal with a stylish action.
Use: light draught, riding and driving.

Friesian

Warmblood
Height: 15 hands.
Colour: black only.
Physique: longish head, crested neck, round hindquarters, good bone, feather and full mane and tail.
Features: good temperament.
Use: in the circus, riding and driving.

Dutch Draught

Coldblood
Height: 16.1 hands.
Colour: bay, chestnut or black.
Physique: tall with a powerful front and deep, strong body.
Features: strength, stamina, and a kind but spirited temperament.
Use: draught.

SWITZERLAND

Franches Montagnes (Freiberger)
Warmblood
Origin: Avenche.
Height: 15.1 hands.
Colour: blue roan or grey; solid colours.
Physique: powerful, compact frame.

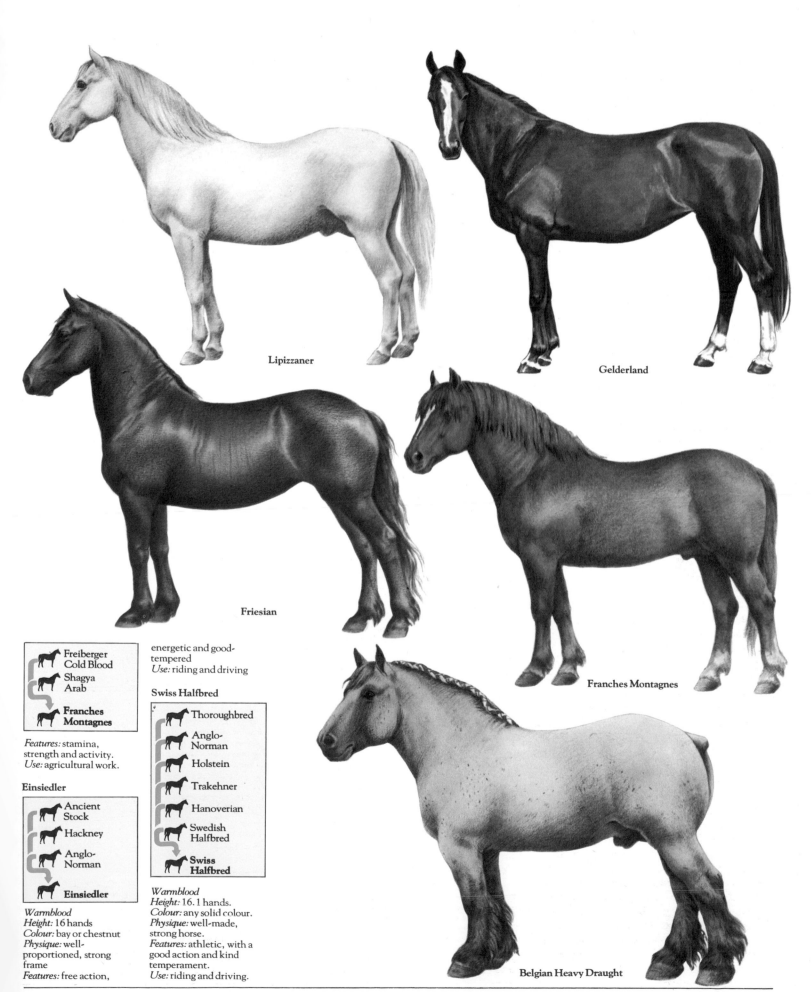

Lipizzaner

Gelderland

Friesian

Franches Montagnes

Belgian Heavy Draught

Freiberger Cold Blood
↳ Shagya Arab
↳ **Franches Montagnes**

Features: stamina, strength and activity.
Use: agricultural work.

Einsiedler

Ancient Stock
↳ Hackney
↳ Anglo-Norman
↳ **Einsiedler**

Warmblood
Height: 16 hands
Colour: bay or chestnut
Physique: well-proportioned, strong frame
Features: free action,

energetic and good-tempered
Use: riding and driving

Swiss Halfbred

Thoroughbred
↳ Anglo-Norman
↳ Holstein
↳ Trakehner
↳ Hanoverian
↳ Swedish Halfbred
↳ **Swiss Halfbred**

Warmblood
Height: 16.1 hands.
Colour: any solid colour.
Physique: well-made, strong horse.
Features: athletic, with a good action and kind temperament.
Use: riding and driving.

Britain and Ireland

Britain and Ireland share a long history of horse breeding. Ireland, in particular, has produced some of the finest horses in the world; for its part, the UK's great contribution to horse breeding has been the development of the Thoroughbred, the world's most valuable and fastest breed.

On the west coast of Ireland, the tough but handsome Connemara pony has run wild for centuries. Its origins are said to be the same as those of the Highland; the difference between the two lies in the cross-breeding that took place between the native ponies and the Spanish jennets and Arabs which came ashore from the shipwrecked Spanish Armada in the sixteenth century.

Ireland has no true native coldblood, for the Irish Draught is a borderline warmblood/coldblood. Its origins are obscure, but it is thought to descend from medieval war horses and some European warmbloods. It was originally a dual-purpose horse – farmers both hunting on it and using it for work in the fields – but, with mechanization, this latter use has dwindled. It was then crossed with the Thoroughbred to produce a high-class riding horse, which now receives considerable government support. This was largely achieved through the Irish Horse Board, formed in 1971 to look after the non-Thoroughbred horse industry.

The foundations for the future British Thoroughbred were laid in the century following the Stuart Restoration to the throne in 1660; during this period, more than 200 Arabs, Turks and Barbs were imported to improve British racing stock. It is still uncertain whether these imports were crossed with the native racing mares – the now extinct Galloway ponies – or whether the foundations were purely Oriental. There is no question, however, that the three greatest influences were the stallions Darley Arabian (originator of the Blandford, Phalaris, Gainsborough, Son in Law and St Simon lines); the Byerley Turk (Herod line); and the Godolphin Barb (Matcham line).

The original Thoroughbreds were only 14.2 hands high, but, over the years, they grew in height to today's average of about 16 hands. During these formative years, the horse also changed in other ways as well. At first, stamina took precedence over sheer speed, but, by the nineteenth century, speed and quicker maturity was deemed to be essential. By this time, too, the British Thoroughbred had established itself all over the world. As no other country could produce a faster horse, all resorted to importing Thoroughbreds from Britain.

The UK's other main export in the horse world has been its native ponies. Nine dis-

Thoroughbred

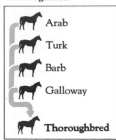

Thoroughbred
Height: 16 hands.
Colour: solid colours.
Physique: varies from close-coupled sprinters with large, powerful hindquarters to big-framed, longer backed, big-boned chasers. Must have an elegant head, long neck, sloping shoulder, prominent wither and silky coat.
Features: fast and spirited.
Use: racing, riding and improving other breeds.

Suffolk Punch

Coldblood:
Origin: East Anglia.
Height: 16.1 hands.
Colour: chestnut, with no white markings.
Physique: short, clean legs, massive neck and shoulders and square

body.
Features: good action, long-lived, frugal and good-tempered.
Use: draught.

Hackney

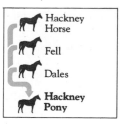

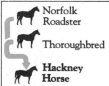

Warmblood and Pony
Height: Horse, 15.1 hands; pony, under 14.2 hands.
Colour: dark colours.
Physique: smallish head, strong straightish shoulder, powerful hindquarters and tail set and carried high.
Features: spirited, with a high-stepping action.
Use: driving.

Fell

Pony
Origin: Cumbria (Westmorland and Cumberland).
Height: 13.2 hands.
Colour: black, brown or bay.
Physique: great substance, minimum 8 inches of bone, fine hair on heels and long curly mane and tail.
Features: strength and

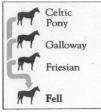

stamina; a fast trotter.
Use: all-purpose; driving, agricultural work, pack and trekking.

Irish Draught

Coldblood/Warmblood
Height: 16 hands.
Colour: bay, brown or grey.
Physique: straight face, short, muscular neck, longish back, strong, sloping hindquarters, good bone, little feather and large round feet.
Features: good-tempered and a good jumper.
Use: multi-purpose, but mainly breeding riding horses.

New Forest

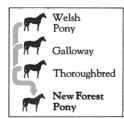

Pony
Origin: The New Forest, Hampshire.
Colour: solid colours.
Physique: great variety – type A, lighter, under 13.2 hands; type B, heavier, between 13.2 and 14.2 hands.
Features: hardy, frugal and friendly.
Use: riding.

Welsh Cob (section D).

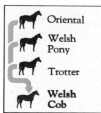

Warmblood:
Height: 14 to 15.1 hands.
Colour: solid colours.
Physique: compact, great substance, quality head, strong shoulder, deep,

powerful back and silky feather.
Features: high knee action, stamina, strength and versatility.
Use: all purpose; driving and riding.

Irish Halfbred

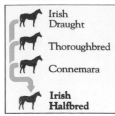

Warmblood
Height: 16.1 hands.
Colour: most colours.
Physique: varies.
Features: strong, good-tempered and athletic.
Use: riding.

Welsh Pony (section B).

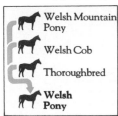

Pony
Height: 12 to 13.2 hands.
Colour: solid colours.
Physique: larger version of Section A.
Features: good action and kind temperament.
Use: riding.

Welsh Pony (section C).

Pony:
Height: under 13.2 hands.
Colour: solid colours.
Physique: cob type, with silky feather.
Features: hardy, active and frugal.
Use: driving and trekking.

Welsh Mountain (section A).

Pony
Height: under 12 hands.
Colour: grey, brown or chestnut.
Physique: Arab-like head, long, crested neck, sloping shoulder, short back and high set tail.
Features: spirited, intelligent, with great powers of endurance.
Use: riding; foundation stock for children's riding ponies.

Welsh pony

Suffolk Punch

Shire

Thoroughbred

Irish Draught

Hackney

tinctive types have emerged, of which the Exmoor claims to be the oldest. Its origins are thought to date back to prehistoric times, when the ancestors of today's Exmoors crossed the land bridge that then linked Britain and Europe.

The Exmoor's near neighbour, the Dartmoor, is larger and not as purebred. However, it still has fewer out-crossings than the New Forest Pony, which, largely because it lives in a more inhabited area, has received admixtures of Arab, Thoroughbred and Galloway blood. Oriental influence can also be clearly seen in the elegance of the Welsh Mountain Pony.

The Welsh Cob was established by the fifteenth century. Since then, these cobs have served Welsh farmers well, working in the fields, drawing carriages, hunting and running in trotting races.

The Fell Pony's home is the Pennines. These ponies stem from the Celtic Pony; the most influential subsequent crossing came with the Friesian blood added in Roman times. Their neighbour to the east, the Dale, has similar origins, but is more of a harness pony. This development came about in the nineteenth century, when a Welsh Cob stallion injected size and strength into the breed, now the largest of the British ponies.

The Highland's ancestry has the same roots as the Fell and Dale. However, additions of Arab and French blood, and Clydesdale to the Garron, has made the Highland quite distinct. Even further to the north are the Shetlands; the ancestry of this small, sturdy breed – a major British export – dates back to 500 BC.

Britain's native ponies also gave rise to a very influential, but now extinct, breed – the Norfolk Trotter or Roadster. Many of these horses were at one time exported, and they served as the foundation stock for most breeds of trotting horse, as well as many riding horses. The closest surviving relation is the eye-catching Hackney, with its spectacular high action.

The only recognized breed of riding/driving horse is the Cleveland Bay. Bred in Yorkshire for more than 200 years, and used, like the Irish Draught, as a dual-purpose horse, its greatest value today is for driving and for crossing with Thoroughbreds, to produce competition horses and hunters.

The largest horse in the UK is the Shire. This is said to be a descendant of the Great Horse of England of medieval times. The smaller, rounder Suffolk Punch, however, has a more definite ancestry. Every member of the breed can be traced back to a horse foaled in 1760. Scotland's heavy horse, the Clydesdale, is thought to share the Shire's ancestry.

Dale

Pony
Origin: Eastern Pennines.
Height: 14.1 hands.
Colour: dark colours; no white, except star.
Physique: powerful frame, straightish shoulder, fine hair on heels and thick mane and tail.
Features: strong, good-tempered and sure-footed.
Use: pack, agricultural work and riding.

Exmoor

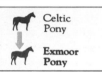

Pony
Origin: Exmoor, Somerset and Devon.
Height: 12 hands.
Colour: bay, brown or dun with black points, light mealy muzzle, no white.
Physique: prominent 'toad' eyes, wide chest, strong quarters and thick, springy coat with no bloom in winter.
Features: strength and endurance.
Use: riding.

Clydesdale

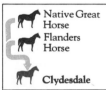

Coldblood
Origin: Lanarkshire.
Height: 16.2 hands.
Colour: dark with white on face and legs.
Physique: long, crested neck, high withers, straightish hind legs, much feather.
Features: active.
Use: draught.

Connemara

Pony
Origin: County Connaught
Height: 13.2 hands.
Colour: grey.
Physique: compact, intelligent head, crested neck, sloping shoulder and deep, strong, sloping hindquarters.

Features: intelligent, sure-footed, hardy; a good jumper.
Use: riding and driving.

Cleveland Bay

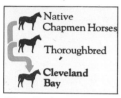

Warmblood
Origin: Yorkshire.
Height: 16 hands.
Colour: bay or brown; white markings not desirable.
Physique: large head, convex profile, longish back, high set tail and good bone.
Features: versatile, long-lived and strong.
Use: riding and driving.

Shetland

Pony
Origin: Shetland and the Orkneys.

Height: 9.3 hands (6.2 hands the smallest recorded).
Colour: black, brown or coloured.
Physique: small head, face usually concave, small ears, short, strong back, full mane and tail; winter coat very thick.
Features: hardy and strong.
Use: general.

Dartmoor

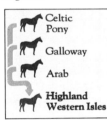

Pony
Origin: Dartmoor, Devon.
Height: 12.1 hands.
Colour: bay, black or brown.
Physique: small head, strong shoulders, back and loins, high set tail, and full mane and tail.
Features: long-lived, sure-footed and tough.
Use: riding.

Highland

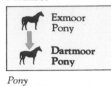

Pony
Origin: Western Isles and mainland.
Height: Mainland (Garron), 14.2 hands; Islands (Western Isles), 13.2 hands.

Colour: Mainland, black or brown varying to dun and grey; Islands, dun with a dorsal stripe.
Physique: Mainland, short ears, powerful loins, strong, short legs, on Islands, smaller.
Features: strength.
Use: Mainland, deer stalking and work for crofters. Islands, children's pony.

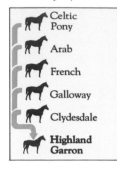

Shire

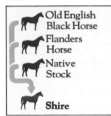

Coldblood
Origin: Central Counties
Height: 17 hands.
Colour: dark with white markings.
Physique: face nearly convex, broad forehead, long, crested neck, broad back, sloping croup and much fine silky feather.
Features: strength; the tallest breed in the world.
Use: draught.

Dale

Cleveland Bay

Exmoor

Shetland

Highland

Connemara

Irish Halfbred

Dartmoor

Southern Europe

Italy was one of the world's first major horse-breeding areas; the Etruscans bred horses there more than 2500 years ago. It was in medieval times, however, that Italy produced its most famous horse – the Neapolitan. Bred from Barb, Arab and Spanish stock, the Neapolitan was used for Haute Ecole in all the major courts of Europe during the sixteenth and seventeenth centuries. It also became the foundation stock for many other breeds.

Nowadays, imported breeds are the most popular ones in Italy. Of the native breeds, the Avelignese is popular for mountain work, but riding horses, such as the Murghese, Salerno and Calabrese are on the decline. Most Italian riding stock now comes from West Germany, France and Ireland.

The horses of Spain have marked Oriental features derived from the Arabs and Barbs brought into the country by successive conquering armies from the Middle East in the Middle Ages. The most celebrated Spanish breed, the Andalusian, is thought to have Oriental, Noriker and Garrano ancestry. It owes its survival largely to the monks of the Carthusian monasteries of Jerez de la Frontera, Seville and Cazello, who continued to breed the horse after it was replaced by the heavier Neapolitan in the Spanish court in the fifteenth century. The Zapata family did much the same at their Andalusian stud, and the two strains have been kept relatively pure up to the present day.

The breeds of Portugal have much in common with those of Spain, for both countries came under the same Moorish influence. Thus the Altér-Real comes from the same basic stock as the Andalusian, and the other Portuguese breed, the Lusitano, also has Andalusian connections. It is a tougher horse than the Altér-Real.

The mountains of northern Portugal are the breeding grounds for the Minho, or Garrano, Pony. The breed has Arab origins and has survived with little change for thousands of years. Close to the Spanish border, in the plains between the Sor and Raio rivers, the tough Sorraia Pony is found. This was one of the first ponies to be domesticated; it is strong enough to be used for herding and agriculture.

Greece was famous for its horses and horsemen in Classical times, but now the country has only a few native pony breeds. The Peneia is used on the farms of the Peloponnese, the Pindos is used in the mountains of Thessaly and Epirus, and the Skyros is a children's pony. Riding horses are usually Arabs or Lipizzaners, though, as riding becomes more popular, a variety of types are being imported.

ITALY

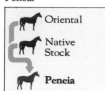

Italian Heavy Draught

Coldblood
Origin: Italy.
Height: 15.2 hands.
Colour: sorrel or roan.
Physique: fine, long head, shortish neck, flat back.
Features: fast, strong.
Use: meat and agricultural.

Salerno

Warmblood
Origin: Maremma and Salerno.
Height: 16 hands.
Colour: solid colours.
Physique: large, refined head.
Use: riding.

Murghese

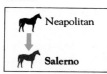

Warmblood
Height: 15.2 hands.
Physique: Oriental features but heavier frame.
Features: versatile.
Use: dual-purpose horse

for agricultural work or riding.

Avelignese

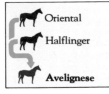

Pony
Origin: Alps and Appennines.
Height: 14 hands.
Colour: chestnut.
Physique: heavy-frame.
Features: sure-footed.
Use: pack, agricultural.

Calabrese

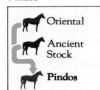

Warmblood
Origin: Calabria.
Colour: solid colours.
Physique: middleweight, short-coupled riding horse.
Use: riding.

GREECE

Skyros

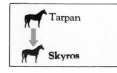

Pony
Origin: Island of Skyros.

Height: 10 hands.
Colour: dun, brown or grey.
Physique: light of bone, upright shoulder and often cow-hocked.
Use: pack, carrying water, agricultural work and riding.

Peneia

Pony
Origin: Peneia, Peloponnese.
Height: 10 to 14 hands.
Colour: most colours.
Physique: Oriental.
Features: frugal, hardy.
Use: pack and agricultural

Pindos

Pony
Origin: Mountains of Thessaly and Epirus.
Height: 12.1 hands.
Colour: grey or dark.
Physique: tough.
Use: riding and light agricultural work.

SPAIN

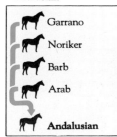

Andalusian

Warmblood
Origin: Andalusia.
Height: 16 hands.
Physique: largish head, almost convex profile, strong, arched neck.
Features: intelligent and athletic.
Use: high school and general.

Hispano Anglo-Arab

Warmblood
Origin: Estramadura and Andalusia.
Height: 15.3 hands.
Colour: bay, chestnut or grey.
Use: competitions, riding and testing young bulls.

TURKEY

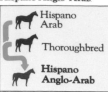

Karacabey

Warmblood
Height: 16 hands.
Colour: solid colours.
Physique: tough.
Use: riding, light draught, agricultural work, cavalry and pack.

MAJORCA

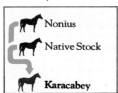

Balearic
Pony
Height:
Colour: bay or brown.
Physique: fine head, usually Roman nose.
Features: good-tempered.
Use: agricultural work and driving.

PORTUGAL

Skyros

Altér Real

Italian Heavy Draught

Lusitano

Salerno

Sorraia

Tarpan → **Sorraia**

Pony
Origin: River Sorraia
district.
Height: 13 hands.
Colour: dun with a dorsal
stripe and stripes on legs.
Physique: primitive
appearance, long head,
straight profile, long ears.
Features: tough and frugal.
Use: runs wild.

Altér Real
Warmblood
Origin: Alentejo
province.
Height: 15.2 hands.

Andalusian
Arab
Thoroughbred
Norman
Hanoverian
**Altér
Real**

Colour: chestnut, bay or
piebald.
Physique: smallish head
with straight profile.
Features: spirited.
Use: riding.

Garrano (Minho)
Pony
Origin: Garranho do

Arab → **Garrano**

Minho, Traz dos Montes.
Height: 11 hands.
Colour: dark chestnut.
Physique: light frame.
Features: strong.
Use: riding and pack.

Lusitano
Warmblood
Origin: Southern and
Central Portugal.
Height: 15.1 hands.
Colour: grey.
Physique: small head,
small ears, large eyes,
thick neck.
Features: frugal.
Use: bullring.

Andalusian

West and East Germany

West Germany is famous for its riding horses, particularly the Hanoverian and Trakehner. Its success stems primarily from the considerable financial support given by both the national and regional governments to the breeding industry, and the thought and control with which breeding has been directed.

The breeds of riding horse in West Germany are defined according to area – hence the Hanoverian in Hanover and the Holstein in Schleswig-Holstein, for instance. The only breeds to be organised on a national basis are the imported breeds – the Thoroughbreds, the Trotters, various breeds of pony, and the Trakehner, whose original home now lies in East Germany.

The most numerous and successful warmblood is the Hanoverian. Originally a heavy war horse, it has been refined for various uses over the centuries.

Before the war, the Trakehner, named after its home of Trakehnan, was thought to be the Hanoverian's superior. The stud was established in 1732, and it survived until 1944, when the advancing Russians forced evacuation. A few stallions and 700 mares reached the west to form the nucleus of today's Trakehner breed.

The Holstein is the other main German breed in international demand. It has been raised on the marshlands of Schleswig-Holstein since the fourteenth century, when Neapolitan and Spanish blood was first imported to improve the local Marsh Horse. More recently, Cleveland Bays and Thoroughbreds have been used to further refine the breed.

The other German warmbloods have relied extensively on these three breeds for foundation stock, and, together with Arab and Thoroughbred blood, still use them for improvement. None of the German warmbloods are pure-bred; outside blood (always pedigree) has been brought in to improve a breed when necessary. Neither is there a pure breed of pony, and, in fact, there is only one native one – the Dolmen, bred on the Duke of Croy's estate.

The heavy horses of Germany, too, were developed largely through the use of imported stock. The Rhineland and the Schleswig Heavy Draught were established during the nineteenth century by crossing foreign breeds.

East Germany is rather isolated as a horse-breeding nation, and, unlike other Eastern bloc countries, makes no great effort to export horses to the west. The two main breeds produced are offshoots of those found in West Germany, the Mecklenburg having similar origins to the Hanoverian and the East Friesian to the Oldenburg.

Hanoverian

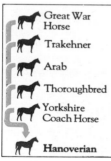

Warmblood
Origin: Hanover and Lower Saxony.
Height: 16 hands.
Physique: powerful.
Features: athletic.
Use: competition and riding horse.

Hessen, Rheinlander and Pfalz-Saar

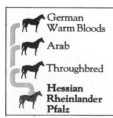

Warmblood
Height: 16 hands.
Physique: strongly built.
Features: good temperament, action.
Use: riding.

East Friesian
Warmblood
Height: 16.1 hands.
Colour: solid colours.
Physique: similar to the Oldenburg but lighter.
Use: riding and light draught.

Dulmen
Pony
Origin: Westphalia.
Height: 12.3 hands.
Colour: black, brown or dun.
Physique: various.
Use: riding.

Württemburg

Warmblood
Height: 16 hands.
Colour: black, brown, bay or chestnut.
Physique: cob type.
Features: hardy.
Use: riding and driving.

Schleswig Heavy Draught
Coldblood
Colour: chestnut, flaxen mane and tail.

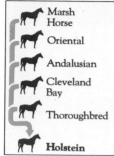

Physique similar to the Jutland.
Use: draught.

Holstein

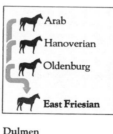

Warmblood
Origin: Holstein.
Height: 16.1 hands.
Colour: black, bay, brown.
Physique: heavier frame than the Hanoverian
Features: a good action.
Use: general uses

Trakehner

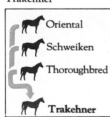

Origin: East Prussia.
Height: 16.1 hands.
Colour: dark colours.
Features: intelligent with an extravagant action.
Use: riding and competitions.

Bavarian

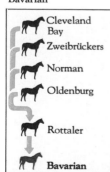

Warmblood
Origin: Lower Bavaria.
Height: 16 hands.
Colour: solid colours.

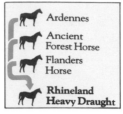

Physique: medium-sized frame, deep girth.
Use: riding.

Rhineland Heavy Draught

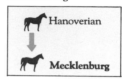

Coldblood
Height: 16.1 hands.
Physique: heavy and compact.
Features: strength, early maturity.
Use: draught.

Mecklenburg

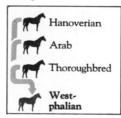

Warmblood
Height: 16 hands.
Colour: solid colours.
Physique: smaller version of the Hanoverian.
Use: riding, cavalry.

Westphalian

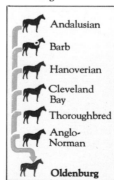

Warmblood
Origin: Westphalia.
Height: 16.1 hands.
Colour: any solid colour.
Physique, Features
Use: Similar to Hanoverian.

Oldenburg

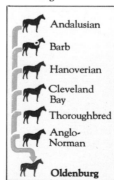

Warmblood
Origin: Oldenburg and East Friesland.
Height: 16.3 hands.
Physique: largest of the German warmbloods;
Use: riding and driving.

Trakehner

East Friesian

Oldenburg

Holstein

Schleswig Heavy
Draught

Hanoverian

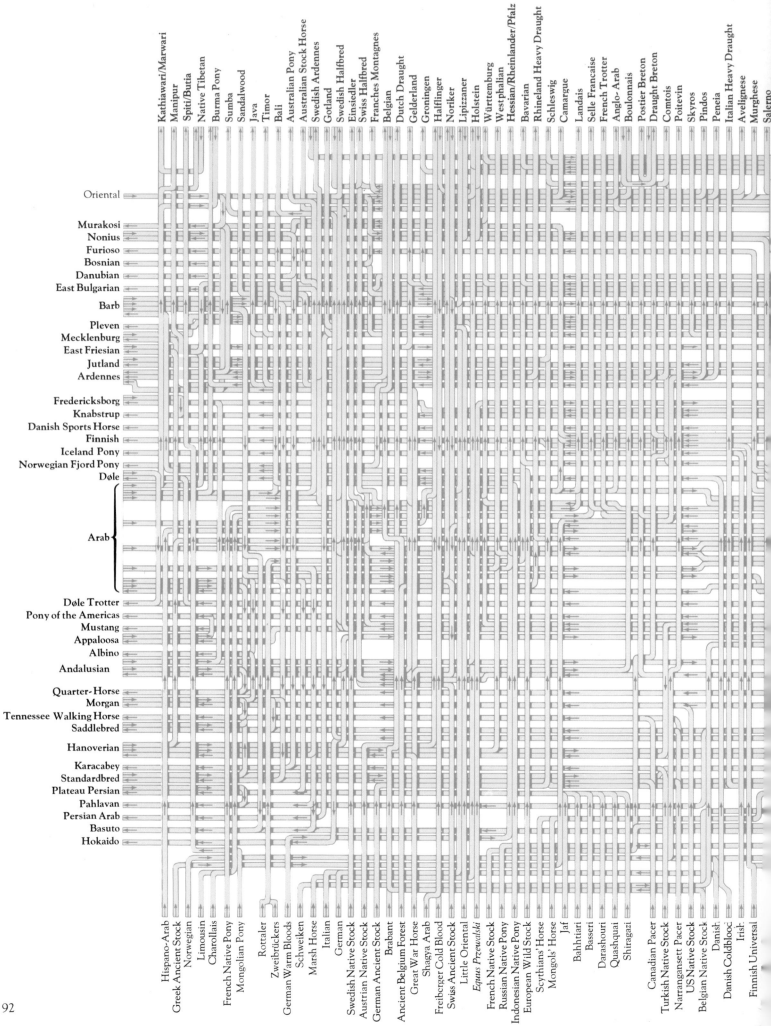

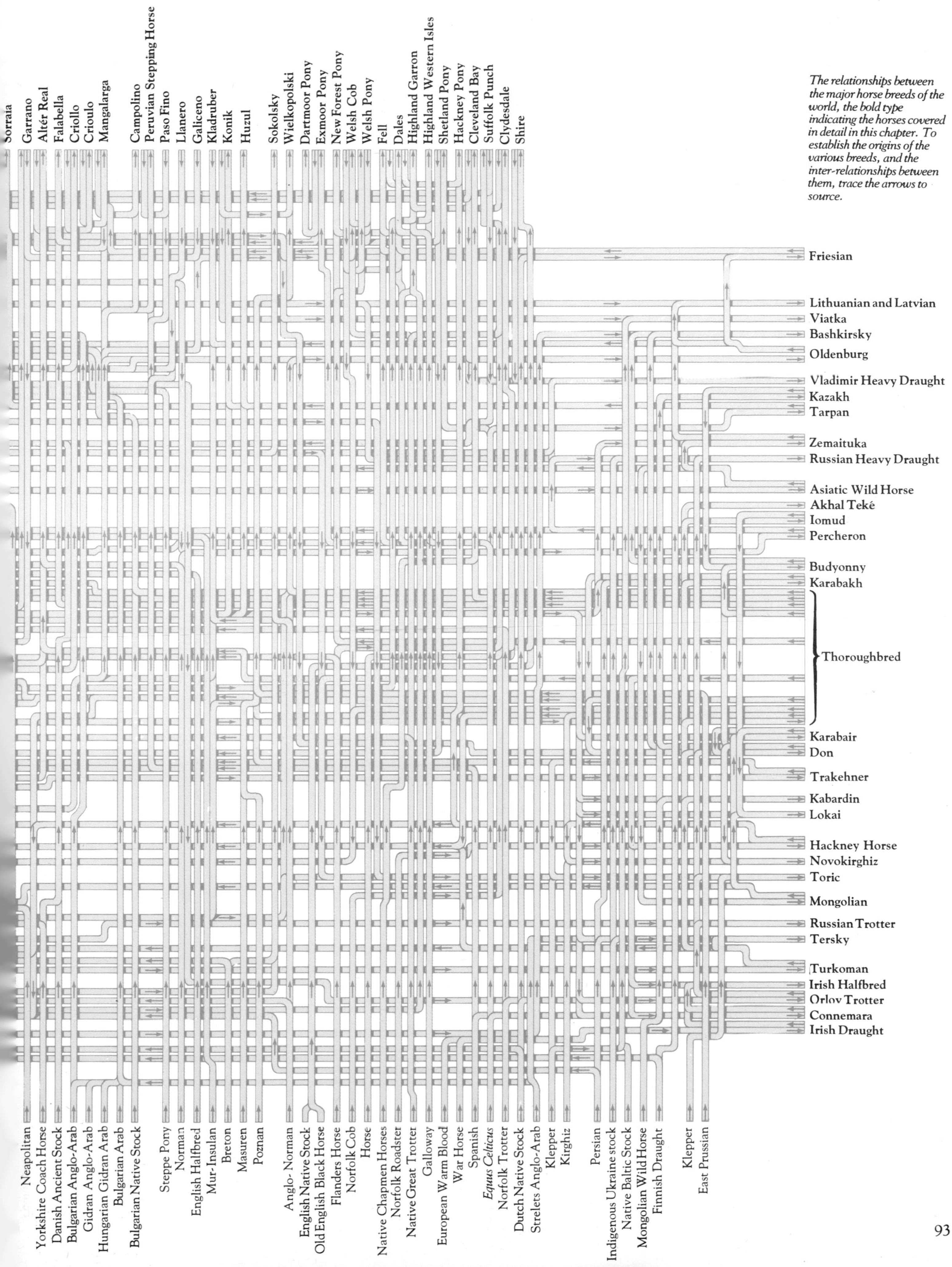
Sorraia
Garrano
Altér Real
Falabella
Criollo
Crioulo
Mangalarga
Campolino
Peruvian Stepping Horse
Paso Fino
Llanero
Galiceno
Kladruber
Konik
Huzul
Sokolsky
Wielkopolski
Dartmoor Pony
Exmoor Pony
New Forest Pony
Welsh Cob
Welsh Pony
Fell
Dales
Highland Garron
Highland Western Isles
Shetland Pony
Hackney Pony
Cleveland Bay
Suffolk Punch
Clydesdale
Shire
Friesian
Lithuanian and Latvian
Viatka
Bashkirsky
Oldenburg
Vladimir Heavy Draught
Kazakh
Tarpan
Zemaituka
Russian Heavy Draught
Asiatic Wild Horse
Akhal Teké
Iomud
Percheron
Budyonny
Karabakh
Thoroughbred
Karabair
Don
Trakehner
Kabardin
Lokai
Hackney Horse
Novokirghiz
Toric
Mongolian
Russian Trotter
Tersky
Turkoman
Irish Halfbred
Orlov Trotter
Connemara
Irish Draught
Neapolitan
Yorkshire Coach Horse
Danish Ancient Stock
Bulgarian Anglo-Arab
Gidran Anglo-Arab
Hungarian Gidran Arab
Bulgarian Arab
Bulgarian Native Stock
Steppe Pony
Norman
English Halfbred
Mur-Insulan
Breton
Masuren
Poznan
Anglo- Norman
English Native Stock
Old English Black Horse
Flanders Horse
Norfolk Cob
Horse
Native Chapmen Horses
Norfolk Roadster
Native Great Trotter
Galloway
European Warm Blood
War Horse
Spanish
Equus Celticus
Norfolk Trotter
Dutch Native Stock
Strelets Anglo-Arab
Klepper
Kirghiz
Persian
Indigenous Ukraine stock
Native Baltic Stock
Mongolian Wild Horse
Finnish Draught
Klepper
East Prussian

The relationships between the major horse breeds of the world, the bold type indicating the horses covered in detail in this chapter. To establish the origins of the various breeds, and the inter-relationships between them, trace the arrows to source.

Buying a horse

For even an experienced rider, buying a horse can be an operation fraught with hazards. For example, the horse can turn out to be unsound, 'nappy', a rearer or a runaway, traffic-shy, bad in the stable, or difficult in company with other horses or when left alone. It may, on the other hand, be a paragon of virtue, but simply not what you are looking for. Buying a horse is as highly personalized a procedure as choosing a wife or a husband.

There are many methods of buying a horse – riding magazines, for example, list horses for sale. But generally, if you are buying a horse for the first time, the soundest course of action is to find a reputable dealer and rely on his judgement. This is far preferable to purchasing a horse at a sale. Sales are sometimes used to unload undesirable horses – the chronically sick, for instance, which have to be kept going on drugs, or those which have serious vices. Of course, if a horse is warranted sound when it is sold and then turns out not to be, the purchaser can return the horse and get the money back. But it is simpler and safer not to get into this situation in the first place.

Few reputable dealers will take advantage of someone who confesses their ignorance. The beginner should therefore admit his lack of experience and trust in the dealer's judgement, though an experienced friend is by far the greatest asset.

Points to watch for

There is a saying that a good horse should 'fit into a box'. This means that a classically conformed horse should, excluding its head and neck, be capable of fitting into a rectangle. A horse of this type is most likely to be, and remain, sound.

Good limbs are, of course, essential. The foreleg should give the overall impression of being 'over', rather than 'back' of the knee. Pay attention, too, to the horse's centre of gravity – the part of the creature on which the greatest strain devolves. Points before or behind the centre are also liable to strain, but a well-conformed horse is far less at risk.

To assess the horse's personality, look it squarely in the eye; the character and intentions of a horse are fairly easy to read and interpret with a little experience. A bold but kind eye, generously proportioned, indicates a reliable, sympathetic temperament. Piggy little eyes, especially if the skull is convex between them and runs down to a Roman nose, are sure signs of an untrustworthy beast.

The role of the vet

Before any purchase is made, always have the horse examined by a veterinary surgeon, who should be first told what the horse is required

Top left Bidding for a horse at an auction, top right a horse being displayed to potential buyers in the sale ring and below a successful purchase. Far left The veterinary examination – an essential stage in any transaction – and left trying out a horse's paces prior to purchase. When buying a horse, the important things to check are the animal's conformation, movements, soundness and suitability for the prospective rider, both in temperament and the uses intended for it.

A vet can help assess the first three points, but the rider is the best judge of the other two. Whenever possible, try out a horse thoroughly. Take it into a large field to test its paces and to make sure that it can be easily controlled, past its stable to check that it is obedient and along a road to ensure that it is not traffic-shy.

for. A general hack, for instance, will not make an event horse. The examination should begin with the horse being 'run up in hand', in order to check that the horse moves straight, and that it is sound. A sound horse can be heard to be going level and evenly, as well as seen to be. An unsound horse will favour the lame leg, keeping it on the ground for as little time as possible. If very lame, it will nod its head as it drops its weight on to the sound leg.

The feet and limbs are then examined, the vet being on the watch for any heat or swelling, exostoses (bony enlargements such as spavins, sidebones, or ringbones), and signs of muscular unsoundness, such as curbs, thorough-pins, or thickened tendons.

If all appears satisfactory, the horse's eyes are examined for cataract; it is then mounted and galloped to check its wind. This is to ensure that there are no latent troubles with breathing or lungs – defects that are betrayed by a 'roar' or a 'whistle'.

Horses with wind afflictions may also have cardiac problems, for the effort of breathing

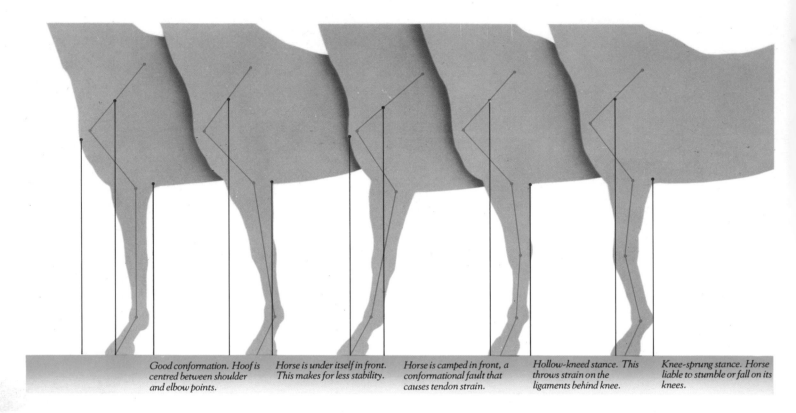

Good conformation. Hoof is centred between shoulder and elbow points.

Horse is under itself in front. This makes for less stability.

Horse is camped in front, a conformational fault that causes tendon strain.

Hollow-kneed stance. This throws strain on the ligaments behind knee.

Knee-sprung stance. Horse liable to stumble or fall on its knees.

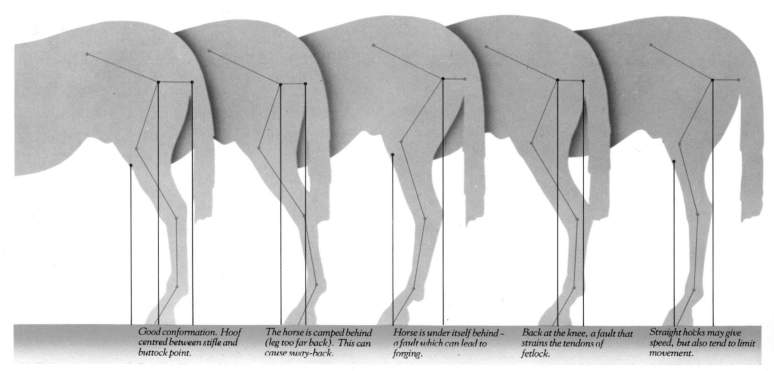

Good conformation. Hoof centred between stifle and buttock point.

The horse is camped behind (leg too far back). This can cause sway-back.

Horse is under itself behind – a fault which can lead to forging.

Back at the knee, a fault that strains the tendons of fetlock.

Straight hocks may give speed, but also tend to limit movement.

in such cases naturally imposes an added strain on the heart. For this reason, after the gallop, the heart is tested with a stethoscope.

The general condition of the horse is also examined and checks made for worms or other parasites. Finally, the vet submits a report of his findings.

Trial before buying
It is sometimes possible to have a horse on trial for a limited period to see if horse and rider are compatible, though usually only if the dealer has a personal knowledge of the buyer. Horses are prone to all kinds of ailments and afflictions, and no dealer should be expected to entrust a horse to an inexperienced prospective purchaser.

A trial period is exceptionally valuable when buying a pony for a child. Here, the normal problems can be further compounded by the child's lack of strength, as well as, possibly, of experience. The safety of the child must be the first priority. Children have been killed when their ponies take fright and bolt – a particular hazard when riding on or near roads. It is therefore of the utmost importance only to buy from people with impeccable credentials. The outgrown family pony is ideal, but often hard to find, as these animals are often passed on to the owner's

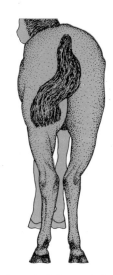

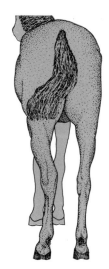

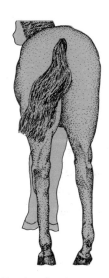

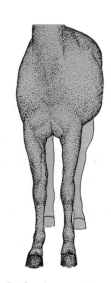

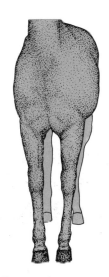

Good conformation. Point of buttock is in line with hock and hoof.

A cow-hocked stance looks awkward, but is no problem if legs strong.

Bow-legged conformation puts strain on hock bones and ligaments.

Good conformation. Point of shoulder is in line with knee and hoof.

Pigeon-toed stance puts strain on the knees. The horse may tend to stumble.

Horse is closed in front. Has little heart room, may tend to brush.

Below *A shallow-bodied horse has little stamina as it lacks lung capacity.*

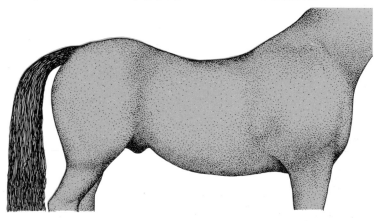

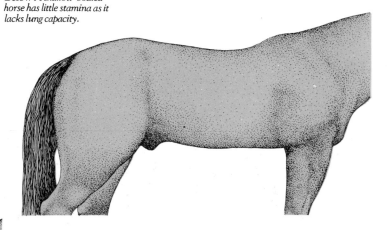

Above *A hollow back lacks strength and flexibility. It can be a sign of age.*

Below *A straight back restricts movement. The horse will lack power.*

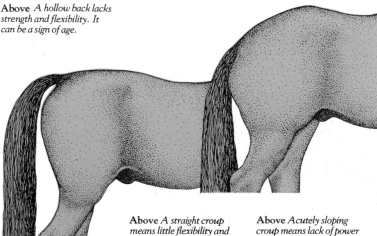

Above *A straight croup means little flexibility and less power in jumping.*

Above *Acutely sloping croup means lack of power in hind quarters.*

friends and relations. Ponies are also sold by their breeders, and breed societies will supply the names of studs.

For a first horse, do not make the mistake of buying too young an animal A well-trained horse that knows its job and is a willing and co-operative ride, is a much better buy than a young, inexperienced one. Two novices together is a bad combination; the horse is very likely to dominate its inexperienced rider.

Thus, a horse of four, five or six years of age is not a beginner's ride. At eight years, it is mature, and, providing it is sound and healthy, it should be useful and active until aged well over twenty. The more nervous the rider, the more docile the horse should be.

It is possible that as a rider becomes more proficient, he or she will look for a horse with more quality. This is a natural and correct progression, but resist the temptation of buy-

ing a horse with too much 'fire in its belly'. This may well pull your arms nearly out of their sockets when, say, in company with other horses. Remember, too, that well-bred horses are far more expensive to keep than, say, a cob, for they usually have to be stabled in winter. A cob, on the other hand, can winter out in a New Zealand rug quite happily, as long as it has access to a shelter and is given hay and one or two feeds a day.

Chapter Six

Breeding a horse

Breeding and raising a foal is one of the most satisfying things involved with horses, but it is a complex business, and should never be undertaken without careful consideration of all the problems involved. For instance, a foal cannot be produced simply for the amount of the stud fee; the additional expenses of veterinary fees, upkeep, and of transporting the mare to and from the stud all have to be taken into account. The vet must be consulted, both to check for hereditary defects and also to ensure that the animal is free from disease – the usual method is to take a cervical and clitoral swab. Most studs require a veterinary certificate to this effect. So, unless the facilities are right and time and money are of no object, think twice about becoming a horse-breeder.

The role of the mare

Mares come into season at regular intervals of between eighteen and twenty-one days, and it is at this time that they can be 'served' (inseminated) by a stallion. However, it is possible for a mare to apparently 'hold' to a service and then to 'return' (come into season again) six weeks later. To make doubly sure, a vet should test a specimen of the mare's blood or urine after 45/100 days and 120 days respectively.

It is best not to ride the mare for a few weeks, until it is certain that she has held to the service. Usually, most studs prefer to keep mares for six weeks in any case, and do not send them back before then unless quite

Sexual organs of the mare

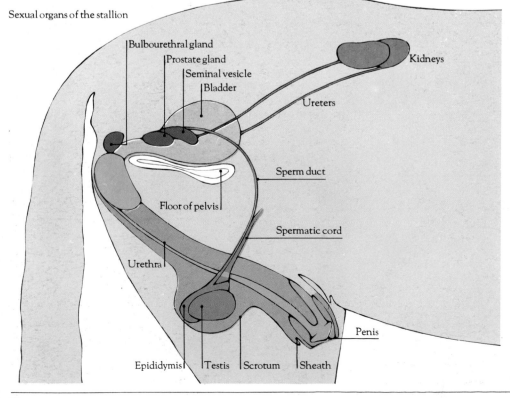

Sexual organs of the stallion

A mare's sexual organs consist of ovaries, Fallopian tubes, uterus, cervix, vagina and vulva. At birth, the ovaries contain thousands of eggs; some of these are released into the Fallopian tubes during the sexual cycle to allow fertilization to occur. A stallion's sexual

organs consist of two testes, in the scrotum, collecting ducts, linked to the the urethra through the spermatic cord, prostate, bulbourethral and vesicular seminal glands, and the penis, in the prepuce. Spermatoza are produced in the testes.

certain that they are in foal. The cost of their keep, of course, raises the price still further.

The mare will not need any special care when she returns from the stud, apart from a more nourishing diet. If she is fed nuts or cubes, buy the stud variety instead of the ordinary horse and pony ones. If she is not, introduce a suitable vitamin preparation and some cod liver oil, which has been especially enriched for animal feeding, into the diet.

Unless it is unavoidable, it is wise not to turn a pregnant mare out with geldings. These may tease or worry her and cause her to 'slip' (lose) her foal.

Choosing a stallion

The choice of stallion depends on the type of horse that you are hoping to breed. Bear in mind that a good quality big horse may be expected to grow into money, while a small one is unlikely to.

Breeding is an uncertain venture at the best of times, with all kinds of risks of hereditary unsoundness. Therefore, choose a stallion that has been certified by a recognized, official body – most countries have regulations covering this. In the UK, for instance, the Hunter's Improvement and National Light Horse Hunter Breeding Society have awarded premiums to sixty Thoroughbred stallions. Each of these has undergone a stringent examination by a panel of vets and they are the only stallions in the country warranted to be sound and free from hereditary disease.

Stallions are generally advertised for

breeding purposes in the spring. At one time they used to travel the roads and railways in the company of a stallion man, staying for the night at various points along the route, where the owners of mares in season would bring them to be served. Nowadays, in most countries, stallions remain on their base farms throughout the spring and early summer, and the mares are brought to them to be served there.

Many novice breeders make the mistake of choosing a stallion purely on the strength of geographical convenience. Nothing could be more short-sighted, for it is essential to select a stallion that will be likely to offset any conformational defects in the mare.

The stallion and the stud

Although it is important to keep a stallion under control, and to demand respect from him, he should never be treated as a dangerous wild animal. Knowledgeable stallion men lead or ride their horses out for daily exercise, and their horses are contented and relaxed. Some owners ride them around the farm and along quiet country roads, while others turn them out to grass with the mares.

At many studs, a horse called a 'teaser' is kept for trying mares, that is, to ascertain whether they are ready for service. Teasers are used to safeguard the stallions that are actually doing the serving, for all horses used at stud are liable to be kicked by an irritable mare at some time during their careers. Some studs insist on hobbling all mares before they are served, in any case, a mare should never be sent to a stud unless its hind shoes have first been removed.

When the attentions of the teaser have satisfied the stud groom that the mare is fully 'on' and ready to accept the stallion – the usual signs are that the mare stands still, with the vulva damp with fluid and opening spasmodically – the stallion is brought out of his box, or from behind the trying gate or wall. The stallion serves the mare in hand, that is, they are both on lead reins and wearing bridles, as a safety precaution. Mating normally takes one or two minutes, during which the mare must be kept as still as possible, especially during ejaculation. The head should be kept as high as possible and, at the moment of mounting, the leg hobble – if used – should be released. To achieve extra con-

trol over the mare during mating, some studs put a twitch on her. This is a loop of rope on the end of a stick, which is twisted tightly around the upper lip.

An instantaneous mating may not immediately ensue, however; horses, like humans, have their foibles. Mares have been known to take immediate and strong exception to the partner selected for them, while stallions also have their likes and dislikes. The premium stallion Little Cloud, for example, son of the Derby winner Nimbus, always refused to serve grey mares unless they were covered by a rug.

Nevertheless, if the mare does not accept the stallion willingly, it may well be that she has some internal illness, such as a cystic ovary. She should be thoroughly examined by a vet, as a reluctance to mate is often an indication that the mare is unlikely to breed. Or the time is not right – either she has passed the fertile period of her season, when the ovum is ready for fertilisation, or she has not yet reached it. Healthy mares are seldom a problem to cover or to get in foal, though excess weight is not an aid to procreation.

Mares generally carry foals for eleven

Right *A stallion with a stud groom. Stallions are exceptionally valuable animals and need particular care in their management. In this, the role of the groom is vital, particularly during the actual covering process. As with all horses, cleanliness and proper grooming, exercise and feeding are essential; a Thoroughbred stallion, for instance, needs a high protein diet, with up to 7kg (16lb) of crushed oats a day in addition to top quality hay. Exercise is usually given on the lunge or by leading, though small stallions can often be safely ridden.*

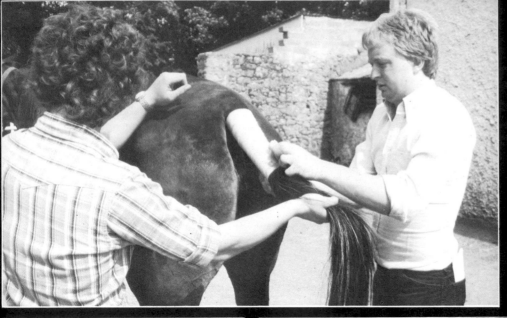

Top left *Bandaging a mare's tail prior to covering,* **centre** *cleaning the mare after covering has been completed and* **right** *teasing a mare with a 'rig' – a second-rate stallion – to find out whether she is ready to be covered.* **Above left** *Cleaning a stallion's penis,* **centre** *putting protective boots on the mare and* **right** *the actual act of covering. Hygiene plus careful management are essential if a successful mating is to be accomplished. The other main reason for teasing, for instance, is to establish what the mare's reactions are likely to be during the actual* covering *process, so that safety measures can be planned accordingly. If she reacts aggressively, then protective boots, or hobbles, have to be fitted to lessen the risk of her injuring the stallion if she kicks out at the end of the process. During the covering, the mare should be held securely, particularly during the period of penetration. The whole process usually lasts a maximum of two minutes, if not less.*

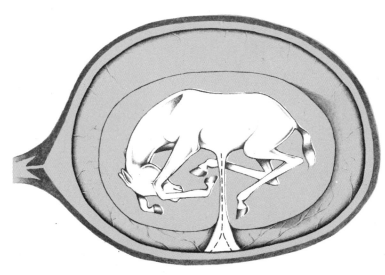

months and a few days – on average, 334 days for colts, and 332.5 days for fillies – but there is a possible variation of some 9.5 days each way, and some mares may be as much as two weeks late. A pregnant mare may safely be ridden to an advanced stage in pregnancy for seven months – as long as she is never over-exerted. Exercise is beneficial for all healthy pregnant animals.

Foaling

Pony mares are usually best left out in a field to foal. They foal quickly and seem to have sufficient natural instinct to produce the foal, clean and dry it, as they would if part of a wild herd, when mare and foal would have to be prepared to move on with the rest of the band soon after birth. The more

Above *The foetus of a foal is protected by an outer membrane called the allantois and an inner one known as the amnion. Both contain fluid in which the foal floats and so is kept insulated from possible shock. The foetus feeds on the blood of its dam through the choriotic villii, buds which link the allantois and the lining of the womb, and the veins and the arteries contained in the navel cord.*

Right *A pregnant mare in the wild. Most types of pony, too, are sturdy enough to bear their foals in outdoor conditions.*

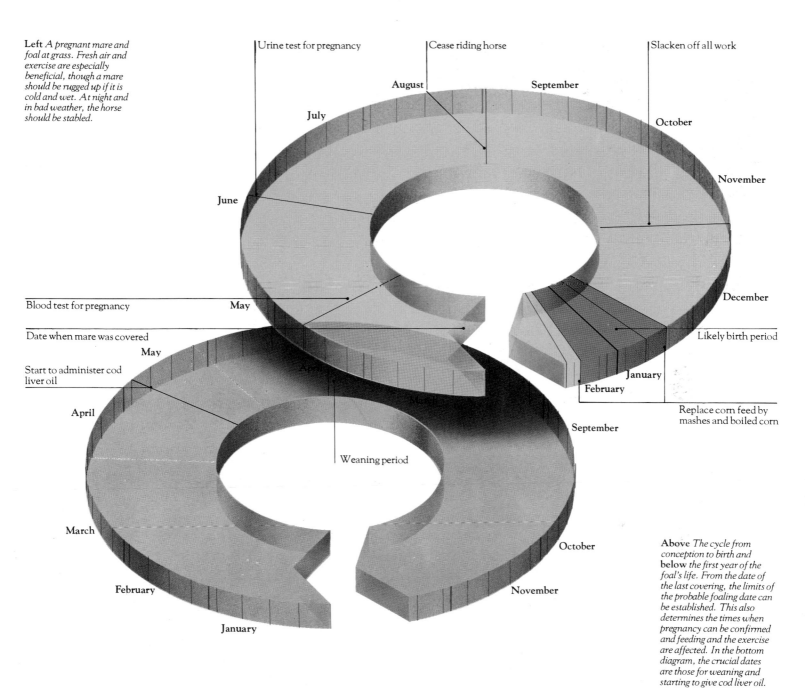

Left *A pregnant mare and foal at grass. Fresh air and exercise are especially beneficial, though a mare should be rugged up if it is cold and wet. At night and in bad weather, the horse should be stabled.*

Urine test for pregnancy

Cease riding horse

Slacken off all work

August

September

July

October

June

November

Blood test for pregnancy

May

December

Date when mare was covered

May

Likely birth period

Start to administer cod liver oil

April

January

April

February

March

Replace corn feed by mashes and boiled corn

September

April

Weaning period

March

October

February

November

January

Above *The cycle from conception to birth and* below *the first year of the foal's life. From the date of the last covering, the limits of the probable foaling date can be established. This also determines the times when pregnancy can be confirmed and feeding and the exercise are affected. In the bottom diagram, the crucial dates are those for weaning and starting to give cod liver oil.*

highly-bred the mare is, the more supervision she will require. Thoroughbred mares almost always foal in the stable, watched over by attendants. At all the major studs, closed-circuit television is employed. This gives the mare the illusion of being alone, while every move is being watched, and help is immediately at hand, if required.

Only a proper stud will have the facilities for sitting up all night for perhaps as long as two weeks – a task that is beyond most private owners. Therefore, it may be advisable to book the mare into a stud as early as possible. Make sure that the stud is reputable and responsible; a vet is a good person to consult.

Giving birth

The first sign of approaching birth is when the mare starts to pace around, showing signs of discomfort at regular intervals, glancing at her sides and swishing her tail. The wax formed on the udder drops off the teats and the muscles on either side of the croup drop inwards.

As the labour pains become strong, the mare lies down. Delivery is imminent when the membranes of the water bag, in which the foal is contained, break to release the mare's waters.

If, however, delivery is delayed and the mare seems to be straining and visibly tiring, veterinary assistance must be obtained immediately, for the cause may well be a malpresentation. In a normal birth, the forefeet are delivered first, followed by the head and the rest of the body. Complications ensue if

the presentation is incorrect – the most common examples being the frontal presentation, in which the foal's head is bent sideways; where the foal is on its chest, with its knees bent; when the head is bent backwards, and one knee half bent; the head bowed beneath the forelegs; and the dorsal presentation, in which the foal lies on its back, with the head and forelegs pointing backwards. Sometimes there may be a breech presentation (hind end foremost), in which the hind feet come first, or some other abnormality, such as the twisting of the foetal membranes or the disintegration of the foetus.

In many of these cases, the foal must be pushed back from the birth canal into the uterus, where there is room to turn the foal round, to straighten its legs, or reposition its head. To accomplish this, professional veterinary help is essential.

Once the foal is born, most mares will instinctively start to wash it. Then, as it staggers to its feet, she gently pushes it towards her udder, where it begins to suckle. This early suck is all-important, for the first flow of milk is proceded by colostrum, a vitamin-rich substance that contains natural protection against several juvenile diseases and also stimulates the bowels of the newly-born foal into action.

The mare frees itself of the afterbirth. This should be retained for inspection by a vet to make sure that it is complete. If, for any reason, release of the afterbirth is unduly delayed, then the vet should be called to free it, or infection will follow.

When the foal is a day or two old – even a few hours old, if it is strong and healthy – a small head collar, made of webbing or soft leather and known as a slip, may be put on it. This always involves a struggle, so it should be undertaken before the foal gets too strong. This will enable you to get it accustomed to being handled and led about, which is essential if it becomes necessary to administer medicines or injections. A good way to accustom the foal to human contact is to bring it

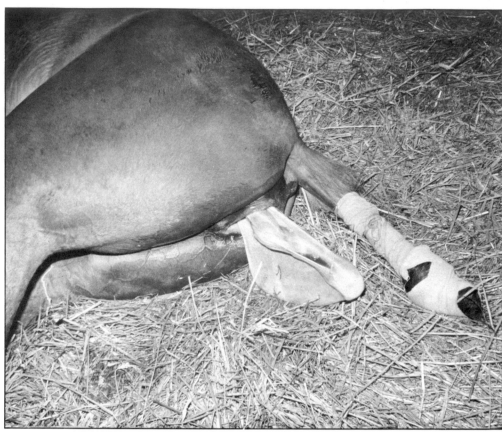

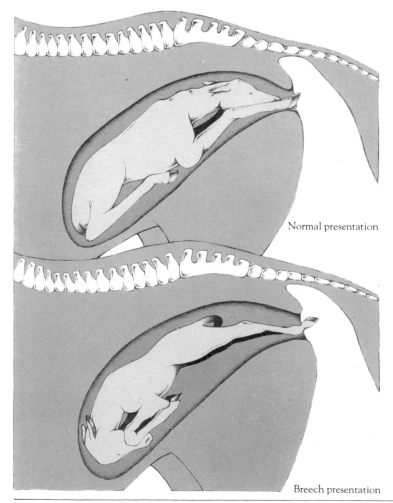

Normal presentation

Breech presentation

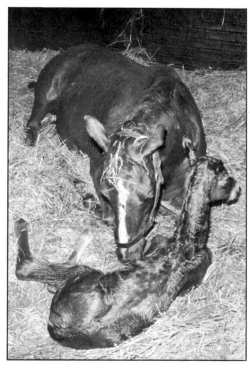

Left *A normal presentation contrasted with a breech presentation, in which the foal is presented hind-foremost. A normal breech presentation presents few difficulties, provided that skilled assistance can be obtained to manipulate the foal. The chief task is to make sure both hind legs are in the birth passage; the chief risk is that the umbilical cord may become trapped, so that the foal is in danger of suffocation. Speed is therefore essential as otherwise the foal will drown in the waters contained in the protective membrane.*

Left *The second stage of labour begins, with the foal's forelegs emerging, and* **right** *its completion.*
Below left *The mare licks her foal clean and* **right** *the two twenty minutes after the birth has been completed, the only visible sign being the afterbirth attached to the mare. Birth starts when the mare's waters burst, after which there is usually a short pause. The next stage is the emergence of the forelegs (in normal birth), wrapped in the amnion, and the process now continues until birth is completed. Help can be given by wrapping a cloth around the foal's fetlocks and applying traction in time with the labour pangs.*

After birth, the mare's licking encourages the foal to stand and, during this process, the umbilical cord usually breaks naturally. If not, it can be cut with sterilised scissors. It should then be drained and disinfected as a precaution against infection. The same applies to the afterbirth, which must be removed by a vet if the mare does not cleanse itself in six hours.

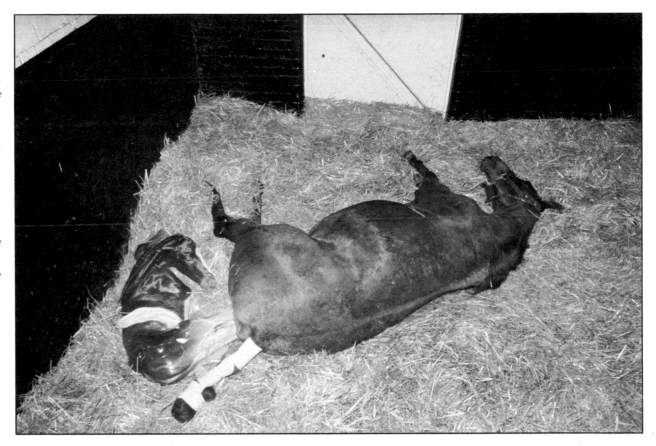

into the stable with its mother at night. This also provides it with a dry bed to sleep on and minimises the risk of chills. If the mare is fed dampened bran and crushed oats, night and morning from a bin on the ground, it will help her condition, and very soon the foal will be eating them too. If you have someone to help, the process of leading the foal in and out of the stall will be a valuable early lesson for the young horse, and may save time and trouble later during the breaking process.

Caring for the foal

With the approach of autumn, the foal must be weaned or it will become a heavy drain on the mother's strength. If she is in foal again, it will rob her of calcium, and the next foal may be born with deformed limbs. Weaning, however, vastly increases the owner's responsibilities. The mare, parted from her foal, bellows night and day, her cries evoking shrill replies from the foal. This lasts until she becomes resigned to the fact that the foal has passed from her care to that of their mutual owner.

The foal should remain in a loose box for at least two weeks; there, where it has become accustomed to eating hard feed together with its mother, it will give little trouble. It will welcome its feeds, which should be generous to compensate for the milk it now lacks. Milk pellets may be added to the feed if it seems to be losing condition.

It is when the two weeks are up, and the foal has to adapt to a new routine of loose box by night and outdoors by day, that the responsibilities mount. First, you must find a companion for your foal to substitute for its mother. Ideally, another foal is the best companion.

It is as well, however, to keep the two foals in different boxes at night. If they are constantly together, one will dominate the other and take most of the food. They will also be so difficult to separate when they mature that you will have a performance almost akin to weaning all over again.

When the warm weather returns, they can stay out all night, and, as the summer days grow really hot, you may consider keeping them in by day and out by night, as a means of protecting them from flies. This should be the pattern of their lives for a couple of years or more, until the time comes for them to be broken. By the second winter, you may decide to let them remain in the field, which does, of course, save a lot of mucking out. Provided you give them some sort of shelter for cold, wet nights, they should not come to much harm. Throughout these early years, have the blacksmith check their feet – say, every six weeks, especially in long periods of dry weather.

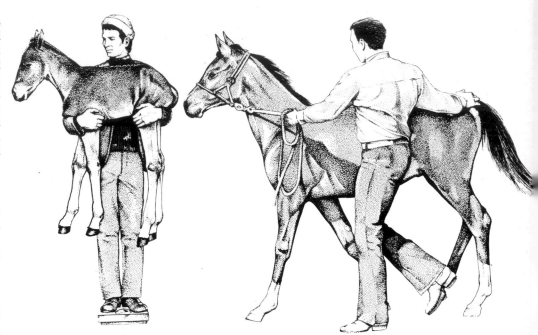

Lifting a foal on to the scales to check its weight. Weighing should be carried out regularly to ensure all is well.

Leading should be done daily, using a halter to control direction and a hand for encouragement.

Right *The result of a year's patience – a healthy foal growing towards maturity.*

If you live in an area of good grass, you can dispense with feeding from late spring to late summer. But as soon as the rains come, corn must be provided, together with as much hay as the young horses will eat.

Breaking and training

If you lack the knowledge or the time to break in a colt yourself, be very careful to whom you send it for training. Every area where horses are concentrated has at least one colt-breaker, and sometimes more. Ask the owner of your local riding school or the blacksmith, to find out which breaker has the best reputation. Make sure to send your colt to someone generally acknowledged to be expert. It takes a long time to 'make' a horse, but a very short time indeed to spoil it.

Owing to the colt's extreme youth, this will not in any case be a making operation, but rather just an erosion of the rough edges. Most breakers prefer to have a horse for a few weeks in the spring of its third year, when it is strong enough to undertake light work, but not powerful enough to put up too much of a fight. Battles may thus be avoided, rather than precipitated.

When to sell

It is always possible that when the foal has been bred and weaned, or even after it has been run on for a couple of years, you may decide to part with it. The horse may have an ungenerous temperament, or is unlikely to grow as tall, or stay as small, as you had hoped. Perhaps it has some conformational fault which you perhaps particularly dislike.

Young horses do not grow in even stages. A good foal, for instance, may go off as a yearling but be a brilliant two year old. On the other hand, a good yearling might become a plain two year old and then develop into a star long before its fourth birthday. However, it is a mistake to keep horses in the hope that they will improve, unless you have unlimited grass to keep them on, or a farm to provide plentiful supplies of corn free of charge. If you possess neither, it is impossible to keep colts without spending a great deal of money. There are also bound to be occasions when the vet must be called, and this is by no means cheap. For instance, if the foal is a male, he will have to be gelded as a yearling.

One way of avoiding disappointment is not to breed from your old mare that has become lame and incapable of work. Unsound stock produces youngsters with a tendency to unsoundness themselves, usually through bad conformation. Buy the soundest mare you can afford, send her to the most suitable stallion, and see, if possible, the stock that either have produced. A really bad horse is likely to be slaughtered when young as being too unsound to work. It is therefore vital that all breeding should be selective – there is no point in producing horses fit only for slaughter.

Remember, too, to decide what the horse will actually be used for well in advance of making the decision to breed. Sending a small mare to a small stallion, for instance, will inevitably produce a small foal.

Chapter Seven

Breaking and schooling

Since man domesticated the horse, its life style has adapted to meet its change in circumstances. Yet the natural instincts of its ancestors still remain firmly embedded in the horse's mind and character, from the most scientifically bred Thoroughbred to the humblest of ponies.

The first, and perhaps the most important, thing to remember is that the horse is an outdoor animal, and, in the wild, lived its life as part of a single community, the herd. In the herd, leadership came from the head horse, the stallion within the group with the most dominant and positive personality. The horse now looks to man for decisions and protection in the same way as once it did to the head horse, and a good trainer must understand and accept these responsibilities as an important part of his task. For instance, a horse with a strong personality should be treated with tact and firmness, while a nervous or less intelligent horse requires sympathy and patience.

Toughness is also a legacy from the horse's past, but so, too, are sensitivity and timidity. So another general principle to bear in mind when handling horses is not to surprise them with any sudden movement or noise. A frightened horse will often take weeks or even months to get over the experience. If a horse is frightened, then the handler must be calm and soothe it with a quiet voice. Do not make an issue of anything that may go wrong, for horses are very perceptive to the emotions of those around them. Such treatment will only confuse the horse; this is something that neither horses nor ponies like and it can often upset them so much that they become uncontrollable.

Thus, the mental approach of the trainer is the basic factor influencing the progress of the training programme. Bad horses are not born – they are made. Observation is the key in establishing the right mental attitude. By watching the horse at liberty, at rest, feeding, by studying how the animal moves and how it reacts to situations around it, the trainer can determine and analyse just how the horse thinks and what he or she is going to do with it during the teaching process.

Handling – the first step

The training programme starts with handling the foal; early handling is just as important as backing and schooling, if not more so. But it must be remembered that, to give the horse time to mature physically, there should be a two to three year interval between early handling and concentrated training. In other words, we may be discussing the handling of a yearling, though it may not actually be backed until its third year.

A trainer should spend the early days with

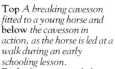

Top A breaking cavesson fitted to a young horse and **below** *the cavesson in action, as the horse is led at a walk during an early schooling lesson.* **Right** *Lungeing with the saddle in position and* **above** *lungeing on the lead, the horse walking in a circle with a helper at its head. The time when breaking and schooling can start varies according to the type and temperament of horse concerned. Some experts believe that it is best to leave half and three-quarter breds until at least the age of three; Thoroughbreds, however, can be worked as yearlings and two-year-olds. Once started in earnest, the basic process of breaking should take about six weeks.*

Two essential items of equipment are the cavesson and the lunge rein. The former is a superior form of head collar, with a well-padded noseband on to which is set a metal plate. This is fitted with three swivelling metal rings, to which the leading or lunge rein is attached. The noseband must be tight enough to prevent the cavesson slipping round, or control will be lost. Its position should be checked carefully; the noseband should be about four fingers above the horse's nostrils, or it will interfere with the breathing. The lunge rein should be at least 6m (20ft) long and made of strong, lightweight material, such as canvas or nylon. The horse should also wear boots, bandages and knee pads.

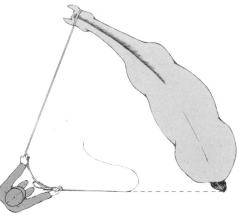

Above *Training a horse to circle left on the lunge. Positioned behind the point of the shoulder, the trainer gradually increases the size of the circle, controlling the head with the left hand and* the hindquarters with the whip in the right. The aim is to get the horse to walk, trot and halt correctly and respond to verbal commands. For the right, the procedure is reversed

the foal just going out to it in the field, patting it, talking to it, feeling it, picking up its legs, and slipping a head collar on and off. The foal can also get used to being led; this should be established as part of the daily routine of bringing the foal in at night.

Through these processes, the foal becomes familiar with its trainer through physical contact, smell and mental 'feel'. The horse is gradually convinced that it has nothing to fear and comes to realize that the trainer will ask certain tasks of it which it will be able to comprehend and perform without harm to itself.

Once the foal is used to being handled and led, the first foundation in its relationship with man has been laid. Next the trainer starts to get the youngster to obey some basic signals. This can be done by teaching it a few basic manners — to give its feet up so that they can be cleaned out, for example. Eventually, the horse will learn to give up each foot from just a touch of the hand.

Then, the horse is taught to move across the box. First, the trainer holds the horse's head still and then, by pointing with a short riding cane or stick, encourages the horse to move its hindquarters over to the left or right. The horse soon learns to move over in its box from the voice alone.

Thus, dressage, of a simple sort, has been started. In this, the whip or stick plays an important part, though it is only an aid to the trainer in communicating with the horse. It is a means of making commands and signals obvious and simple, not a means of punishment or of enforcing the trainer's own will upon the creature. The young horse should have complete confidence in the whip; it must not be afraid of it.

Leading in hand
Serious work with a young colt or filly starts with teaching it to be led in hand. This is the phase of training where many young horses can be spoilt for life. The basic aim of all training must be to encourage the horse to move willingly and quietly through all its paces, without loss of energy and balance, while carrying a rider. The handler should be level with the animal's shoulders and, above all, should not restrict its free forward movement.

The process can start quite early — even before the foal is weaned. Real control from the lead-rope, however, can be left to this later stage. The simplest exercise involved is teaching the young animal to come to the halt. This can be done in the stable yard, say, by walking the horse around, and every now and then standing still, while giving the command 'stand'. The trainer restricts the forward movement by standing still himself,

but not by pulling backwards on the lead.

At first, the young horse will stop with the forehand, though the hindquarters may continue to move, describing a quarter circle. But the animal will quickly realize that this is a waste of energy; after a few lessons, it will teach itself to come completely to the halt, provided that the head has not been pulled about in the initial process.

These early lessons should only last about ten to fifteen minutes a day. Discipline between trainer and horse has now been established, but the essential key remains co-operation; the animal puts up no physical resistance and the trainer avoids the use of force, which is totally counter productive.

Lungeing

Lungeing starts when the trainer is certain that the horse is physically fit enough to undergo a more extensive work programme. Boots, bandages and knee pads should be worn. The lunge cavesson now takes the place of the head collar, with the lunge rein fitted to the central 'D' ring. A helper, lightly holding the cavesson, walks the horse around in a circle at the end of the lunge rein, with the trainer standing in the centre forming a triangle between him or herself, the lunge rein, the lunge whip and the horse.

The same routine of stopping and starting is followed as that already established in the yard. But now, when the trainer asks the horse to walk on, the signal is given with the lunge whip and the voice – the most important aid in lungeing.

Gradually, the helper moves away from the horse towards the trainer at the centre of the circle. Success is achieved when the youngster walks willingly around the trainer at the end of the lunge rein.

Lunge work can then start at the trot. The horse now realizes that the control is coming from one central point and is receptive to the commands being given.

The breaking roller

The first purpose of the roller is to familiarize the youngster with the feel of a girth; later, it

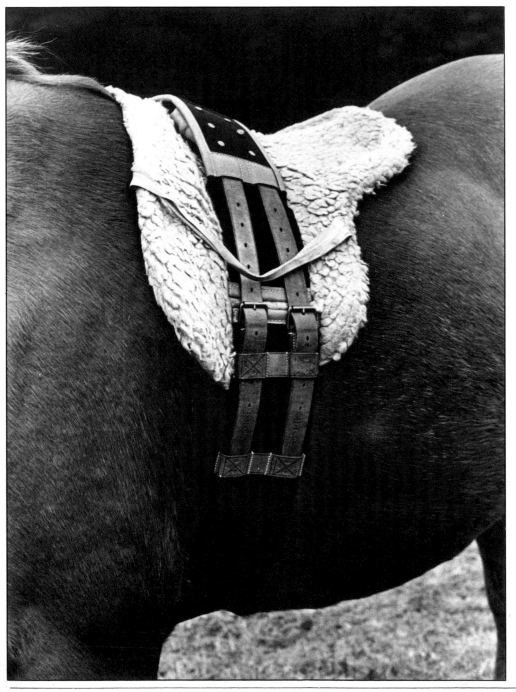

Above *A mouthing bit and* **below** *a horse accustoms itself to the feel of the bit in its mouth. The animal is wearing a cavesson in addition to its bridle. Fitting a bit correctly is extremely important; care and patience are both required, so as not to startle or hurt the horse. If the bit is positioned too high, it will damage the bars of the mouth, but, if the position is too low, the horse may well start putting its tongue over the bit. This is a serious vice and one which is very difficult to cure. Once bridle and bit are fitted, leave them in place for a time, but keep the horse secured. Otherwise it may rub its head, catch the bit in its mouth and so frighten itself and destroy its confidence.*

Left *A horse in a breaking roller and* **right** *a bit and bridle under a cavesson. After initial lungeing off the cavesson's rings, the lunge rein is attached to the bit's rings as well. The horse comes to associate pressure on the corners of the mouth with the signals from the cavesson. The breaking roller gets the horse used to something being tightened over its back and under its belly before the final stage of backing. It is kept in place with a breastplate at first; used on its own, the roller will either be too tight or loose enough to slip. In both cases, the horse will buck. Once fitted, it should be kept in position for a couple of days. The breaking roller must be well padded and kept supple.*

is necessary for the fitting of side reins. A breast plate should be used to keep the roller in place at first as otherwise it will be much too tight. The plate can be dispensed with when the roller can be tightened without the horse bucking.

One of the ways of helping both trainer and horse is to place a stable rubber under the roller and to attach some pieces of cloth to the side-rings of the roller (two rubbers do the job well). These will help the horse to begin to understand the feeling of the saddle and the rider that will follow later. If the horse has been handled confidently and quietly, it will not object to this. If it does seem nervous, put the cavesson on, then the roller with the rubbers, and turn the horse loose in the school. The shrewd trainer who wants to produce really good horses will use every opportunity to let the horse learn for itself.

Mouthing

The secret of making a good mouth is to encourage the horse to accept the bit as a 'natural' part of its mouth. This takes time and patience. To accept the bit, the horse must learn to swallow and produce its normal saliva with it in his mouth. A wet mouth, within reason, is a sign of a sensitive mouth, and a dry mouth a sign of an insensitive one.

Mouthing is accomplished by leaving the mouthing bit in the youngster's mouth for short periods each day. The trainer should watch for any sign of objection; at the slightest sign of this, the bit should be removed, and the process repeated the following day. The same routine is followed until the horse accepts the bit completely. Take care, however, not to encourage the development of vices, such as putting the tongue over the bit.

During this process, the horse should be worked on the lunge with a bridle fitted under the lunge cavesson and the lunge rein still attached to the centre 'D' ring.

Introducing the saddle

The saddle can now be substituted for the roller. This should ideally be done in an

enclosed space. Having removed the stirrup leathers and irons, let the horse have a look at it first, say, after a lungeing session. A helper stands at the horse's head while the trainer lifts the saddle up and down just above the horse's back until the animal stands quite still and calm, showing no fear of the saddle at all. Then the trainer gently places the saddle over the back.

Once the saddle is in place, the horse should be thoroughly petted. The next day, the process is repeated and the girth secured. Once the horse has worked on the lunge quietly with the saddle, the leathers and irons can be put back on it. Work should now continue with these pulled down.

Long reins and side reins
Before backing, there is one final stage of training to accomplish – the introduction and use of the reins. There are two methods – long reining and side reining – but the former should be left to real experts.

The use of side reins should be combined with that of a dropped noseband. With the horse in a simple snaffle bridle and drop noseband, the lunge cavesson goes over the top again and the lunge rein is once more attached to the centre 'D' ring. The side reins are then hooked to the rings of the bridle and buckled by a loop through the girth straps.

Allow the horse to relax thoroughly and just saunter around on the lunge at a slow walk. Eventually, it will 'reach' to make contact with the bit itself, and the process can then be repeated at the trot. The trainer should be able to tell when the time is right to start shortening the side reins until they finally reach a length corresponding to that which a rider would use on the horse. The art here, as in the entire programme, is to get the horse to learn from experience.

Backing
There are many different schools of thought on backing, but the essential part is to remember that, as in the introduction of the saddle, the rider must be introduced in stages. For this, two competent helpers are required; the trainer's job is to hold the horse's head to keep the horse calm and for safety, while one helper actually mounts the horse.

First, the helper stands next to the youngster and reaches up and touches the saddle. Then he or she is given a leg-up so that their body is simply resting over the saddle, and, finally, completes the task by putting the leg across the horse and sitting down in the saddle. Once there, the helper should sit quite still, with the feet out of the irons, holding a neck strap or the saddle's pommel for security. All the time both trainer and helper should be talking to the horse, and

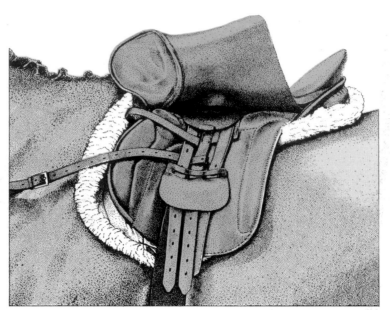

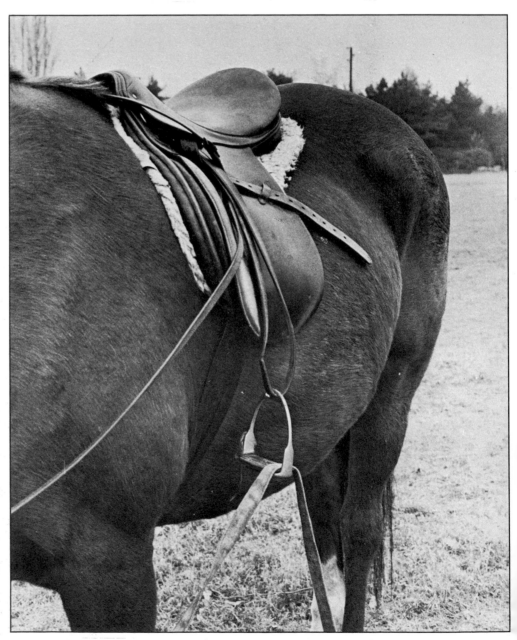

Left *How side reins are attached to the saddle for lungeing and* **below** *preparation of tack before long reining in a saddle and bridle. The best place to attach side reins is just above the girth buckles; they should never be tight enough to pull the horse's head down. Long reins run from cavesson and bit through the stirrups to the trainer, a cord under the belly stopping the irons from flapping about during a turn.*

Long reining is a useful exercise when preparing for backing. If done well, the horse will be going forward when backed, not moving about like an eel. The purpose of side reining is to get the horse to come on to the bit The engagement of the hind legs lightens the forehand and lengthens the line of back and neck.

petting it when backing has been successfully completed.

Schooling under saddle

The prime aims of the trainer should now be to produce (1) a horse that goes forward freely with a balanced rhythm; (2) a horse with a steady head carriage; (3) a horse that is balanced in all gaits; (4) a horse that moves 'straight'; (5) a horse that is supple and confident of its physical ability; and (6) a horse that willingly obeys the rider's aids. Once again, it must be remembered that these processes take time. Horses learn through routine, repetition and reward.

Moving forward freely

The first step in showing the horse that it must learn to await the rider's instructions is to teach it to stand still when being mounted. The trainer can achieve this by getting a helper to stand by the horse's head while he gets on and off several times. The horse will soon realize that it must stand still and await the command to move forward. It is worth doing this from both sides of the horse, as this will encourage the animal to remain calm and help it to keep its balance under the weight of the rider.

The horse is now ready to learn the first leg aid to walk on. The trainer asks the horse to

Above *Long reining off the bit, the horse being taught to turn left, right and to halt with the reins used as substitute leg aids. After this stage has been completed successfully, the horse can be worked steadily in the reins.*

Right *Lungeing with saddle, bridle and side reins. The correct pace for side reining is the trot, as it is the only pace at which the horse can be active while keeping its head still. At both the walk and canter, the horse's head moves slightly from side to side, so, to avoid pressure and the risk of damage to the mouth, side reins should not be used at these paces.*

As in normal lungeing, work with side reins is carried out in circles. If the circle is a large one, the reins should be almost equal in length; if, however, it is of small diameter, then the inside rein should be shortened slightly. However, care should be taken not to shorten this rein too much. If this happens, the horse will throw its weight on to its inside shoulder, the quarters will swing out and the animal will be on its forehand. This is a fault to be avoided at all costs.

walk forward with the leg aid, backing this up with a light touch of a dressage whip on the hindquarters, if necessary. As soon as the horse understands the signal, the whip can be dispensed with. The same process is repeated for the trot, but the canter should not be attempted until the horse is ready for training in balance and collection.

Changes of direction should be quite simple at this stage, with, again, no collection being asked of the horse but only free forward activity. The aim is to educate the animal to the squeeze of the rein and to get it to bend its body in the direction it is travelling. At first this can be done at the walk by simply raising and squeezing the 'asking' rein, closing the inside leg to the girth, and positioning the outside leg slightly behind it, to get the horse to move out of one corner of the school and walk across to the one diagonally opposite for another change of direction.

Checking the pace
To teach the horse to check its pace, the animal should be walked in a straight line. About a third of the way along this, the trainer closes the hands to resist the forward movement, and, with the voice, encourages the animal to check its walk. Then, after a couple of yards, he or she opens the fingers, closes the legs to the girth, and encourages the horse to walk forward again in an active rhythm. At first, the horse may resist, but, if the trainer shows patience and understanding, it will soon realize what is wanted and begin to enjoy it.

Once the horse has understood the signals at the walk, the same exercise is repeated at the trot. It will not be long before the young- ster has an active, forward movement.

The head, balance and collection
The chief reason for teaching a horse to carry its head correctly is the additional weight and movement of the rider on its back. Running free, a horse will alter the position of its head and neck according to the pace or direction in which it is moving. With a rider, however, a new balance has to be learned.

There are two dangers which must be avoided during this stage of training. The first is that the horse's head must not be allowed to go up; a high head-carriage will force the horse to hollow its back, affecting balance and decreasing the activity and length of stride of the hindlegs. In addition, once the horse gets into this habit it will

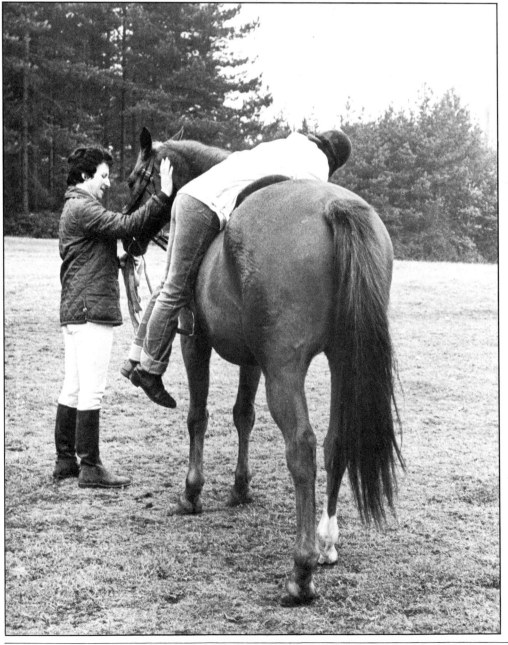

realize that control from the bit and the hands can be evaded.

Likewise, the horse's head must not get too low for exactly the same reasons. If this happens, the horse will round its back and be encouraged to stiffen the jaw and set the neck muscles against the pressure of the bit.

Another problem at this stage can involve what are termed the stiff side and the soft side of the horse. Just as people are left handed or right handed, so the vast majority of horses tend to favour one side of their body at the expense of the other. The side that the horse favours is known as the soft side; the hard side is the one on which the horse resists. The trainer must correct this to bring the body back into balance, and to 'straighten' the horse. At the same time, he or she should take advantage of the situation to get the

horse to 'give' its jaw.

To find out which side is which, walk the horse on a free rein. Quietly pick up the left rein only and ask the horse to move to the left. If there is immediate response – the horse turning its head, neck and body to the directing rein – the left is the soft side. Confirm this by following the same procedure to the right. The horse should resist, first with its mouth and then with its body.

Once this has been established, the processes of 'straightening' and bringing to full collection can begin. The trainer first puts his or her horse into a steady, even trot. Once the horse is relaxed, a firm, but light, contact is taken on the soft side rein. If the horse's soft side is its left, the animal is ridden clockwise around the school – vice versa if the right.

The trainer then closes the fingers of the right hand in a squeezing action and slightly raises the right rein hand, so bringing pressure to bear on the right side of the horse's mouth and the corner of the lips. This is a request for the horse to 'give' (relax) its jaw from the hard side, where it would normally resist. The horse's response should be to give its jaw and lower the head; the trainer will feel this through a lighter contact on the right rein hand. The signals are backed up with the leg aids to maintain activity and bring the horse down on to the bit.

This exercise should only be carried out for short periods, say, at the beginning of a training session, but repeated over the following days until the horse understands what is required of it. Throughout the process, the aim is to bring the horse into what is termed

Left to right *Three crucial stages in backing. The rider puts her full weight on the horse, patting it with her offside hand. From this position, the horse can be led forward until fully familiar with carrying a weight. As a consequence, the horse makes no objection when the rider mounts fully, patting the horse and talking to it quietly throughout the procedure. Finally, the horse is led forward with the rider in the saddle. It remains on the lead until it is fully confident.*

Backing requires two people – the trainer should stand at the horse's head while the assistant mounts. After being given a leg-up to lie across the saddle, the rider lies quietly for a few moments to let the horse get used to the weight. Then the horse is led forwards slowly, turned and led back again. This stage should take about a minute and is repeated over several days until the horse is fully relaxed. Next, the rider quietly sits astride – without putting the feet in the stirrups – and again walks around on the lead. If all the preliminary work has been done satisfactorily, the horse will be confident and know what is required of it.

full collection, with the head carried 'natur-ally' just behind the perpendicular. Once success has been achieved, the horse can go on to more advanced work, such as circles and transitions.

Work at the canter

Work at the canter is one of the last stages in schooling the horse on the flat. The impor-tant thing here is to get the horse to follow the correct sequence of leg movements, so that it remains balanced.

If the horse is cantering to the left, the leading front leg must be the near-fore; to the right, the off-fore. This must be achieved without any loss of impulsion or change in the head carriage. The body must be 'bent', too; if the animal is on the left rein, then the body must curve to the left so that the horse will naturally go into a left-lead canter bal-ance and with what trainers term cadence. The horse must not be allowed to lead from the shoulder; it should bend into its turn all the way from nose to tail.

To establish this, trot down the long side of the school, keeping the horse trotting evenly and relaxed at the jaw. On approach-ing the corner, ask for the bend to the left, with the left hand closed and left leg close to the girth. Simultaneously, sit down in the saddle, close both legs to the horse's flanks, with the right leg slightly behind the girth, and, with the seat aid, ask the horse to canter. If the horse does not strike-off with the correct leg, come back to the trot and start again. The process should be repeated until the horse changes its pace correctly.

Once this has been achieved consistently, the horse can start working in circles. Finally, comes the advanced stage of changing from one leading leg to the other. The first step in this is to ride in two circles, the first on the left lead. Then slow down to a trot for a few paces, and then ride into the canter again on a right-hand circle, this time with the right lead. The trotting period can be shortened with each session, until, eventually, the horse will change its leg while still in the collected canter.

Further exercises

At this stage, the trainer can start such exer-cises as the turn on the fore-hand, the shoulder-in and the haunches-in. The first gives the horse practice in obeying the trainer's aids; the other two help to supple its body.

The best method of training the horse to lengthen and shorten its stride, while pre-serving its balance and energy, involves the use of cavalletti. These are to the horse trainer what wall bars are to the gymnastics coach. Their use also helps to build up body

Below *Schooling over poles on the ground and* **inset** *riding on the lunge and walking independently. It takes about six weeks to reach this final stage from backing. The first step is to repeat the lungeing process,* *the horse still being controlled by the trainer and not by the rider. The reins should only be actively used if the horse lowers its head to buck. After this, the rider can start working on his or her own, developing the use* *of the aids and progressing through exercises like the one shown here. These should be as varied as possible, with plenty of changes of directions and transitions of pace, which will keep the horse interested.*

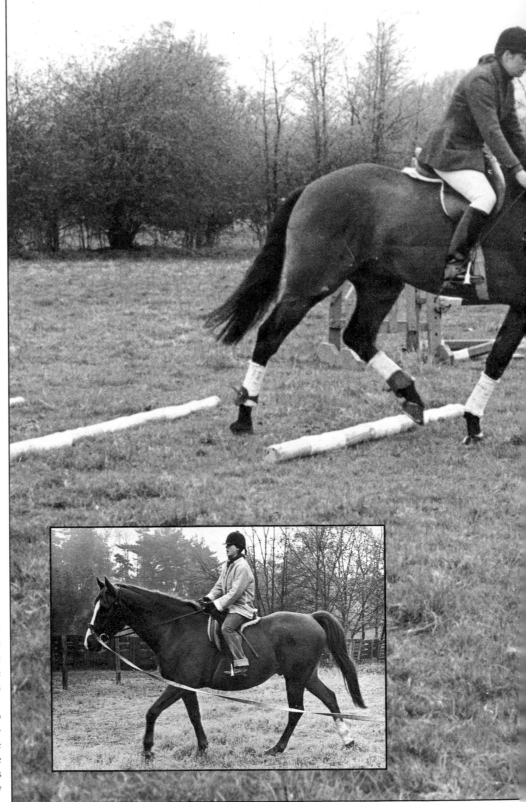

muscle, as well as extending the horse's mental powers and making it calmer under the concentrated control of the rider, preparing it for the stress of jumping.

Two sets of cavalletti should be laid out in the school – one set to short strides (about 1m apart), and the other to long strides (about 2m apart). Start off with the poles in their lowest position and simply walk the horse over them to gain confidence. Then, work at the trot, allowing the horse to teach itself how to shorten and lengthen its stride, but making sure that it maintains energy and collection. Gradually, the cavalletti can be raised; this enables the horse to exercise its muscles and brings its joints to maximum flexion.

Learning to jump

When schooling a horse to jump, the same principles apply as those involved in schooling on the flat – that is, to encourage the horse to perform as naturally as possible while coping with the weight and signals of a rider.

During basic training, the young horse has learned to trot over poles in cavalletti work, so these can now be brought into use in elementary jumping training. Again, two sets are used; this time, however, the last cavalletti are raised to represent a jump – a vertical jump on one side of the school, and a spread jump on the other. The young horse is started off on the lunge and trotted down the two grids and over the jumps. If possible, this should be done on both reins to give the horse confidence.

The technique is exactly the same with a rider; the trainer rides the horse on a free rein and virtually allows it to teach itself. The more the trainer can encourage this, the better competition jumper the horse is likely to become.

Following this, schooling can take place in the jumping lane and, finally, over practice fences.

The secret of success

Work, perseverance and patience are the secret of successful horse-training. The schooling figures – circles, figures of eight, and so on – are the tools of the trade and not an end in themselves. The aim is to control the horse as sensitively as possible, so that it seems as if it is performing entirely on its own – gracefully and independently, with the minimum of interference from its rider.

Anticipation is the hallmark of the artist in the saddle. In addition, the discipline that a good system of training demands to produce successful results brings a understanding between rider and horse – the partnership which forms the basis of the sport of equitation at all levels.

Chapter Eight

Basic riding

The key to learning to ride is basically one of confidence. The rider must have faith in his or her ability to communicate with, control and work with the horse; equally, the horse must have confidence in its rider. The only way to achieve this is to find a good instructor, who has the knack of encouraging his or her pupils to approach their lessons in a calm and relaxed manner. Riding is supposed to be a pleasure, so do not go to a hectoring instructor or trainer, who may turn this wonderful sport into a weekly nightmare.

The search can be a bewildering one, as level, competence and type of instruction often varies. Approval by a recognized riding association is always a sign of quality. In the UK, the British Horse Society (BHS) and the Association of British Riding Schools both publish lists of stables that have been inspected and approved; in the USA, the American Horse Shows Association does the same. In Australia, though there is no national system of assessment as such, the magazine *Australian Horse and Rider* publishes similar surveys.

The clothes to wear

At first there is no need to spend money on a full riding kit, but certain items are essential for both safety and comfort. A hard riding hat, or, better still, a racing-style crash hel-

met, is one of them, but make sure that the brand you buy meets national safety requirements. Jodhpur boots, western riding boots, or rubber riding boots (these are far cheaper than leather ones) are also vital. Plimsolls can slip through the stirrup irons and rubber wellingtons are not really the right shape.

Otherwise clothes can be adapted to purse and needs. A thick, close-fitting pair of jeans (not the 'flared' variety), or a pair of 'chaps', worn cowboy-style over a pair of trousers, can take the place of breeches or jodhpurs at first. These should be worn with a thick sweater or windcheater in winter, or, in hot weather, a tee-shirt or sports shirt. A riding mackintosh is a good investment, as is a pair of string gloves. Wet reins, especially if also slippery with sweat, can be almost impossible to grip.

Handling, mounting and dismounting

At first, the horse should be 'made ready' for you, but it is a good idea to ask if you can bring your mount out of its box and into the yard to get used to being around such a big animal. Greet the horse calmly and move to its shoulder, talking to it as you do so. Then, run your hand down the shoulder and give it a pat. Move to its head, undo the head-collar and lead the horse out of the box.

The next stage is to mount the horse — either unaided, or assisted by a leg-up. Begin-

The principles of classical riding were laid down by a sixteenth century Neapolitan riding master Federico Grisone in 1550. In them, the horseman used a straight leg and fixed-hand reins controlling the horse with a powerful curb bit and spurs. The rider dominated the horse completely, forcing it into intricate dressage movements. Grisone's influence was widespread and long-lasting, particularly in the various high schools of the royal courts of Europe. A present day survival is the Spanish School in Vienna and its famous Lipizzaner horses (left).

With the dawn of the twentieth century came a revolution in riding which transformed the art of equitation. This was the creation of the Forward Seat by an Italian cavalry officer, Federico Caprilli (1867–1907). His system was based on a partnership between horse and rider, the aim being to interfere with the horse as little as possible and so allow it to move freely and with natural balance.

Riding hat

Shirt and tie

Show jacket

String and leather gloves

Breeches

Leather boots

At shows, it is important to be smart with dark jacket, collar and tie, breeches, hat and boots.

Well-fitting riding hat

Weatherproof jacket

String or leather gloves

Well-fitting jeans

Rubber riding boots

Riding clothes must be practical, like this warm jacket, close-fitting trousers, boots and hat.

No hat

Scarf

Woollen gloves

Baggy trousers

Flapping coat

High-heeled shoes

Flapping clothing which can distract a horse and get tangled in trees and bushes is not suitable.

Holding the headpiece in the left hand, put the reins over the horse's head and neck first. The horse will then be under control while the headpiece is being fitted. Make sure that no part of the bridle trails on the ground.

Hold the headpiece up in the right hand and cradle the bit on the thumb and forefinger of the left. Then slip the left hand under the horse's muzzle and insert a finger between its front and back teeth on the offside to open the mouth.

Having slipped the bit into the mouth, use both hands to bring the headpiece over its ears, one at a time. Smooth the forelock down over the browband and check that this is clear of the ears. See that no part of the headpiece is twisted.

Then fasten the throatlash and nose band. There should be a hand's width between throatlash and jaw and noseband. See that the bit is not low enough to rest on the teeth, or high enough to wrinkle the horse's lips.

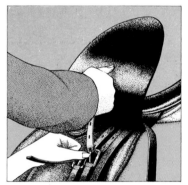

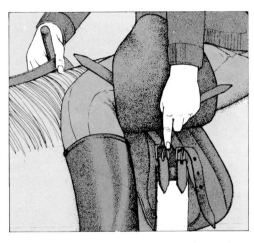

With the horse tied up, smooth the saddle area of the coat before picking up the saddle by its front arch and cantle, and placing it lightly but firmly on the horse's withers. Then slide it back enough to let the horse's shoulders move freely.

Check that all is smooth under saddle flap, then move to the offside and let down girth, which has been lying over saddle. Return to nearside and buckle the girth firmly, so that a hand can just be slipped beneath it. Saddling can be done in one operation.

Right *After riding for a few minutes, the girth will usually need a further tightening. There is no need to dismount as this can be done in the saddle. Take the foot from the nearside stirrup iron and move the leg forward, so that the saddle flap can be lifted and tucked under the thigh, out of the way. Adjust the girth strap in the same way as a stirrup leather, tightening it by a hole or two while keeping a finger on the buckle prong. Then release the flap and replace the foot in the stirrup iron.*

ners should always have a groom standing at the horse's head to ensure that the animal stands still while being mounted.

Always mount a horse from the near (left) side. Before doing so, check the girth for tightness; if it is too loose, the saddle may slip as the rider's weight comes on to the stirrup. Gather the reins in the left hand, maintaining a light contact with the horse's mouth. Take care not to keep the left rein too short, or the horse may start to circle as you mount.

Place the left hand on the pommel of the saddle and then turn the body so that your back is to the horse's head with the left shoulder parallel with the horse's left shoulder. Take the left stirrup iron with the right hand, turn it clockwise towards you and place the ball of the left foot in the iron, keeping the toe as low as possible. If it digs into the horse's flank, it will act as a signal to the horse to move forward.

Place the right hand over the waist of the saddle, and, with the weight of the body on the left foot, spring upwards from the right foot, using the right hand as a lever. Bring the right leg over the saddle and then gently lower yourself into it. Place the right foot in the offside iron and take up the reins with both hands.

To dismount, take both feet out of the irons and collect the reins in one hand.

Then, swinging the right leg well over the cantle of the saddle, gently, but briskly, vault off, landing on both feet.

Adjusting the stirrups
Once in the saddle, the next thing to do is tighten the girth again and then adjust the stirrup leathers to the correct length. The initial temptation at the start of a ride is to have the leathers too short. As the ride progresses, and the seat comes properly down into the saddle, it will be necessary to lengthen them.

To establish the correct length, take the feet out of the irons and let them hang down naturally. The iron should just touch the inside point of the ankle bone. Adjust the leathers accordingly, making sure that they are both the same length.

The seat
The seat is the rock on which all good riding is founded; without a correct position in the saddle, no pupil can hope to go on to advanced equitation successfully. A correct seat means that the rider is in balance — secure, light, and responsive to the horse's every movement. It is used in rhythm with the animal's action; the pushing down of the seat bones on the horse's back encourages it to lengthen its stride.

The rider sits into the middle and lowest part of the saddle, the body position being upright and free from stiffness, especially round the waist. The rider is in fact sitting on a triangle, two points being the seat bones and the third the crotch of the body.

The back should be straight, but relaxed and supple, with the shoulders held square. The head should always be held up and looking to the front. Never look down, or the back will become rounded and the chest hollowed. As a guide, place a hand behind you flat on the saddle. There should be room for the flat hand between you and the cantle.

The temptation to grip with knees and calves must be avoided. Otherwise the body will be stiffened, the seat raised out of the saddle and the position made rigid. The thighs and legs should wrap around the horse and mould themselves to the correct position. A simple routine to help achieve this is to open the legs away from the horse's flanks and then draw the thighs into position from behind. This will bring the large inside-thigh muscle under and to the back of the thigh, flattening the area and allowing it to rest close to the saddle and the horse. Then, by pushing the weight down on the ankles, the rider will feel the seat lower into the saddle.

The lower leg should hang down to rest lightly against the horse's sides, just behind

When mounting place left hand on the saddle pommel and put ball of left foot into iron with right hand, keeping toe low.

Next place right hand over waist of saddle and, keeping the toe under the horse against the girth, spring smoothly and lightly up.

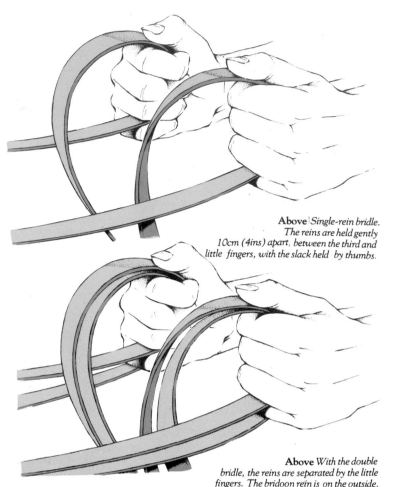

Above Single-rein bridle. The reins are held gently 10cm (4ins) apart, between the third and little fingers, with the slack held by thumbs.

Bring the right leg over, keeping it well clear of the saddle and the back of the horse. This should be done in one smooth movement.

Dismounting. First take both feet from the stirrup irons, transfer the reins to the left hand and grip pommel with the right hand.

Above With the double bridle, the reins are separated by the little fingers. The bridoon rein is on the outside.

Next, leaning forward lightly swing both legs clear of the horse, keeping weight on right hand and holding reins with the left.

Land lightly on both feet, facing the saddle and still keeping control with the reins in gentle contact with the horse's mouth.

Left When mounted adjust stirrups by pulling the top leather up against the buckle under the saddle skirt. Keep a finger on the buckle spike – the leather can then be easily adjusted up or down. **Below left** The iron should hang level with the point of the ankle bone. **Below right** Secure top leather through keeper on saddle.

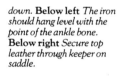

the girth with the heel pressed down. This is where the rider's weight is balanced. Holding the lower leg too far forward or too far back must be avoided, because it affects the position in the saddle and makes it difficult to apply the leg aids correctly. Only the ball of the foot should rest in the stirrup iron, and both feet should be held parallel with the horse's sides.

If the position is correct, the rider's ears, shoulders, hips and heels should be in line with each other. The stirrup leather should be at right angles to the ground when the rider is mounted.

The arms should hang down naturally to the elbow. The hands, with thumbs uppermost, are held as if carrying two glasses of water. The rider should not get into the habit of bending the wrists inwards or of flattening the hand. A straight line should run from the elbow through the hand to the bit in the horse's mouth.

The best place to work on the correct saddle position is on the lunge rein, where most of the student's early work is usually done in any case. When working on the lunge, the rider should be holding a neckstrap, and not the reins. The horse is being controlled from the lunge; two people trying to direct it, one with the lunge and the other

from the bridle, will only confuse the animal.

A strong independent seat can only be achieved by regular active riding, assisted by suppling exercises and riding without stirrups. These are essential for developing balance and confidence.

The aids
The aids are the system of signals used to control the horse. They fall into two categories; first come the natural aids of hands, legs, seat and voice, and second are the artificial aids of whip, spurs, draw reins, drop nosebands, martingales and so on. The only one a beginner should use is a whip.

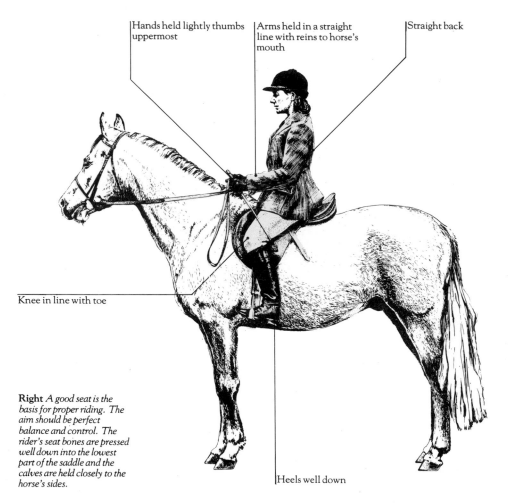

Hands held lightly thumbs uppermost

Arms held in a straight line with reins to horse's mouth

Straight back

Knee in line with toe

Heels well down

Right *A good seat is the basis for proper riding. The aim should be perfect balance and control. The rider's seat bones are pressed well down into the lowest part of the saddle and the calves are held closely to the horse's sides.*

All riding is based on controlling the natural impulsion of the horse. This is achieved by combined use of the rider's legs and seat. The aim is to get the horse moving freely and actively forward in the desired direction, and not evading the aids when they are applied. The rider can usually tell this through the hands; if the horse is resisting, there will be little 'feel' on the reins when activity is being asked for, and 'pull' if the horse is being checked.

The legs are used in a squeezing action just behind the girth. A quick, light squeeze, repeated if necessary, is more effective than prolonged pressure. Use of the heels should be avoided.

If the horse does not respond to the legs, the whip can be used to reinforce the aid. A tap on the horse's ribs, just behind the rider's leg, is usually adequate. Note that the whip is only an extension of the aid. It should not be used as a punishment except in extreme cases of disobedience.

Use of the hands

The hands control, never create, pace and direction through the use of the reins. Contact with the mouth should therefore be light and steady; pulling on the reins will only hurt and upset the horse. The wrists should be supple and flexible enough to follow the horse's natural rhythm; the aim is to achieve a passive hand, not a rigid one with the wrists set in a fixed position.

It is essential therefore to hold the reins correctly. With a single-rein bridle, the reins should pass between the little finger and the third finger of each hand. The remainder of the reins pass through the finger and thumb, with the thumb on top of the rein to aid the grip. Double bridles, however, can be held in several different ways. One of them is to divide the reins with the little finger of each hand, with the curb (lower) rein crossing inside to pass between the third finger and little finger. Again, the reins pass out through the index finger and thumb, with the remainder crossing over to the left.

The walk

All early work should be done at the walk until the pupil has established the basic confidence required to move on to the other paces. Take up contact with the mouth and apply the aids to make the horse walk on. Keep the hands relaxed when the walk has been established, however, or the horse may be tempted to go into a trot.

Any unwanted increase in pace should be checked by closing the hands to resist the forward movement, closing the legs to the sides and pushing down in the saddle with the seat bones. In response, the horse checks its pace. After a few strides, the rider should give with the hands, increase the pressure of the leg and seat aids and ask the horse to walk on again.

To ask for the halt, the rider applies both leg and seat pressure at the same time as lightly resisting the forward movement with the hands. The horse should stand still on all fours when it comes to the halt.

Changes of direction should also be learned and practised at the walk. The inside leg and hand ask for these, while the outside hand and leg control the pace. To go to the right, ask with the right hand, keeping the left one passive. Both legs should be closed to the horse to maintain the walk, but apply the left leg more strongly to prevent the swing of the quarters. To turn to the left, reverse the procedure.

The rider should make a conscious effort to think right or left. This concentration can act as a reinforcement to the physical aids being applied.

The trot

This is a two-time gait, in which the horse moves its legs in a diagonal sequence of near-fore, off-hind, off-fore and near-hind. Near-fore and off-hind make up what is known as the left diagonal; off-fore and near-hind the right. The rider can either sit in the saddle and follow the natural rhythm of the trot, or rise (post) slightly out of the saddle for one beat of the gait.

To achieve the transition from walk to trot, sit down in the saddle, close the legs and feel the inside rein. As the horse gets into its trot, sit into it for a few strides, using the legs to maintain the activity.

In the rising trot, the rider rises out of the saddle on one beat of one diagonal and descends on the other, with the weight of the body supported by the ankles, heels and stirrup irons, but not by the knees. These must act purely as a hinge. Rise from the hip, keeping the lower leg still. The thigh and body should remain at the same angle. Keep the horse moving forward and a light and even contact with the animal's mouth.

The seat should never be allowed to come completely out of the saddle and the reins should never be used as a lever when rising. In addition, always regularly change from one diagonal to the other. Like human beings, horses tend to favour one side of their body to the other, and this means that it is very easy to always remain on, say, the left diagonal during a prolonged period at the trot. This is bad for the horse as well as for the rider.

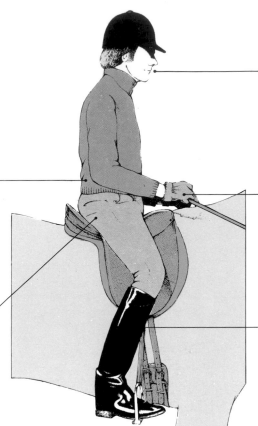

Right *The natural aids are the movements which communicate the rider's intentions to the horse. The body, legs and hands work together in complete harmony. If the horse is positioned and prepared correctly it can obey the rider's instructions more easily.*

The back muscles affect the seat. They make it more secure and enable the rider to maintain balance. Straightening the spine, combined with corresponding leg and hand actions conveys the rider's intentions to the horse.

Pressure from the seat encourages the horse to move forward from the hindquarters. A firm, deep seat enables the rider to use the legs correctly.

The voice can be used to soothe or check the horse.

The hands should be light and responsive, being used in a give-and-take action. They regulate the energy created by the calves, and control the forehand.

The calves control impulsion and energy in the hindquarters and guide their direction.

lead the horse to increase the speed of its trot.

The horse should always lead off into the canter with the correct leg. The sequence always begins with a hind – off-hind if going to the left and near-hind to the right. The near-fore and off-fore are the two leading front legs respectively. A horse that starts to canter with the wrong lead is said to be cantering 'false'.

It is easier to establish the correct lead if the aids for the canter are applied on a bend, when the horse's body should be bent in the direction it is going. Thus, it usually balances itself naturally to take up the canter on the desired leg. The best way to establish a good canter, therefore, is to work in a large circle. The horse should maintain an active, rhyth-

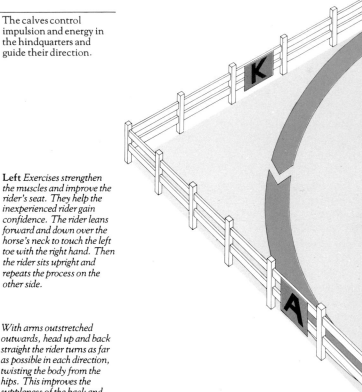

To change diagonals, simply sit down in the saddle for two beats, and then start rising again on the other diagonal, using the leg to give added impulsion if there is resistance. Diagonals should always be changed with each change of direction. For example, if trotting to the right on the left diagonal and then changing the rein to the left, the rider should shift his or her weight to the right diagonal. This keeps the horse level, balanced and gives it a 'breather'. In long distance riding, or hacking, the diagonal at the trot should be changed regularly.

To return to the walk, sit well down in the saddle, close the hands firmly and apply the leg aids until the horse walks forward freely. Give with the hands but keep applying the leg aids until the momentum of the walk is firmly established.

The canter

The canter is a three-time gait, with one beat coming from each of the forelegs and the third from the hindlegs. The rider relaxes with this rhythm, keeping a steady, even contact with the mouth. Sit deeply into the saddle, allowing the back to follow the movement from the hips, and avoid the temptation to be tipped forward. Over excitement – and kicking hard with the heels – will only

Left *Exercises strengthen the muscles and improve the rider's seat. They help the inexperienced rider gain confidence. The rider leans forward and down over the horse's neck to touch the left toe with the right hand. Then the rider sits upright and repeats the process on the other side.*

With arms outstretched outwards, head up and back straight the rider turns as far as possible in each direction, twisting the body from the hips. This improves the suppleness of the back and waist. This exercise can be practised at the halt or when the horse is moving at a walk.

With arms folded, the rider leans back to rest on the horse's quarters, then sits upright again. The legs should remain in the correct riding position during the exercise. Do not attempt this, or any other, exercise on an inexperienced horse which may be frightened by the movements involved.

Right *Riding schools often use an enclosed arena. The area is divided up by letter markers to help the rider learn to judge distance accurately. This is particularly important in dressage training. In a lesson, the instructor usually stands in the centre of the arena and directs the riders individually or as a group. The rider can work in circles or straight lines, or use a combination of both. The arena is suitable for most types of schooling on the flat, and for jumping.*

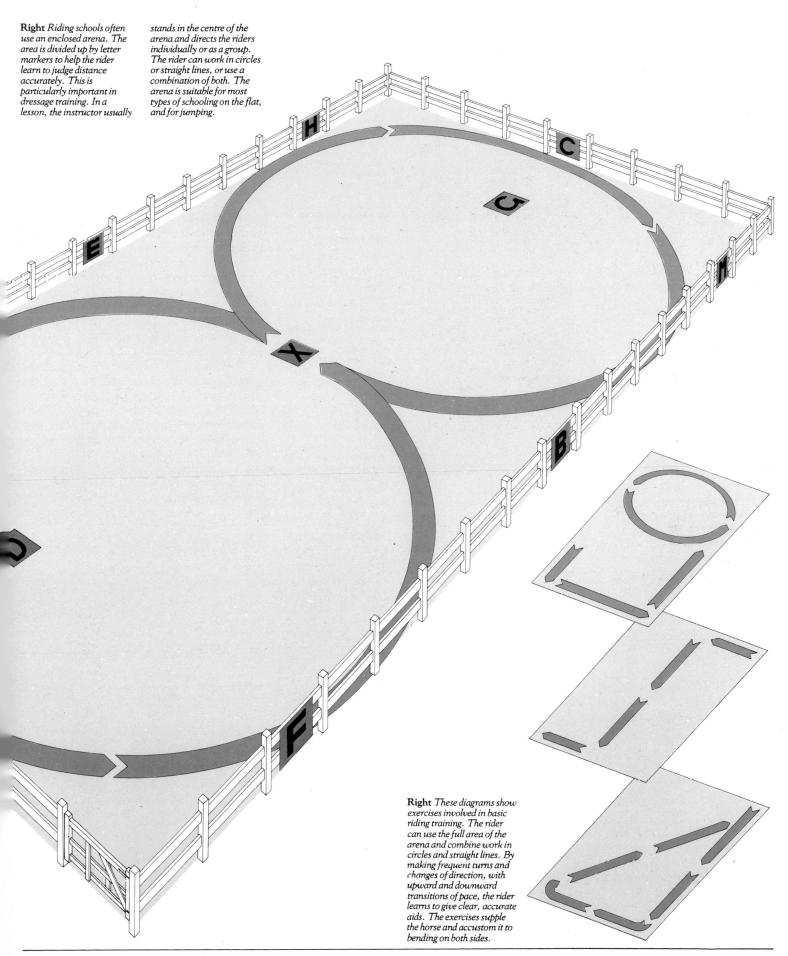

Right *These diagrams show exercises involved in basic riding training. The rider can use the full area of the arena and combine work in circles and straight lines. By making frequent turns and changes of direction, with upward and downward transitions of pace, the rider learns to give clear, accurate aids. The exercises supple the horse and accustom it to bending on both sides.*

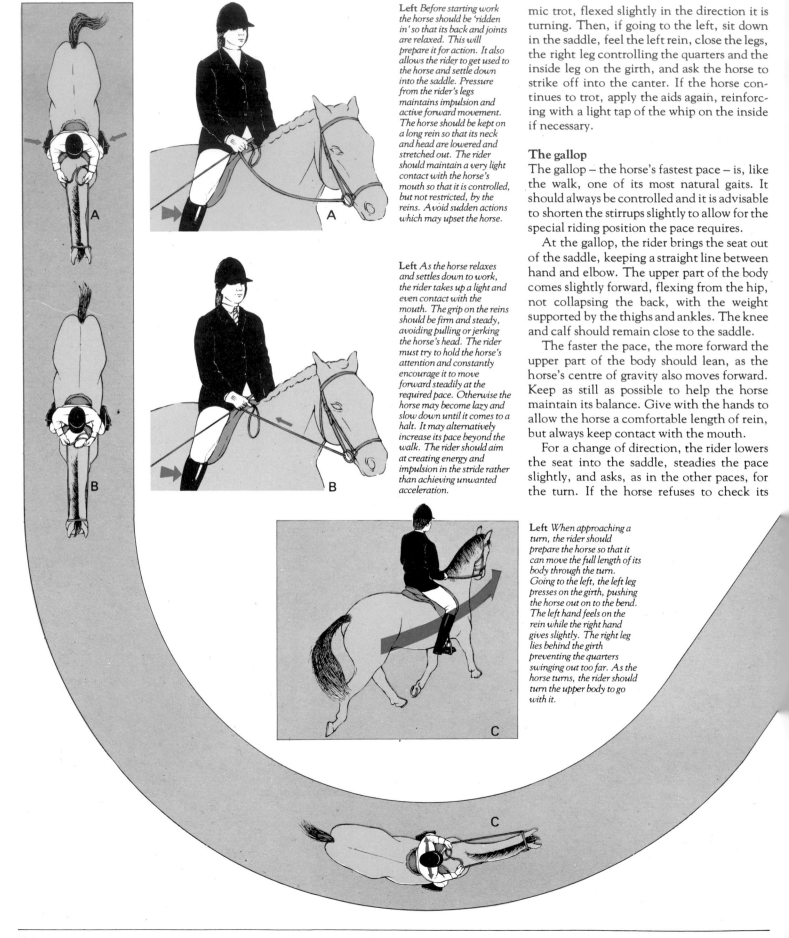

Left *Before starting work the horse should be 'ridden in' so that its back and joints are relaxed. This will prepare it for action. It also allows the rider to get used to the horse and settle down into the saddle. Pressure from the rider's legs maintains impulsion and active forward movement. The horse should be kept on a long rein so that its neck and head are lowered and stretched out. The rider should maintain a very light contact with the horse's mouth so that it is controlled, but not restricted, by the reins. Avoid sudden actions which may upset the horse.*

Left *As the horse relaxes and settles down to work, the rider takes up a light and even contact with the mouth. The grip on the reins should be firm and steady, avoiding pulling or jerking the horse's head. The rider must try to hold the horse's attention and constantly encourage it to move forward steadily at the required pace. Otherwise the horse may become lazy and slow down until it comes to a halt. It may alternatively increase its pace beyond the walk. The rider should aim at creating energy and impulsion in the stride rather than achieving unwanted acceleration.*

Left *When approaching a turn, the rider should prepare the horse so that it can move the full length of its body through the turn. Going to the left, the left leg presses on the girth, pushing the horse out on to the bend. The left hand feels on the rein while the right hand gives slightly. The right leg lies behind the girth preventing the quarters swinging out too far. As the horse turns, the rider should turn the upper body to go with it.*

mic trot, flexed slightly in the direction it is turning. Then, if going to the left, sit down in the saddle, feel the left rein, close the legs, the right leg controlling the quarters and the inside leg on the girth, and ask the horse to strike off into the canter. If the horse continues to trot, apply the aids again, reinforcing with a light tap of the whip on the inside if necessary.

The gallop

The gallop – the horse's fastest pace – is, like the walk, one of its most natural gaits. It should always be controlled and it is advisable to shorten the stirrups slightly to allow for the special riding position the pace requires.

At the gallop, the rider brings the seat out of the saddle, keeping a straight line between hand and elbow. The upper part of the body comes slightly forward, flexing from the hip, not collapsing the back, with the weight supported by the thighs and ankles. The knee and calf should remain close to the saddle.

The faster the pace, the more forward the upper part of the body should lean, as the horse's centre of gravity also moves forward. Keep as still as possible to help the horse maintain its balance. Give with the hands to allow the horse a comfortable length of rein, but always keep contact with the mouth.

For a change of direction, the rider lowers the seat into the saddle, steadies the pace slightly, and asks, as in the other paces, for the turn. If the horse refuses to check its

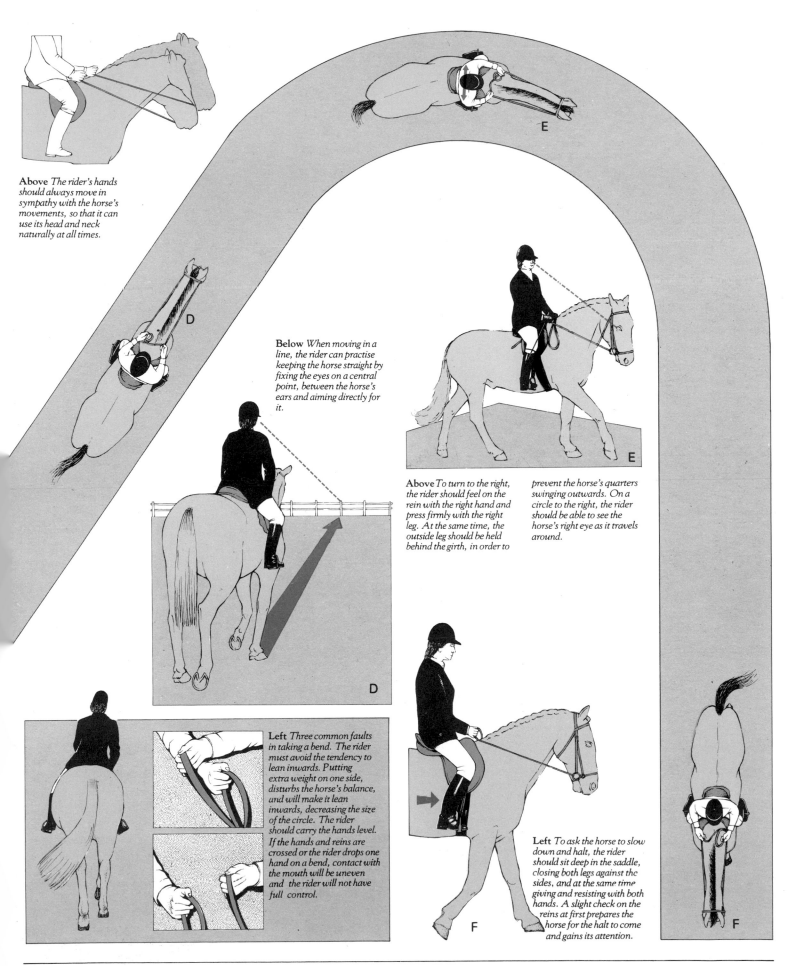

Above *The rider's hands should always move in sympathy with the horse's movements, so that it can use its head and neck naturally at all times.*

Below *When moving in a line, the rider can practise keeping the horse straight by fixing the eyes on a central point, between the horse's ears and aiming directly for it.*

Above *To turn to the right, the rider should feel on the rein with the right hand and press firmly with the right leg. At the same time, the outside leg should be held behind the girth, in order to* *prevent the horse's quarters swinging outwards. On a circle to the right, the rider should be able to see the horse's right eye as it travels around.*

Left *Three common faults in taking a bend. The rider must avoid the tendency to lean inwards. Putting extra weight on one side, disturbs the horse's balance, and will make it lean inwards, decreasing the size of the circle. The rider should carry the hands level. If the hands and reins are crossed or the rider drops one hand on a bend, contact with the mouth will be uneven and the rider will not have full control.*

Left *To ask the horse to slow down and halt, the rider should sit deep in the saddle, closing both legs against the sides, and at the same time giving and resisting with both hands. A slight check on the reins at first prepares the horse for the halt to come and gains its attention.*

pace, the best course of action is to sit upright and turn the horse in a circle. Above all, never pull – the horse will only pull back.

Jumping

Riding over jumps is just as much a matter of confidence as the basic process of learning to ride. All elementary jumping techniques should therefore be learned and practised at the trot, before increasing the pace to a controlled canter. With full confidence and control, jumping comes easily; the basic rule is to aid the horse as much as possible and not to hinder it. When jumping, the stirrups should be slightly shortened.

There are many exercises which can be practised by novice jumpers to help them to learn to jump correctly. For the first lessons, the rider should use a neck strap; this lessens the risk of a nervous pupil pulling on the reins and so jabbing the horse in the mouth with the bit. Jumping without stirrups is also an excellent way of improving balance and developing muscles.

The first step to practise is the approach. Sit well down in the saddle, keeping a very close contact with the horse with thighs, knees and calves, and use the seat and legs to build up impulsion. Support the weight of the body by thighs and ankles - not by the hands - and bring the upper part of the body forward so that it is just off the perpendicular. Never look down, always ahead, and ride for the middle of the obstacle, keeping a light even contact on the reins. The rider must allow the horse freedom of the head and neck.

As the horse starts to leave the ground, bring the hands well down on either side of the neck to allow it to lower and stretch, while bending the body forward from the hip upwards over the centre of gravity. The weight of the body comes slightly out of the saddle. Keep the thighs as close to the horse as possible and the lower leg and feet in the same position as for riding on the flat, making sure that they do not go back in the air.

Once in the air, the rider should give the horse the maximum freedom to complete its jump. Follow the horse's mouth with the hands, but maintain contact. Bring the body well forward from the hip and down close to the horse. As the horse starts to come down to land, begin the return to the normal riding position to balance the animal.

One useful exercise to help achieve a good position is to work with cavalletti in the school. The idea is not to present the rider with real fences, but to simulate them, so that he or she can concentrate on position in the saddle and learn to regulate the horse's stride and direction. The cavalletti can be arranged as a box in the centre of the school, or down one side of it.

Right To rise to the trot the rider leans slightly forward and eases the seat from the saddle to go with the movement of the horse.

Below Three common faults in the trot. In the first diagram, the rider is exaggerating the rise; this stiffens the position and leads to loss of balance. Rising with a hollowed back throws the shoulders forward and the seat back. A slouched back is equally bad, the spine should be straight.

Below The sitting trot is used particularly during schooling. The rider does not rise to the trot but sits deeply, absorbing the bumps with the small of the back.

Left When making the transition from the trot to a canter, the rider should ensure that the horse leads on the correct leg. This will give a balanced and flowing movement. The rider should sit deeply into the saddle and feel the rein in the direction the horse should lead. The rider squeezes with both legs. The outside leg presses behind the girth – this instructs the horse that its outside hind leg should be first to leave the ground as it changes to the canter. The inside leg is placed on the girth to maintain impulsion. The rider should sit still and follow the natural movement of the canter with the back and hips. The position should be relaxed, but not loose in the saddle. The pace of the canter should always be steady and controlled.

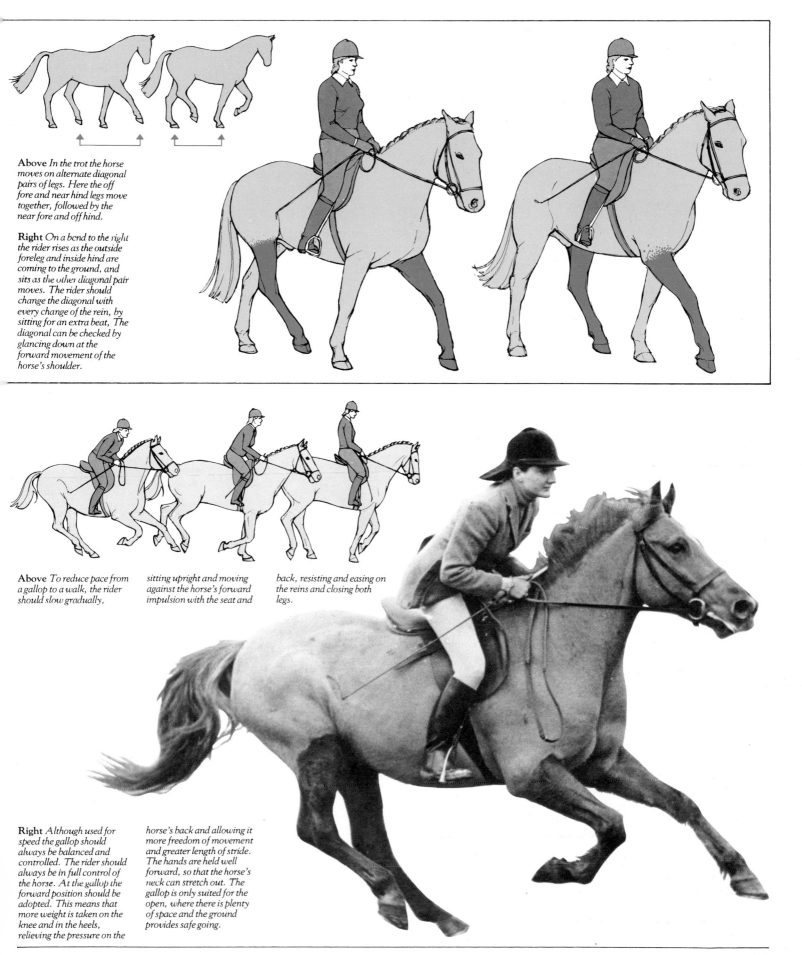

Above *In the trot the horse moves on alternate diagonal pairs of legs. Here the off fore and near hind legs move together, followed by the near fore and off hind.*

Right *On a bend to the right the rider rises as the outside foreleg and inside hind are coming to the ground, and sits as the other diagonal pair moves. The rider should change the diagonal with every change of the rein, by sitting for an extra beat. The diagonal can be checked by glancing down at the forward movement of the horse's shoulder.*

Above *To reduce pace from a gallop to a walk, the rider should slow gradually,* *sitting upright and moving against the horse's forward impulsion with the seat and* *back, resisting and easing on the reins and closing both legs.*

Right *Although used for speed the gallop should always be balanced and controlled. The rider should always be in full control of the horse. At the gallop the forward position should be adopted. This means that more weight is taken on the knee and in the heels, relieving the pressure on the* *horse's back and allowing it more freedom of movement and greater length of stride. The hands are held well forward, so that the horse's neck can stretch out. The gallop is only suited for the open, where there is plenty of space and the ground provides safe going.*

127

Trot around the school in the sitting-jumping position – this means sitting in the same way as for riding on the flat, but with the upper part of the body bent slightly forward. From any corner of the school, turn to approach the box, coming up into the poised jumping position as you do so. This means that the rider raises the seat out of the saddle, taking the weight on thighs, ankles and heels, without using the reins for support. Then, looking directly ahead, ask the horse to trot through the box. On reaching the other side, return to the original position and trot on around the school on the opposite rein to the one first used.

This exercise enables the rider to practice various angles of approach. It also enables the pupil to control the pace of his or her mount while concentrating on developing the right position in the saddle.

Another, more advanced, exercise with cavalletti helps improve rhythm and timing. Cavalletti are placed at various intervals down one side of the school, one set being combined to create a spread element. The rider soon learns to use the leg and seat aids to lengthen and shorten the horse's stride as necessary.

Through the use of such jumping exercises, a good basic technique can be developed. This is essential before going on to more advanced forms of jumping.

Below *The correct forward jumping position can be practised on a stationary or moving horse. The rider adopts a spring-like position to balance and move with the horse over the jump.*

Body bending forward from hips

Straight back

Head up looking in forward direction

Hands and arms forward and down side of neck

Knees resting on saddle

Shortened stirrups to allow ankles and knees to absorb movement

Weight in heels

Right *Trotting over cavalletti helps the rider develop the forward seat position. This is the correct seat for galloping and jumping.*

Cavalletti are useful for numerous schooling exercises for horse and rider. Schooling over cavalletti is good preparation both for jumping and riding on the flat.

Right *A more advanced exercise is to slightly extend the distance between poles, remove one, or add a small jump. This teaches horse and rider to judge distance and place their strides. The rider should trot over the first poles and then canter in the direction indicated.*

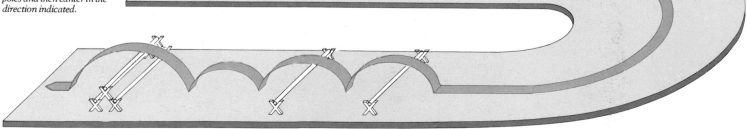

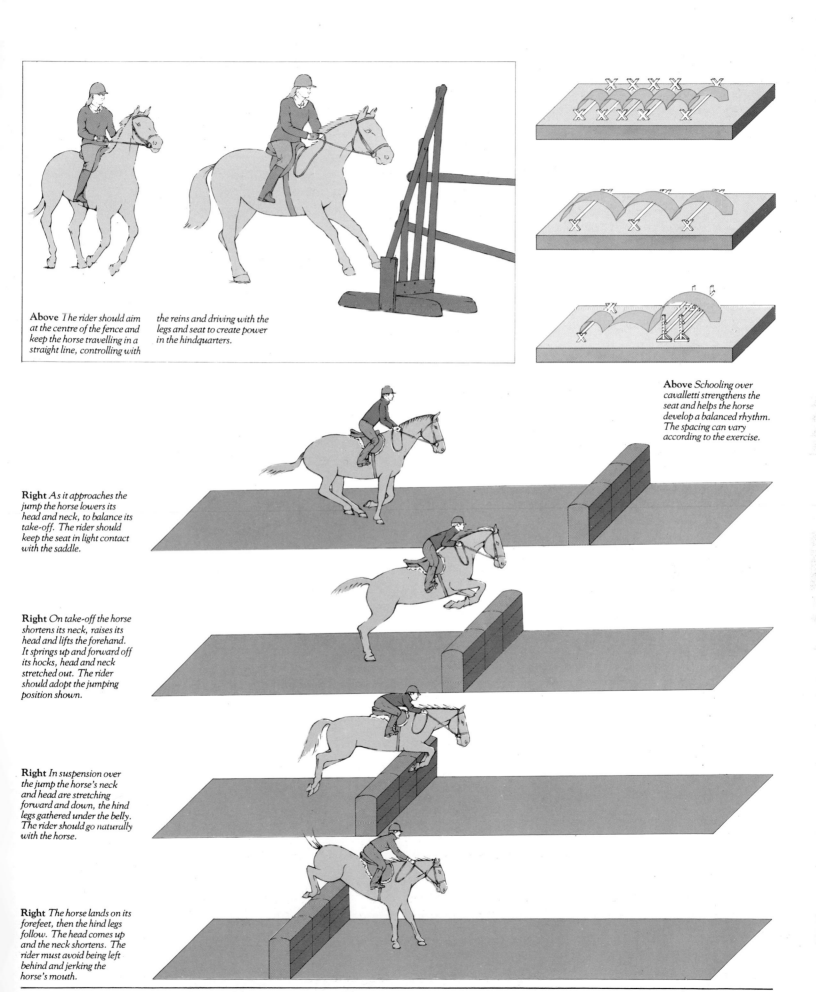

Above *The rider should aim at the centre of the fence and keep the horse travelling in a straight line, controlling with the reins and driving with the legs and seat to create power in the hindquarters.*

Above *Schooling over cavalletti strengthens the seat and helps the horse develop a balanced rhythm. The spacing can vary according to the exercise.*

Right *As it approaches the jump the horse lowers its head and neck, to balance its take-off. The rider should keep the seat in light contact with the saddle.*

Right *On take-off the horse shortens its neck, raises its head and lifts the forehand. It springs up and forward off its hocks, head and neck stretched out. The rider should adopt the jumping position shown.*

Right *In suspension over the jump the horse's neck and head are stretching forward and down, the hind legs gathered under the belly. The rider should go naturally with the horse.*

Right *The horse lands on its forefeet, then the hind legs follow. The head comes up and the neck shortens. The rider must avoid being left behind and jerking the horse's mouth.*

Chapter Nine

Looking after the horse

Looking after and caring for a horse or pony is perhaps the greatest responsibility any rider faces. Having learned to ride, many riders aim at eventually having a horse of their own. It is worth remembering, though, that looking after a horse unaided – especially if it is stabled – can be a full-time occupation. One answer is to board the horse out at livery, which can be very expensive. Another is to get someone to help out during the day. Most of the other factors involved, such as feeding, watering, exercising and grooming, are mainly matters of common sense, combined with willingness to ask for and take expert advice whenever necessary.

Horses can either be stabled, kept at grass or the two systems can be combined. This means that the horse can run free during the day and have the shelter of a stable by night – except in hot weather, when the procedure should be reversed. Which system is adopted is a matter of choice, practicality, and the type of horse concerned. Ponies, for example, are usually sturdier and more resilient to extremes of climate than horses, particularly thoroughbreds and part-breds. Some thoroughbreds, for instance, should not be left out over the winter. Nor can a horse being worked hard in, say, competitions be really kept fit enough except by being cared for in a stable. At the very least, it must be fed extra food in the field. The amount of extra feeding required should be worked out using the same guidelines as those for a stabled horse. In the case of a field-kept animal, however, the total amount involved should be divided into three, rather than into four.

The combined system can also be adapted to suit the needs of a rider who is using his or her horse frequently, but cannot spare the time to keep it fully stabled. If the horse is

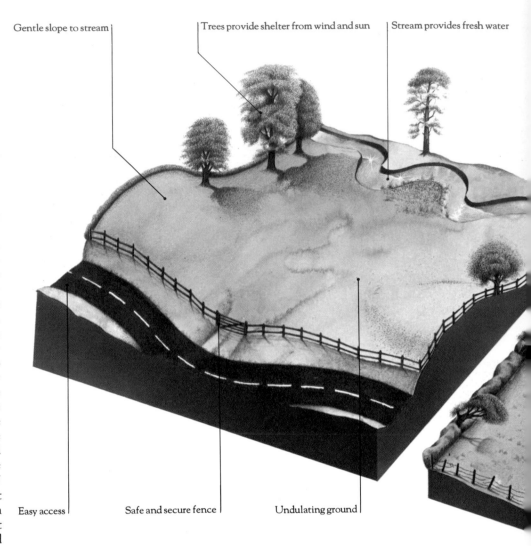

Gentle slope to stream

Trees provide shelter from wind and sun

Stream provides fresh water

Easy access

Safe and secure fence

Undulating ground

Below Horses may roll to relax after being ridden, or just to deal with an irritating itch. Rolling can also be a symptom of colic, but generally it is simply a sign of pure enjoyment.

Below The life cycle of the redworm, or large strongyle. The eggs are dropped in the dung of infected horses. Larvae hatch when conditions are warm and moist to be absorbed during grazing. Inside the horse they reach the gut. Piercing the gut wall, they migrate through the internal organs and blood vessels, returning to the gut to mature and lay eggs, which are passed out in the dung to repeat the cycle.

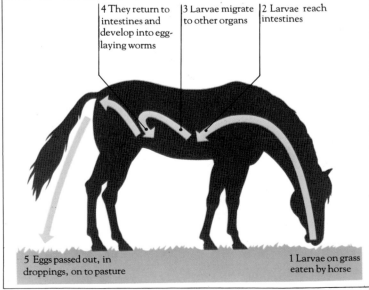

4 They return to intestines and develop into egg-laying worms

3 Larvae migrate to other organs

2 Larvae reach intestines

5 Eggs passed out, in droppings, on to pasture

1 Larvae on grass eaten by horse

Stagnant water

Coarse rank vegetation – unsuitable for feed

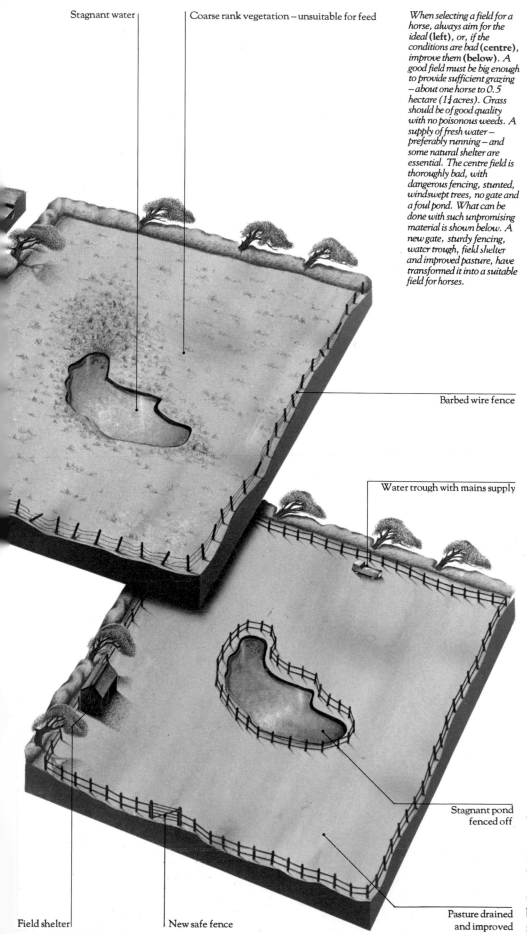

Barbed wire fence

Water trough with mains supply

Stagnant pond fenced off

Field shelter

New safe fence

Pasture drained and improved

When selecting a field for a horse, always aim for the ideal (left), or, if the conditions are bad (centre), improve them (below). A good field must be big enough to provide sufficient grazing – about one horse to 0.5 hectare (1¼ acres). Grass should be of good quality with no poisonous weeds. A supply of fresh water – preferably running – and some natural shelter are essential. The centre field is thoroughly bad, with dangerous fencing, stunted, windswept trees, no gate and a foul pond. What can be done with such unpromising material is shown below. A new gate, sturdy fencing, water trough, field shelter and improved pasture, have transformed it into a suitable field for horses.

being worked regularly in the spring or summer, say, it is a good idea to bring it into the stable first thing in the morning for the first extra feed that will be required. If the horse is to be ridden more than once that day, the same routine is followed as for the stabled horse until the afternoon, when the animal can be turned out for the night. If only one ride is possible, it can be turned out after the second feed, or, if it cannot be exercised at all, it can be turned out after the first.

Keeping a horse at grass

Looking after a horse kept at grass is less time-consuming than looking after one kept in a stable. Among the pluses are the natural vitamins and the exercise the horse gets, but equal responsibility is still demanded from the owner. Statistics show that more accidents happen to horses left unattended in a field than those in a stable. They can kick each other, get tangled up in fences or gates and quickly lose condition either through illness or just plain bad weather. Also, a horse should be visited every day, even if it is not being ridden. Horses are gregarious creatures – ideally, a horse should be kept in company with others – and require affection. Neglect will only make them difficult, if not impossible, to catch.

The ideal field is large – between six and eight acres. It should be undulating, well-drained, securely fenced by a high-grown hedge reinforced by post-and-rail fencing, with a clump of trees at one end and a gravel-bedded stream to provide fresh water. But this situation is often hard to achieve. It is usually considered that about 1 to 1½ acres per pony is adequate, provided that the grass is kept in good condition. Because horses are 'selective grazers' – that is, they pick and choose where and what they eat – a paddock can become 'horse sick'. Some places will be almost bare of grass, while others will be overgrown with the rank, coarse grasses the horses have found unpalatable. In addition, the ground will almost certainly be infested with parasites, the eggs of which horses pass in their dung. If action is not taken, the horses are sure to become infected with worms. These fall into two categories, of which roundworms are by far the most important and potentially destructive. Of these, the most dangerous are red worms *(Strongyles)*, which, untreated, can lead to severe loss of condition. Even though the horse is well-fed, it looks thin and 'poor', with a staring coat; in the worst cases, anaemia may develop or indigestion, colic and enteritis.

As far as an infected horse is concerned, the treatment is regular worming, but it is far better to tackle the problem at source by making sure that the field is maintained properly. A large field should be subdivided so that one area can be rested while another is being grazed. Ideally, sheep or cattle should be introduced on the the resting areas, as they will eat the tall grasses the horses have rejected. They will also help reduce worm infestation, as their digestive juices kill horse worms. Harrowing is also essential as it aerates the soil, encouraging new grass to grow, and also scatters the harmful dung. Failing this, the manure must be collected at least twice a week and transferred to a compost heap.

Mowing after grazing, coupled with the use of a balanced fertilizer, also helps keep a field in good condition, but horses should not be returned to their grazing too soon after it has been so treated. If in doubt, allow three weeks.

Bots are another problem for field-kept horses, for which veterinary treatment is necessary.

Food, water and shelter

All grassland is composed of a mixture of grasses and other plants. Some have little nutritional value, though the horse may well like them, but the three most important are Perennial Rye Grass *(Lolium perennae)*, Cocksfoot *(Dactylis glomerata)* and Timothy *(Phleum pratense)*. Some White Clover *(Trifolium repens)* is useful, but beware of a heavily-clovered pasture. This may prove too rich and lead to digestive problems.

Even if clover is not present, grass itself can cause problems. This is especially the case in the spring when excessive greed can lead a horse to put on too much weight, and sometimes to the painful disease called laminitis, or founder. Also, a horse or pony can only exist on grass alone for the summer months – from about the end of April to the beginning of September. By October, supplementary feeding becomes essential. Start off with hay and then provide oats or beans, if required. The more refined the breed, the more extra feeding that will be necessary.

Water is another essential; field-kept horses must have easy access to a plentiful supply of fresh water. Remember that a horse drinks about 35 litres (8 gal) a day. If the water supply is in the form of a stream, check that it can be reached by means of a gentle slope; if the banks are steep or muddy, it is safer to fence the stream off and provide a water trough instead. Similarly, always fence off stagnant pools and ponds.

The most convenient form of trough is one connected to a mains water supply, controlled either by a tap or automatic valve. Custom-made troughs are on the market, but cheaper alternatives are an old domestic cistern or bath. Remember to remove all sharp

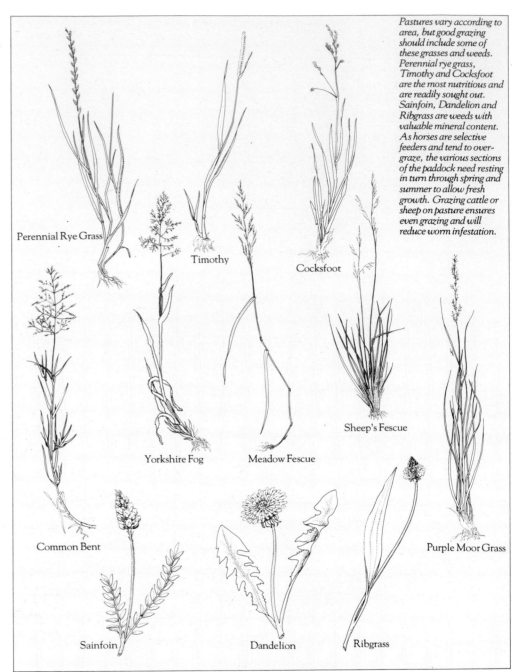

Pastures vary according to area, but good grazing should include some of these grasses and weeds. Perennial rye grass, Timothy and Cocksfoot are the most nutritious and are readily sought out. Sainfoin, Dandelion and Ribgrass are weeds with valuable mineral content. As horses are selective feeders and tend to overgraze, the various sections of the paddock need resting in turn through spring and summer to allow fresh growth. Grazing cattle or sheep on pasture ensures even grazing and will reduce worm infestation.

Perennial Rye Grass

Timothy

Cocksfoot

Sheep's Fescue

Yorkshire Fog

Meadow Fescue

Common Bent

Purple Moor Grass

Sainfoin

Dandelion

Ribgrass

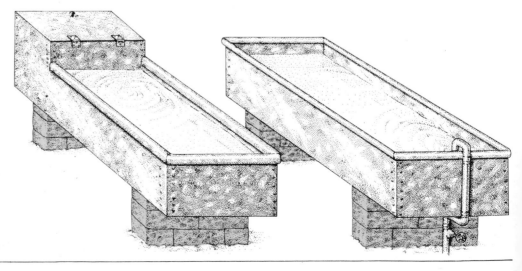

Fencing and gates

Sound and strong fencing is essential for safety. A fence must be high enough to prevent horses from jumping over it – 1.3m (3ft 9in) is the absolute minimum. Bars must also be fitted; two rails are usually adequate for containing horses, with the bottom one about 4.5cm (18in) from the ground. Small ponies, however, can wriggle through incredibly small gaps, so a third or even a fourth rail should be added for them. This type of fencing is known as post-and-rail, or 'Man O' War'.

Of all the types of fencing available, timber is the safest but most expensive. Hedges run a close second, but should be regularly checked, as otherwise a determined pony might well push his way through. Gaps can be reinforced with timber, but avoid filling a gap with wire. Concealed by a hedge in summer, it could be hard for a horse to see and so could lead to accidental injury. Stone walls are also attractive, but, they, too, will need regular checking, especially after a hard winter when frost may have loosened the mortar.

However, wire is perfectly adequate as fencing on its own, as long as the correct type of wire is used. Avoid barbed wire, chicken mesh or sheep wire and use a plain heavy gauge galvinized wire instead. For safety and effectiveness, the strands must be stretched so that they are evenly taut and then stapled to the inside of the posts. Strong stretcher posts, should be positioned at regular intervals. Check regularly for signs of weakness, such as loose posts, broken wires or sprung staples. If each strand of wire ends in an eye bolt attached to the end posts, the wire can be tightened from time to time.

Gates are another safety factor. The only criterion is that they should be easy for people to open and close, but that it should be impossible for the horse to do so. A five-

projections, such as taps, and to give the inside a thorough cleaning before putting into use. If there is no piped water supply, use a hose or fill the trough with buckets.

Buckets alone are totally insufficient. A horse can easily drink a whole bucket of water at one go, and, in any case, a bucket can all too easily be kicked over. Daily checks of the water supply are vital, especially in winter, when ice may form and must be broken. A child's rubber ball left floating on the surface of a trough will help to keep the water ice-free, except when frosts are severe, when the ice must be broken daily.

Winter and summer also bring the problem of shelter. From a horse's point of view, the worst elements are wind, rain and sun. Even if the field possesses a natural windbreak, an artificial shelter is a good addition. It need not be complicated – a three-sided shed the size of a large loose box is usually adequate. Make sure that the open side does not face the sun.

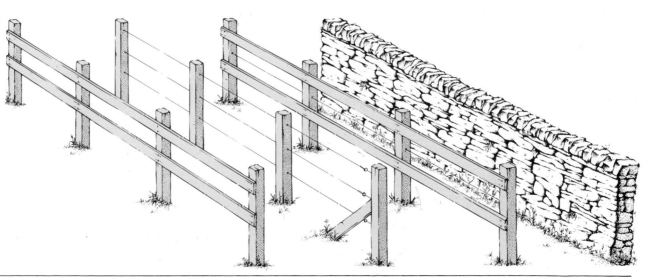

Yew

Tutu

Castor oil plant

False acacia

Privet

Deadly nightshade

Ragwort

Hemlock

Horsetail

Ngaio

Purple milk-vetch

Avocado

Rangiora

Yellow star-thistle

Oleander

Buckthorn

St. John's wort

Many trees, shrubs and plants are poisonous to horses. **Above** are some commonly found in various parts of the world. Great care should be taken to check the pasture and to eradicate any that may appear in fields where horses are kept.

Some plants remain poisonous even when the plant itself dies. Sprayed and uprooted plants should not be left to wither in the field, but should be removed and burned. Many plants are just as poisonous after drying and long storage.

Hay and bedding should, therefore, be examined and any harmful plants removed. Horses will eat a toxic plant, like ragwort, when it is fed to them dried in hay, although they will not touch it growing in the field because of its bitter taste, which, however, disappears with drying.

Fortunately, horses are not attracted to some of the most toxic plants. They will only eat deadly nightshade, for example, if virtually starving. However, some equally poisonous ones, like yew and privet do get eaten occasionally.

Garden hedges and their clippings can also be a source of poisoning. Make sure that a horse does not snatch at them while out riding. Poisonous, exotic plants, less easy to identify than familiar native ones, may grow in gardens and parks too.

Poison can be quickly fatal, or it may take as long as a month to work. Symptoms include loss of condition, lack of appetite, jaundice, staggering and nervous spasms. The horse may have a normal temperature throughout the period.

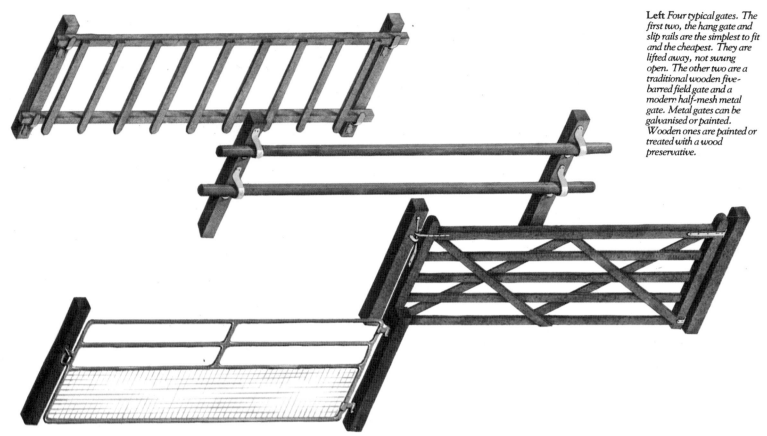

barred farm gate, hung just clear of the ground so that it swings freely when unlatched, is ideal. It should be fitted with either a self-closing latch, or with a simple chain fitted with a snap lock and fastened to the latching post. Slip rails and hang-gates are cheaper alternatives.

'Turning out', exercise and grooming

Before a pony or horse is turned out into a field, always check it carefully. Inspect the gate and fencing, strengthening any weak points. Make certain that there are no poisonous plants either in the field or within reach of the fence. See that there is an adequate supply of water, and check that there are no man-made hazards, such as broken bottles, tin cans and plastic bags lying about, which could injure the horse; a pony can die if it swallows a plastic bag, for example. Have any rabbit holes filled in to avoid the risk of a cantering horse catching its feet in one, falling, and perhaps breaking a leg.

When you are satisfied with the state of the field, turn the horse out. If it is not to be ridden for some time, say over the winter, have the shoes removed. This will lessen the danger of injury in the event of any kicking contest with other horses kept in the field.

Before exercising, always check the horse for cuts, bruises and other injuries. This procedure should also be carried out during the daily visits. Pick out the feet, noting the condition of the shoes. Also check the teeth

regularly. Left unattended, they can develop rough edges, which make eating difficult. If this happens, they will need to be filed.

Remember, too, that the horse will be in what is known as 'grass condition'. Its soft muscles and its extra layers of fat will make it incapable of any prolonged period of hard work, without sweating heavily and exhibiting other signs of distress. Forcing a horse to do so will only damage wind and limbs. If, as at the start of the school holidays, say, the horse is being ridden frequently for the first time in some months, it is a good idea to start a supplementary feeding programme a few weeks before, as grass is not a high-energy food. In any case, exercise should always be gradual, slowly building up from walking to a full exercise programme.

After exercise, the horse may well be sweaty, particularly if the animal has a long, shaggy coat. It is best to turn it out immediately and not to wait until the sweat has completely dried, or there is the danger of colds or, in extreme cases, colic. Conversely, in winter remember that the grease in a horse's coat helps to keep it warm, so restrict after-exercise grooming to remove any mud. A clipped horse should always wear a New Zealand rug in the field in the winter.

Groom with a dandy brush, taking care to get rid of all dried and caked mud and any sweat marks. Groom the mane and tail with a body brush and, finally, sponge out eyes, nostrils and dock.

Gate fastenings must be impossible for horses to open, but simple for human beings. Here are three secure kinds. **Top** *A simple catch with a lug held in a notch.* **Centre** *A catch with a release mechanism.* **Below** *A spring catch with a bar held forward against a retaining hook.*

The stabled horse

There are two main reasons for keeping a horse in a stable. The first is that the horse may be too well-bred to live out in all weathers, without seriously losing condition. The second is the amount of work the rider requires the horse to do. If a horse is being ridden a great deal, it must be fit enough to cope with its rider's demands without showing signs of distress, such as excessive sweating and blowing. Such a degree of fitness takes time to achieve and can only be maintained in a stable.

The ideal stable is also often easier to provide than the ideal field. It should be roomy, warm, well-ventilated yet draught-free, easy to keep clean, have good drainage and be vermin proof. It should face away from prevailing winds and have a pleasant outlook – preferably on to a stable yard or at least an area where something is often going on. The horse could be spending some 22 hours a day in the stable and unless there is something to hold its attention, it may well become bored. This can lead, in turn, to the development of vices, such as weaving (rocking from side to side), box walking, (a constant restless wandering around the box), or crib-biting (gripping the manger or stable door with the teeth and drawing in a sharp breath). The first two vices may lead to loss of condition, the third to broken wind.

Buying, renting or building

Any stable, whether it is bought, rented, converted or specially built, must conform to certain basic standards. If a stable is being converted, say, from a garage or barn, or being built from scratch, make sure that these standards are followed.

In the latter case, an architect can either design a stable to your individual specifications or one can be bought ready-made. This type of stable is usually delivered in sections and erected on a pre-prepared concrete base. But, before committing yourself, always check your plans out with the local authority concerned. They may well have to grant planning permission, and will certainly have regulations governing such crucial health factors as drainage.

The choice of site is very important. As far as possible, it should be level and well-drained, with easy access to the electricity and water supplies. The stable itself should be situated with the doorway facing the sun and the general lay-out should be planned to have all the essential elements – stable, feed room, tack room and manure heap – conveniently close together.

The stable can either be a straight stall or a loose box; the latter is much more commonly used today, particularly in the UK and USA.

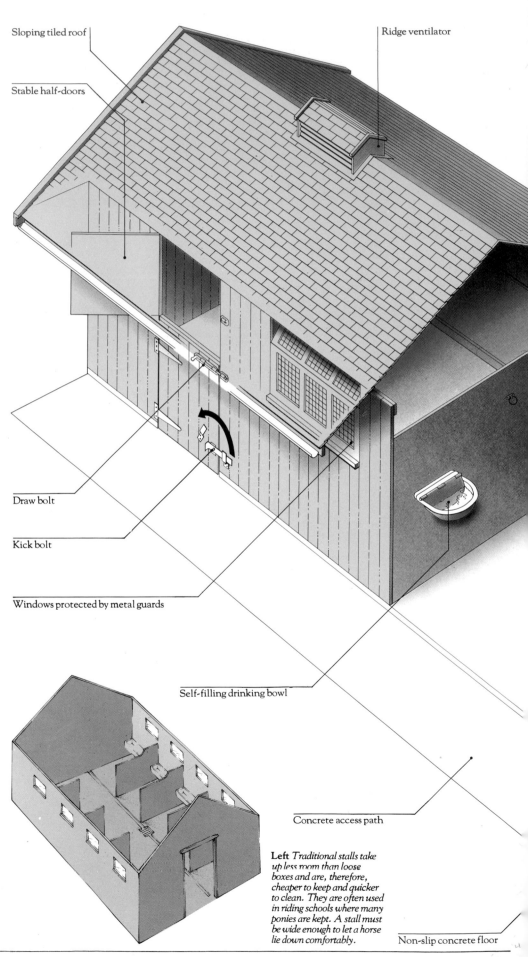

Sloping tiled roof

Ridge ventilator

Stable half-doors

Draw bolt

Kick bolt

Windows protected by metal guards

Self-filling drinking bowl

Concrete access path

Left *Traditional stalls take up less room than loose boxes and are, therefore, cheaper to keep and quicker to clean. They are often used in riding schools where many ponies are kept. A stall must be wide enough to let a horse lie down comfortably.*

Non-slip concrete floor

Corner manger Kick board Louvred ventilator

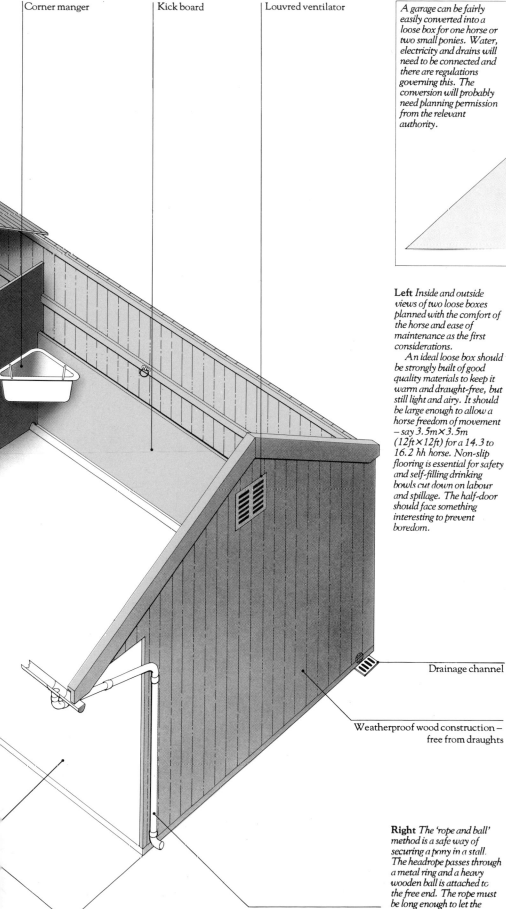

A garage can be fairly easily converted into a loose box for one horse or two small ponies. Water, electricity and drains will need to be connected and there are regulations governing this. The conversion will probably need planning permission from the relevant authority.

Left *Inside and outside views of two loose boxes planned with the comfort of the horse and ease of maintenance as the first considerations.*

An ideal loose box should be strongly built of good quality materials to keep it warm and draught-free, but still light and airy. It should be large enough to allow a horse freedom of movement – say 3.5m × 3.5m (12ft × 12ft) for a 14.3 to 16.2 hh horse. Non-slip flooring is essential for safety and self-filling drinking bowls cut down on labour and spillage. The half-door should face something interesting to prevent boredom.

Drainage channel

Weatherproof wood construction – free from draughts

The chief advantage of a stall is that it can be relatively small, so making cleaning easier. But, as it is open at one end, the horse has to be kept tied up. The usual method is known as the rope and ball system, where the halter rope is passed through a ring on the manger and attached to a hardwood ball resting on the horses' bed. This helps to safeguard the horse against possible injury, while still allowing it some freedom of movement.

Most horse owners prefer the loose box, as it allows the horse far more freedom to move around and so more comfort. Size is here all-important; cramming a 16hh hunter into a loose box built for a Shetland pony can only lead to trouble. As a rough guide, 3½m (12ft) square is probably the optimum size, rising to 4m (13ft) for horses over 16 hands. It is worth bearing in mind that a child's first pony, say, will be outgrown in time, so the bigger the box the better.

Boxes should be square rather than oblong, so that the horse can more easily determine the amount of room it has to lie down or to roll. The box must be big enough to minimize the risk of the horse being 'cast' – that is, rolling over and being trapped on its back by the legs striking the wall. In its struggles to get up, the horse may injure itself severely. The ceiling height should allow plenty of clearance for the horse's head; 3m (10ft) is the bare minimum.

Brick and stone are both durable and at-

Right *The 'rope and ball' method is a safe way of securing a pony in a stall. The headrope passes through a metal ring and a heavy wooden ball is attached to the free end. The rope must be long enough to let the horse lie down comfortably.*

PVC gutters and drainage pipes

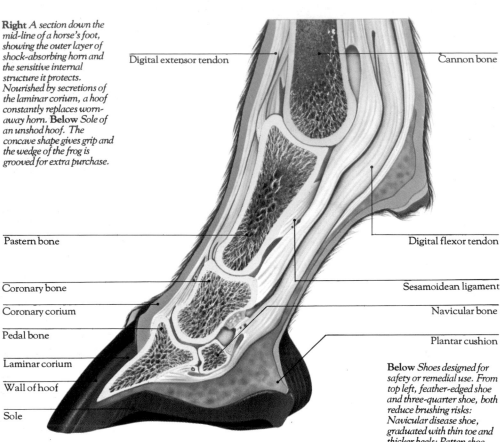

Right *A section down the mid-line of a horse's foot, showing the outer layer of shock-absorbing horn and the sensitive internal structure it protects. Nourished by secretions of the laminar corium, a hoof constantly replaces worn-away horn.* **Below** *Sole of an unshod hoof. The concave shape gives grip and the wedge of the frog is grooved for extra purchase.*

Digital extensor tendon

Cannon bone

Pastern bone

Digital flexor tendon

Coronary bone

Sesamoidean ligament

Coronary corium

Navicular bone

Pedal bone

Plantar cushion

Laminar corium

Wall of hoof

Sole

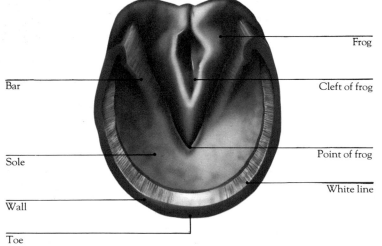

Frog

Bar

Cleft of frog

Sole

Point of frog

Wall

White line

Toe

Below *Shoes designed for safety or remedial use. From top left, feather-edged shoe and three-quarter shoe, both reduce brushing risks: Navicular disease shoe, graduated with thin toe and thicker heels: Patten shoe with raised heels and bar to rest injured tendon: Shoe with heel set to ease pressure on corn: 'T' shoe for contracted heels: Hind shoe with rolled toe against over-reaching injury: Hunter hind shoe with calkin and wedge heels for extra grip.*

Re-shoeing is needed when the clenches have risen through the hoof wall.

Here the shoe has worn extremely thin and should be replaced.

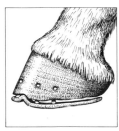

This shoe is loose and likely to be cast. The hoof must be re-shod.

A newly-shod hoof showing well-positioned clenches and a close-fitting shoe.

tractive building materials, but breeze blocks, solid concrete blocks or timber may be cheaper. Both walls and roof should be insulated, which will keep the stable warmer when the weather is cold and cooler when it is hot.

The floor must be hard-wearing, non-absorbent and slip-proof. A well compacted concrete base is perfectly adequate, provided that it is made with a loam-free aggregate and treated with a proprietary non-slip coating after laying. Alternatively, roughen the surface with a scraper before the concrete sets. Make sure that the floor slopes slightly – a slope of about one in sixty from front to rear is ideal – so that urine can drain away easily. An alternative is to cut a narrow gulley along one inside wall leading to a channel in the wall and so to an outside drain. The channel should be fitted with a trap to stop rats getting in and cleared of dirt and debris daily.

The usual type of stable door is made in two halves, the top half being kept open for ventilation. This should be planned to ensure that the horse gets plenty of fresh air but no draughts, as these can lead to it catching colds and chills. The best position for a window is high on the wall opposite the door so that sufficient cross-ventilation can be provided. Make sure it is fitted with shatter-proof glass, and covered with an iron grill. Otherwise, vents can be built in the roof to allow stale air to escape. They should be protected by cowls.

Doors must be wide and high enough for a horse to pass through without the risk of injury; 1.5m (4ft) is the minimum width, 2.25m (7½ft) the minimum height. Make sure that the door opens outwards so that access is easy and that strong bolts are fitted to both halves of the door. On the lower door, two bolts are necessary – an ordinary sliding bolt at the top and a kick bolt, operated by the foot, at the bottom. The top half needs only one bolt. Remember that the material used must be strong enough to withstand the kicking of a restless horse. Inside the stable, kicking boards, usually cut from

A farrier displays his skill in hot shoeing. After cutting clenches he removes the old shoe with pincers (**above**) and trims away overgrown horn with a drawing knife (**right**). The farrier's forge and tools are seen (**below left**). The new shoe is forged (**top right**) and fitted hot to reveal unevenness (**below right**). The new clenches are smoothed off with a rasp after fitting (**extreme right**).

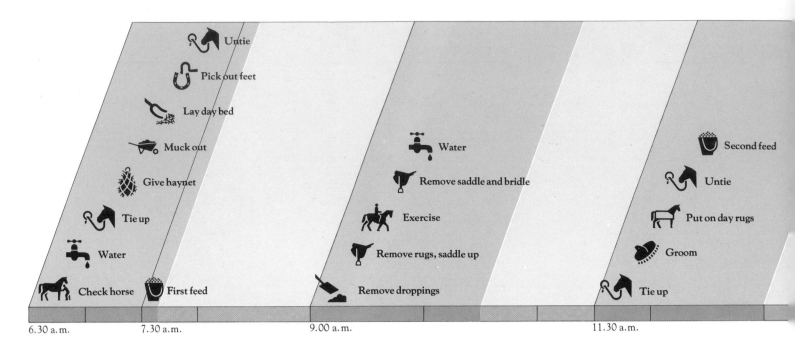

6.30 a.m.   7.30 a.m.   9.00 a.m.   11.30 a.m.

hardwood and some 5ft high, will help with this problem.

Electricity is the only adequate means of lighting. The light itself should be protected by safety glass or an iron grill and all wiring should be housed in galvanized conduits beyond the horse's reach. Switches must be waterproof, properly insulated, and, whenever possible, fitted outside the stable.

Shoeing the horse

Any horse being ridden regularly on a hard surface, such as a road, must be shod, or the wall of the hoof will be worn down quicker than it can grow. This will cause friction, soreness and lameness. Hardy ponies, working lightly and solely on grass, can do without shoes, but their hooves should still be looked at regularly by a blacksmith.

Inspections should take place at regular four to six week intervals. The signs that a horse needs to be reshod are a loose shoe; one that has been 'cast' (lost); a shoe wearing thin; one in which the clenches (securing nails) have risen and stand out from the wall; and if the foot is overlong and out of shape.

Horses can be either hot-shod or cold-shod. In hot-shoeing, the red hot shoe is shaped to the exact size of the hoof. In the latter, the shoes are pre–cast and fitted cold. Whichever method is used by the blacksmith, always check the following points after shoeing has been completed.

Make sure that the shoe has been made to fit the foot – not vice versa. Check that the shoe is suitable for the work you want the horse to do, and that the weight of the shoes is in the right proportion to the horse's size.

As a rough guide, a set of shoes for a horse should usually weigh around 2kg (4½lb). Look at the heel and toe of the foot to make sure that its length has been reduced evenly. See that the foot is in contact with the ground. Check that the right size and number of nails have been used and the clenches are correctly formed, in line and the right distance up the wall. Finally, make sure the clip fits securely and that there is no gap showing between the newly-fitted shoe and the hoof.

Fixtures and fittings

The basic rule to follow is the fewer fittings the better, to minimize the risk of possible injury. The only essential is a means of tying the horse up. Normally, this consists of two rings, fixed to bolts which pass right through the stable wall. One ring should be at waist

Mucking out is the first job done each morning in the stable. Soiled straw and dung are separated from the cleaner portions of the night bedding by tossing with a fork. The cleaner straw is then heaped at the back of the stall to be used again.

The soiled straw and droppings are put into a barrow for removal to the manure heap. In fine weather much of the night bedding can be carried outside to air in the sun. This will freshen it up, restore its springiness and make it last longer.

When the bulk of soiled straw has been removed and the cleaner straw reserved, the floor should be swept clean of remaining dirt. It should be left bare to dry off and air for a while. The clean straw is then spread as a soft floor-covering for the day.

The soiled straw and dung are tossed on the manure heap. Take care to throw the muck right on to the top of the heap, as a neatly built heap decomposes more efficiently. Beat the heap down with a shovel after each load to keep it firm and dense.

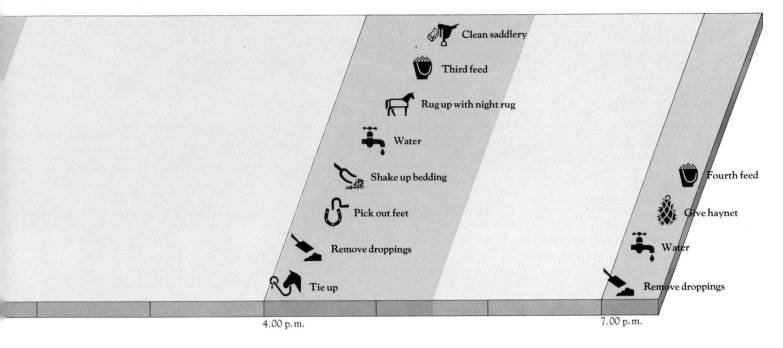

Clean saddlery

Third feed

Rug up with night rug

Water

Shake up bedding

Pick out feet

Remove droppings

Tie up

Fourth feed

Give haynet

Water

Remove droppings

4.00 p.m.   7.00 p.m.

Above *The daily routine for a fully-stabled horse, showing the order of work and the times at which different tasks are carried out. The feeding schedule will vary according to the size and work-load of individual horses. Many owners prefer the less time-consuming combined system, in which horses spend part of the day out in the field.*

height and the other at head height. All other fittings and fixtures are a matter of individual preference.

Fixed mangers positioned at breast level and secured either along a wall or in a corner of the loose box are found in many stables. They should be fitted with lift-out bowls to facilitate cleaning and have well-rounded corners. The space beneath should be boxed in to prevent the horse from injuring itself on the manger's rim – this space makes a good storage place for a grooming kit. However, a container on the floor, which is heavy enough not to be knocked over and which can be removed as soon as the horse has finished its feed is adequate.

Fitted hay racks are found in some stables, but they are not really advisable. They force the horse to eat with its head held unnaturally high and hayseeds may fall into its eyes. The best way of feeding hay is to use a haynet. It is also the least wasteful, as haynets permit accurate weighing. The net should always be hung well clear of the ground and be fastened with a quick-release knot to one of the tying-up rings.

Water is as essential to the horse in the stable as for a horse in the field. Automatic watering bowls are one way of providing a constant supply – but never position them too close to the haynet and manger, or they may get blocked by surplus food. Buckets are satisfactory, provided, again, that the bucket

is heavy enough not to be accidentally upset. Use of a bucket means that it is possible to control the amount of water the horse drinks – important after exercise, for instance, when a 'heated' horse must not drink too much – and also to check how much it is drinking more easily. This is especially useful in cases of suspected illness.

Stable routine

The daily programme for looking after a stabled horse takes up a great deal of time. All the stages have to be carried out, though some, such as the number of feeds, will vary from case to case. Skimping will only lead to problems later.

1. Tie up the horse and check over for injuries which may have occurred during the night. Replenish its water, if necessary, and fill the haynet. Muck out the stable. Quarter the horse thoroughly. Pick out feet with a hoof pick. Lay the day bed.
2. First feed.
3. Allow the horse time to digest – at least 1¼ hours – and then saddle up and exercise. On returning to the stable, refill water bucket and remove droppings.
4. Tie up and groom thoroughly. Put on day rug (blanket) if used. Check water again and refill the haynet. Give the second feed.
5. Pick out feet again and remove droppings. Shake up bedding, replace the day rug (blanket) with a night rug, and replenish water.
6. Third feed. Clean tack.
7. Remove droppings, and lay the night-bed. Replenish the water and re-fill the haynet. Final feed. Put on a night rug (blanket), if worn.

The only way of short-circuiting this

routine is to adopt the combined system of care. This has considerable advantages in time and labour, but is not suited to all horses, especially those being worked hard. Otherwise, board or livery is the only alternative. Some riding schools offer what is termed half-livery; this means that the horse gets free board in exchange for use as a hack. The risk is that the horse may be roughly treated by inexperienced riders even in a supervised lesson. Full livery is extremely expensive; in the UK it can cost as much as £30 a week. In either case, always check that the stable you choose is officially approved by a recognized riding authority.

The principal areas of a horse-owner's day, however, are not as complex as they seem. They can be broken down into various tasks, all of which are relatively simple to carry out.

Bedding down and mucking out

The purpose of bedding is to give the horse something comfortable to lie on, insulate the box, absorb moisture and prevent the horse's legs jarring on the hard stable floor. It must be kept clean – hence the daily task of mucking out. This is usually done first thing in the morning, and, with practice, can be carried out quite quickly.

Straw is the best possible bedding material, though other kinds can be substituted. Wheat straw is excellent, because it is absorbent and lasts well. Barley straw may contain awns, which can irritate the horse's skin. Oat straw should be avoided, because horses tend to eat it and it tends to become saturated.

Of the substitutes, peat makes a soft, well-insulated bed; it is also the least inflammable of all bedding materials. However, it is heavy to work. Damp patches and droppings must

Wheat straw (**left**) makes ideal bedding. It is warm, comfortable, easy to handle and absorbent. Wood shavings (**centre**) make cheaper bedding and are often laid on a base of sawdust to reduce dampness. Droppings have to be removed frequently. Peat moss (**right**) makes a soft bed, but tends to be dusty when first laid down and needs frequent raking.

be removed at once, replacing with fresh peat when necessary. The whole bed requires forking over and raking every day, as the material can cause foot problems if it becomes damp and compacted.

Wood shavings and sawdust are usually cheap but can be difficult to get rid of. Both need to be checked carefully to see that they do not contain nails, screws, paint, oil or other foreign matter. Wood shavings can be used alone, but note that they can cause foot problems if they become damp and compacted. Sawdust is best used in combination with other materials.

There are two types of bed – the day bed and the night bed. The first is a thin layer of bedding laid on the floor for use during the day; the second is thicker and more comfortable for use at night. With materials such as peat or wood shavings, laying the bed is very simple. Just empty the contents of the sack on the floor and rake them level, building up the material slightly higher around the walls to minimize draughts.

Laying a straw bed requires slightly more skill. As the straw will be compacted in the bale, it has to be shaken up so that the stalks separate, and laid so that the finished bed is aerated, springy and free from lumps. A pitchfork is best for the purpose.

Some owners prefer the deep litter method of bedding, where fresh straw is added to the existing bed every day, removing only droppings and sodden straw beforehand. After a time, the bed becomes as much as two feet deep, well-compacted below and soft and resilient on the surface. At the end of a month, the whole bed is removed and restarted. This method should be used only in loose boxes with first-rate drainage. In addition, the feet must be picked out regularly, as otherwise there is a major risk of disease.

Feeding and fodder

Heredity has given the horse a very small stomach for its size and the food it eats takes up to 48 hours to pass through the digestive system. This system is in itself complex. It depends not only on the right amounts of food at the correct time for smoothness of

Laying a night bed of straw requires some skill. First (above) clean straw saved from the day bed is tossed and shaken well with a pitchfork before being spread evenly over the floor as a foundation.

Next new straw is taken from the compressed bale and shaken well to free the stalks and make the bed springy. The floor must be thickly and evenly covered to encourage the horse to lie down.

Last the straw is banked up higher and more thickly around the sides of the box. This cuts down draughts, keeps the horse warmer and gives the animal extra protection from injury during the night.

operation, but also on an adequate supply of water and plenty of exercise. In the wild, horses drink twice a day, usually at dawn and dusk. In between, their day is divided into periods of grazing, rest and exercise. Field-kept horses can duplicate this pattern to some extent, but stabled horses cannot do so.

It is essential to follow a basic set of feeding rules. Otherwise the horse's sensitive digestion may well be upset, encouraging the risks of indigestion, impaction, formation of gas in the stomach or sudden colic attacks.

The basic rules are to feed little and often, with plenty of bulk food – grass or hay – and according to the work you expect the horse to do. Make no sudden change in the type of food, or in the routine of feeding, once the diet and time has been established. Always water the horse before feeding, so that undigested food is not washed out of the stomach. Never work a horse hard straight after feeding or if its stomach is full of grass. Let it digest for $1\frac{1}{4}$ hours or so, otherwise the full stomach will impair breathing. Similarly, never feed a horse immediately after hard work, when it will be 'heated'.

The staple diet of the horse is grass, or, in the case of a stabled horse, hay. The best type is seed hay, usually a mixture of rye grass and clover, which is specially grown as part of a crop-rotation programme. Meadow grass, also commonly used, comes from permanent pasture and so can vary in quality. The best way of judging this is by appearance, smell and age. Hay should smell sweet, be slightly greenish in colour and at least six months old. Blackened, mouldy or wet hay should never be used as fodder.

Of the other types of hay, clover is too rich to be fed to a horse on its own, and the same rule applies to alfalfa, or lucerne, common in the USA and Canada. Alfalfa is extremely rich in protein, so feed small quantities until you can judge how much is needed.

Concentrates for work

Ponies and horses in regular, hard work need additional food to keep them in a fit, hard-muscled condition. In other words, they need energy rather than fatness. This is provided by the feeding of concentrated foodstuffs, usually known as 'short' or 'hard' feeds. Of these, the best is oats, which can be bruised, crushed or rolled to aid digestion. Manufactured horse cubes or pellets are a useful alternative.

Oats have no equal as a natural high protein, energy-giving food and are an essential part of the diet for all horses in work. Good quality oats are plump and short, and pale gold, silver grey or dark chocolate in colour. They should have a hard, dry feel and no sour smell. Take care, however, not to feed to much, or a horse may speedily become unmanageable. This caution applies particularly to children's ponies, which are often better off without oats at all.

Cubes and pellets are manufactured from various grains and also usually contain some grass meal, sweetners such as molasses or treacle, extra vitamins and minerals. Their nutritional value is about two-thirds that of oats, but they are less heating and so ideal for ponies. Their chief advantage is that they provide a balanced diet on their own, as they do not have to be mixed with other foodstuffs. However, they are expensive.

Other grains can be used in addition or as alternatives to oats, but they are all of lesser quality. Flaked maize (corn) is used in many parts of the world as a staple feed. It is high in energy value, but low in protein and mineral content. Like oats, it can be heating for ponies and is usually fed to animals in slow, regular work, such as riding school hacks. Boiled barley helps to fatten up a horse or pony in poor condition and is a useful addition to the diet of a stale, or overworked horse. Beans, too, are nutritious, but, again, because of their heating effect, they should be fed sparingly, either whole, split or boiled.

Other useful foods

Bran makes a useful addition to a horse's diet, as it helps provide roughage. It is either fed dry mixed up with oats – the combined mixture should be slightly dampened – or in the form of a mash. This is a good 'pick me up' for a tired or sick horse. The mash is made by mixing $\frac{2}{3}$ of a bucket of bran with $\frac{1}{3}$ of boiling water and is fed to the horse as soon as it is cool enough to eat. Always remove any remains, as the mash can quickly go rancid. Oatmeal gruel is an alternative. This is made by pouring boiling water on to porridge oats and leaving to cool. Use enough water to make the gruel thin enough in consistency for the horse to drink.

Linseed, prepared as a jelly, mash or tea, is fed to horses in winter to improve condition

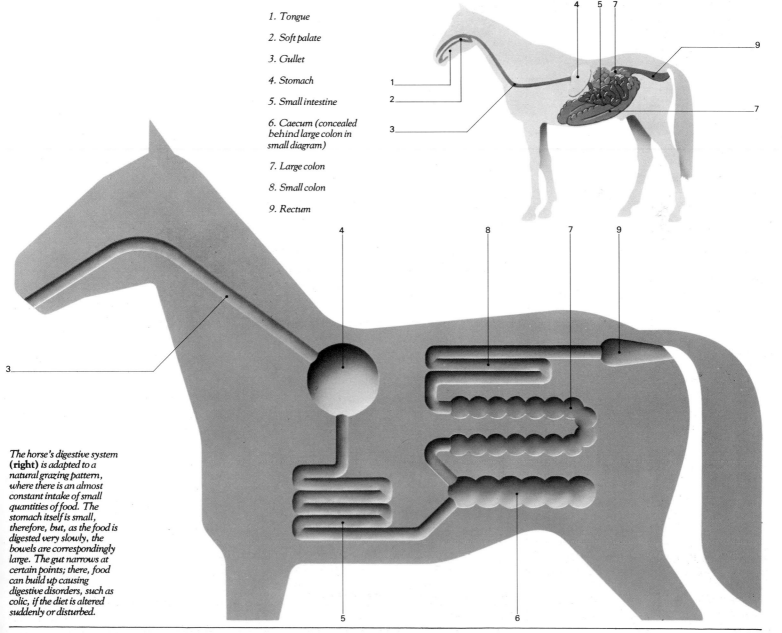

1. Tongue

2. Soft palate

3. Gullet

4. Stomach

5. Small intestine

6. Caecum (concealed behind large colon in small diagram)

7. Large colon

8. Small colon

9. Rectum

The horse's digestive system (right) is adapted to a natural grazing pattern, where there is an almost constant intake of small quantities of food. The stomach itself is small, therefore, but, as the food is digested very slowly, the bowels are correspondingly large. The gut narrows at certain points; there, food can build up causing digestive disorders, such as colic, if the diet is altered suddenly or disturbed.

Left Basic concentrated foods are an essential part of the diet for horses in hard, regular work. 1 Pony nuts are a compound food which contain all essential nutrients and can be fed, dry, instead of oats. Add chaff or bran to aid digestion. 2 Bran is rich in protein, vitamin B and salt. Fed as a mash, or slightly damp, with oats, it has a laxative effect. 3 Hay contains all nutrients needed to keep horses fit, if at grass, or only lightly worked. 4 Linseed fed as jelly, tea or cake has a high oil content and laxative properties. It is good for conditioning as it makes the coat glossy. 5 Oats are a balanced, nutritious and easily digested food, high in energy-giving carbohydrate, Vitamin B and muscle-building protein. They are fed whole, bruised or crushed. 6 Sugar beet cubes provide bulk for horses in slow work. They must be soaked before use, or will swell in stomach and cause colic. There is also a great danger of the horse choking. 7 Maize, fed flaked for digestibility, is energising, but low in protein and minerals. It contains vitamin A. 8 Barley, unsuitable for horses in long, fast work, is fed, boiled, as a general conditioner; it should be crushed if fed raw. It contains vitamin B. 9 Peas are protein-rich; feed them sparingly for energy or conditioning. 10 Chaff has little food value but gives bulk and helps mastication. Add 450g (1lb) to every feed ration.

and to give gloss to the coat. It must be soaked then well cooked to kill the poisonous enzyme present in the raw plant. Let the mix cool before giving it to the horse. Dried sugar beet is another good conditioner, because of its high energy content. Most horses like it because of its sweetness. It must be always soaked in water overnight before it is added to a feed. If fed dry, the beet is likely to cause severe colic, as it swells dramatically when wet.

Roots, such as carrots, turnips and swedes, again help condition and are also of particular value to delicate or fussy feeders. Always wash the roots first and then slice them into finger-shaped pieces. Small round slices may cause a pony to choke.

Molasses or black treacle can be mixed with food to encourage a finicky feeder. In any case, all feeds ideally should contain about ·45kg (1lb) of chaff – chopped hay. Chaff has practically no nutritional content, but it does ensure that the horse chews its food properly, so helping to minimize the risk

Proper feeding with the correct balance of vitamins is essential for health. The diagram (right) shows how particular vitamins work throughout the system and what effects they have. Any deficiency of these vitamins, A B1, B2, B6, D and E, in the horse's diet, will lead inevitably to debility and general loss of condition.

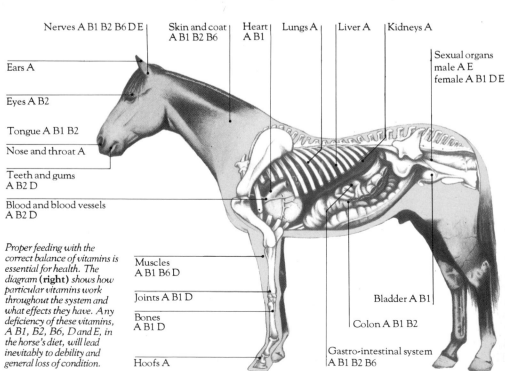

Nerves A B1 B2 B6 D E
Skin and coat A B1 B2 B6
Heart A B1
Lungs A
Liver A
Kidneys A
Sexual organs male A E female A B1 D E
Ears A
Eyes A B2
Tongue A B1 B2
Nose and throat A
Teeth and gums A B2 D
Blood and blood vessels A B2 D
Muscles A B1 B6 D
Joints A B1 D
Bones A B1 D
Bladder A B1
Colon A B1 B2
Gastro-intestinal system A B1 B2 B6
Hoofs A

of indigestion. It also acts as an abrasive on teeth. Finally, a salt or mineral lick – left in the manger – is essential for all stabled horses. Field-kept animals usually take in an adequate amount of salt during grazing, but a lick is also a good safeguard.

Vitamins and minerals

An adequate supply of vitamins and minerals is vital in addition to the required amounts of carbohydrates, proteins and fat. Vitamins A, B1, B2, B6, D and E are all essential; otherwise the horse's resistance to disease will certainly be lessened, and actual disease may well result. Normally, good-class hay and grass, bran and carrots will contain most of the vitamins a horse needs; oats, barley, flaked maize and sugar beet pulp are also all useful. Vitamin D, however, can only be artificially administered through cod liver oil, or left to the action of sunlight on the natural oil in the coat.

The absence of a sufficient supply of minerals can be even more serious than a lack of vitamins, especially in the case of a young horse. The essential minerals required are: calcium and phosphorus, for the formation of healthy teeth and bones; sodium, sodium chloride (salt) and potassium, for regulation of the amount of body fluids; iron and copper, vital for the formation of haemoglobin in the blood to prevent anaemia; while magnesium, manganese, cobalt, zinc and iodine are all necessary. Magnesium aids skeletal and muscular development; manganese is needed for both the bone structure and for reproduction; zinc and cobalt stimulate growth; while iodine is particularly important in control of the thyroid gland.

However, of all these minerals, the most important is salt. This is why it is vital to provide a horse with a salt lick in either stable of field.

As with vitamins, the chief source of these minerals is grass or hay, together with the other foods mentioned above. However, if the horse needs extra vitamins and minerals, always take the advice of a vet first – an excess of vitamins or minerals can be as dangerous as an underdose. These are many suitable proprietary products on the market. These usually come in the form of liquid, powders and pellets, designed to be mixed in with other food for ease of feeding.

Signs of lack of vitamins are usually seen on the skin and coat; examination of the teeth, gums and eyes can also give warning of possible deficiency. But, with sensible and controlled feeding, the problem should not arise.

Quantities to feed

There is no hard and fast guide to the exact

A separate food store is essential. It should be clean, dry and near to the water supply. Foodstuffs kept in the stable can easily become spoiled or contaminated. The horse is a fastidious feeder, and musty or dusty food, as well as being un-appetizing, may be harmful. The simple food store (below) provides a clean, secure and compact area where foodstuffs can be measured out and mixed. Large establishments often keep a chaff cutter and an oat crusher. Scales are also useful to check the weight of filled haynets periodically.

Foodstuffs should be kept in separate bins, or sections of one large bin, and only mixed at feedtime. A scoop is used to measure out each ration. Where several horses are kept a check list for feeding should be pinned up near the bins so that each receives its appropriate diet.

The feed can be dampened slightly with water before being mixed by hand in a bucket and then fed to horse. Grain keeps fresh and dry in galvanised bins. These should have close-fitting lids to keep out vermin and heavy enough to prevent a horse from raising them.

amounts of food a horse should be fed, as much depends on the type and size of horse and the work it is expected to do. However, as far as a stabled horse is concerned, the amount should certainly not be less than the horse would eat if it was grazing freely.

If the horse concerned was 15·2 hands, say, it would eat approximately 26½lbs of grass a day. Bigger horses require an extra 2lbs for every extra 2ins of height; smaller ones need 2lbs less.

With this basic total established, it is possible to plan a feeding programme, varying the amounts of bulk and concentrated food according to the demands being made upon the horse. Taking as an example a lightweight 15·2 hand horse that is being hunted, say, three days a fortnight in addition to other regular work, the emphasis will be on an almost equal balance between concentrates and hay or grass. The horse should be getting some 14lbs of concentrates a day to some 15lbs of hay. If, however, the horse is being lightly worked – or not worked at all – the

amount of hay will rise and the quantities of concentrates diminish.

Remember, too, that most horses feed much better at night, so it is important that the highest proportion of food be given in the final feed of the day. If the horse is being given three feeds a day, for example, the proportions are ten per cent in the morning, thirty per cent at midday and sixty per cent at night.

The best guide of all is simple observation. If a horse is too fat, it will need its rations reduced; if too thin, it will need building up. Always reduce the amount if food is left uneaten.

Exercising the horse

All stabled horses must have regular and adequate exercise. Otherwise they can develop swollen legs, azoturia and colic (see p. 159) – and will, in any case be spirited and difficult to manage when ridden. They can also become bored and develop bad habits. The amounts needed vary with the type and

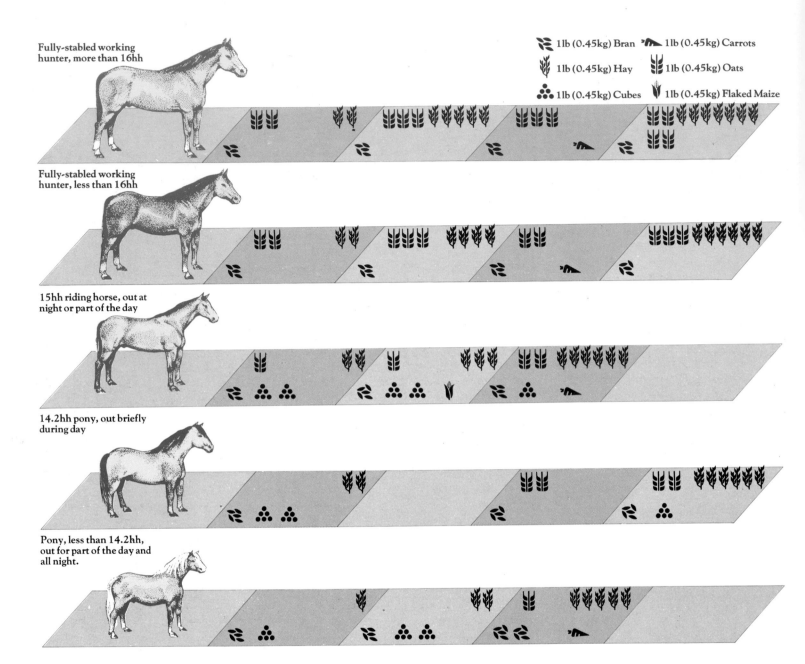

Fully-stabled working hunter, more than 16hh

Fully-stabled working hunter, less than 16hh

15hh riding horse, out at night or part of the day

14.2hh pony, out briefly during day

Pony, less than 14.2hh, out for part of the day and all night.

1lb (0.45kg) Bran   1lb (0.45kg) Carrots

1lb (0.45kg) Hay   1lb (0.45kg) Oats

1lb (0.45kg) Cubes   1lb (0.45kg) Flaked Maize

weight of horse and the work it is expected to do; a hunter needs more exercise than a hack.

As with feeding, there are a few basic rules to remember. Most importantly, never exercise a horse until 1½ hours after a heavy feed; 1 hour after a small one. In any case, always remove the haynet an hour before exercise. Horses full of hay find breathing difficult when being worked hard.

The point of exercise is to get and keep the horse fit enough for the demands being made on it. A horse brought up from grass, say, is likely to be in 'grass condition'. In such a case, fitness can be achieved only through a rigidly controlled programme of exercise and feeding. Restrict exercise to walking, preferably on roads, for a week. Then combine walking with slow trotting. Soon, work can start in the school, while the period of road work can also be extended. Increase the

Above *The amount of food a horse requires varies according to its size, temperament and the type of work it will be doing. This chart gives basic*

specimen diets for horses with an even temperament. The amount and type of food given to each individual horse should be adapted according to observation.

amount of grain fed in proportion to the extra in work. By the end of six weeks, the horse should be ready to be cantered over distances not exceeding 0.8km (½ mile). In the ninth week, it can have a gallop for up to 1.2km (¾ mile), but this should be strictly controlled so that the horse does not gallop flat out at full speed.

Indications of success are an increase in muscle and the disappearance of the profuse, lathery sweat of the out-of-condition horse. Never try to hurry the process; a horse cannot be conditioned through cantering and galloping, but only by slow, steady, regular work. This applies just as much to stabled horses

and ponies.

Always aim to end the exercise with a walk so that the horse comes back to its stable or field cool and relaxed. Once the tack has been removed, inspect the horse for cuts and bruises, pick out its feet, and brush off the saddle and sweat marks. Then rug up or groom. If you have been caught in the rain trot the horse home so that it is warm on arrival. Untack, and then give the horse a thorough rubbing down, either with straw or a towel. When this has been completed, cover the back with a layer of straw or use a sweat sheet. It is vital to keep the back warm to avoid the risk of colds and chills.

A thorough drying is essential if the horse is very hot and sweaty, but it will need to be sponged down first with lukewarm water. Either restrict sponging to the sweaty areas — usually the neck, chest and flanks — or sponge the entire body. Then, scrape off the surplus water with a sweat scraper, taking care to work with, and not against, the run of the coat. Next, rub down and, finally, cover with a sweat sheet. If possible, lead the horse around until it is completely dry.

Horses that have been worked exceptionally hard – in hunting, say, or in competitions – need further care. On returning to the stable, give the horse a drink of warm water. Then follow the procedures outlined above. Feed the horse with a bran mash and then leave it to rest. Return later to check that the animal is warm enough or has not broken out into a fresh sweat. Check for warmth by feeling the bases of the ears. If they are cold, warm by rubbing them with the hand and then put more blankets on the horse. If the latter, rub down again and walk the horse around until it is completely dry.

Grooming the horse

The chief point of grooming is to keep the horse clean, massage the skin and tone up the muscles. Field-kept horses need less grooming than stabled horses, particularly in winter, but some must nevertheless be carried out.

A good grooming kit is essential. This should consist of a dandy brush, to remove mud and dried sweat marks; a body brush, a soft, short-bristled brush for the head, body,

legs, mane and tail; a rubber curry comb, used to remove thickly-caked mud or matted hair, and a metal one, for cleaning the body brush; a water brush, used damp on the mane, tail and hooves; a hoof pick; a stable rubber, used to give a final polish to the coat; and some foam rubber sponges, for cleaning the eyes, nostrils, muzzle and dock.

Where more than one horse is kept, each animal should have its own grooming kit, kept together in a box or bag and clearly marked. This helps to prevent the risk of infection in cases of illness.

Grooming falls into three stages, each of which is carried out at a different time of the day. The first of these is quartering, normally done first thing in the morning before exercise. Tie up the horse. Then, pick the feet out and, next, clean the eyes, muzzle and dock with a damp sponge. If worn, rugs should be unbuckled and folded back and the head, neck, chest and forelegs cleaned with a body brush. Replace the rugs and repeat the process on the rear part of the body. Remove any stable stains with a water brush. Finish by brushing the mane and tail thoroughly with the body brush.

Strapping is the name given to the thorough grooming which follows exercise, when the horse has cooled down. Once again, tie the horse up and pick out its feet.

Follow by using the dandy brush to remove all traces of dirt, mud and sweat, paying particular attention to marks left by the girth and saddle and on the legs. Work from ears to tail, first on the near side and then on the off. Take care to use the brush lightly to avoid irritating the skin.

Next, comes the body brush. This must be used firmly for full effect. Start with the mane, pushing it to the wrong side to remove scurf from the roots. Brush the forelock. Then, start on the body, working from head to tail and grooming the nearside first, as before. Work with a circular motion, finishing in the direction of the hairs, and flick the brush outwards at the end of each stroke to push dust away from the body. At intervals, clean the brush with the curry comb, which is held in the other hand. It can be emptied by tapping on the floor at intervals.

Brush the head, remembering that this is one of the most sensitive areas of the horse. So use the brush firmly, but gently, and take particular care when grooming around the eyes, ears and nostrils. Finally, brush the tail – a few hairs at a time – so that every tangle is removed.

The next stage is wisping, which helps tone up the muscles and also stimulates the circulation. A wisp is a bundle of soft hay, twisted up to form a rope. Slightly dampen it,

Specimen exercise routine
based on a 16hh hunter

Exercise	Care and Management	Special Features	Exercise	Care and Management	Special Features
Week 1			**Week 5**		
20 mins walking on the first day, increasing gradually to one hour	Gradually increase food concentrate, begin strapping	During the pre-work week the horse's feet must be checked and shod. All horses require one rest day each working week	After first walking and trotting, the horse may have a short, slow canter on soft ground. Then decrease pace gradually	Four feeds a day – increase concentrates and reduce time at grass. Re-shoe if necessary	At this stage the coat should shine and the muscles should be hardening
Week 2			**Week 6**		
Walking for 1¼–1½ hrs over a 6–8 mile circuit	Check condition of legs and feet, watch for skin galls. Increase corn and vitamin supplements	Quiet lanes and roads with good surfaces are best for road work	A medium canter of reasonable length. Work at a sitting trot can now be started	Increase concentrate ration. Maintain thorough strapping	Schooling can be intensified by trotting in smaller circles, and work at the canter
Week 3			**Week 7**		
Always walk the first ½ mile. Then introduce very short spells of trotting, increasing their length gradually	Stable the horse at night and establish a regular routine	Schooling and lungeing in large circles can now be started	Canters can speed up. A short half speed gallop may be added at the end of the week (on good ground). Jumping can begin	The horse will sweat and should wear a rug at night	The final phase of building up to full work. It is useful to introduce the horse to travelling and to company at this stage
Week 4			**Week 8**		
1½–2 hrs work daily – split into schooling, lungeing and road work. More frequent, periods of trotting	Increase food concentrates	Trotting up gentle slopes can commence and increase slowly	On day 2 the horse can gallop at half speed up a gentle slope. Always walk the final mile	Full rations of concentrate. The horse should gallop on alternate days, and do steady work on the others. Renew shoes	When the horse is fully conditioned thorough exercise must be maintained on days when it does not work

Exercise needs always differ, according to the size of horse, the type of work it is doing and what it is being prepared for. Vary the routine accordingly

Left *The grooming kit. Ideally every horse should have its own to reduce the chance of any infection being passed from one to another. Keep the kit in a wire basket or bag so that no item is mislaid. Clean the equipment from time to time with a mild disinfectant. 1 Mane combs are used when mane or tail is plaited, trimmed or pulled. 2 Sponges, one for cleaning eyes, lips and nostrils, the second for cleaning the dock. 3 Can of hoof oil and brush, used to improve appearance of hoof and treat brittle feet. 4 Dandy brush (hard) to remove dried mud and sweat. 5 Body brush (soft) to remove dust and scurf. 6 Water brush (soft), for laying mane and tail and washing feet. 7 Sweat scraper, to remove water and sweat from coat. 8 Rubber curry comb, removes dirt from body brush; can also be used in place of dandy brush. 9 Metal curry comb, for cleaning dirt from body brush (never used on the horse). 10 Stable rubber used for final polishing of coat. 11 Hoof pick, for taking dirt and stones from the feet.*

and use vigorously on the neck, shoulders, quarters and thighs, concentrating on the muscular areas. Bang the wisp down hard on these, sliding it off with, not against, the coat. Take care to avoid bony areas and the tender region of the loins.

Sponge the eyes, lips, and muzzle and nostrils. Then, with a second sponge to minimize the risk of possible infection, wash round the dock and under the tail. Lift the tail as high as possible, so the entire region can be adequately cleaned. 'Lay' the mane with the water brush. Then brush the outside of the feet, taking care not to get water into the hollow of the heel. When the hooves are dry, brush hoof oil over the outside of each hoof as high as the coronet.

Finally, work over the horse with the stable rubber for a final polish. The object is to remove the last traces of dust from the coat. Fold the rubber into a flat bundle, dampen it slightly, and then go over the coat, working in the direction of the lay of the hair.

Strapping takes from between half to three-quarters of an hour with practice. It will normally take a novice slightly longer, largely because of the unaccustomed strain it imposes on the groom's muscles. 'Setting fair' – the last grooming of the day – takes far less time. Simply brush the horse lightly with the body brush, wisp and then put on the night rug (blanket), if one is normally worn.

Travelling with a horse

Careful planning when entering for a horse show, say, or going for a day's hunting, is essential if the horse is to arrive fit enough to undertake the tasks demanded of it. The first essential is to plan the journey; a fit horse can be hacked for up to ten miles, walking and trotting at an average speed of no more than six mph (a grass-kept pony's average should not be more than four mph). However, if the distance involved is greater than this, transport will be needed.

Horse boxes or car-towed trailers are the usual method of transport over long distances. Apart from the obvious mechanical checks that should be carried out before each journey, the horse's own requirements, too, need attention. A hay net is one essential; this should be filled with hay and given to the horse during the journey, unless the animal is expected to work hard immediately on arrival. Others include a first aid kit; rugs (day and sweat); bandages; grooming kit; a head collar; a water bucket and a filled water container. This last item is essential if the journey is to be a particularly long one, when the horse will need to be watered perhaps once or even twice en route.

In some cases – when hunting, for example

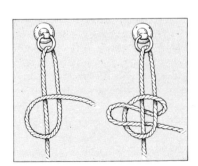

Above *How to tie a quick-release knot. This type of knot, which is easy to undo in an emergency, should always secure a horse. A quick tug on the free end releases the knot, but the more a horse pulls against it, the tighter it becomes.*

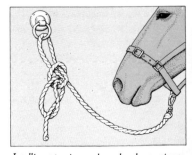

Intelligent ponies can learn by observation to pull at the free end of the quick-release knot and so get loose. If a pony learns to free itself in this way, it can usually be out-witted if the free end of the rope is passed back through the loop again (above).

To pick up a horse's foot, stand facing its tail. Warm it first by sliding a hand down from its shoulder to its fetlock. This can also encourage the horse to move its weight over to the other legs. It also helps to keep a young horse calm.

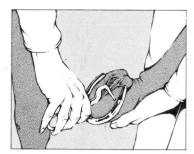

Working from the frog to the toe and concentrating on the edges first, use the point of the hoof pick to prise out any foreign objects lodged in the foot. Pebbles wedged between the frog and the bar can cause lameness. Take care not to push the point into the frog.

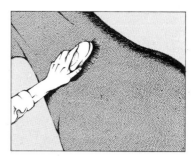

The dandy brush is used to remove heavy dirt caked mud and sweat stains, particularly from the saddle region, belly, points of hocks, fetlocks and pasterns. As it is fairly harsh it should not be used on the more tender areas, or on a recently clipped horse.

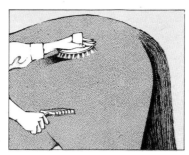

A body brush has short, dense bristles designed to penetrate and clean the coat. It should be applied with some pressure, in firm, circular movements. After a few strokes clear it of dust with a curry comb. A gentler brushing should be given round the head.

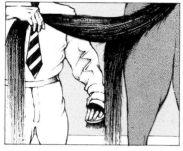

The body brush is also used to groom the tail. This should be brushed a few hairs at a time, starting with the undermost ones. Remove all mud and tangles, taking care not to break any hairs. Finally, the whole tail should be brushed into shape from the top.

Wring out a soft sponge in warm water and sponge the eyes first, wiping outwards from the corners. Carefully sponge round eyelids. Wring out the sponge and wipe over the muzzle, lips and nostrils. A separate sponge should be used to sponge the dock area.

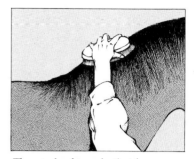

The water brush is used to 'lay' the mane. The tip of the brush is dipped in a bucket of water and thoroughly shaken before it is applied. Keeping the brush flat, make firm, downward strokes from the roots. The mane should be left neat and slightly damp.

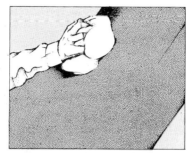

As a final touch to the grooming go over the whole coat with the stable-rubber to remove any trace of dust. This cloth is used slightly damp and folded into a flat bundle. Work along the lie of the hair. The stable-rubber leaves the coat gleaming.

– the horse can travel saddled-up, with a rug placed over the saddle, but, in the case of competitions, a rug alone should be worn. Travelling bandages should always be used, as well as a tail bandage to stop the top of the tail from being rubbed. In addition, knee caps and hock boots should be worn as an added protection.

Preparation of the horse itself must start the night before, with an especially thorough grooming. Both mane and tail should be washed. A grass-kept horse should be kept in for the night, if possible. The next morning, follow the normal stable routine, with the addition of a drawn-out strapping. Remember that, in the case of a show, the mane should be plaited; this can be started the night before to ease the task of getting the mane into shape, but will need to be completed the following day.

Loading the horse

Getting a horse into a box or trailer is an easy enough task, provided that the process is tackled calmly and without undue haste. The simplest way is for one person to lead the horse forward, walking straight forward and resisting the temptation to pull at the head. A couple of helpers should stand behind the horse in case help is required, but out of kicking range.

The main reason for a horse showing reluctance to enter a box is usually its fear of the noise of its hooves on the ramp. This can be overcome by putting down some straw to deaden the sound. Loading another, calmer, horse first, or tempting a horse forward with a feed bucket containing a handful of oats, also act as encouragements.

A really obstinate horse, however, will have to be physically helped into the box. The way to do this is to attach two ropes to the ramp's rails, so that they cross just above the horse's hocks, with two helpers in position – one at each end of the ropes. As the horse approaches the ramp, they tighten the ropes to propel the animal into the box.

Tack – care and maintenance

Care of saddles and bridles is just as important as care of the horse itself. Ill-fitting, dirty or worn tack is not only unpleasant and uncomfortable for the horse; it can also be extremely dangerous for the rider. Therefore always keep tack clean and check it regularly for wear. With saddles this applies particularly to girths and stirrup leathers – a badly-worn girth is a potential killer. Bits should never be allowed to become worn and rough.

All tack should be stored in a cool, dry place – a purpose-planned tack room is the best. A warm, damp atmosphere will cause

Above A half-completed wisp. The wisp is used after body brushing, when strapping a horse. It should be rubbed vigorously over the muscular areas, avoiding the head and sensitive parts. Wisping stimulates circulation, gives a form of massage and shines the coat. The wisp is used damp and brought down with a bang in the direction of the lay of the coat.

A wisp is made from soft hay, dampened slightly and then twisted round a core of twine to form a rope about 2m (7ft) long. This is formed into a firm, fist-sized pad by making two loops and weaving the rest of the rope through them as shown above in loose form. A properly made wisp should be hard and firm and no larger than can conveniently be grasped in the hand.

Clipping is done chiefly for comfort, as the thicker winter coat grown during the autumn can lead to heavy sweating during exercise. Removing all, or part, of it prevents this, lessens the chance of a horse getting chilled and makes it easier to groom. The trace clip (top right) is the minimum clip, removing hair only from the chest, belly, upper legs, elbows and up the back of the quarters. It keeps the protective warmth of the coat, while preventing heavy sweating. The blanket clip (centre) is slightly cooler, leaving a blanket-shaped area of body hair and all the leg hair on for warmth. In the hunter clip (bottom) all the coat is clipped, leaving only the leg hair as protection from thorns and scratches. Sometimes a saddle patch is left. This prevents the saddle rubbing and increases the comfort of horse and rider.

Pulling a mane or tail is done mainly for smartness. Pulling a mane thins it, makes it lie flat and evens the edge. Tail pulling slims the tail by removing short hairs from the top. Grass-kept horses, however, need the protection of a natural, thick tail to keep themselves free from flies, which can be very troublesome in the summer.

Trace clip

Blanket clip

Hunter clip

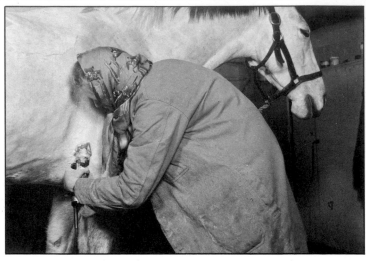

Above Clipping the horse is a lengthy and delicate operation, care should be taken not to upset the animal. The coat should first be dry and well-groomed.

Right Pulling the mane. Remove the longer under-hairs, starting from the withers and working towards the head. It is best done when the horse is warm after exercise. Lift the top hairs clear with a comb, then wind a few strands around the fingers – and pluck them out.

leather to crack, break or develop mould. Similarly, metal parts will tarnish or rust. Always hang bridles up on a bridle rack; saddles should be placed over a saddle horse, or on a wide padded bracket screwed firmly to the wall.

Tack should be cleaned daily; at the very least, sweat marks should be removed and the bit thoroughly cleaned. The equipment needed is as follows: a rough towel or large sponge for washing; a small, flat sponge; a chamois leather; saddle soap; metal polish or wool; a couple of soft cloths; a dandy brush; a nail, to clean curb hooks; a bucket; hanging hooks for bridle, girths and leathers; a saddle horse; and a vegetable oil.

When cleaning the saddle, place it on the saddle horse and remove all fittings, such as girths and stirrup leathers. These should be cleaned separately. Wash the leatherwork with lukewarm water to remove dirt, dried sweat and grease – but take care not to get the saddle saturated. If the lining is of leather, it can also be washed. Otherwise scrub it down dry with a dandy brush.

With the chamois leather slightly dam-pened, dry the saddle off. Apply saddle soap liberally with the damp sponge, working it well into the saddle to get the soap into the leather without creating a lather. Allow some time for the leather to absorb the soap. Then rub over with a moist sponge and, finally, wipe down with the chamois leather. Clean the leather pieces that have been removed with saddle soap, and the metal ones with metal polish. Clean out the holes of stirrup leathers with a match or a nail. Leather girths should be oiled on the inside. Web string and nylon ones should be brushed down with a dandy brush and washed occasionally, using pure soap. Then, reassemble.

As a preliminary to cleaning, it is a good idea to take the bridle to pieces so that the stitching can be thoroughly checked for wear. Reassemble, and, starting with the bit, wash with lukewarm water. Dry, soap the leather and polish the metal in the same way as the saddle. If the leather needs oiling, take the bridle apart once cleaning has been com-pleted. Oil each piece individually. Then fit the parts together again, taking care that the bit is in the correct position.

Bridles and bits

All commonly-used bridles have the same purpose – to hold the bit in the mouth. It is through use of this, in conjunction with seat and legs, that the horse is guided and control-led. There are two main types of bridle – the snaffle bridle, with one bit, and the double bridle, with two. The latter has two bits and two sets of reins.

All modern bits are based on one of two principles – either the snaffle or the curb. The snaffle is a mild bit. It consists of a metal bar, either jointed or plain, with a ring at either end to which the rein and headpiece of the bridle are attached. Pressure on the bit via the rein causes it to act on the corners of the horse's mouth, with a nutcracker action if the bit is jointed.

The curb is also of metal; it may have a hump, called a port, in the middle. It is fitted with shanks at either end, the cheekpieces being attached to the top of the shanks and the rein to rings at the bottom. The shanks are linked by a chain which lies in the chin groove.

Pressure on the rein has a leverage effect –

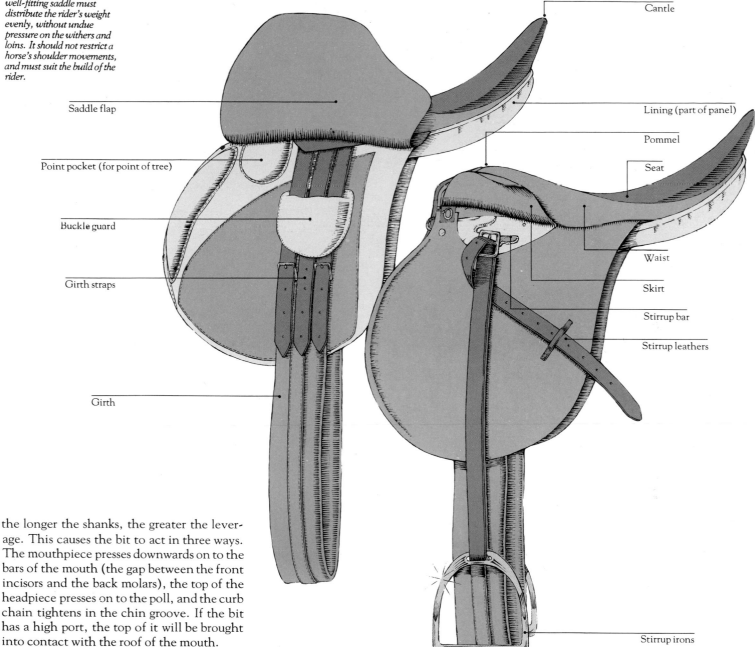

Cantle

Saddle flap

Lining (part of panel)

Pommel

Point pocket (for point of tree)

Seat

Buckle guard

Waist

Skirt

Girth straps

Stirrup bar

Stirrup leathers

Girth

Stirrup irons

the longer the shanks, the greater the leverage. This causes the bit to act in three ways. The mouthpiece presses downwards on to the bars of the mouth (the gap between the front incisors and the back molars), the top of the headpiece presses on to the poll, and the curb chain tightens in the chin groove. If the bit has a high port, the top of it will be brought into contact with the roof of the mouth.

There are many variations of these two basic types of bit. The double bridle, for example, uses a jointed snaffle bit (a bridoon) in combination with an English curb — a curb fitted with short, straight shanks and a lip-strap to keep the curb chain in the correct position. Always use the mildest bit possible. A severe bit often produces exactly the opposite result to the one intended, as the horse can easily become upset, excitable and harder to control. Above all, avoid using the bit insensitively, as this will only lead to the horse developing a hard mouth. Signs of this are the corners of the mouth and the tongue becoming calloused through constant pressure from the bit. If this happens, remedial action should be taken immediatley.

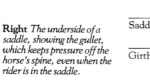

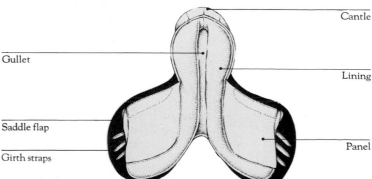

Right *The underside of a saddle, showing the gullet, which keeps pressure off the horse's spine, even when the rider is in the saddle.*

Cantle

Gullet

Lining

Saddle flap

Girth straps

Panel

Selecting a saddle

As with bridles and bits, there are various types of saddle – some designed for a particular task, or, as in the case of the Western saddle, a specific style of riding. The most important thing to remember is that the saddle must fit the horse properly. An ill-fitting saddle will make the horse and rider very sore; and it will also make it impossible for the rider to position himself correctly.

The framework of the saddle is called the tree and determines the final shape, so it must be correctly made. Many riding associations, such as the Pony Club, have their own approved patterns and it is always safest to look for one of these. The commonest form in use today is the 'spring tree' – so-called because it has two pieces of light steel let into it under the seat to increase resilience. Treat the tree with care. If a saddle is dropped the tree may break. The saddle cannot then be used until it is professionally repaired.

The rest of the saddle consists of layers of webbing, canvas, serge, and finally, leather. The padded part, which rests on the horse's back, is usually made of felt or stuffed with wool. It is important that this padding is arranged so that the rider's weight is distributed evenly over the back and carried on the fleshy part rather than the spine. This helps to preserve the horse's strength and stamina and prevents sores from developing. If additional protection is necessary, a pad – known as a numnah – can be placed beneath the saddle.

Girths keep the saddle in place, so they must be strong. They should be inspected

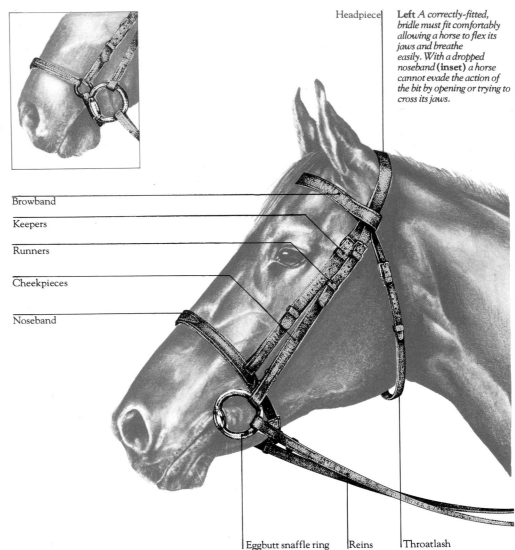

Headpiece

Browband

Keepers

Runners

Cheekpieces

Noseband

Eggbutt snaffle ring   Reins   Throatlash

Left A correctly-fitted, bridle must fit comfortably allowing a horse to flex its jaws and breathe easily. With a dropped noseband **(inset)** a horse cannot evade the action of the bit by opening or trying to cross its jaws.

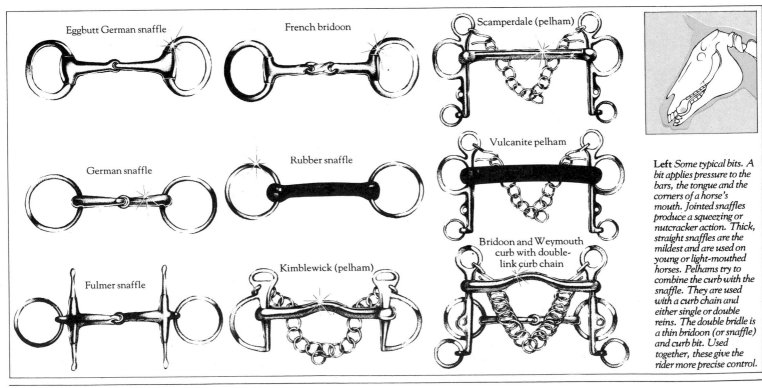

Eggbutt German snaffle

French bridoon

Scamperdale (pelham)

German snaffle

Rubber snaffle

Vulcanite pelham

Fulmer snaffle

Kimblewick (pelham)

Bridoon and Weymouth curb with double-link curb chain

Left Some typical bits. A bit applies pressure to the bars, the tongue and the corners of a horse's mouth. Jointed snaffles produce a squeezing or nutcracker action. Thick, straight snaffles are the mildest and are used on young or light-mouthed horses. Pelhams try to combine the curb with the snaffle. They are used with a curb chain and either single or double reins. The double bridle is a thin bridoon (or snaffle) and curb bit. Used together, these give the rider more precise control.

A double bridle is mainly used by experienced riders on well-trained horses in shows or for dressage. It is not for the novice.

The headcollar should fit comfortably, and be made of strong leather. It is used for leading a horse or tying it up.

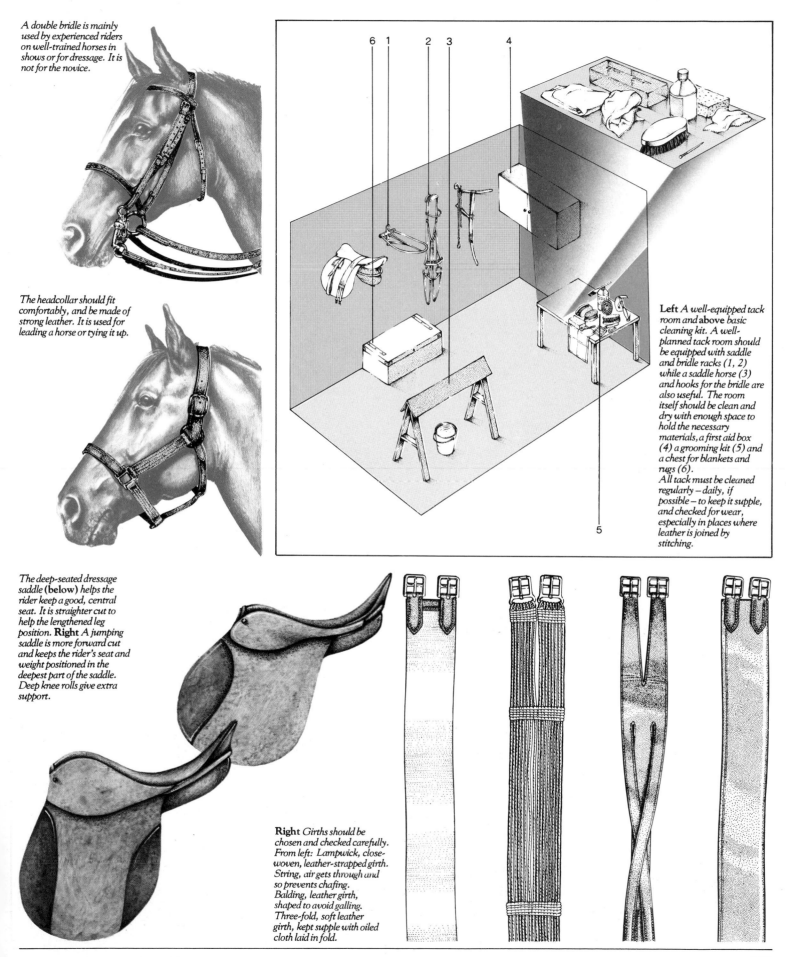

6 1 2 3 4

Left A well-equipped tack room and **above** basic cleaning kit. A well-planned tack room should be equipped with saddle and bridle racks (1, 2) while a saddle horse (3) and hooks for the bridle are also useful. The room itself should be clean and dry with enough space to hold the necessary materials, a first aid box (4) a grooming kit (5) and a chest for blankets and rugs (6).
All tack must be cleaned regularly – daily, if possible – to keep it supple, and checked for wear, especially in places where leather is joined by stitching.

5

The deep-seated dressage saddle (**below**) helps the rider keep a good, central seat. It is straighter cut to help the lengthened leg position. **Right** A jumping saddle is more forward cut and keeps the rider's seat and weight positioned in the deepest part of the saddle. Deep knee rolls give extra support.

Right Girths should be chosen and checked carefully. From left: Lampwick, close-woven, leather-strapped girth. String, air gets through and so prevents chafing. Balding, leather girth, shaped to avoid galling. Three-fold, soft leather girth, kept supple with oiled cloth laid in fold.

Top *New Zealand rug, an outdoor rug of waterproof canvas partly lined with wool, with straps* (inset) *to keep it in place.* Left centre, *woollen day rug, bound with braid, worn for warmth in stable during day or for travelling.* Right centre, *sweat sheet, open cotton mesh, used to cool an overheated horse, or under a night rug if horse sweats.* Below right *Wool-lined night rug, of hemp or jute, for warmth at night in stable.* Below left *Woollen blankets worn under day or night rugs for extra warmth are put well forward on neck and clear of tail. Any surplus is folded back over rug.*

regularly for wear. They can be made of leather, webbing, or nylon string – in the case of webbing, two girths should be used for additional safety. Stirrup irons, too, should always be chosen with safety foremost in mind. Safety irons, often used by children, are specifically designed so that the foot will come free in a fall. Adults should always check that there is 12mm (½in) clearance on either side of the foot, measured at the widest place of the boot or shoe, so that it does not become jammed.

Horse clothing

Many different types of clothing have been developed to keep the horse warm, protect it from injury, or give its limbs added support. Chief amongst these are rugs and bandages.

Rugs are especially useful as protection after a horse has been clipped, but special types are used for other purposes as well. In all cases, it is vital that the blanket should fit properly and be securely fastened. A roller must be used to keep a night rug in place.

Bandages fall into three categories. Tail bandages are used to make the top of the tail look neat and to protect it during a journey. Stable bandages, covering the area from the knee right down is underneath the fetlock, keep the legs warm, and, similarly, are used as protection during travelling. Exercise bandages, support the back tendons and protect the legs from thorns.

Clipping

Horses are clipped to maintain comfort and, less importantly, for smartness. Removing all

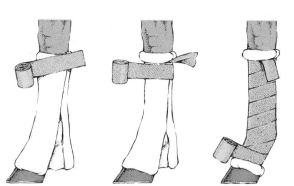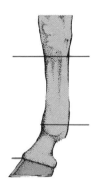

Right Four stages in fitting a stable bandage. Pad beneath all bandages with cotton wool or an equivalent. Wool stable bandages are rolled evenly down from below the knee or hock to the coronet, then upwards to the start and tied on side of leg. Far right Placing of crêpe exercise or pressure bandage to support back tendons and protect the leg. These bandages are applied firmly and often stitched in place for greater security.

or part of the coat by clipping prevents heavy sweating during exercise in winter and therefore lessens the risk of a horse catching a chill. It also enables the horse to dry off more quickly.

There are various types of clip; choice should depend on what the horse is expected to do, and how much it sweats doing it. Remember that a clipped horse will need to wear rugs for warmth during cold weather, if it is kept in either a stable or a field.

Health and the horse

Horses are tough creatures, but, like any animal, they can fall ill or be injured. A healthy pony or horse is alert, bright eyed, and takes a keen interest in all that goes on around it. Ribs and hip bones should not be prominent, and the quarters should be well-rounded. The animal should stand square on all four legs. The base of the ears should be warm to the touch.

Signs of illness vary, but there are some general symptoms which can give warning of trouble to come. A field-kept pony which stays for a long time in one place, a horse which goes off its food, a willing horse which suddenly becomes 'nappy' – all these signs are indications that something is wrong. Other symptoms include: discharge from the eyes or nostrils; stumbling for no apparent reason; restlessness; dullness of eye or general lack of interest; sweating; kicking or biting at the flank; lameness; diarrhoea; persistent rubbing of the neck or quarters against a wall or fence; apparent difficulty in breathing; coughing.

It is essential, therefore, to have a reliable vet, and, if ever in any doubt, to call him without hesitation. Better to pay for a visit than to run the risk of mistaken self-diagnosis leading to a more serious illness, or even death. Nevertheless, all horse owners should have a practical knowledge of first aid, and a first aid kit is an essential part of any stable.

Brushing boots of felt or leather, and rubber over-reach boots, are often worn for protection in training and eventing, or when a horse moves too closely in front (top left), so knocking one leg with the other, or hits the heel of its forefoot with toe of hind foot (top right).

Fitting a stockinette tail bandage. Dampen hair with water brush. Unroll short length of dry bandage and place this beneath tail, close to dock.

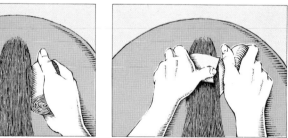

Holding the end of the bandage against the tail, make one turn to secure the bandage. Then continue the bandaging evenly downwards.

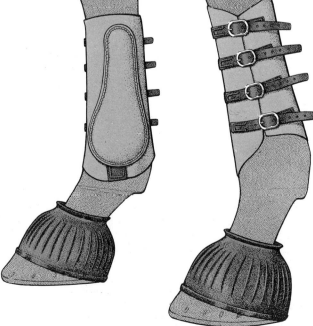

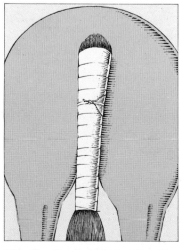

The tail bandage should stop just short of the last tail bone and the remaining length should be bandaged upwards and secured with tapes.

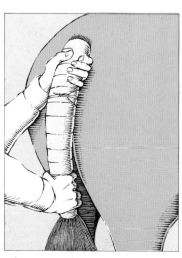

Finally bend the tail into a comfortable position. Tail bandages should not be left overnight. Slide them off, downwards, with both hands.

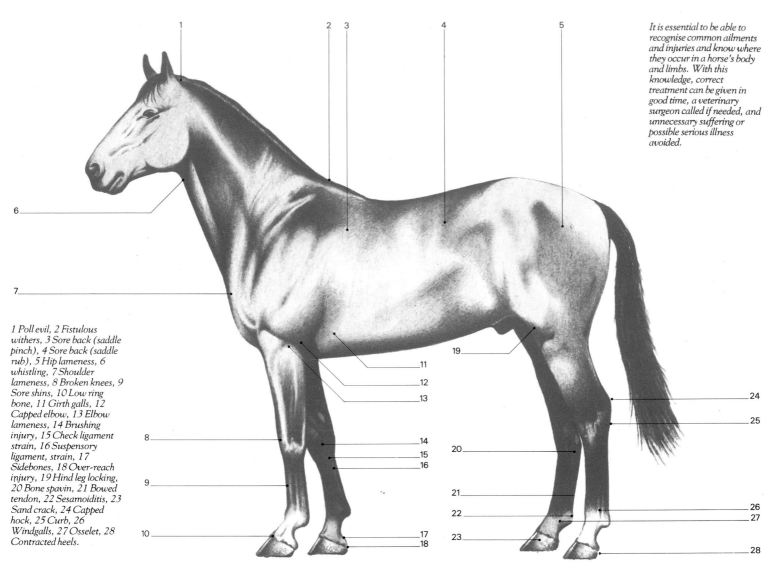

1 Poll evil, 2 Fistulous withers, 3 Sore back (saddle pinch), 4 Sore back (saddle rub), 5 Hip lameness, 6 whistling, 7 Shoulder lameness, 8 Broken knees, 9 Sore shins, 10 Low ring bone, 11 Girth galls, 12 Capped elbow, 13 Elbow lameness, 14 Brushing injury, 15 Check ligament strain, 16 Suspensory ligament, strain, 17 Sidebones, 18 Over-reach injury, 19 Hind leg locking, 20 Bone spavin, 21 Bowed tendon, 22 Sesamoiditis, 23 Sand crack, 24 Capped hock, 25 Curb, 26 Windgalls, 27 Osselet, 28 Contracted heels.

It should be placed where it can be easily found in an emergency.

Lameness

Lameness is the commonest form of disability in the horse. Treating most forms of it is usually best left to an expert.

To find the source of the lameness, first establish which leg is causing the pain. Do this by having the horse led at a slow trot – downhill, if possible. If one of the forelegs is lame, the horse will nod its head as the other leg touches the ground. Similarly, if the hind legs are involved, the horse's weight will fall on the sound leg. Next, feel for heat, pain and swelling. Start with the foot, as 90 per cent of all lameness is centred there.

Causes of lameness can range from a simple stone in the foot to actual disease. Consult the chart for details and possible treatment. The most serious disease is laminitis (founder), when prompt veterinary attention is essential to avoid the risk of permanent injury to the horse. This is one of the most painful conditions from which the horse can suffer.

Wounds and other injuries

Wounds and injuries are another common problem. Puncture cuts, caused by thorns, say, can easily occur during exercise. This is one of the reasons why exercise bandages should always be worn. Always call the vet if the wound looks deep, or if you think stitching is required.

First bring the bleeding under control. Small cuts should cease bleeding on their own within 20 minutes, but, if the cut is serious or bleeding does not stop, apply a pressure bandage. Clip the hair from the skin around the wound and clean it thoroughly. Gently trickle cold water over it from a hose pipe, or wash the area with saline solution. Then coat with an anti-biotic powder and dress, if possible. Do not bandage too tightly; a tight bandage will cause pain if swelling occurs. Keep the wound clean and check.

The most serious of all infections is tetanus, caused by bacteria in the soil penetrating the skin through the wound. All horses should be immunized against the disease by an initial course of injections, followed by regular 'boosters'. If in any doubt, it is best to

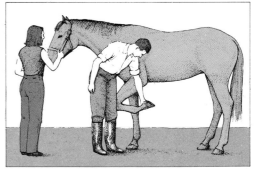

Above Lifting a front foot helps keep the horse still during examination.

Below Kicking is unlikely, when handling hind legs, if tail is held firmly down.

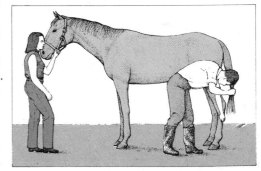

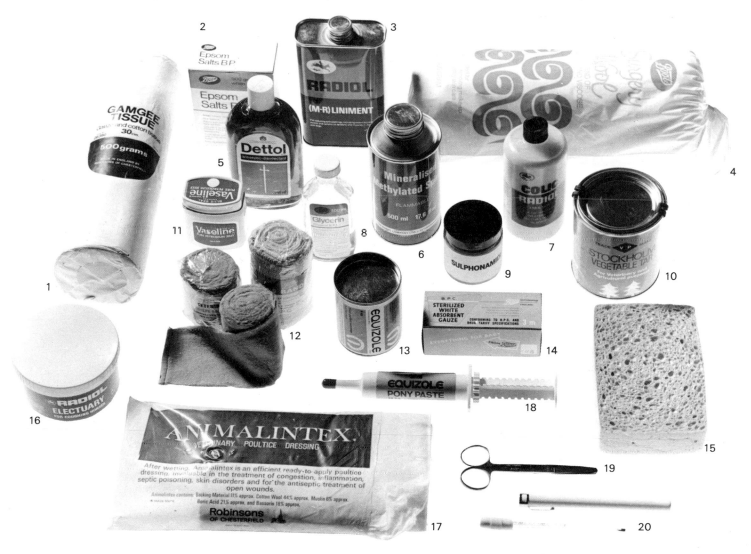

Every stable should have a medicine chest stocked with a first aid kit and medicines for everyday ailments. It should be conveniently

placed and kept clean and tidy. Clear identification of the kit and contents is essential. **Above** A typical basic kit containing:

1 Gamgee tissue, 2 Epsom salts, 3 Liniment, 4 Roll of cotton wool, 5 Antiseptic, 6 Methylated spirit, 7 Specific for colic, 8 Glycerine, 9

Sulphonamide powder, 10 Stockholm tar, 11 Petroleum jelly, 12 Assorted bandages, 13 Worming remedy, 14 Sterilized gauze,

15 Sponge, 16 Coughing electuary, 17 Ready-to-apply poultice, 18 Worm paste in dispenser, 19 Round-ended surgical

scissors, 20 Thermometer. Substitutions can be made to this selection. Opinions vary as to the amount of equipment needed.

have the horse immunized again. The injections cannot kill – tetanus will, unless treatment is administered speedily.

Other injuries are normally the result of falls, kicks, or irritations – the latter frequently the result of ill-fitting tack. Mouth injuries should be treated with salt water washes. Do not use a bit until the mouth has healed and check that this was not the initial cause of the injury. Girth galls and saddle sores should both be treated with fomentations. After they have healed, harden the affected areas with salt water or methylated spirit. Do not ride the horse with a saddle until the sore has completely healed.

Broken or cut knees can happen as the result of a fall. If the injury is more than skin deep, the vet should be called. Otherwise treat with cold water, as with a cut, and then

apply a soothing poultice. Carefully tie a figure of eight bandage.

Capped knees and hocks are usually the result of kicks or a blow. Treat the first with a rest, massage and a pressure bandage. The treatment for the second is cold water, and then a poultice. If any swelling persists, blister the area of the injury mildly.

Skin diseases
Like humans, horses can easily catch skin diseases, particularly in unhygienic conditions. Lice, for example, are a constant pest to a long-coated, field-kept horse, particularly in February. Other skin diseases include ringworm; sweet itch; mud fever; cracked heels; pustular dermititis (acne); warbles; and nettle rash. For their treatment, see the chart. Many of these diseases are highly con-

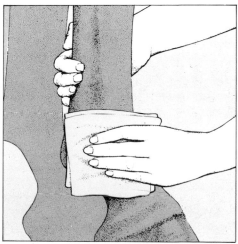

Above Direct pressure is applied to stop persistent bleeding from a vein. A folded handkerchief should always be carried, as this can serve as a pad.

Ailment and injury chart

Feet

Symptoms:	Causes:	Treatment:
Bruised sole		
Lameness. Horse may ease the weight of the foot when at rest	Bruising by stones or rough going and hard ground	Rest. If necessary, new shoes. Keep farrier informed
Corns		
Lameness. Heat in foot. Horse more lame on turn than straight	Ill fitting shoe causing pinching. Shoe which has moved in. Bruising	Call blacksmith or vet to cut out corn and advise further treatment
Laminitis (Founder)		
Obvious pain in the feet. Horse is reluctant to move and stands with its front feet pushed forward and its hind legs under it so that its weight is taken on the heels. May shift weight from one foot to another. Possibly a high temperature. Always apparent in front feet first but may affect all four feet	Over feeding and not enough exercise. Grass-fed horses are especially prone to the disease after eating excessive amounts of new spring grass. The feet become engorged with blood and the sensitive laminae in the hoof become inflamed and may separate	Call vet at once as prompt treatment can help the condition considerably. In the meantime cool the feet in running water from a hosepipe and try to get the horse to walk, as exercise helps the feet to drain. Remove from grass and give light starvation diet
Nail blind		
Lameness soon after the horse has been shod	Shoe nail driven home too close to the sensitive areas of the foot	Call blacksmith, who will remove nail and replace it correctly
Navicular disease		
Intermittent lameness, usually slight, followed by pointing, in which one forefoot is rested in front of the other on the toe. Gradual increase in tendency to stumble. Later, foot will contract at the heels	May be hereditary. Otherwise probably due to jarring of the foot through excessive roadwork or strain in hunting and jumping. This brings on lesions on the navicular bone	Consult vet
Overreach		
Cuts and bruises to bulbs of heel	Toe of hind shoe hitting front heel	Bathe wound in salt solution. Call vet if wound is severe. Prevention is better than cure – horse should be fitted with overreach boots
Pedal ostitis		
Intermittent lameness, later permanent	Severe jarring, brought on by too much roadwork or by jumping when the ground is very hard. This leads to inflammation of the pedal bone and bony growths on the bone	Rest. Bathing foot in cold water. Special shoeing may help
Quittor		
Lameness. Infection breaking out around coronary band	Infection in the hoof working its way upwards to form abscess	Consult vet
Sandcrack		
Crack or split in the wall of the hoof, extending upwards into coronary band	Mineral deficiency which makes hoof unusually brittle	Consult blacksmith who may fit special clips to hold edges of crack together, or put on special shoes
Seedy toe		
Revealed when trimming the hoof during shoeing. The outside of the hoof wall appears normal but a cavity is revealed when the horn is pared away	A legacy of laminitis. Tight shoes may also be a cause	Call blacksmith who will pare away the damaged horn. Then treat liberally with Stockholm tar

Legs

Symptoms:	Causes:	Treatment:
Bog spavin		
Swelling in the front of the hock and on both sides at the back	Excess fluid in hock joint	None. Bog spavins look unsightly but cause no trouble
Brushing		
Sudden acute lameness. Injury around the fetlock joint	One leg striking against the other	Rest and hosing the affected part with cold water. Prevent recurrence by fitting brushing boots. Consult blacksmith
Capped elbow		
Swelling on the point of the elbow, level with chest. If infected, horse may be lame	Persistent irritation or rubbing of the elbow when lying down or because bed is too thin	Cold poultice the swelling and call vet if infected. special shoeing and provide thicker bed
Capped hock		
Similar swelling to capped elbow, but this time on hock. It is usually permanent but rarely painful	Knock or kick on affected area	None. Cold poulticing sometimes helps to reduce swelling
Cracked heels		
Sore patches, often suppurating, and deep cracks on the heels at the back of the pastern	An irritant in the soil which affects the heels and legs after they have been covered in mud. White legs are more prone to the condition	Apply ointment, using one with a cod liver oil or zinc oxide base. Alternatively, dry poultice with dry warm bran, and bandaging
Curb		
Lameness. Outward bowing of line from point of hock to cannon bone	Sprain to ligament connecting point of hock with cannon bone	Rest. Cold poulticing application of liniment
Ringbone		
Lameness. Swelling of pastern	Blow, sprain or jarring which causes extra bone to form on first or second pastern bones or both	Rest. Seek professional advice and be prepared for pony to be permanently lame
Speedy cutting		
Sudden fall or lameness. Cuts or bruises just below knee	One leg interfering with another	Rest. Bathe affected part with cold water
Splints		
Lameness. Heat and swelling in affected leg	Formation of bone between the splint and cannon	Rest. Cold water poultices. Once splint has formed, lameness disappears, leaving a permanent lump
Sprained joints and tendons		
Heat and swelling. Lameness in some cases	Jarring. Twisting of joint. Inflammation of the tendon	Cold water dowsing. For tendons, pressure bandages. Rest
Sprung tendon		
Bowed tendon	Sprain to the tendon	None. This is an indication of a former sprain
Thoroughpin		
Swelling just above the hock which can usually be pushed from one side to the other	Strain	Pressure bandage to reduce swelling. Keep soft by massage or by applying goose grease

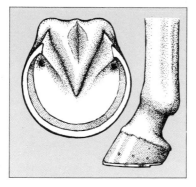

Above *Corns (bruises) occur on sole in angle of wall and bar. After treatment, seated shoes* (**inset**) *relieve pressure.*

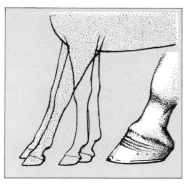

Above *Laminitis, inflammation of inner hoof wall, causes this stance. It can lead to ridging on hoof* (**inset**)*.*

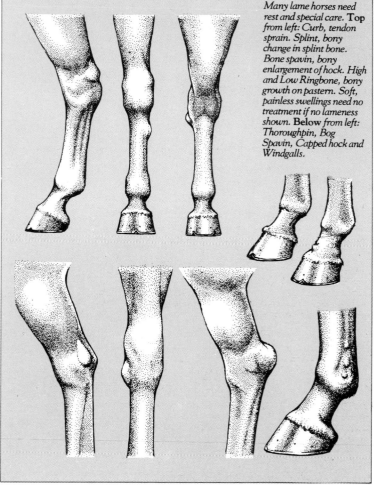

Many lame horses need rest and special care. **Top** *from left: Curb, tendon sprain. Splint, bony change in splint bone. Bone spavin, bony enlargement of hock. High and Low Ringbone, bony growth on pastern. Soft, painless swellings need no treatment if no lameness shown.* **Below** *from left: Thoroughpin, Bog Spavin, Capped hock and Windgalls.*

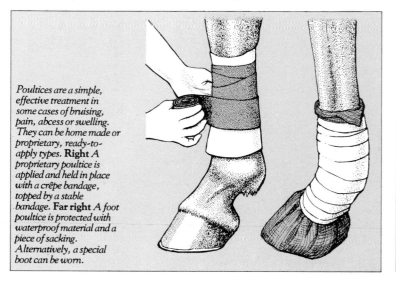

Poultices are a simple, effective treatment in some cases of bruising, pain, abcess or swelling. They can be home made or proprietary, ready-to-apply types. **Right** *A proprietary poultice is applied and held in place with a crêpe bandage, topped by a stable bandage.* **Far right** *A foot poultice is protected with waterproof material and a piece of sacking. Alternatively, a special boot can be worn.*

tagious – ringworm, for instance, can be transmitted to humans, as well as horses, in certain cases. Therefore, always observe strict sanitary precautions in the stable.

Chills, coughs and chest diseases
Refusing food, discharge from nostrils and eyes, listlessness, coughing and high temperature are all indications of a chill. Keep the horse warm and consult the vet, who will probably prescribe antibiotics in severe cases.

Coughs, too, should always be treated by the vet if they are persistent. Causes can vary from simple irritation, the result of feeding with dusty hay, to severe diseases, such as epidemic cough and strangles. Other respiratory diseases include equine influenza; whistling; roaring; high blowing; and broken wind. For details, consult the chart.

If the horse is coughing, never work it hard. Rest and warmth are most important. Galloping a horse with a cough can, in extreme cases, lead to broken wind, which is incurable.

Digestive problems
Teeth and stomach can both give the horse problems. Both demand prompt attention if anything does go wrong.

Uneven wear on the teeth can lead to sharp edges developing. These make chewing food painful; in addition, the mouth and cheeks may get cut. The remedy is to have the teeth filed (rasped). This must be done by an expert.

Restlessness, sweating, biting and kicking at the flank, lying down and getting up again are all signs of colic – acute pain in the abdomen. Colic falls into three types. These are spasmodic colic, so-called because the pain comes in spasms; flatulent colic, caused by a gas build-up because of a blockage in the bowel; and twisted gut, where the bowel itself, or the membrane supporting it, becomes twisted, so cutting off the blood

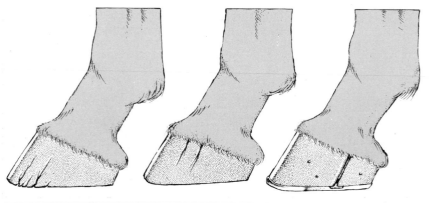

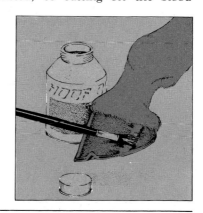

*Hoofs of unshod horses at grass can become cracked if they are neglected. Grass cracks (**far left**) split up from base of wall. They grow out if the hoof is treated appropriately by the farrier. Sand cracks (**centre left**) split down from the hoof head. These are much more serious and need veterinary care. After treatment, they can be controlled with seated shoes (**left**), which take the pressure off the crack. Hoof cream and hoof oil (**right**) applied daily, help prevent cracks by keeping hoof healthy.*

Strangles

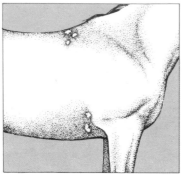
Saddle sores and girth galls

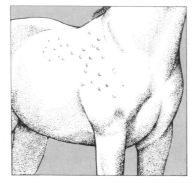
Ringworm

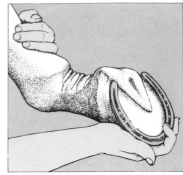
Cracked heels

Head

Symptoms:	Causes:	Treatment:	Symptoms:	Causes:	Treatment:
Blocked tear duct			**Colds and Coughs**		
Tears running down face	Sand, grit or mucous causing blockage of tear ducts	Call vet, who will probably clear blockage by using a catheter to force sterile liquid through the duct	Thin discharge from nostrils; coughing	Infection; sometimes dusty hay or allergy	Isolate animal and keep warm; give regular doses of cough medicine. Consult vet
Broken wind			**Influenza**		
Persistent cough, rapid exhaustion, double movement of flank	Breakdown of air vessels in the lung from overworking the horse	Incurable, may be alleviated by keeping horse out, work gently and dampen food	Lethargy, cough, high temperature. Horse refuses food	Virus infection	Isolate. Keep warm. Rest. Call vet. Prevention by inoculation is possible
Catarrh			**Strangles**		
Thick yellowish discharge from the nostrils	Inflammation of mucous membrane May be cold infection preceding cough or allergy, beware of infecting other horses	Clean nostrils with warm boracic solution and smear with petroleum jelly In summer, turn out to grass	Similar to those of influenza, plus swelling of lymph glands under the jaw, which eventually form abscesses	Contact with infected animal or with contaminated grooming kit, feed buckets, etc	Isolate. Call vet. Feed hay and bran mashes and keep horse warm. Rest is essential

supply and causing severe pain.

All forms of colic are exceptionally painful, as the horse is incapable of vomiting to obtain relief

Colic must be treated quickly, as real suffering is being caused. As long as the horse is not completely exhausted, lead it around gently and, if at all possible, prevent it from lying down. If the animal lies down and rolls, it may well injure itself. Keep the horse warm and the box or stall well bedded.

Treatment varies according to the type of colic involved, but, if no improvement occurs after an hour or if the pain is obviously severe, call a vet immediately. For spasms, give a colic drink (one should be kept ready made-up in the first aid kit) and for wind administer a laxative to open the bowels. A half to a pint of linseed oil, depending on the size of the horse involved, is a standard re-

medy. Linseed oil, too, is good in cases of constipation.

Constipation and diarrhoea present fewer problems, but worms – parasites present in all horses – can be a menace if not strictly controlled. They present particular problems to the owners of field-kept horses; here, prevention is better than cure (see p. 142). All horses, however, should be regularly wormed, by treating with a deworming medicine, as part of stable routing. Consult the vet as to the best dosage.

Azoturia is not strictly a digestive disease, but it is closely connected with correct feeding. It can occur when a horse is worked hard after being rested on a full working diet, though the exact cause of the disease is unknown. The first signs are slackening of pace and stiffness of muscles, particularly in the quarters. If the horse is urged on it will

eventually stagger, come to a halt and may even collapse. Always arrange for it to be transported back to the stable – never try to ride home. The vet must be called.

Treatment is rest, warmth, massage, plenty of water and a laxative diet. However, once infected, it is likely that the disease will reoccur. Therefore, always reduce the feed according to the amount of work actually being done by the horse.

Nursing the horse

Like all animals, horses take time to recover form illness. The vet will always instruct the owner in what to do, but, largely, successful nursing is merely a matter of common sense.

Giving medicine, for example, can present problems. The simplest way is in the feed, provided that the medicine is suitable and the horse is eating. Soluble medicines can be

Digestive system

Symptoms:	Causes:	Treatment:	Symptoms:	Causes:	Treatment:
Colic			**Diarrhoea**		
Severe abdominal pain, characterised by pawing of the ground, restlessness, sweating, rolling, lying down and getting up, kicking, biting and looking at the stomach, groaning, cold ears	Poor or irregular feeding, wrong sort of food, exercise or drinking straight after food, too much food when horse is tired. Worm infection	Call vet immediately. meanwhile do what you can to relieve the pain. Keep horse warm, apply hot water bottle to belly. Try to discourage horse from lying down or rolling	Very loose, watery droppings	Excessive fresh grass. Worms	Mix dry bran with food or add kaolin. Feed with hay. If persistant, call vet
			Worms		
			Loss of condition, in spite of careful feeding	There are several types of intestinal parasites collectively known as worms	Regular doses of worming powder or paste, coupled with regular maintenance of pasture

Skin and coat

Symptoms:	Causes:	Treatment:	Symptoms:	Causes:	Treatment:
Heat bumps (Humor)			**Sweet itch**		
Various forms of size and shape. Rarely seen all over horse	Probably overheating from too much protein in system	Give bran mash with addition of two tablespoons of Epsom salts.	Extreme itchiness of areas around mane and tail, apparent only in late spring, summer and early autumn	Unknown, probably an allergy	Apply calamine lotion to relieve itching. Keep mane and tail clean. Lard and sulphur applied to the area can be soothing. Consult vet
Lice			**Warbles**		
Itching, dull coat, appearance of small grey or black parasites on the coat	Unknown. Appears in spring on grass-fed horses or on animals which have been in poor condition and are now improving	Dust affected areas liberally with delousing powder, obtainable from vet. Keep grooming kit separate	Maggot of the warble fly	Painful swelling on back	Bathe in warm water which will keep the lump soft and help to 'draw' the warble from a small hole on the top of the swelling. The maggot can be gently squeezed out, but do not do this before consulting the vet
Ringworm					
Usually circular bare patches on the skin of varying sizes which may or may not be itchy	Fungus infection which is highly contagious	Apply tincture of iodine to affected parts. Disinfect rugs and sterilise grooming kit. Keep horse isolated			

Left A healthy horse is alert and attentive, taking a keen interest in its surroundings. It carries its head high, ears pricked, eyes bright and wide open. Its coat is smooth and glossy.

Lack of work and boredom can cause severe stable vices like crib-biting (below) and weaving (right).

mixed in with the drinking water. Otherwise the vet will advise.

The golden rules of nursing are gentleness, cleanliness, and the ability to ensure the horse's comfort and rest. When treating a wound always try to keep the dust down in the stable. Reduce concentrated foods for a horse suddenly thrown out of work by lameness and substitute a mild laxative instead. Gentle sponging of eyes and nostrils will help refresh a horse with a raised temperature.

Care when old

Horses and ponies are frequently remarkably long lived. Some ponies, for instance, are still leading useful lives at thirty, but caring for an elderly horse presents its own set of problems.

Teeth must be regularly filed (rasped), as the molars will probably become long and sharp if left untreated. Select the diet carefully; boiled barley, broad bran, chaff and good quality hay form the best mixture for an old horse.

Eventually though, some horses just lose interest in life. If the lustre goes out of the eyes or the appetite wanes for no apparent reason, it is then kinder to have the horse put down. A vet will arrange this. A humane killer is used, and death is instantaneous.

Chapter Ten

The horse in leisure and sport

Riding is fast becoming one of the most popular leisure sports in the world. In the UK alone, more than 250,000 people of all ages ride each week; in other countries, the figure is even higher.

Riding for leisure falls into two main categories. Many people ride solely for enjoyment, with little thought for sports or competitions. There is little more exhilarating, say, than riding out for a good hack across country. Secondly, there are organized activities, such as hunting, show jumping, and eventing, with which this chapter is chiefly concerned. Some of these are now becoming more and more professional, but the basic theme is still enjoyment – whether at a local gymkhana or at an international event.

Leaving the formality of the riding school for an hour or so's riding around the roads or across country is usually the rider's first real test of responsibility. The rules are few and simple, and can be summed up in the two words consideration and safety. Remember that traffic regulations, for example, apply just as much to riders as to other road users; it is extremely dangerous, say, for a ride of a dozen horses to be allowed to straggle across a road. On a winter afternoon, wear something light – a luminous armband is ideal – so that you will be easily visible when riding back in the twilight. A light, attached to the stirrup iron, is also a good idea.

As far as actual riding is concerned, remember the lessons of the school. Always show consideration and courtesy to pedestrians and keep to authorized bridle paths and riding tracks, if they are marked. Above all, never ride at speed near animals or people; if they are frightened, they may well inadvertantly frighten your horse.

As far as children and teenagers up to the age of twenty are concerned, many of these lessons are part of the basic teaching of the Pony Club – a world-wide organization which attracts many young riders. Originally found-

Right A group of children clean tack at Pony Club camp and **inset** *four typical scenes of riding activity, ranging from a lesson to an outdoor hack. The Pony Club is a world-wide organization with the aim of teaching horsemanship in all its aspects and, to this end,*

many activities, such as camps, working rallies, gymkhanas and technical lectures, are organized. Branches, too, have special activities according to geographical location; bush and trail rides, for instance, are both very popular in Australia and the USA.

ed in the UK in 1929, there are now branches all over the English-speaking world; Canada, Australia, New Zealand and the USA in particular have very strong memberships. The first US branch was formed in 1935, though this lapsed during the Second World War, and the Club was not refounded there until 1950; the first Australian branch was set up in 1947.

The object of the Club is to teach horsemastership in its broadest aspects. The teaching, done by qualified volunteers, is backed up by a system of optional examinations. In the UK and the USA, these tests range in difficulty from D to A – D being fairly simple and A being of a very high standard indeed. Australia follows the same system, with two extra tests — the K, for the active rider, and the H, for horsemastership.

The gymkhana — an import from India

Though the upper age limit for Pony Club membership is twenty, many adult riding clubs follow the same basic pattern. Adult riders, too, enjoy all the thrills and spills of the gymkhana just as much as their younger counterparts.

The word itself comes from gymnastics and the Hindustani *gend-khana* (sports ground); the idea of such mounted games was brought back to the UK by officers serving in India in the 19th century. From Britain, it spread throughout the horse world. There are many different events, ranging from simple jumping competitions to tests of agility and speed, such as Chase Me Charlie and bending races.

Both riders and mounts – ponies are usually

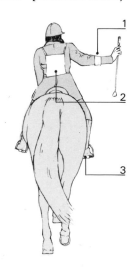

Right A rider wearing safety clothing clearly signals to traffic her intention of turning right (1). Safety first is the order of the day when riding on a road. Horses should never move two abreast unless an inexperienced young animal or rider needs escorting by a more experienced companion. The luminous back cloth (2) and stirrup light (3) are both vital in the twilight. **Left** *The usual method of transport over long distances is a horsebox. The interior is padded so that the horse cannot injure itself during a journey, but, in addition, knee caps, hock boots, travelling and tail bandages should be worn for protection.*

more successful than horses because of their greater manoeuvrability – have to be fit, though not as fit as they would have to be for a day's hunting, for instance. Grass-kept ponies and horses are quite capable of taking part in such events once a week, say, during the summer season without any ill effects.

Hunting

Another sport which appeals to many riders is hunting – the oldest surviving horseback sport. Originally the stag was the chief quarry – it still is in France – but, in English-speaking countries, fox hunting now has the largest following (though drag hunting is gaining in popularity). In all cases, the etiquette of hunting is the same, based as it is on traditions that date back for hundreds of years. The USA and Canada have some 140 hunts between them, though by far the greater number are in the US. Virginia has the highest individual total with twenty. Both there and in Australia, hunting follows the British model, though, in Australia, other animals, such as the wallaby, are sometimes hunted in place of foxes.

Permission to hunt has to be obtained in advance from either the Secretary or the Master of a pack. This can be either for a day, in which case a fee known as a 'cap' – so-called because it is usually collected on the spot in a hunting cap – is paid, or a subscription can be taken out for a season.

On arrival at the Meet, the first thing to do is to identify the various Hunt officers, whose instructions must be instantly obeyed during the day. The Master is in overall charge, assisted by a Field Master, whose task it is to control the hunt-followers. The Huntsman, in charge of the hounds, is similarly assisted by one or two Whippers-in, who chase up any stragglers in the pack and generally help keep the hounds under control.

Hounds work by scent and once this has been 'found' (discovered) in the covert, things can happen very quickly. The hounds will begin to 'speak' and then take up the scent. The field then follows, taking care not to overtake the Master and the pack.

It is best for inexperienced riders to stay near the back of the field until they gain in confidence, and, if possible, pick a more experienced member of the hunt to follow. However, whether inexperienced or experi-

enced, no rider should get carried away by excitement; a cool head is better than a hot one. Remember, too, that the excitement of the hunt affects the horses and they are only too willing to gallop on even when close to exhaustion. At the end of the day, therefore, care of the horse becomes the absolute priority, so that it can recover from its exertions as quickly as possible.

Hunter trials and point-to-points

Two activities closely connected with hunting are Hunter trials and point-to-points. The first is a kind of mini cross-country competition, in part judged against the clock. Riders race over a predetermined course of 1½ to 2 miles, jumping conventional fences. Other tests can include dealing with the sort of hazards commonly found in the hunting field – a gate to be opened and closed, say, or a slip rail to be removed and replaced.

Point-to-points, or hunt races, first started in the UK several centuries ago, but, unlike the gymkhana, they have not been universally adopted by the horse world. However the USA has a few, while Australia has its less

formal equivalent in the so-called picnic races of the Outback.

Eventing

Most equestrian sports developed from hunting, but eventing – one of the toughest all-round tests that any horse and rider can face – is a notable exception. Its roots lie in the battlefield rather than in the hunting field. The sport officially became part of the Olympics in 1912, but it is only since the Second World War that it has risen to its present immense popularity. Today, such nations as Australia, the UK, the USA, West Germany and the USSR are all world leaders in the sport.

To succeed in eventing, horse and rider must be proficient in all three of its disciplines – dressage, cross country, and show jumping. In one day events, all three stages are held on the same day; in the three day event, one day is allocated for each test. The standard set varies from novice upwards; at the very top, it is extremely demanding indeed. In addition, the competitors also have to face extra endurance tests over roads and tracks and a steeplechase course.

Some hold that the first phase – dressage – is the most important part of the event and that the standard of training demonstrated in it by horse and rider is the crux of the matter. The test lasts for seven and a half minutes and is ridden from memory. Though the standard set is not as high as in pure dressage competitions, the judges still look for correct carriage and obedience in the performance of the various movements. These include coming to the halt from the canter; half passes; extended trot; extended canter; and the counter canter.

It is unarguable that a good performance in the dressage arena, with the horse showing implicit obedience, gives a competitor a head start of his or her rivals. But, above all, champion riders are never less than superlative in the age-old art of riding across country. This test of speed and endurance is the key to success in the sport, as the competitors pit their wits and skills against the wiles of the cross-country course builder, negotiating up to thirty-five fences, many with difficult approaches.

The distance to be covered varies; at Olympic level, it is about 30k (18.6 miles).

In the Olympics, or competitions such as the world-famous Badminton Three Day Event, there are four phases – roads and tracks, steeplechase, roads and tracks again, and, finally, the cross-country itself.

On the roads and tracks stages, the horse must cover the ground at approximately 240m (262yd) a minute to keep up with the set time; this means that a very fast trot is necessary. The steeplechase, usually between 3k (2 miles) and 4k (2½ miles) long, has to be tackled at a good gallop; again to avoid time penalties, the horse must average nearly 40kph (25mph). After the second road and track phase, there is a compulsory ten-minute rest period before competitors start the cross country.

In the cross country, the course builder takes full advantage of the natural terrain in planning what many regard as the ultimate test for horse and rider. The course itself can be between 6km (4 miles) and 8km (5 miles) long, and a speed of 570km (623yd) a minute is required. The height of the various fences is fixed at a maximum of 1m 20cm (4ft) and the width at 1m 80cm (6ft), though Olympic fences can be six inches wider.

Left A rider takes a fence in an Irish hunt and inset a Master of a hunt and his pack. Formal riding dress is required in the hunting field.

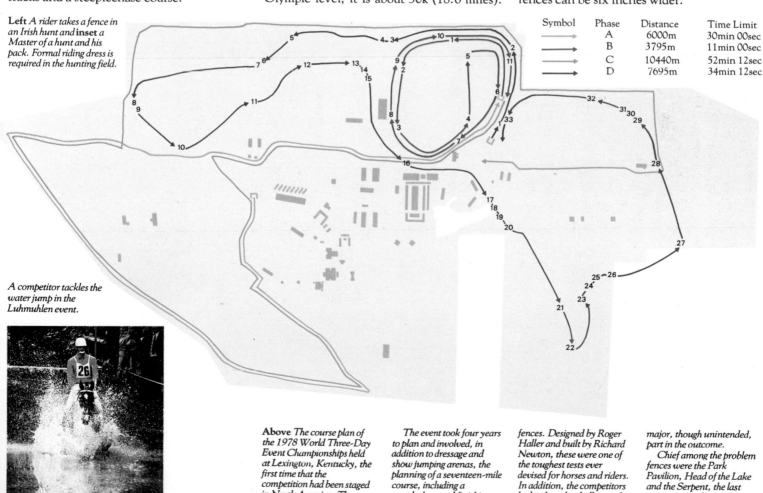

Symbol	Phase	Distance	Time Limit
	A	6000m	30min 00sec
	B	3795m	11min 00sec
	C	10440m	52min 12sec
	D	7695m	34min 12sec

A competitor tackles the water jump in the Luhmuhlen event.

Above The course plan of the 1978 World Three-Day Event Championships held at Lexington, Kentucky, the first time that the competition had been staged in North America. The forty-seven entrants represented the cream of world eventing talent.

The event took four years to plan and involved, in addition to dressage and show jumping arenas, the planning of a seventeen-mile course, including a steeplechase and finishing with a cross-country of nearly five miles, with thirty-three fixed and varied

fences. Designed by Roger Haller and built by Richard Newton, these were one of the toughest tests ever devised for horses and riders. In addition, the competitors had to face the challenge of intense humidity and an extremely high pollution rate, both of which played a

major, though unintended, part in the outcome.

Chief among the problem fences were the Park Pavilion, Head of the Lake and the Serpent, the last causing nine eliminations and retirements, eight falls and three refusals among the competitors.

Among the most taxing fences the rider has to face are the coffin and the water jump. The coffin, named after a fence first devised at Badminton, consists of three elements – a fence, a ditch and then another fence. It is the ditch which usually causes the problems. Success at the water jump depends on persuading the horse to overcome its natural reluctance to jump into water.

Errors are heavily penalized. In addition to time faults – these are so important that riders usually wear several watches to check their time – twenty penalties are added for a refusal and sixty for a fall. Riders can be eliminated for three refusals.

Before the final show jumping stage, the horse must pass a thorough veterinary examination to make sure that it is fit enough to continue. The show jumping test itself is primarily one of fitness and suppleness. It is devised to show that the horse is still capable of negotiating a small, twisting course of obstacles after the gruelling ordeal of the previous day.

The rider, too, needs to be alert. Often, the competitors are so close together after the cross country that a single fence down can alter the whole finishing order.

Show jumping

The rules governing eventing are laid down by the Fédération Equestre Internationale (FEI); they are reviewed annually in the light of current experience. So, too, are the rules of show jumping, a sport which had its origins in the later half of the nineteenth century and rose from these beginnings to become probably the most popular equestrian sport in the world today – with the sole exception of racing.

There are four types of competition. In the first, competitors are faulted if they knock down a fence (four faults); for a fall (eight faults); and for disobedience (first disobedience, three faults, a second, six, and a third, elimination). In case of a tie, a jump-off is held, frequently against the clock. Time also enters into the other three types of competition. In the first two, faults are penalized by time penalties, while the third is ridden solely against the fixed time limit the judges have decided for the course.

Most international competitions adopt the first method of scoring. Most demanding of these is the *Prix des Nations*; in this, the fences number thirteen or fourteen in all, the highest being approximately 1.60m (5ft 3in) and the lowest 1.30m (4ft 4in). Each team consists of four riders, each of whom jump the course twice. The best three scores are the ones that count in the final placing.

The nature of the fences follow a basic standard laid down by the FEI. They are of two main types – the upright and the spread. Common examples of the first are gates, walls, poles, and poles and brush; of the second, the triple bar, parallel bars and the double oxer. A water jump, between 3m (10ft) and 5m (16ft 5in) wide, is also usually included.

The course designer works within the limits set down by the sport's governing body, but, within these, he has several alternatives. In planning a course, he has to consider, above all, the level of the competition involved, together with such problems as the size of the arena, the number of fences available, and so on. Generally speaking, he plans what is known as the 'track' of the course first – making sure that competitors will have to change direction once at least – and then goes on to plot the position of the fences. He may decide to test the riders' ability further by varying the distance between them, which means that the horse will have to vary its natural stride. He finally chooses the type of fences. Usually, upright and spread fences are alternated, progressing upwards in order of difficulty after a few easy fences first to 'settle' the horse. With the twin exceptions of puissance and speed competitions, there is at least one combination included.

Preparation of horse and rider is vital.

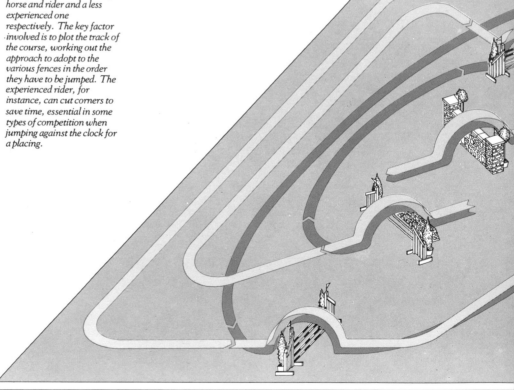

Right *A typical show jumping course, showing the approaches taken by two competitors – an experienced combination of horse and rider and a less experienced one respectively. The key factor involved is to plot the track of the course, working out the approach to adopt to the various fences in the order they have to be jumped. The experienced rider, for instance, can cut corners to save time, essential in some types of competition when jumping against the clock for a placing.*

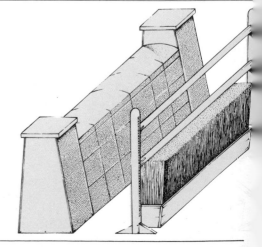

Left to right *Five common types of fence – a wall, brush and rail, parallel bars, a gate, and triple bar. Fences normally fall into two types; these are the upright, in which, as the name implies, the structure is built up vertically from the ground, and the spread, where width is combined with height. When tackling uprights, the horse should be well collected, its rider making sure that the take-off point is calculated so that the horse can clear the obstacle with the minimum possible effort. This means starting the jump from further back than* would be the case with a spread. When jumping a spread, on the other hand, the take-off point is nearer to the fence. Such fences are best approached at speed; the important thing here is to ensure that the horse has sufficient impulsion to clear the width of the obstacle. The best take-off point is one at a distance of 1 to 1¼ times the fence's height. The horse judges this from the groundline (the base of the fence); the rider should estimate the distance from a higher point, as, in some cases, the ground line can be misleading.*

Walking the course before the event, working out the track, the strides between each fence and the elements of a combination, is as important as riding it later. Related distances and fences make it essential to ride the course as a rhythmic, flowing whole. The horse must be well-trained and responsive, so that its stride can be lengthened or shortened at will while maintaining impulsion.

Training should be a matter of patient progression. After basic schooling, the horse should be introduced to the kind of fences it will face in competition, starting off at a low height and gradually building up to a higher one. Two main points can be established

here. The horse should be encouraged to bascule, that is, to arch its head, neck and back while in the air. Any tendency to flatten at this point should be corrected through gridwork and by jumping a series of wide, low parallels. Secondly, work can be done on the basic stride to overcome two common faults – the tendency to slow down in the approach to the jump and taking off too close to it. The rider should also practise jumping at an angle, increasing pace and cutting corners – all vital elements in speed tests.

Before the actual competition, a good warm-up period is essential, but the work done then should vary according to the per-

sonality of the horse. A lazy horse may need stirring up, an excitable one calming down.

Top riders all have very individual styles, though in many cases there is also the influence of national training and tradition. The West Germans, with their strong, powerful horses, their dominant style of riding and training and their emphasis on dressage, or schooling on the flat, are without doubt the world's leading show-jumping nation at the moment, and likely to remain so. Also in the top rank are the UK, Italy and the USA, with individual riders from many nations, including Australia, Canada, Belgium, France and Ireland, following close behind.

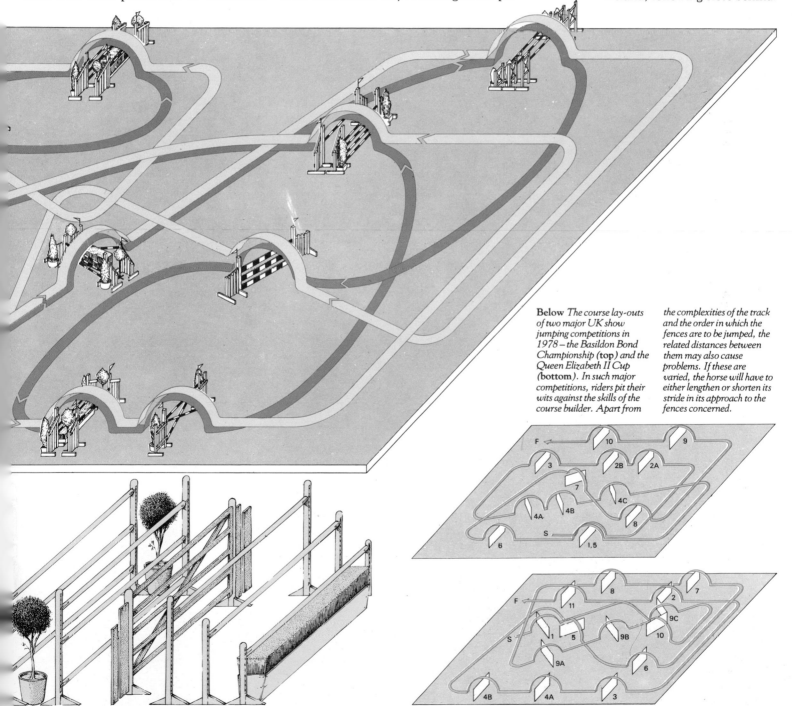

Below *The course lay-outs of two major UK show jumping competitions in 1978 – the Basildon Bond Championship (top) and the Queen Elizabeth II Cup (bottom). In such major competitions, riders pit their wits against the skills of the course builder. Apart from the complexities of the track and the order in which the fences are to be jumped, the related distances between them may also cause problems. If these are varied, the horse will have to either lengthen or shorten its stride in its approach to the fences concerned.*

Right *Show jumping scenes from around the world, including the Derby Bank at Hickstead (bottom right), one of the sport's most celebrated obstacles. Show jumping has greatly developed since 1868, when a competition for a 'high leap' and a 'wide leap' was included in the first horse show of the Royal Dublin Society, Ireland, to test the qualifications of horses for the hunting field. In 1881, a course of permanent fences was laid out and in use at the Dublin show's new permanent show ground at Ballsbridge. The first US National Horse show was held at Madison Square Gardens, New York, in 1883, and in Paris seventeen years later three jumping competitions were held in conjunction with the Olympic Games. Britain's first international horse show was held at Olympia, London, in 1907.*

In those early days, conditions were very different to those of today. The rules for jumping were virtually non-existent; for instance, circling before a fence, now penalised as a refusal, was permitted, while the wooden slats placed on each fence were removed as often by the wind as by the horses themselves. Today, however, show jumping is a highly sophisticated sport, and, in many cases, very big business indeed. At one end of the scale, a teenager can jump at a local show for nothing more than a rosette. At the other are the top-class professional riders, many now sponsored by industry, who win large sums of money each year in major competitions. Such is the demand for horses at this level that a good one can easily fetch a small fortune.

Dressage

Dressage (the name comes from the French *dresser*, to train) is a highly specialised sport. Its practitioners are rarely household names, as the discipline lacks the obvious excitement of eventing or show jumping, but nevertheless it is one of the most skilled forms of riding. The history of the sport goes back to late medieval times, when *Haute Ecole* (high school) became established in the royal courts of Europe. Today, it has its place in many competitions, including the Olympic Games, while its Classical traditions are maintained by institutions such as the Span-

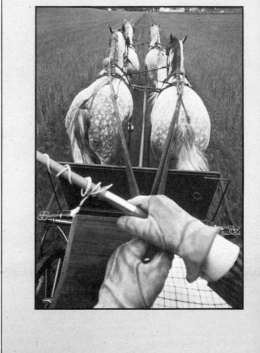

Above *Christine Stuckelberger, one of the world's youngest dressage stars, in action on her horse Granat,* **left** *Elena Petouchkova, a leading Soviet rider, competing in Copenhagen, and* **below** *the German dressage team – the present world champions – at Goodwood, UK, in 1978. Even at the basic*

levels, where only walk, trot, canter and halt are required, training a dressage horse takes considerable time and patience. Ideally, the horse should give the impression of doing what is required of it of its own accord, moving freely and regularly with harmony and grace in all its movements at the desired paces.

ish Riding School in Vienna and the Cadre Noir at Saumur, France.

The object of dressage is to teach the horse how to be supple, agile and keen to ride, while at the same time developing a perfect understanding with its rider. To achieve all this takes considerable time. At the most advanced level – the Olympic dressage test – training a horse takes at least four years and often considerably longer. Marks are given for each section of the test, on a scale from zero to ten, with additional assessment of the general impression both horse and rider give the judges.

The rider demonstrates a wide range of movements, working at collected, medium and extended paces, with smooth transitions between each one. Basic movements include the rein-back; halt; counter canter; change of leg; pirouette; and turn on the forehand. Lateral movements, in which the horse moves simultaneously sideways and forwards are also required; these include the leg yield, the travers, and the half pass. Two other

complex movements are the piaffe, a trot on the spot, and the passage, a measured, very collected, elevated and cadenced exercise.

The tests are performed in an arena on either sand or, at less advanced levels, grass, bordered by a 30cm (1ft)-high fence. The arena's size varies from 20m (22yd) by 40m (44yd) for novice to medium grades to 20m by 60m (65yd) for advanced dressage. The rider must make full use of the arena, especially in figure work. Figures include the vole, a circle of 6m (19½ft) in diameter, the serpentine and the figure of eight.

Driving

Dressage, too, plays its part in the relatively new sport of combined driving, the equivalent of a three day event on wheels, which has been steadily gaining in popularity since it was founded in 1969. Competitors are assessed on both presentation and dressage before they compete in the cross-country marathon, covering up to eighteen miles during which they have to negotiate six hazards,

such as narrow turns between trees or descents into lakes. The final obstacle-driving phase, which takes the place of show jumping in the ridden test, consists of driving between closely-set plastic bollards without knocking them, or the markers on them, over.

Private driving, or showing, however, is confined to the show ring. The emphasis here is on smart presentation of horse, or horses, vehicle and driver. Known as 'the whip', he or she circles the ring at a trot, changing direction as requested by the judges. The general presentation is then assessed, and, after this, the driver gives a short

solo performance, finishing with a halt and rein-back.

Show horses and ponies

Riding horses and ponies, too, are frequently shown in classes ranging from show ponies, hunters and hacks to saddle horses in the USA. All such competitions have as their basic purpose the improvement of the breed or type concerned; in the UK they started some 200 years ago.

The crucial test for any show pony or horse is conformation, though there are other qualities judges look for as well when selecting the prize winners. Pony classes are divided by height, with an upper limit of fifteen hands for working ponies. The best of these change hands for large sums of money, often in excess of £10,000 ($20,000). Hunter classes, on the other hand, are divided by weight into lightweight, middleweight and heavyweight divisions. Other classes include Ladies' Hunter, where the horse must be ridden sidesaddle, small hunter and working hunter. The horse has to show off its paces, particularly the gallop, and is then ridden by a judge to assess the quality of ride it gives. In the USA, in competitions in the Hunter Divi-

Below A four-in-hand team of Swiss-bred stallions drive through the shallows of Lake Movat, Switzerland, in the marathon stage of a combined driving competition; **inset** *a team of Lipizzaners, viewed from the whip's position, two scurry racing scenes and a troika racing through the snow outside Moscow. In the world of equestrian sport, the two activities of combined driving and obstacle driving have a considerable international following. Combined driving, the harness*

equivalent of the three-day event, was founded in 1969. It has three stages — dressage, the marathon (the equivalent of the cross-country), and obstacle driving (the equivalent of show jumping).

Obstacle driving on its own is usually held in indoor arenas, when teams of ponies, like the ones above, hurtle round a twisting course pulling scurries in a battle against the clock. Up to twenty obstacles, each topped by a ball, have to be rounded. Ten seconds is added for each fault.

sion, such as the Maclay, the horses have to jump a small course of fences, but in the UK and Ireland only working hunters are asked to leave the ground.

Although hunters comprise the majority of show horses, hacks also have a following. In the last century, there were two types – park hacks, suitable for fashionable riding and covert hacks, which were ridden to a hunt meet and then exchanged for a hunter. Now there is simply the show hack, an elegant well-trained horse with good conformation and manners. Again, there are three classes – small, large and ladies. The basic requirement is for the horse to walk, trot and canter to the judges' satisfaction, though the rider also has the opportunity to ride an individual test. As with the hunter, the judges assess the ride the horse gives themselves, and, finally, have the horse run up in hand as a last test.

The USA has one extra showing division, that of the saddle horse. These horses are shown as three-gaited, five-gaited or fine harness animals. The three-gaited horse demonstrates the usual paces of walk, trot and canter, but the five-gaited one has the extra paces of slow gait and rack. In both of these, each foot touches the ground individually, though the rack is slightly faster than the gait. Harness horses draw light buggies at walk, trot and park gait (a more lively version of the trot).

A showy, even flamboyant, turnout is very important for both horse and rider, and the spectacle, usually held in an indoor arena and compèred by a ring-master, attracts large crowds. Madison Square Gardens is the most important show.

Polo

Polo is one of the oldest horseback sports, and, today, is probably the most expensive of all. It is believed to have originated in Persia more than 2,000 years ago, though it was played in varying forms in China, Mongolia and Japan. The game was taken to India by the Moslems and Chinese; there, English planters in Assam discovered it in the mid-nineteenth century.

Polo reached the UK in 1869, where it was dubbed by spectators 'Hockey on horseback.' Six years later, the first English rules were issued, and a year after that the game was taken to the USA. There, it quickly spread, with the founding of such international competitions as the Westchester Cup, to reach a golden age between the two world wars.

Since 1945, however, the sport has been dominated by players from Argentina, who maintain a stranglehold in the one remaining international tournament, the Cup of the Americas. The USA comes second in the

Top left *An American saddlebred,* **top right** *miniature horses from South America,* **left** *the champion Working Hunter of 1978 at the Horse of the Year Show, Wembley, UK, and* **below** *an English-bred hack, ridden side-saddle by its elegant rider, shows off its paces. Showing classes are held at horse shows throughout the world. The types of horses competing in them vary widely, but the basic aim is always the same – the winners are the ones the judges consider likely to improve the breed. The three chief qualities assessed are conformation, paces, and the quality of ride given.*

Top right *Polo in Abadan, Iran,* **below** *chukka in progress at Cowdray Park, UK. Because of its expense, the game is probably the most expensive equestrian sport in the world. The qualities demanded of good polo ponies are considerable. Usually about 15.1 hands high, they are required to gallop flat out, stop in their own length, turn on a sixpence, swing round in a pirouette, and start off again at top speed from a standstill. They also have to ride off other ponies, be able to neck rein and perform flying changes of leg, which must come as second nature to the animal.*

world rankings.

The demands made by the game on the ponies are exacting: considerable courage and stamina are required. The ability to neck-rein is all-important as the animal is ridden only with one hand.

The teams are made up of two forwards, a centre-half and a back. All the players have handicaps, based on goal-scoring potential and ranging downwards from ten to zero (in some countries minus two). These are totalled and used to give a team with a handicap disadvantage an equal start in a match.

The centre-half initiates attacks on the opposing goal and covers the back in defence. He should be a long and accurate hitter. The forwards follow up the centre-half's attacking moves and mark the opposing centre-half and back. A game lasts for between four to six 'chukkas' of seven and a half minutes each, with a three minute interval between each chukka. A single pony plays only two chukkas, so reserves are necessary.

In Australia, an alternative to polo has developed. This is polo-crosse, which by 1946, was so popular that the Polocrosse Association of Australia was formed. The game is now played in every state, with 300 affiliated clubs. It is a combination of polo,

Left *Polo players in action in the USA. Between the wars, US polo teams led the world rankings in the sport, but now Argentina holds first place. A player must have a good natural eye for a moving ball; this is more important than outstanding horsemanship, though a strong seat and good balance are both essential.*

Today, the rules are primarily concerned with safety. Any player riding after the line of the ball has the right of way – vital when speeds of 30 mph are being achieved – and, for safety reasons too, players are also forbidden to hold their sticks in their left hands. The game is also stopped for falling or lame ponies, accidents to the ponies' gear, lost helmets, or when the ball goes out of play.

The rules are enforced by two mounted umpires and a referee, who sits centrally on one side of the ground to act as arbiter in cases of disagreement between them. Because of the speed of the game, these can occur fairly frequently. Fouls are penalized by penalties; these can vary in severity according to the nature of the offence. A penalty goal can be awarded, for example, or a free hit taken from a point determined by the umpires. This can be anywhere from the centre of the ground to the goal mouth.

lacrosse and netball; players are required to have neat riding gear with approved headwear and only one pony per player is allowed.

Trail and distance riding
In Australia and the USA in particular, long distance riding is also extremely popular. There are more than 500 distance rides in the USA, the most celebrated being the Tevis Cup and the Green Mountain Ride; in Australia, the Quilty Cup is equally famous, while in the UK the Golden Horse Shoe Ride is held annually over 121km (75 miles) of the Exmoor National Park.

Basic requirements are a fit horse and a fit rider, and, to ensure that the first condition is met, veterinary standards are extremely high, with inspections being held at regular stages of the ride. Normally, such competitive rides are organized in one of two ways; either a fixed time is laid down for the various stages, with riders arriving ahead of, or behind, this time being penalized, or the results are decided on finishing position. This can be a real test of endurance and only horses with considerable stamina should be entered for it.

Many long distance rides, however, are organized purely for pleasure, with no competitive element included. The most basic is pony trekking, which even a relatively inexperienced rider can enjoy.

Western riding
Another form of riding gaining in worldwide popularity is western riding – the style of riding that US cowboys use to herd cattle on the American range. It is closely linked with distance riding and with the flourishing spectacle of rodeo, extremely popular in both North America and Australia.

The Western style of riding differs from the European style in four main points. First, the appearance of the saddle is very different. It was originally designed to make long, hard days in the saddle checking stock as comfortable as possible for the rider, and to make the task of actual stock control easier. Thus, there is a horn mounted on the pommel for carrying a rope or young steer – or for fixing the rope to when lassoing cattle for, say, branding. The seat of the saddle is designed to give 'bounce' to the rider for increased comfort at the sitting trot. Second, the rider's hands are held high and a single-reined, long-cheeked curb bridle or bitless bridle is used for light, quick and accurate control. Thirdly, the stirrup leathers are designed to encourage a 'straight leg' position to keep the rider deep in the saddle; they are also adjusted to be extremely long. Finally, the horse itself is trained to 'neck rein', that is, to move right or left instantly from the pressure of the rein on the neck. For example, to turn to the

right, the rider's hands move across to the right, the signal to the horse being the pressure of the left rein on its neck. The reason for the development of this unusual technique was that the cowboy often had to control his horse with one hand, the other being needed, say, to throw a rope.

Entrants to shows in the Western Division of US riding can choose any one of three classes. In the Stock Horse section, they first demonstrate their horse's paces at the walk, jog (the western term for the trot), and lope (canter). They then perform a dressage test; this includes the sliding halt and a reining-back test. Some of the competitions involve

working with cattle.

The Trail Horse section is very much like a British Hunter Trial, with the additional demonstration of the horse's paces. These, too, have to be demonstrated in the Pleasure Horse section, while, in the Parade Class, turn-out is all important. Both horse and rider are gaily bedecked in spectacular tack and riding clothes.

Rodeo
Rodeo (the Spanish word for a cattle ring) is a survival from frontier days in the USA. Then, the trail gangs held informal competitions after a cattle drive to demonstrate their

Left *Long distance riding in Hungary,* **above** *pony trekking on Dartmoor in the UK and* **below** *trail riders in the desert near Tucson,* *USA. Endurance riding is another form of equestrian sport which has gained in world-wide popularity in recent years.*

skills in the arts of roping, bareback broncho riding, steer wrestling, steer and calf roping, bull riding, and so on. From these beginnings, the spectacle of rodeo was born.

As far as is known, the first public rodeo was held on 4 July (Independence Day) 1866 in Arizona. By the turn of the century, the Wild West show had come into being, adding an element of circus and carnival to the exhibition, with demonstrations of fancy shooting, riding and chuck wagon racing. Public interest is now on an international scale. In the USA, today, according to the Rodeo Cowboys' Association, more than 500 professional rodeos are held annually, as well as the hundreds of amateur contests. The total audience runs into the millions, while prize money, too, can be considerable. For its part, the Australian Rough Riders Association has a membership of over 12,000 and organizes rodeos in every state. The National Finals Rodeo is the highlight of the Australian rodeo season.

There are five traditional rodeo events; calf roping; steer wrestling; and broncho, bull, and saddle broncho riding. All of them require considerable skill and nerve from both horse and rider. In calf roping, for instance, a young calf is released into the arena from a chute; the cowboy's task is to gallop after it and lasso the animal. The horse then comes to a sliding halt and backs away to maintain the tension on the lariat, which is secured to the saddle horn. This is all part of a good western horse's basic training. The cowboy dismounts, runs over to the calf, turns it on its side and quickly ties three of its legs together. The contestant with the fastest time wins.

Another test of skill, in which the risk of injury can be considerable, is bronco riding. In saddle bronc riding, the bronc wears a saddle and the rider tries to stay seated in it for a minimum of ten seconds. His only security is a halter rope, which he holds with one hand. In bareback bronc riding, the saddle is replaced by a surcingle strap with a leather handhold. The stipulated minimum time is eight seconds.

In both events, the contestants score points up to a maximum of twenty-five, awarded by two judges on the basis of the riders' skill and the horse's wildness. To increase this, the rules stipulate that the animal must be spurred (on its shoulders) as it leaps from the chute, while hard spurring during the ride wins bonus points.

Women riders, too, feature on the rodeo circuits; the Girls' Rodeo Association in the USA was formed as early as 1948. Rewards for successful riders are considerable, but expenses are also high. Competitors have to pay their own entry fees, and there is also the cost of travelling the thousands of miles involved to be taken into consideration. There is, too, the constant risk of injury – or even death.

This is one of the reasons for the employment of clowns and pick-up riders at rodeos. As well as entertaining the crowds, part of the clowns' task is to attract the attention of a bull or broncho so that a fallen rider can be brought to safety. Pick-up riders, as their name implies, have the job of helping successful competitors off their mounts by riding alongside and lifting them to safety.

Below *A calf-roping contest in the Calgary Stampede,* **inset** *a cowboy in an American stock yard and broncho busting in a US rodeo, while* **far right** *chuck wagons race for victory, also at the Calgary Stampede. Rodeo originated in the US wild west in the nineteenth* *century, when cowboys tested their skill against each other at the end of cattle drives. It grew to become a major spectacle, attracting vast audiences in both North America and Australia, where it spread in the 1940s. Both male and female contestants take part.*

Hazers, on the other hand, have a less humanitarian role. Their task is to gallop alongside the bull in bull wrestling events to make sure that it keeps to a reasonably straight line. In some ways, their role is not unlike that of the picadors' in the bull ring, just as rodeo itself, particularly in its display and spectacle, has some links with bull fighting. The picadors' task is to bait the bull in preparation for the toreador and to help ensure his safety. Traditionally, toreadors fought on foot, the picadors being mounted. Recently, however, mounted bullfighting has gained considerably in popularity.

Cutting horses, too, compete in rodeos, though they also have their own competitions and events. These are extremely popular in the USA and Australia; in the latter country, such was public demand that the National Cutting Horse Association was formed in 1972 to organize the sport. Watching the horse at work is almost like watching a sheepdog, as it cuts out a steer apparently without assistance from its rider.

Riding for the disabled

Another form of horseback leisure activity is also growing in importance, as its value is

for the Handicapped Association was formed. There are similar organizations in Australia and New Zealand, as well as many in Europe.

Teaching starts off with confidence-building exercises; there then follows hacking, mounted games and even jumping. In addition to qualified teachers, considerable volunteer help is needed, as it can take three people to look after a severely handicapped child rider adequately.

An enclosed school is an obvious essential, as disabled children cannot be expected to ride in the rain. The horses and ponies used need to be selected carefully for quietness, while only simple forms of tack should be used. Some extra items, however, are usually needed; these include basket saddles for the legless and long lopped reins for the armless. In addition to the customary hard hat, a belt is also necessary, so that a helper can grasp it in case of an emergency.

Throughout, the aim is to let the children, or adults, do as much as possible for themselves, though the volunteers play an essential role. In the UK, seven grades of competency certificate are awarded by Riding for the Disabled to encourage this.

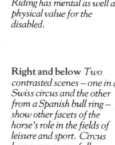

Above *A disabled child is taught to ride at a purpose-built school in the UK. Riding has mental as well as physical value for the disabled.*

Right and below *Two contrasted scenes – one in a Swiss circus and the other from a Spanish bull ring – show other facets of the horse's role in the fields of leisure and sport. Circus horses are as carefully trained as their dressage equivalents, while mounted bull-fighters expect an equal degree of skill from their specially-bred mounts.*

increasingly recognized. This is riding for the disabled. Modern medical opinion holds that riding gives a crippled child, both the benefit of physical exercise and a powerful psychological stimulus.

The therapeutic value of riding was recognized many centuries ago; in ancient Greece, and in imperial Rome, the chronic sick were encouraged to exercise on horseback. In modern times, the first notable disabled rider was Liz Hartel. Despite being crippled by polio, she won silver medals for Denmark in both the 1952 and 1956 Olympic Games.

Riding for the disabled groups now exist all over the world. In the UK, the Riding for the Disabled Association was founded in 1969; in the same year, the North American Riding

Horse racing

Horse racing has developed over the last century into a vast, colourful entertainments industry with perhaps half a million thoroughbreds involved either in racing or breeding throughout the world. However, its origins are difficult to trace. The Chinese, the Tartars, Mongols, Greeks and Romans all engaged in the sport in one form or another. On racing days, every citizen of Rome wore the colour of his favourite team of charioteers and prepared to do battle with the supporters of other teams in the stands around the track. Even in the uttermost corner of the Roman Empire, in Britain, the garrisons of Wetherby and York are known to have held races.

The founding Thoroughbreds

All racing Thoroughbreds are descended from three stallions of Arabian stock – the Byerley Turk, the Darley Arabian, and the Godolphin Barb. The Byerley Turk was captured when Budapest was taken from the Turks in 1686–87 and his new owner, Colonel Byerley of the Dragoon Guards, rode him at the Battle of the Boyne in 1690. Impressed by his speed and agility, especially when compared to the Dragoons' usual mounts, Byerley brought his charger home and installed him as a stud stallion first in County Durham, and later in Yorkshire. The ancestry of such famous racehorses as Tetrarch and Tourbillon can be traced back to the Byerley Turk through his son Jig.

The Darley Arabian, foaled in 1700 on the edge of the Syrian Desert, was sold four years later by Sheik Mirza to Thomas Darley, the English Consul in Aleppo. The Sheik tried to go back on the deal, and gave orders that anyone who tried to remove the horse should be killed. Undeterred, the Consul enlisted the help of some British sailors from a warship that was visiting the port. They rowed ashore in the dark, overpowered the stable guards, and returned to their man o'war with the horse. Furious, the Sheik wrote to Queen Anne, claiming his incomparable stallion was 'worth more than a King's ransom and had been foully stolen by one of her subjects'.

His plea was ignored, but the Sheik's opinion of the horse was amply justified. During the next twenty-five years, the Darley Arabian sired a whole race of champions among whose descendants were St Simon, Gainsborough, Blandford and – perhaps the noblest of them all – the great Eclipse.

The Godolphin Barb, foaled in 1724, was given to Louis XV of France by the Sultan of Morocco. The horse was later acquired by Lord Godolphin and became the ancestor of another great line of racehorses. The influence of these three stallions on Thoroughbred breeding was at once appar-

ent, during the early Georgian period a further 24 Arabian stallions were imported.

The English Jockey Club, founded in 1752, soon became the foremost authority in all racing matters. The same year too, saw the first recorded steeplechase, held over $4\frac{1}{2}$ miles of hunting country between Buttevant Church and St Leger Church in Ireland. By the end of the century, two-year-old races had been instituted. These were soon equalling and even surpassing in popularity the three- and five-year-old races which were all that had been permitted until then.

The spread of racing

In France, racing did not become fully established until after the French Revolution, though the first regular French course was laid out in the Plaine des Sablons as early as 1776; one two-mile race held there in the same year offered a prize of 15,000 francs for the winner.

In 1833 Lord Henry Seymour, a British nobleman living in Paris, founded the French Jockey Club, and three years later the Prix du Jockey Club, over the classic distance of $1\frac{1}{2}$

A horse and jockey of the second century BC. In the ancient world, the Greeks were ardent racegoers.

miles, was run for the first time. In 1857, a track was laid in the Bois du Boulogne; set in picturesque woodland just a few minutes' from the centre of Paris, Longchamp was to become one of the most fashionable of the world's racecourses.

Other nations were swift to follow France's example. The first Japanese meeting was held in 1852, Australia established the Melbourne Cup in 1861, while Ireland and Germany each founded its own Derby in 1866 and 1869 respectively. In the USA, the Belmont Stakes, first of the three classic races that together compose the American Triple Crown, was set up in 1867; the other two, the Preakness Stakes and the Kentucky Derby entered the calendar in 1873 and 1876.

There were no horses in Australasia until at least 1788. Only 11 years later, breeding was firmly established and the first official race meeting was staged at Hyde Park, Sydney, in 1810. The sport flourished with the

continued importation of Thoroughbred stallions and in 1840, the Australian Race Committee issued a manifesto setting out the aims of the Australian breeding industry. South Africa had instituted its own racing almost half a century before; the first meeting was held on Green Point Common, near Cape Town, in September 1797.

American breeding

The first US race course was laid out in 1665 on Long Island, but the sport did not become established there until later. Then the purchase of the 21-year-old stallion Diomed proved an immensely shrewd and important move by American breeders. Winner of the first Derby to be run at Epsom in 1780, he had not been a success at stud in England and was eventually sold for a paltry 50 guineas to a Virginian breeder, who, in turn, quickly sold him to another breeder for 1,000 guineas. Diomed proved a prolific sire of winners in America, and was still covering mares at the age of twenty-nine.

Once the Civil War was over, American racing boomed. By 1897, there were 314 racetracks operating in the United States and 43 in Canada. But, at the turn of the century, legislation against betting and racing was passed in many states and this for a time had a disastrous effect on the sport. By 1908, only 25 courses were still open, and in 1910 a yet more severe anti-betting law brought New York racing to a standstill. Most of this legislation remained in force until the 1920s.

The role of the trainer

Training racehorses is a time-consuming, highly-skilled art. Many trainers complain that there are simply not enough hours in a day to cope with their numerous tasks, and, as a result, most modern stables now employ secretaries and assistants to look after the ever-increasing paper-work and administration. Training methods differ enormously from stable to stable and country to country but their basic task is to bring a horse to a state of complete physical fitness, so enabling it to run faster than its rivals, with sufficient stamina to maintain its speed.

Generally, the process begins with the trainer buying a yearling for a particular owner. This might be done at the numerous bloodstock auction sales held annually, or he might prefer to buy or lease a horse direct from a stud. The horse is then broken in, lunged on a long rein, saddled, and ridden away, a task that must be accomplished with patience and gentleness. It may therefore be some considerable time before the horse is ready to be ridden out each morning with the rest of the stable's string.

Later, the trainer decides on the horse's

LES COURSES DE STEEPLE
Le saut de la rivière

Top *The scene at Sadlers Wells racecourse, London, in 1826 and* **above** *a steeple chase at Auteuil, France, in 1903. The nineteenth and early twentieth centuries saw the establishment of racing as a major sport.*

exercise routine, the most suitable distance for him to race, the right type of going and the most suitable jockey. Then, when he feels the horse is almost ready to run, he enters it for its first races.

The trainer's routine begins before dawn when he gets up to watch the daily gallops.

Paperwork occupies his morning before he leaves to watch whatever races are being held in which he has an interest. He then returns home to look over each horse at evening stables.

A large staff is employed, including apprentice jockeys, and most important of all a head stable lad who runs everything in the trainer's absence and usually has charge of feeding. Trainers charge a set monthly fee with the addition of such expenses as veterinary care, transport, and gallops. The sharp increase in feed and labour bills has greatly increased the price of keeping a horse in training in many parts of the world. It remains a rich man's sport, though lately, partnerships and syndicates have enabled some of the less well-off to experience the pleasure of owning a racehorse.

Trainers, like jockeys, earn a percentage of any prize money their horses win. Many also bet and make money by dealing, buying and selling horses.

In Europe, trainers have their own stables from which the horses are taken to each race, while in the US, hundreds, and sometimes thousands, of horses lodge briefly at each consecutive meeting. When the meeting comes to an end, the whole set-up moves on to the next course.

In 1977, Vincent O'Brien, the leading British trainer of the last decade, won a record £439,124 from a mere eighteen victories on British tracks, a figure that was considerably increased by his many successes in France and Ireland. In America, the prize money won by the leading trainers is substantially more than this. The 1966 record of $2,435,450 set by Eddie Neloy, is now regularly surpassed by several trainers each year.

The role of the jockey

The trainer teaches the racehorse its job, yet his fame seldom reaches beyond the ears of the more expert punters. A successful jockey, on the other hand can, and often does, become a national celebrity.

In the USA, Willie Shoemaker set a world record of riding winners as long ago as 1970 when he equalled Eddie Acaro's figure of 6,032. By mid-1978, 'The Shoe', as he is nicknamed, was still going strong with more than 7,300 wins to his credit, having ridden 172 winners in 1977 alone. In Britain, the record set by the legendary Sir Gordon Richards of 4,870 is still unbroken. Sir Gordon was champion of the flat 26 times: his most splendid feat was 1933 when he rode 12 consecutive winners.

The British flat racing season lasts only from mid-March to early November. In America, races are held all the year round, with programmes of up to twelve races a day. This gives US jockeys the opportunity to achieve much higher totals than their British counterparts. Steve Cauthen, who started his riding career in 1976, set an astonishing record in 1977 by winning 488 races around the USA.

US jockeys have agents who seek out and

secure rides for them. In return they earn between twenty and twenty-five per cent of whatever their jockeys collect. Harry Silbert has worked as Willie Shoemaker's agent since he rode his first race in 1949. In Britain, many top jockeys are retained by one, or sometimes two, stables – they do not employ agents. Unquestionably the best jockey in Britain is Lester Piggott, who in the 1960s, broke from convention by going freelance. His reward has been innumerable victories, including a record eight wins in the Epsom Derby – the last in 1977.

Modern flat jockeys throughout the world ride with very short stirrup leathers and a low, wind-resisting crouch, a style imported from America at the end of the last century. It is generally accepted that Tod Sloan was the first man to introduce this style to Europe but in fact, he was preceded by another American, Willie Simms. His style was so ridiculed that he packed his bag and returned home. Sloan, however, was made of sterner stuff. His crouching style was so successful in English races that UK jockeys soon abandoned their old-fashioned, upright postures and copied him.

Sloan won so many races perched high in the saddle, that he became known as the 'monkey up the stick'. After Sloan came two more Americans who both topped the jockeys' list in Britain — Danny Maher and Lester Reiff. Australian jockeys, such as Brownie Carslake and Frank Bullock, were also successful in Britain at about this time.

The lightest jockey ever recorded was Kitchener who died in 1872; he weighed only 49lbs when he won the 1844 Chester Cup on Red Deer. The youngest winning jockey was Frank Wootton, later English champion, who gained his first success in South Africa aged 9 years and 10 months, while the oldest was Levi Barlingame who was eighty when he rode his last winner in America in 1932.

By the 1970s, professional women jockeys were making an impact in several racing countries. The breakthrough came first in America where a number of women regularly began to ride winners.

Male or female, every jockey weighs in before each race on specially-designed scales and the first four must weigh in again after it. They sit on the scales holding their saddles but not their crash helmets. Jockeys are paid a set riding fee plus a percentage, varying between 7½% and 10% of the prize money

How betting works

Betting is the lifeblood of racing throughout the world. Most countries operate a totalisator system, called the pari-mutuel in France and the USA, and the Tote in Britain. The racing authorities keep a set percentage for the considerable running costs of the industry, and a further percentage is taken in tax, while the remainder is redistributed to the lucky winners.

This system is efficient and has the obvious advantage of being reasonably easy to run, but punters often have to queue for a considerable time to place their bets and are denied the opportunity to shop around for the best available price. Britain is in the unusual position of allowing both bookmakers and Tote to operate in competition both on and off the racecourse, and there is little doubt that most punters prefer to use the bookmakers.

The extent of the huge annual betting

Above *The equipment required by a jockey and a race horse and* **right** *the two combined in action. By far the most important and expensive item is the special* racing saddle, weighing from between 2 to 9lb. On average, jockeys need three of these in different sizes to suit both their mount and the weight carried.*

Left *Swimming a horse to help it tone up its muscles is today a common feature of the training programme, as this scene shows.*

turnover in America can be gauged by the figures, released by the New York Racing Association, from the meetings held at Aqueduct, Belmont Park, and Saratoga in 1977. Turnover that year was $711 million dollars—and that from just three of the 106 tracks in the country.

France, too, benefits greatly from the pari-mutuel system, while in Australia, though rules differ from state to state, bookmakers are allowed to operate only at race-meetings. The result is that betting markets are much stronger than in Europe or the USA.

Racing's hall of fame

What are the qualities that make a racehorse great? Shakespeare wrote of a nobleman's horse:

'round-hoofed, short-jointed, fetlocks shag and long,
Broad-breast, full eye, small head and nostril wide,
High-crest, short ears, straight legs, and passing

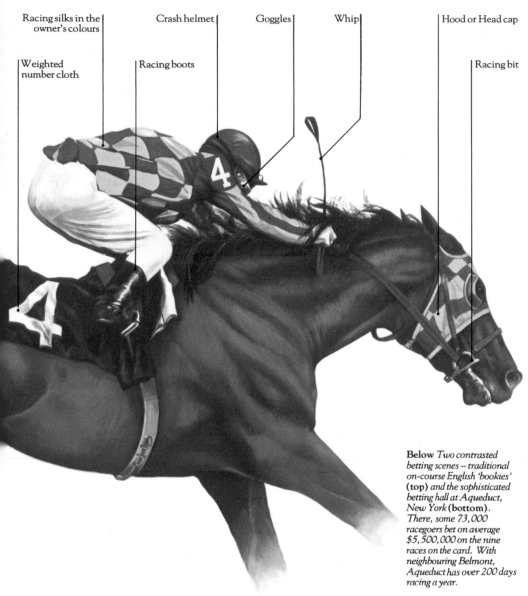

Racing silks in the owner's colours

Crash helmet

Goggles

Whip

Hood or Head cap

Weighted number cloth

Racing boots

Racing bit

or so before the Derby, his health deteriorated day by day. Sometimes he looked dreadfully ill and would not eat, but, in the race itself, he led on the last turn and battled home to hold the nearest challenge by a neck. Just over two weeks later, Humorist ended a brief gallop with blood from a broken blood vessel gushing from his nostrils.

In the following week, Sir Alfred Munnings, the great horse painter, began a portrait of Humorist, but before it could be completed, the horse lay dead amid pools of blood in his box. A post-mortem showed he had suffered from consumption and a severe haemorrhage of the lungs. Yet in this condition, he had won the Derby.

Trainers look for different attributes when buying horses. Breeding is the most important, especially on the dam's side; a good pace, when allied to a bright, intelligent head, long ears, clean joints and strong quarters, is also attractive. But breeding can be misleading. Some of the best-bred animals turn out to be very slow and history has proved time and again, that conformation and good looks do not guarantee success in racing.

Famous races and racecourses

Epsom, on the edge of the Surrey Downs, is the home of the Derby – the most famous race in the world and the third of the five English Classics to be run. In some respects it is an unlikely site on which to stage the supreme test for three-year-old Thoroughbreds. Epsom has an awkward, undulating left-handed horseshoe track, so that horses are seldom running on an even keel.

From the start of the one-and-a-half mile course, the ground rises continuously some 150 feet over six furlongs, until it bears left downhill towards Tattenham Corner, a sharp left-handed curve into the four-furlong straight. The final half-mile is also downhill until the last 50 yards when there is a sudden climb to the winning post. Throughout the straight there is a sharp camber towards the far rail; this causes problems for many jockeys when their tired mounts start to 'hang' and veer under pressure.

The Derby is held on the first Wednesday of June. Each year, upwards of a quarter of a million spectators attend the race, many of them watching from the free enclosures on the inside of the horseshoe, where they are entertained by the traditional fair that operates throughout the week.

The origins of the Derby are linked to another Classic race, The Oaks. In 1778, at a party given by Lord Derby at his home, 'The Oaks', near Epsom, it was decided to stage a race the following year and to name it after his lordship's house. The 1779 Oaks was such

Below *Two contrasted betting scenes – traditional on-course English 'bookies' (top) and the sophisticated betting hall at Aqueduct, New York (bottom). There, some 73,000 racegoers bet on average $5,500,000 on the nine races on the card. With neighbouring Belmont, Aqueduct has over 200 days racing a year.*

strong,
Thin mane, thick tail, broad buttock, tender hide. . . !'

Dame Julyana Berners, writing in the first sporting publication in England in 1481, listed several other desirable features:
'Of a man, bolde, prowde, and hardy;
'Of a woman, fayrbrested, fayr of heere, and easy to leape upon;
'Of a fox, a fayr taylle, short eeres, with a good trotte-
'Of a haare, a grete eye, a dry hede, and well runnynge,
'Of an asse, a bygge chyn, a flatte legge and a good hoof'.

While both authors include many of the attributes that make a great racehorse, every judge has a different idea about perfect conformation. Soundness, good-health, and the highest ability, for example, are worth nothing if not matched by courage.

Humorist, the 1921 Derby winner, was a creature of matchless courage. In the month

a success that a further race was suggested for 1780. The toss of a coin, between Lord Derby and Sir Charles Bunbury, determined the name of this second contest. Sir Charles at least had the consolation of seeing his own colt, Diomed, win the first Derby, then run over a mile. Later in 1784, the distance was increased to one and a half miles.

The first Derby was worth just over £1,000 to the winner, compared with £107,530 in 1977, when The Minstrel beat Hot Grove by a neck. The Minstrel was later sold for a world record figure of $10,000,000. Stud values of winners have naturally kept pace with the increases in prize money. Mahmoud, winner in 1936, was sold for a mere £21,000 to America where he later sired the winners of more than £2½ million in stakes.

The three longest priced winners in Derby history are Jeddah (1898), Signorinetta (1908) and Aboyeur (1913), all at 100–1. There were two dead heats in 1828 and 1884. In recent years, the race has been dominated by American-bred horses trained in Ireland by Vincent O'Brien and ridden by the incomparable British jockey Lester Piggott. The Minstrel gave Piggott a record eighth Derby victory in 1977.

Ascot, the only racecourse in England which belongs to the Royal Family was founded by Queen Anne in the early 1700s. Royal Ascot, held in June, at the height of summer, is one of the most sparkling events in the world's racing calendar. A Royal procession down the racecourse opens the proceedings on each of the four days, all of which glow with racing of the highest quality. The principal race of the meeting is the Ascot Gold Cup, a 'stayers' race run over a course of two-and-a-half miles.

Prize money is even higher in the King George VI and Queen Elizabeth Diamond Stakes, recently sponsored by the De Beers group, which is held at the July meeting at Ascot. First run in 1951, the race provides a fine test between the best staying colts and fillies of three and four years. The Diamond Stakes is one of the most prestigious and profitable races in the world; the 1977 winner, The Minstrel, made his owner richer by £88,355

A right handed course, with the last six furlongs run up a gradual gradient, Ascot is a test of stamina. The round course (1½ miles) is supplemented by a straight mile used for such races as the Royal Hunt Cup.

Other famous English racecourses include Newmarket, Doncaster, Aintree and Cheltenham. Newmarket, centre of English racing for over 300 years, stages the first two Classics of each season – the One Thousand and Two Thousand Guineas. The former,

first held in 1814, is run over the straight Rowley mile (the name comes from Charles II's nickname 'Old Rowley') at the Newmarket spring meeting. It was set up as the fillies equivalent of the Two Thousand Guineas – a race for colts.

The Thousand Guineas, coming early in the season for three-year-old fillies, is still the major English contest for female milers. The stiff mile, with its undulating course and uphill finish, is a stiff test which soon discovers specialist sprinters. Prize money for the 1978 Canadian-owned winner Enstone Spark, was £41,130. Thirty-four winners of the Thousand Guineas have completed a double by also winning The Oaks.

The 2,000 Guineas was originally financed by a sweepstake of 100 guineas for each entry. Coming a month or so before the Derby, it is an ideal preparation for the Epsom Classic and by 1977, no fewer than 34 horses had achieved the double triumph of winning both in the same year.

Doncaster stages the last of the season's five Classics, the St Leger, at its September meeting. Run over one mile, six furlongs and 132 yards, it is a real test of stamina and form, with the Two Thousand Guineas and the

Derby, the third leg of the so-called Triple Crown. Only 12 horses have ever gained this coveted honour in British racing – the last of which was the great Nijinsky in 1970.

Aintree is the home of what is the most famous steeplechase in the world – the Grand National. Founded in 1839, the fences are noted for the stamina they call for from both horse and rider. The most taxing is the Chair, the last but one on the first circuit, but the most famous is undoubtedly Becher's Brook, named after Captain Becher, one of the riders in the first Grand National.

Cheltenham, deep in the heart of the Cotswolds, annually provides the setting for the most important meeting of the jump season, the March National Hunt Festival. Spread over three days, this fixture offers one of the finest spectacles of action over hurdles and fences to be seen in the world. The two most important races are the Cheltenham Gold Cup, steeplechasing's premier prize, and the Champion Hurdle.

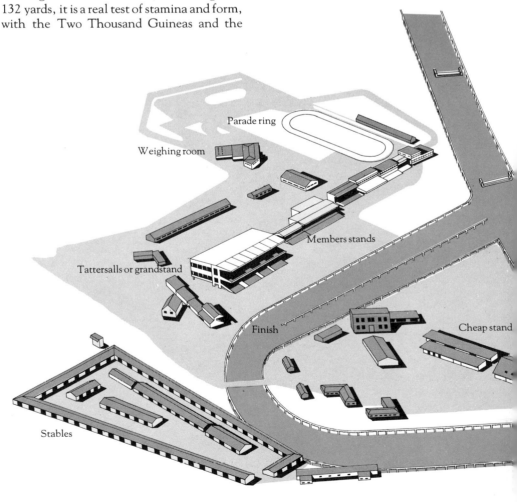

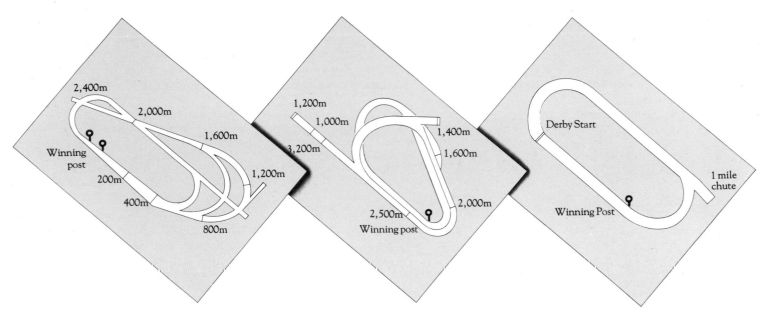

Longchamp, home of the Prix de l'Arc de Triomphe, is probably the best known of the French racecourses. Opened in 1857, it has round course of 2,400m (1½ miles) and a straight one of 1,600m (1 mile), used for another famous race, the Grand Criterium.

Flemington is the home of Australia's most prestigious race, the Melbourne Gold Cup. In addition to its flat-racing course – just under 2,400m (1½ miles) round, with a run in to the finish, it has a shorter straight track and also a separate steeplechase circuit.

Churchill Downs is the home of the Kentucky Derby, founded in 1875 and run over a distance of 2,000m (1¼ miles). It is a flat, oval course and, in common with most US racecourses, has a dirt surface, not a grass one. Races are flat out from start to finish.

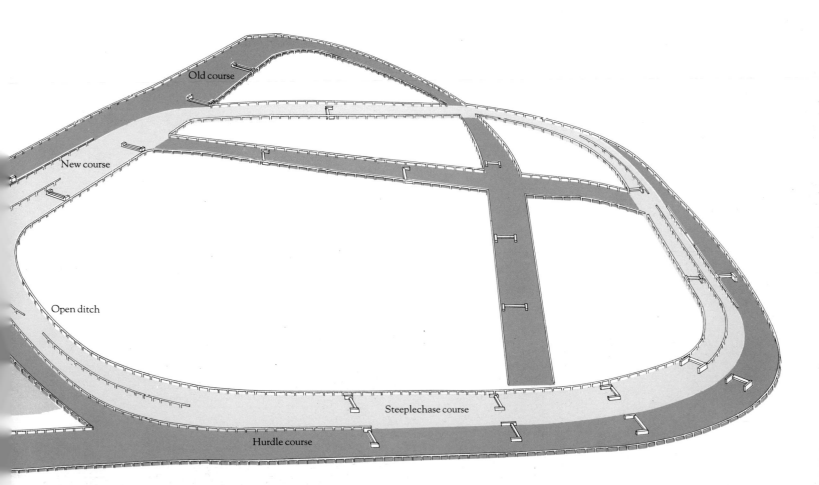

The layout of a typical racecourse. Behind the scenes at every major meeting, there is a massive organization at work, headed by the Clerk of the Course, to make sure all runs smoothly. Spectators, jockeys, owners, trainers and bookmakers all need their specialized facilities. Apart from the course itself, the paddock, where horses parade before a race, is the chief centre of interest, together with the winner's enclosure after it. On the course, one of the chief innovations of recent years is the use of mobile starting stalls in flat racing, replacing the traditional tapes. Stalls make it far easier for the starter to ensure that all the runners get an equal chance, while photo-finish cameras and a TV patrol both help to ensure fairness during the actual running of a race.

Left *Jockeying for position in a race at Kempton Park, UK, in 1976;* **inset** *racing over snow in Switzerland and a tense start at Ascot, UK.* **Above top** *The saddling enclosure at Flemington Racecourse, Melbourne, and* **below** *mud-splattered horses and riders strain every nerve in a Canadian flat race. The appeal of racing is such that it attracts thousands who have probably never been near a racecourse, while among the actual spectators, few realize the months and years of preparation that go into producing, say, a British Derby winner.*

The trainer's role in this is all important. Together with his back-up team – stable jockey, assistant, head lad. senior lads, apprentices and others – his day starts at dawn and finishes at dusk.

His responsibilities are immense, as he can easily have a million pounds worth of horses in his care.

To the spectator, however the key figure on the day of the race is without question the jockey. Competition to succeed in this field is so intense that, for every world-class star who emerges, such as the top British jockey Lester Piggott, literally hundreds of aspiring hopefuls vanish into obscurity. Nevertheless recruits to the profession still come forward, particularly now that racing has opened its doors to women jockeys as well as men.

A jockey is either retained by a stable under contract for, say, a season, or is booked for rides as a freelance. At the top, skill and expertise bring considerable financial

dividends – in the UK a top jockey can earn in the region of £50,000 a year, while in the USA, because of its all-year race programme, the amounts are considerably more. But, at the bottom, the rewards can be relatively small. Jockeys work a six-day week, though working conditions vary considerably. In the UK, for example, there is far more travelling involved than , say in France or the USA. Because of the nature of American racing, with its larger meetings, US jockeys can spend more time on a particular circuit.

In addition, all jockeys face the key physical problem of weight. Diet has to be strictly controlled, while vital ounces often have to be sweated off speedily in a Turkish bath or a sauna.

Ireland

All five Irish Classics are held at the Curragh, for centuries the home of Irish racing. Situated thirty miles south of Dublin, the Curragh, which belongs to the Turf Club, is also the main training centre of Ireland. The Irish Derby attracted little attention outside the country until it was given a major injection of funds by the Irish Sweepstake Organisation in 1962. Since then, the race has become progressively more important in the pattern of European three-year-old classics.

Ireland also has a unique racecourse at Laytown Beach, north of Dublin. Racing is held just once a year on the beach, and the date depends entirely on the state of the tide. Stewards have to wait for the tide to go out before marking off the course with poles and ropes and the only permanent building on the course is a concrete public convenience.

France

Longchamp, in the wooded Bois de Boulogne just a few minutes from the centre of Paris, provides the golden autumnal setting for Europe's richest race, the Prix de l'Arc de Triomphe, which is run early in October. First held in 1920, the Arc is the most important race in France and attracts the best European staying three-year-olds to pace their qualities against a handful of older horses. The one snag is that a number of top class horses miss the race because it comes too late in the season; all the same, it can still fairly claim to attract the most international competition of any race held in Europe. In 1977, the winner, Alleged, earned the huge sum of $281,690 in prize money.

Only slightly less prestigious than the Arc is the Grand Prix de Paris, for three year olds, which is run over one mile, seven furlongs, and 110 yards on the last Sunday in June.

Longchamp is one of the most attractive racecourses in the world. The panoramic grandstands, the quiet, tree-lined paddock and the long sweeping right hand turn leading to the wide straight, are beautiful in themselves as well as offering racing at its best. Beauty, however, is the keynote of many French racecourses, among them Chantilly, where the French Derby and Oaks are held. Here, the runners pass a magnificent château before turning right-handed into the final straight.

Australia

Flemington is the home of Australia's most famous race, the Melbourne Cup, which is run on the first Tuesday in November. Four miles from the centre of Melbourne, Flemington was named after a local butcher, Bob Fleming, whose shop stood opposite the course when it was built in the 1840s. Surrounded by stands that can hold 100,000 or more, the flat course at Flemington is just under 1½ miles round with a short run — little more than two furlongs — to the post. There is also a straight six furlong track and a separate steeplechase circuit.

The Melbourne Cup, run over two miles, was first held in 1861, and since then has attracted almost every good stayer in Australia and New Zealand. Though the Victoria Derby, and VRC Sires Produce Stakes and other important races are also held at Flemington, the Melbourne Cup reigns supreme. Parliament, courts and indeed the entire nation, halts and rushes to its television sets to watch the race. Stars of the past are still revered — like Archer, who won the first two Melbourne Cups in 1861 and 1862, a feat not equalled until Rain Lover completed the same double in 1968 and 1969.

A neck-and-neck battle at Florida Downs race track, Tampa, USA. One of the jockey's chief skills is to know when to use the whip on his horse.

Flemington too, was the scene of the first triple dead heat in Australia, in November 1956, when three horses crossed the line perfectly together. All three had their ears back, their heads held low, and their off fore legs extended exactly the same length, as if locked by remote control.

Melbourne's other course is Caulfield, where the famous Caulfield Cup is run, just seventeen days before the Melbourne Cup. The Caulfield Cup, the second most important race in the Australian racing calendar, was first competed for in 1879.

The United States

The most important leg of the American Triple Crown is the Kentucky Derby, held on Churchill Downs, Louisville, Ky., on the first Saturday in May. The race provides a marvellous spectacle for the over 100,000 spectators who come to see the best three year olds in training being put to the test over the one-and-a-quarter mile circuit. In 1875, the race's inaugural year, the first prize was $2,850; by 1977, this had risen to $208,000. A Derby museum is open on the racecourse throughout the year, though only in the mornings on race days and the Churchill Downs executive struck a bronze medal in 1974 to commemorate the 100th running of the race. The Kentucky Derby is always enacted with pomp, circumstance and musical accompaniment, which includes a trumpet solo version of The Star Spangled Banner and a massed bands rendering of My Old Kentucky Home.

Most American races, including the Kentucky Derby, are run on dirt tracks, oval in shape and completely flat. However the Washington International, which justifies its name by attracting runners from all over the world, is run on a grass track at Laurel Park.

Racing in America is organised on completely different lines from those familiar in Europe. Race meetings are staged at the same tracks for up to two months, with as many as a dozen races on each card. Santa Anita Park, Los Angeles, for instance, started its 75 day meeting on New Year's day, 1978, when, despite heavy rain, 42,711 customers wagered $4,557,676 through the Pari-Mutuel — more or less the American equivalent of the British Tote.

The Far East

Since the Second World War, astute buying of bloodstock on a vast scale has helped Japan emerge as one of the world's leading racing nations. No less than six Epsom Derby winners now stand at stud there, as well as many other well-known imported stallions. Japanese racing is thriving, and the Japanese Derby, first run in 1933, is now worth $190,000 to the winner. Even Hong Kong's racecourse has proved so popular that sometimes the gates are closed on a capacity crowd an hour or more before the first race. Now a second Hong Kong course is being built.

The sport of Trotting

Trotting and pacing have never been so popular as thoroughbred racing, but during the 1960s, interest in the sport began to increase in many parts of the world. The modern equivalent of chariot racing, trotting first became popular in Europe, Russia and the USA in the eighteenth century. Now harness racing is big business and one in which horses have won as much as £750,000 in prize money during their careers.

Both pacers and trotters are known as Standardbreds, a breed which originated as long ago as 1790, when an English Thoroughbred, Messenger, was exported to Pennsylvania. In both trotting and pacing, Standardbred horses maintain a specified gait while pulling a driver sitting on a two-wheeled carriage, known as a sulky. Trotters move their left front leg and right back leg simultaneously, while pacers move both legs on the same side forward together. Because pacers wear hobbles, they are less likely to break into a gallop during a race.

By the 1960s in the USA, the sport had become so popular that more people watched trotting than American football. One track in New York took $2,000,000 in bets a night, six nights a week. In Australia, fifty-one tracks opened in New South Wales alone, while, in France, punters bet $8,000,000 on one race. In 1961, the champion French trotter, Jamin, was sold to an American breeder for $570,000.

This might suggest that the sport had suddenly found new wealth; but in fact as far back as 1903, the brilliant Dan Patch (1896–1916), nicknamed 'The Immortal' was barred from racing for the simple reason that he totally outclassed all his potential rivals. There was not one horse capable of giving him a race, so instead, he made exhibition runs against the stop watch. He was reputed to have run the mile 73 times in under two minutes and to have earned a highly satisfactory $4 million of prize money during his career.

In America, in 1935, a trotter called Greyhound won $33,000 in the Hambletonian, one third of the trotting Triple Crown and three years later, set speed records unequalled for three decades. On one occasion at Lexington, he clocked 1 minute 57¼ seconds over the mile – a time not beaten until 1966. Another record was set in 1965, when the well-bred Speedy Streak was sold at public auction for $113,000. He repaid his new owner's faith by winning the Hambletonian two years later.

The US trotting Triple Crown consists of the Yonkers Futurity in New York, the Hambletonian at Du Quoin, Illinois, and the Kentucky Futurity at Lexington, though the Roosevelt International is widely recognized as the world championship for trotters.

In Australia, the biggest events are the Interdominion Championship and the Australasia Championship, run annually in Melbourne since 1963. In 1976, the Grand Final offered a new record prize of $40,000 for a pacing event.

New Zealand is so keen to encourage trotters that at least two events at every race meeting are set aside for them.

Two harness racing scenes. This type of racing has gained considerably in international popularity in recent years, though it has always been a major sport in the USA, Australia, New Zealand, France and Germany.

Races fall into two categories – trotting and pacing. The difference between the two is that the latter is an artificial pace – the pacer is trained to trot on the laterals rather than the diagonals, the natural trotting gait.

In trotting, just as in motor racing, the competitors have a short runup to the start. They then race round the circuit, the chief rule being that the specified gait must not be broken. If a horse goes into a canter, for instance, the driver must immediately check the pace, thus losing vital seconds. A handicap system also operates; the faster horses have to start behind their slower competitors.

Chapter Eleven

Great horses

Simona

Be Fair

Laurieston

Mill Reef

Simona

This chestnut mare will always be remembered as the mount of West Germany's Hartwig Steenken, who died tragically after six months in a coma following a motor accident in 1977. She carried him to victory in the European Championship in Aachen in 1971, and, a year later, won him a team gold medal at the Munich Olympics. Most glorious of all was her performance at Hickstead in 1974, where the partnership won the World Championship. Simona has now retired to stud.

Be Fair

The chestnut mount of leading British rider Lucinda Prior-Palmer when she won her first European title at Luhmuhlen, West Germany, in 1975. The son of Sheila Willcox's Fair and Square, Be Fair's first major victory was at Badminton in 1973, after which he was selected for the European Championship team in Kiev. He was also in the British team for the 1974 World Championships in which it was unsuccessful, and for the 1976 Olympics. There, however, he slipped a tendon off his hock after going clear across country – an injury which ended his competitive career.

Laurieston

The mount of Richard Meade, one of Britain's leading male event riders, when he won the individual gold medal at the 1972 Munich Olympics; the UK also won the team event. Laurieston was bred in the UK by Major Derek Allhusen by the premium stallion Happy Monarch out of Laurien by Davy Jones. Laurien, too, had a successful international career; ridden by her owner, she took part in the European Championships in Copenhagen in 1957 as a member of the winning British team.

Mill Reef

Mill Reef, bred in America by his multimillionaire owner Paul Mellon, was later sent to the UK to be trained on the Hampshire downs by Ian Balding at Kingsclere. There, his early work convinced his trainer that Mill Reef was the best two-year-old he had ever handled. His belief was confirmed when Mill Reef bounced out of the stalls at Salisbury, and galloped home four lengths ahead of his nearest pursuer. He gained another easy victory at Royal Ascot, and was just beaten in France after a miserable journey and the worst possible draw. He won twice more as a two year old and shrugged off defeat by Brigadier Gerard in the Two Thousand Guineas, a distance too short for him, to win the Derby in 1971 with an explosive surge of speed and power. Continuing his triumphs into his third year, Mill Reef won the Eclipse Stakes at Sandown from the French hope, Caro, as a prelude to a runaway success in the King George VI and Queen Elizabeth Stakes at Ascot.

After a short rest, he achieved his finest victory, the Prix de l'Arc de Triomphe, at Lonchamp, in a new record time of 2 minutes 28.3 seconds over the mile and a half course.

Mill Reef had beaten Sea Bird II's time, and was the first English-trained winner of the Arc for twenty years. He was back at Longchamp the following spring for a ten length success over Amadou in the Prix Ganay, but a glorious second triumph in the Arc was denied him by his broken leg.

Red Rum

Red Rum's extraordinary career came to an untimely conclusion in April, 1978, in full view of the world's television cameras on the eve of what would have been his sixth consecutive Grand National over the daunting Aintree fences. Withdrawn through injury

Red Rum

Arkle

The Poacher

Gladiateur

less than 24 hours before the race he had dominated for so much of the decade, 'Rummy', as the horse was nicknamed, could do no more than parade before a huge crowd of 60,000 well-wishers in an emotional farewell to the racing scene.

He ran in five Grand Nationals, winning a record three and finishing a gallant second in the other two. His fame spread across the world and by the close of his career in the spring of 1978, Red Rum Ltd were charging up to £750 for each personal appearance he made. He opened nightclubs, fetes, attended functions and was greeted wherever he went as a true equine superstar.

Red Rum ran in exactly 100 races over fences and hurdles, winning twenty-four. Though his earnings were the jumper's record of £114,627, yet he originally changed hands as a yearling for a mere 400 guineas.

Rummy won his first two Nationals in 1973 and 1974, the first in a desperate finish after he had made up fully 100 yards to catch the fine New Zealand horse, Crisp. Already a legend, Rummy was then beaten into second place in 1975 and 1976, handicapped by extra big weight, and came back at the age of twelve, ridden by Tommy Stack, to complete the historic hat-trick in 1977.

Arkle
Red Rum will always be the King of Aintree but Arkle was surely the finest steeplechaser who ever lived.

Arkle ran in 35 races, three on the flat as part of his education, and six over hurdles. Over fences, he was beaten only four times — twice through a handicap of too much weight, once by an unlucky slip, and the last time when he incurred the injury that brought his marvellous career to a tragic end. He won £78,825 in prize money and the affection of all those who appreciate the sight of a brave horse and jockey jumping at speed.

Arkle won three Gold Cups in effortless style, but in other races found himself increasingly taking on the handicapper. For the first time in racing history, the handicapper was forced to formulate two handicaps – one if Arkle ran and another if he was withdrawn.

Adored by steeplechase fans on both sides of the Irish Sea, Arkle reigned supreme. A big, bright bay with an intelligent head and a bold, heart-stopping spring, he dominated steeplechasing for three and a half magical seasons until he fractured a bone in his foot in the King George VI Chase at Kempton Park on Boxing Day, 1966.

Gladiateur
Gladiateur, was the first French horse to win the Epsom Derby. His sparkling three length victory was a blow to the boasted supremacy of the British Thoroughbred. His form as a two year old was hardly memorable, but he won the 1865 Two Thousand Guineas well enough at 7 – 1 and went on to win the Derby fifty years to the month after Napoleon's defeat at Waterloo. In the same year, he added the French Derby, (The Prix du Jockey Club), to his list of triumphs, and in the autumn completed the Triple Crown despite intermittent lameness. His last race and victory in the Ascot Gold Cup still ranks as one of the most remarkable performances in racing history.

The Poacher
One of the leading British event horses of the late 1960s and early 1970s. Ridden by his owner, Captain Martin Whiteley, The Poacher won the individual silver medal at the 1967 European Championships; however, at the Mexico Olympics the following year, the horse was ridden by Staff Sergeant Ben Jones because of its owner's bad back.

Richard Mcade's association with The Poacher began in 1970, when he rode him to victory at Badminton. The following year, he rode the horse again in the winning British team for the European Championships at Burghley.

Kilbarry

Halla

Secretariat

Kilbarry

Though Irish-bred, Kilbarry was one of Britain's greatest three-day event horses, with a string of almost unbroken successes until his untimely death in a one-day event. Ridden by his owner, Colonel Frank Weldon, he won European silver medals in 1953 and 1954; in 1955 he won a European gold. The following year, he won Badminton, and a team gold and an individual bronze at the Stockholm Olympics.

Secretariat

In the stands at Belmont on June 9, 1973, the massive Secretariat, a powerful chestnut with three white socks, was being hailed as the greatest racehorse of all time. Just 250 yards away, hidden among the vast complex of 2,500 boxes, the subject of all the adoration was munching his way through a meal sufficient for three ordinary horses.

An hour earlier on the dirt course on Long Island, New York, he had run away with with the Belmont Stakes, final leg of his US Triple Crown, winning by the astonishing margin of

thirty-one lengths. Meanwhile, the thirty-two optimists who had paid $190,000 each in the previous winter for a share in his future, were viewing their syndication figure of $6,080,000 with the satisfaction of men who had just scooped the jackpot.

Statistics alone cannot convey the genius of this unique horse, sired by a champion, Bold Ruler, out of a mare, Something Royal, who never won a race. One breeding expert summed it up when he suggested; 'This is probably the best horse there has ever been. He's what everyone has been trying to breed for the past 100 years; one that sprints for one-and-a-half miles'.

First winner of the American Triple Crown for a quarter of a century, Secretariat won 16 of his 21 races in a meteoric career that spanned barely 16 months. Nicknamed 'Big Red' by his legion of admirers, he collected $1,316,808 in prize money. He won the Kentucky Derby in style by 2½ lengths from Sham in a record time, then came close to beating the record for the Preakness when defeating Sham again. After this, he shat-

tered the world record for 1½ miles on a dirt track while completing the Triple Crown in the Belmont Stakes. In an incredible solo display of power and speed, Secretariat made nearly all the running, drew clear of his toiling rivals at the half-way point, and won by thirty-one lengths, beating the previous best time for the race by 2.6 seconds. He was travelling so fast as Ron Turcotte began to pull him up, that he also set a new world record for thirteen furlongs.

Halla

Halla became nearly as famous as the man she brought to the forefront of world show jumping, Hans Günter Winkler of West Germany. A brown mare by the trotting sire Oberst out of the half-bred mare Helene, she started her career as a racehorse and then was tried as an eventer before being sent to Winkler by her owner, Gustav Vierling.

Halla won her first competition in 1952 and then the pair rocketed to fame and fortune. In 1953 they won in Rome, Madrid, Paris and Pinerolo; the following year, having started with three wins in Dortmund, the championship in Rome and one of the biggest classes in Lucerne, Halla took Winkler to the world title in Madrid. On the autumn circuit in the USA, she was equally consistent and successful.

Riding Halla in 1955, Winkler retained his world title in Aachen. The pair also won their first Hamburg Derby, which they retained in 1956, as well as winning an Olym-

Boomerang

The Rock

Doublet

pic team and individual gold medal in Stock-holm. Four years later, in Rome, they won another team gold medal.

Boomerang

The present mount of Eddie Macken, Ireland's leading international rider is Boomerang. He is the top Grand Prix horse in Europe in 1978, and has won the British Jumping Derby at Hickstead three times in succession, a feat no other horse has achieved. The last of these wins was in 1978, though, in the same month, he was beaten in the World Championship in Aachen by a fractional time penalty and cheated of the double title. Together they make one of the most popular combinations in modern show-jumping.

The Rock

The Rock was mount of the Italian rider Colonel Piero d'Inzeo, brother of Raimondo d'Inzeo, when he won the Olympic individual silver medal in Rome in 1960. A handsome grey Irish horse, he emerged dramatically on to the international scene in 1957, when he won in Paris, the Puissance contest in London (with the wall at 7ft 1in), a class in Dublin and two in Geneva. In 1958, he won two competitions in Rome, including the coveted Grand Prix, a class at Aachen and two – again including the Puissance – in London. The following year Paris again saw his first win of the season, followed by two in Aachen and two at Wembley, London. Show

jumping often seems to be a family affair as the d'Inzeo brothers demonstrated.

Doublet

The two horses with which H.R.H. Princess Anne is chiefly associated in her eventing career are Doublet and Goodwill. Doublet was bred by Queen Elizabeth II by Doubtless II out of an Argentinian polo pony mare. The high spot of his career was winning the European individual title at Burghley in 1971, but the horse had to be destroyed after breaking a hind leg during a dressage test at Windsor, a tragic set-back to the career of Britain's riding princess.

Democrat

Democrat was the best show jumper with which Billy Steinkraus, captain of the US team through six Olympics, from Helsinki to Munich, thought himself ever likely to be associated. Democrat's long career began in 1940 when, ridden by Colonel F. F. Wing, he first competed at the National Horse Show, Madison Square Gardens, New York, where

he was to become a by-word, winning the Grand Prix on his first outing in top company. In 1941, he won two competitions there; and, after an enforced retirement during the war, he staged a comeback in 1946, winning in New York and Toronto. This feat he repeated the following year. He was then sent to Europe for the Olympic Games. As part of the US team's pre-Olympic preparations, he won in Lucerne, Aachen, London and Dublin, while, in the Olympics themselves, he finished fourth individually.

In the same year, however, the US Army team was disbanded and Democrat went into retirement. In 1952, however, at the age of nineteen, he was brought back into the US Olympic team and, ridden now by Major John Russell, helped the USA to win the team bronze medals. On his return to the USA, he went on the autumn circuit of shows and, ridden by Bill Steinkraus, won every class in which he was entered at three major international meetings – one in Harrisburgh, four in New York and three in Toronto. After this, he went into final retirement.

Irish Cap

Goodwill

Cornishman V

Ballycor

Irish Cap and Might Tango

The two horses on which Bruce Davidson of the USA won his first World Horse Trials Championship in 1974 at Burghley in the UK and retained the title in 1978 at Lexington, Kentucky, respectively. Irish Cap, who also competed in the 1974 Olympics, was bred in Ireland and sold to the USA as an unbroken four-year-old. There, he remained unbroken until the age of six, as his girl owner was too small and too frightened to ride him.

Goodwill

After Doublet's tragic death, Princess Anne's chief partner was Goodwill, a former champion working hunter. Selected for the European Championships as individuals at Kiev in 1972, they were forced to retire after a fall at the second cross-country fence, but two years later they finished as runners-up to Lucinda Prior-Palmer and Be Fair at Luhmuhlen, West Germany. However, another fall at the 1976 Olympics put them well behind the leaders, though they finished the course. After Princess Anne's temporary retirement from the sport during her pregnancy, they were short-listed for the 1978 British team for the World Championships in Kentucky.

Cornishman V

The mount of leading British rider Mary Gordon-Watson when she won the European Championships in 1969 and the world title in 1970. Bred in Cornwall by Golden Surprise out of a point-to-point mare, Polly V, Cornishman was bought by Mary Gordon-Watson's father as a potential event horse for his daughter, even though Cornishman bucked him off into a muck heap when he first tried him. However, in the 1968 Olym-

pics, Cornishman was ridden by Richard Meade, as Mary Gordon-Watson had broken her leg three months before. In 1972, he won his second Olympic team gold medal in Munich, with his owner this time riding.

Ballycor

The mount of the US rider Tad Coffin when he won the Olympic individual gold medal at Bromont in 1976, the year after the horse had won the Pan American gold medal. A dark bay mare, 16.3 hands high and thirteen years old when she took part in the World Championships in 1978, Ballycor is a thoroughbred, by Cormac out of Bally Lickey, and was bred in America by Dr Charles Reid. In 1977, also with Tad Coffin, she won the Blue Ridge Advanced competition for the Gladstone Trophy; she was also the leading mare in American three-day events.

Sea Bird II

Of all the horses to have won Epsom's Derby this century, Sea Bird II probably has the highest reputation; yet his dam was sold to a

butcher for £100 long before he ever ran for the first time, in September 1964. Sea Bird II was something of a late developer, but he showed sufficient promise in the autumn of his second year to be aimed by his trainer at the leading events of 1965. Two victories in France made him an automatic favourite for the Epsom Derby. He did not let his supporters down. One moment he was cruising along handily placed behind the leaders, the next he had sprinted past the opposition to run home an early winner. It was a breathtaking achievement, enhanced by the subsequent victories of his nearest challenger, Meadow Court, first in the Irish Sweeps Derby, then in the King George VI and Queen Elizabeth Stakes.

Sea Bird II left Epsom to add the Grand Prix de Saint Cloud to his laurels, then settled down for his major test, the Prix de l'Arc de Triomphe. The field included Meadow Court, Reliance, unbeaten in five runs including the French Derby, Tom Rolfe, winner of the American Derby and Preakness Stakes, and a dozen other top class

Sea Bird II

Pele

Kelso

Foxhunter

thoroughbreds who had already proved themselves in competitive European contests.

Yet which horse would win the first prize of 1,084,747 francs was not in doubt for one moment. Settled by his jockey Pat Glennon in an ideal position close to the leaders, Sea Bird surged past his rivals in the straight to win by six lengths from Reliance.

Pele

Eddie Macken's previous mount was Pele. In 1974 they finished as runners-up to Steenken and Simona in the World Championship. Three years later, with Pele now re-christened Kerrygold, they were again runners-up for the European Championships in Vienna, beaten by a mere one-tenth of a second.

Kelso

Kelso's record as Horse of the Year in America for five consecutive seasons, from 1960 – 65, has never been equalled. He won a total of $1,977,896 racing on dirt and grass tracks and had an enormous following, including

his own fan clubs, in a career that started on September 4, 1959.

Kelso raced 63 times, winning 39 races outright, coming second twelve times, third twice, and fourth five times. He was unplaced in only five races and was the most consistent performer in the history of North American racing. He won at varying distances from six furlongs to two miles, on all types of going, and on twelve different courses ridden by six different jockeys. Three times runner-up in the much publicised Washington D.C. International, held at Laurel Park towards the close of each year, he finally won this elusive event on November 11, 1964, for the biggest prize – $90,000 dollars – of his long and distinguished career.

Kelso was probably the world's most famous gelding. Having recovered from the operation, carried out at the start of his career, he ran three times at Atlantic City, winning his debut race at 6 – 1, the best starting price ever offered him, and coming second in his other two races. An injury kept him off the course for the next nine months, after which he won

at Monmouth Park in June, 1960, for his new trainer, the former jockey Card Hanford. Beaten only once in 1960, in the Arlington Classic, he was voted Horse of the Year. He continued to dominate American racing for several years, usually winning but occasionally finding himself outmanoeuvered by the handicapper. Flat-racing horses tend to deteriorate after two or three seasons, but Kelso raced as honestly and bravely as ever until his retirement in 1966.

Foxhunter

One of the first really famous post-war British show jumpers, in partnership with his rider, Colonel Harry Llewellyn, Foxhunter started show jumping at the age of five in 1946. A year later, he was bought by Harry Llewellyn to begin their long association.

During his career, Foxhunter was consistently successful at international level. In 1948, he competed with the British team in the Olympics; a week after the Olympics closed, he won the King George V Gold Cup. Subsequent victories in this competition in 1950 and 1953 made him the only horse ever to win this prestigious trophy three times. Having triumphed at Grand Prix and Puissance competitions all over Europe and in North America, he then, at Helsinki, played a leading part in the UK's first and only Olympic show jumping victory.

Idle Dice

High and Mighty

Man O'War

Idle Dice

Ridden by the leading American professional, Rodney Jenkins, Idle Dice is the most
renowned show jumper in the USA. A brown
gelding, standing 17.1 hands high, he has
won more prize money than any other horse
in the history of the sport. Grand Prix Horse
of the Year in 1977, he has won the American Gold Cup three times, as well as the
American Invitational, the President's Cup
and many other major championships. In
1978, he was loaned to the US world championship by his owner, Harry Gill. In common
with most other American show jumpers,
Idle Dice was a failed race horse.

High and Mighty

British event horse who, ridden by Sheila
Willcox, won Badminton in both 1957 and
1958. In 1957, too, they took the individual
and a team gold medal in the European
Championships at Copenhagen. However,
as the three-day Olympic event was at that
time still closed to women riders, they were
never able to compete in the Games. Sheila
Willcox went on to become one of the UK's
leading eventing trainers.

Man O'War

Man O'War's deserved reputation as the finest American-bred racehorse has withstood a
series of challenges from such famous modern
candidates as Kelso and Secretariat. Foaled in
Kentucky in 1917 and sold a year later at the
Saratoga Sales for $5,000, Man O'War – a
richly coloured chestnut with a powerful,
stocky, frame – proved to be the ultimate

racehorse. Beaten just once in 21 starts, he
won a total of $249,465 and caught the
imagination of the nation throughout his
brief career of only seventeen months.

Nicknamed 'Big Red', a label also given to
Secretariat nearly fifty years later, Man
O'War was a giant of a horse, with en-
thusiasm and courage to match his outstanding ability. News of his startling home gallops
made him a celebrity before he had even run
in public; his first race confirmed these
rumours when he won a modest $500 dollar
maiden event at Belmont Park. He started
odds-on that day, a pattern that was maintained in all his races. He won six races in a
row before being beaten in a six furlong race
at Saratoga, owing to the over-confident
riding of his jockey, Johnny Loftus. Man
O'War was trapped on the rails and shut in
despite a small field, but once clear he made
up ground rapidly and failed to catch the
winner by only half a length. Having won
three more races in 1919, he took an eight

month break from racing.

Despite his non-appearance at the Kentucky Derby, his fans thought the wait worth-
while, for he strolled home in the second and
third legs of the Triple Crown. Man O'War
won all his eleven races as a three-year-old,
breaking seven track, American, or world
records during the year. Three times he
started at the remarkable odds of 100 – 1 on,
and once he won by no less than 100 lengths.
His last race and victory came in a match
against the Canadian, Sir Barton, the American Triple Crown winner in 1919. Setting
out to make all the running, Man O'War
galloped clean away from his illustrious rival,
breaking the ten furlong track record by 6⅘ of
a second.

His devoted owner, Samuel Riddle, retired
him to stud in 1921, and restricted him to the
unusually low figure of 25 mares a year to
conserve his strength. The wonder horse
lived to 1947, siring the winners of more than
$3,500,000 in stake money.

Ribot

Mister Softee

Ali Baba

Ali Baba

Ali Baba was one of a long succession of French-bred Anglo-Arabs which carried Pierre Jonqueres d'Oriola to a series of dazzling victories. The partnership came together in 1952 in Rome; they collaborated so well that they were selected for the Olympics, where they won the individual gold medal. D'Oriola repeated this feat on Lutteur at Tokyo in 1964.

Ribot

The calm and peaceful pastures of West Sussex were the unlikely setting for the birth of Italy's greatest racehorse. Ribot was born there in 1952, as the result of a union arranged by breeding genius Frederico Tesio who, sadly, did not live to see his finest achievement prove his methods on the track.

When still very young, Ribot returned to Italy with his dam. Small and backward, he looked insignificant and was so unprepossessing that he was not even entered for the

Italian classics. But his puny frame disguised a burgeoning ability, that, for a brief and glorious period, was to capture the imagination of the racing world.

Ribot won his first race, easily beating a more fancied stable mate in the process, and, without being extended, soon proved himself the champion two year old of Italy. Champion again at three, despite missing the classics, he won all his races with consummate ease before heading for Europe's most contested prize, the Prix de l'Arc de Triomphe at Longchamp in October, 1955. The French treated the invader with contempt in the hulabaloo of the days leading up to the race, and consequently, he was allowed to start at the amazingly generous 9–1. Never in the slightest danger of losing his unbeaten record, he cantered home unchallenged, three lengths ahead of his nearest rival.

Next season, as a four-year old, Ribot travelled to Ascot, for the prestigious King George VI and Queen Elizabeth Stakes, run over unusually heavy ground for high summer. His five length win was labelled by the critics, somewhat unkindly, as laboured and unimpressive. Then, after another easy win in Milan, Ribot headed for Longchamp once more, in a bid to become the fifth horse to complete a double in the Prix de L'Arc de Triomphe.

The opposition was particularly strong, with winners of many major European races competing in the field. Ribot, however, swept through them all in a performance of stunning power. Seldom has a horse dominated a champion field so completely. Jockey Enrico Camici settled him in third place as

Fisherman set a furious gallop, closed on the leader effortlessly on the final bend, then simply sprinted away. At the post, he was six lengths clear and increasing his lead with every stride.

Unchallenged in sixteen races spread over three seasons, Ribot returned to an equally successful and prolific career at stud, first in Europe, then from 1960 onwards in Kentucky. His influence is still enormous on both sides of the Atlantic. Tom Rolfe, Graustark, Molvedo, Ribocco, Ribero, Ribofilio, and Arts and Letters are only a few of the champions he sired before his premature death.

Mister Softee

Favourite mount of the distinguished British show jumper David Broome. An Irish horse, bought at Dublin Horse Show as a three-year-old after he had been lunged over a pole, Mister Softee won the European Championship in London in 1962 when ridden by David Barker – but he really made his name after joining the Broome team in 1965. The following year, the two proved unbeatable in major UK competitions, winning the King George V Gold Cup, the British Jumping Derby at Hickstead, the Olympic Trial and the Victor Ludorum at the Horse of the Year Show. In 1967, they won the European Championship at Rotterdam, retaining it at Hickstead in 1969, after jumping-off with Alwin Schockemohle on Donald Rex. In the intervening year, they won an Olympic bronze medal in Mexico for Great Britain, becoming one of the most popular combinations in British and international show-jumping.

Sympatico

Ormonde

Jet Run

Sympatico

An eighteen-year-old thoroughbred gelding when bought by a Canadian syndicate in 1976, Sympatico is now owned by 25-year-old Terry Leibel, whose father paid a reputed $300,000 for the horse. Sympatico's reputation more than explains the price; he was the leading Grand Prix horse in the USA from 1972 to 1975, setting the world Puissance record at a towering 7ft 4in in New York in 1974.

St Simon and Ormonde

These two horses, born two years apart, dominated British racing in the late nineteenth century. The great jockey Fred Archer, who killed himself in tragic circumstances at the height of his career, rode both horses but clearly held St Simon in the higher esteem.

Ormonde, winner of the elusive Triple Crown – the Two Thousand Guineas, the Derby and the St Leger – was unbeaten in all his races but proved a hopeless failure at stud. St Simon, on the other hand, cost only 1,600 guineas, never ran in a Classic, but won all his races with contemptuous ease (though his earnings in prize money were a mere £4,676) and became one of the most important sires in the history of the turf. His first stud fee, in 1886, was no more than 50 guineas, but by

1899, he had become such a prolific sire of winners that his price rose to 500 guineas for each mare he covered.

Ormonde's failure as a stallion contrasts sadly with his brilliance as a racehorse. There have been few Epsom Derby winners to match his excellence, for in his three years on the turf he was never beaten. He won £28,625 in prize money, and started at the astonishing price of 100-1 on in the 1886 Champion Stakes.

Ormonde won the first leg of the Triple Crown, the Two Thousand Guineas, at the generous odds of 7-2 from the supposed certainty, Minting. He went on to triumph in the 1886 Derby in runaway style from the Bard, who himself had been undefeated in 16 races as a two year old. By October that year, his reputation was so formidable that the owners of the Bard and Melton, winners of the 1885 Derby and St Leger, each paid a £500 forfeit rather than risk their horses against him in a private sweepstake at Newmarket. Despite growing problems with his

wind, as a four-year-old, he won three more races and even beat the top sprinter, Whitefriar, by two lengths over six furlongs, a tremendous feat even for a Triple Crown winner.

Ormonde might well have continued to dominate his rivals, but his wind problems cut short his career, and he was eventually sold by his owner, the Duke of Westminster, to an Argentinian breeder in 1889. Four years later, he was sold again, to a US buyer, but he proved an abject failure at stud, and managed to sire only 16 foals in 11 years. One of the finest racehorses in the history of the Thoroughbred, he ended his life infertile, and was put down in 1904.

St Simon headed the sires' list in England nine times, was twice second and three times third. His influence was immense, for he sired the winners of no less than seventeen Classics and three Ascot Gold Cups. Altogether, his offspring won 571 races and £553,159 in prize money. In 1896, he led the stallions list with his son St Serf second, and his own sire, Galopin, third.

Posillipo

Flanagan

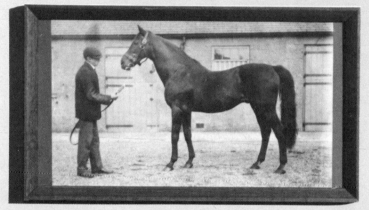

St Simon

St Simon died in 1908 as he was returning from exercise; his skeleton was given to the British Museum. Despite the affection inherent in his trainer's account St Simon did cause a few problems at the Welbeck stud. On one occasion, he was given a stable companion to quieten him down. The plan misfired, for he seized the poor animal, tossed it against the ceiling of the box, and trampled it to death.

Jet Run

A nine-year-old, 16.2 hands bay gelding, Jet Run is one of the biggest winners in North America. Originally owned by the Mexican Fernando Senderos, he won New York's Grand Prix in 1974 and a Pan American gold medal in 1975.

After touring Europe with Jet Run in 1977, Senderos sold him to the American owner F. Eugene Dixon, Jr., who made him available to the US equestrian team. Ridden by Michael Matz, he won the American Jumping Derby in Rhode Island in 1977, as well as the Grand Prix at the Royal Winter Fair in Toronto and the Valley Forge Grand Prix. In 1978, he was one of the four finalists in the world championship.

Posillipo

Mount of the Italian rider Colonel Raimondo d'Inzeo, Piero d'Inzeo's brother, when he won the Olympic individual gold medal in Rome in 1960. However, this Italian thoroughbred had a comparatively short working life as an international show jumper, especially when compared with Raimondo d'Inzeo's own favourite horse, Bellevue, now in his twenties.

Flanagan

For many years, Britain's Pat Smythe was the most successful woman rider in the world, and the most consistent of her mounts was the Irish-bred chestnut Flanagan. Foaled in 1948, he started his career as a three-day event horse, but, under Pat Smythe, he became one of the world's leading show jumpers. Among many top international prizes, he won her the Ladies' European Champion-ship at Spa in 1957, Deauville in 1961, Madrid in 1962 and Hickstead in 1963. He was also a member of the Olympic team in 1956 and 1960.

Phar Lap

No champion has ever started life with less likely credentials than Phar Lap. Unplaced in his first four races in 1929, he did at last win a modest race at his fifth attempt, but then reverted to his more customary position of an also ran in his next three outings. Yet this most famous of Australasian race-horses was to improve so rapidly that he won no fewer than 37 of his 51 races.

As a three year old, he landed the A.J.C. and Victoria Derbys as well as the Craven Plate, before running third in the Melbourne Cup. After a rest, he returned to win another third place before beginning a sequence of nine straight wins. The big ugly duckling, as the horse was affectionately described, had sprouted wings. He continued to improve, winning the nickname Red Terror, and duly won the Melbourne Cup at odds of 8 – 11 despite carrying the burden of 138lbs.

The next step was a trip to America, where Phar Lap won the Mexican Agua Calienta handicap. But, sadly, this was his last race. Shortly afterwards, he died after eating grass which had been sprayed with insecticide.

The glossary

Aachen One of the chief world centres for show jumping and dressage; the purpose-built stadium, just outside the city, was erected after the Second World War. The stadium is equipped with excellent exercise areas and blocks of permanent stabling, as well as a large covered grandstand and uncovered seating. Audience capacity is 50,000.

Aachen is the most popular show in the world with riders. There are two main reasons for this; in Hans-Heinrich Brinckmann, a pre-war German cavalry officer, it has the finest course builder in the world, while the prize money, too, is extremely high. The event often attracts fifteen to twenty full international teams; the Nations' Cup is thus a reliable guide to world form, with the best teams competing over an extremely testing course, while it takes an Olympic-standard horse to win the Grand Prix.

Accoutrements The tack – saddles, bridles and bits – worn by the horse. The earliest surviving examples come from the Near and Middle East, where horses were at first harnessed and controlled in pairs under a yoke, with a nose ring. By 1700 BC, however, the first bits had been introduced; a surviving bronze example from Gaza has a plain bar mouthpiece and circular cheek pieces, with a barbaric spike on their inner surfaces. More elaborate bits have been found in Luristan, in western Iran. These date from the 7th to 10th centuries BC, with the cheek pieces cast in the form of horses or moufflons.

As the chariot horse was replaced by the ridden horse, bits, too, changed their form. Hungarian bits of the 15th century BC had soft mouthpieces of rope, gut or rawhide. Greek bits of the 6th and 7th centuries BC had bar or arc-shaped cheek pieces, while early Italian bronze bits of the 9th to 7th centuries BC were made with jointed mouthpieces.

The first mounted troops appeared in Assyria in the 9th century BC, riding on animal skins held in place by breastbands. By the 6th century BC, the Persians were also using saddle cloths and, by about AD 100, the Romans had a leather military saddle, secured by an overall roller, a crupper and a breastplate.

Stirrups made their first appearance with the Huns, though they were not developed in western Europe until Charlemagne's wars against the Avars of Hungary and there is no evidence of their general use until the 9th century AD. They revolutionised the art of riding, however, and led to the soft saddle being replaced by a rigid structure, with a pair of shaped boards, padded and stuffed top and bottom, lying on either side of the horse's spine. The boards were joined by two iron arches. The next stage, with more agile horses, was a saddle with a deeper seat, giving the rider greater contact with the horse.

With the Middle Ages, curb bits came into common use, as warhorses became heavier and greater collection was required of them. In the Renaissance, schooled horses wore single-rein curbs; training, however, started with a cavesson in order not to spoil their mouths, after which the curb was first used with 'false reins' attached to its top rings to form a pelham. To suit this dominant style of riding, a variety of extremely severe bits was developed, but, slowly over the centuries, they, too, were replaced by less severe ones. The ultimate development came with the use of double bridles and snaffles, together with the introduction of different types of saddles for various activities. This was part and parcel of the forward seat style of riding, originated by Federico CAPRILLI of Italy in the early 20th century.

Aging Age in the horse is determined by the examination of its six incisor teeth. When all the permanent incisors have fully erupted, the horse is said to have a full mouth. From then on, age is assessed from the changes that occur on the wearing surfaces of the lower incisors, and the angle at which they meet those of the upper jaw. Up to the age of eight, the age can be accurately estimated; after that, however, the system is less precise, which is why horses over the age of seven are described as 'aged'.

In assessing age, it is important to note that all Thoroughbreds are likely to be born early in the year and other breeds in the spring. Thus, in the Northern Hemispere, the age of a Thoroughbred is judged to date from January 1; of other breeds from May 1. A Thoroughbred foal born in late December is therefore deemed for racing purposes to be a year old the following month.

The lifespan of a healthy horse varies enormously according to the care it receives and the work it does. The greatest age so far recorded is that of Old Billy, a barge horse who died at sixty-two. Generally, a horse is considered mature at between six and seven according to its size and type, and in its prime at eight. It can work hard until it is aged between twelve and fourteen and do light work up to the age of twenty – and in some cases even after this.

Aids The various means employed by the rider to transmit his or her wishes to the horse. There are two types – the natural aids (legs, hands, seat and voice) and the artificial aids (whip and spur). Other differentiations are lateral and diagonal aids, combinations of hand and leg aids on the same side of the horse or on opposite sides.

In early training, lateral aids are used as they are more readily understood by the horse. In later, more advanced, training, diagonal aids are employed. Both hands, sometimes known as the upper aids, control pace, speed and direction by acting, resisting or yielding. The legs, the lower aids, produce forward movement, and shift or hold the haunches in the same manner.

Airs Above the Ground The name given to High School movements in which the horse jumps into the air. Examples are the *ballotade, croupage, courbette, capriole* and *levade*.

Airs, Classical The aim of classical equitation is to develop and perfect the natural movements of the horse. Exercises on the ground, of the kind required in dressage tests, range from walk, trot and canter on a single track, through lateral work, when the horse moves sideways as well as forward, to the *piaffe* and *passage*. The airs above the ground, developed from the natural leaps of the horse, are the *levade* and *pesade*, with the horse rising on its deeply bent haunches, the forelegs folded under its chest, and the *capriole*, with the hind legs kicking vigorously simultaneously. When not kicking out, the horse performs a *ballotade*. In the *courbette*, it leaps several times on its hind legs without touching the ground with its forelegs. A single leap on the hind legs is called a *croupade*.

From the sixteenth to the eighteenth centuries, these airs were part of the training of a school horse and they were used in mock jousts and tournaments. Today, they are best displayed in the art of the Spanish Riding School of Vienna.

Amateur and professional A controversial area of riding, particularly at the top international level. For some years, for example, the International Olympic Committee and others have levelled charges of 'shamateurism' at the leading show jumpers of many nations; in the UK, for instance, some horses are now sponsored by companies in exchange for a change of name to advertise their products. Thus, in 1972, the International Equestrian Federation announced that every national federation must declare its professionals. Britain led the way, with forty-six riders taking out professional licences, in the hope that other countries would follow suit. Ironically, the I.O.C. has now found a compromise solution to the problem.

Badminton The Cotswold home of the Dukes of Beaufort in Gloucestershire, England, is the setting for the Badminton Three-Day Horse Trials, one of the chief fixtures in the eventing calendar since its foundation in 1949. Many top riders have competed there, including Richard Meade,

Lucinda Prior-Palmer and H.R.H. Princess Anne, and the results are a good guide to world ratings in the sport.

Bareme The name given to the table under which a jumping competition is judged. Table A covers jumping only, and Table C speed.

Barrage The alternate name for a jump-off, in which horses with equal scores at the end of a competition compete against each other again. The result can either be decided by the number of faults, time against the clock, or a combination of the two.

Bitless Bridle A bridle without a mouth-piece, the horse being controlled by pressure on the nose. Its alternate name is a hackamore.

Brushing The term applied when a horse strikes its fetlock with the shoe on the opposite foot. It is usually a result of faulty action.

Buck Over-fresh horses can 'get their backs up' and kick into the air, either during a ride when, say, a change of pace is asked for, or when the rider is settling in the saddle.

Burghley The seat, near Stamford in Lincolnshire, of the Marquess of Exeter, is the home of Britain's principal autumn three-day event, the Burghley Horse Trials, which started in 1961. It has been the scene of two World Championships in 1966 and 1974, and three European Championships in 1963, 1971 (when the individual title was won by H.R.H. Princess Anne on Doublet), and 1977, when Lucinda Prior-Palmer won her second title and the British team won the team title back from the USSR.

Byerley Turk An Arab stallion who was one of the three founders of the English Thoroughbred. The Byerley Turk was captured from the Turks at the siege of Budapest and brought back to England by Captain Byerley – hence the name. Never raced, the horse proved to be a top-class sire, though it covered relatively few mares. One of the Turk's most distinguished descendants was Herod, who was foaled in 1758.

Caprilli, Federico (1868–1907) Italian cavalry officer who originated the chief modern style of riding. Caprilli's influence began when he succeeded Cesare Paderni as instructor at Pinerola. There, he abolished the accepted classical method of riding, regarding this as totally unsuitable for riding across country, and, after private experiment, introduced his celebrated Forward Seat to replace it. This met with great opposition from traditionalists, and, to prove his theories, Caprilli negotiated the famous *Scivalone* (slide) at Tor di Quinto in this position. He also won numerous competitions, as well as the army championship, riding his Irish horse Pouf.

Caprilli, however, wrote only a few notes on his innovations; these appeared in 1901 in the *Revista di Cavalleria*. In December 1907, he died while riding his horse at a walk at Turin, either from a heart attack or as a result of an old head wound. In the same year, the seat was adopted by the entire Italian cavalry and army officers from all over the world were sent to Italy to learn to ride in this manner. Their teaching on their return home did much to establish the seat's reputation, as did Italian successes in international competitions.

Cavalletto Small fence consisting of a squared-off pole, supported at each end in an X-shaped support. Cavalletti are used for schooling, either in the form of a grid or built up to make a fence.

Chaff Chopped-up hay or oat straw. It is mixed with corn or bran to form a bulk feed.

Chef d'équipe Term used in the horse world to describe a team manager. Show jumping teams and eventing teams all have their chef d'équipe, whose role is organizational and strategical.

Cob Name given to a stocky, short-legged horse, not much over or under 15.1 hands, with good bone and body and up to weight. The best ones are good rides and have the ability to gallop willingly and freely.

Collect To pull a schooled horse together by creating impulsion with the legs and containing it with the hands. As a result, the horse brings its hind legs more under its body.

Colt Term used to describe a young male horse under four years old.

Combined Training A dressage and show-jumping competition, possibly including a cross-country test, as in the three-day event.

Cow hocks A conformational weakness of the horse. In it, the points and the joints of the hocks incline towards one another.

Crib biting A stable vice, in which the horse gets hold of the door or manger with the incisors and swallows air. This leads to indigestion.

Curb A prominence situated a hand's breadth below the point of the hock, caused by sprain of the calcaneometatarsal ligament. It is conspicuous when the horse is viewed from the side and is a serious blemish as far as a show horse is concerned. In racing, however, the curb is tolerated as long as the horse is sound.

Curb Bit A bit consisting of a straight mouthpiece to which are attached two hooks. These hold the curb chain, which fits into the chin groove on the lower jaw. The bit works by leverage on the lower jaw, exerting pressure on the chin groove by means of the chain. It is one half of a DOUBLE BRIDLE, the other being the SNAFFLE.

Curry Comb A large, flat metal comb, used to clean the body brush – never the horse.

Darley Arabian The most important of the three founders of the English Thoroughbred, the horse was imported to Britain from the east by a Mr Darley in the early eighteenth century. Foaled in 1700, he was a bay horse with a blaze and three white socks, and stood about fifteen hands high. Out of the famous mare Betty Leedes, he sired the two brothers Flying Childers and Bartletts Childers. He was also the sire of Bulle Rock, the first Thoroughbred to go to the USA.

Derby (Jumping) The prototype show jumping Derby was held in Hamburg in 1920. It proved so successful and spectacular that its formula of cross-country-type show jumping over a long course, with permanent fences such as banks, sunken coffin-type fences, table fences, ditches and stone walls, has been enthusiastically adopted elsewhere. The most notable examples are the British Jumping Derby, held at Hickstead in Sussex, and the French equivalent, held at the seaside resort of La Baule.

The Hamburg version did not produce a single clear round until 1935. The British one, which started in 1961, produced its nineteenth clear round in 1978, when it was won for the third consecutive year by Eddie Macken and Boomerang for Ireland. He and Harvey Smith have each won it three times, but Smith has had two different mounts.

Dope tests Under the International Equestrian Federation's rules for international sport, the use of stimulants, sedatives and anabolic steroids is absolutely prohibited. However, the use of painkilling drugs, such as phenylbutazone or butazolidine is only forbidden for dressage horses – a ruling that is causing considerable controversy, particularly in the three-day event field.

Urine tests, to discover whether drugs have been used, are taken at all international meetings. If the horse does not produce a sample within an hour, it is up to the discretion of the organizers as to whether blood or saliva tests shall be taken instead. Because of the quite understandable fear of infection, some riders refuse to allow blood samples to be taken in the unsterile atmosphere of a showground.

Double Two fences with only a short distance between them, which the rider has to jump as a combination.

Double Bridle A showing bridle, also used by some riders in the hunting field and dressage arena. It consists of two bits, a CURB and a SNAFFLE, each with separate cheek pieces and its own rein. The double bridle is more sophisticated than the snaffle, which merely raises the head; the curb causes the horse to flex its neck and to bring its nose in.

Drag Hunt A form of hunting gaining increasing popularity. Instead of chasing a live quarry, the hunters and hounds follow a scent which has been put down artificially, often using an aniseed trail laid by a runner.

Draw rein A rein fixed to the girth and passing through the rings of the bit to the rider's hand.

Driving Competitions (International) The sport of combined driving, based on the ridden three-day event, is a relatively new one. It has become increasingly popular during recent years, especially in the UK, where one of its most prominent supporters is Prince Philip. The West Germans and the Poles are also very successful, as are the Dutch with their Friesians and the Hungarians with their little blood horses.

Entire The term used to describe an ungelded horse.

F.E.I. (Fédération Equestre Internationale) The international governing body of competitive equestrian sport. Based in Brussels, its president is H.R.H. The Prince Philip, Duke of Edinburgh.

Fillis, James (1834–1913) Influential British riding master, who spent most of his life in France. At eight, Fillis was already riding difficult horses well, largely due to the influence of his fine teacher François Caron, himself a pupil of François Baucher, one of the greatest French trainers. Fillis devoted his life to training horses for Haute Ecole, including a period at the Champs-Elysee circus from 1873 to 1886. Of small stature, he had great strength in his legs, which he maintained were of more importance to the horseman than hands.

Fillis created his own school, based on the classical precepts. This is still followed today, although Caprilli maintained that Fillis imposed an artificial balance on the horse. His methods were especially influential in Russia and in 1898 he was appointed riding master to the School of Cavalry for Officers in St Petersburg, a position he held until 1910. He died in Paris three years later.

Filly The name given to a young mare, under four years old. It is chiefly associated with racing.

Gag A gag snaffle bit has cheek pieces which pass through holes in the top and bottom of the rings and lead right on to the reins. It is a severe bit and should only be used by a rider with good hands.

Gaited horses A prominent class of American show horse. The horses have five gaits, the two extra ones being the stepping pace and the rack. Both of these are cultivated artificially, though there is some

hereditary ability involved.

The stepping pace is a slow gait with a slight break in cadence from the pace, in which the near fore and near hind feet strike the ground simultaneously, followed by the off fore and off hind. The rack, which used to be known as the single foot, is a smooth, fast gait, in which each foot strikes the ground separately. Gaited horses also carry their tails high; this is the result of an operation which severs the tail's depressor muscles.

Galls Areas on an unfit horse's body which have been rubbed raw by ill-fitting girths and saddles. They are a sign of bad horsemanship and stable management. Work should cease until the galls are healed and the skin has hardened.

Godolphin Arab or Barb The third stallion to play a part in the foundation of the English Thoroughbred. The Godolphin Arab was bought in Paris in 1729 by a Mr Edward Coke of Derbyshire. A lop-eared bay, standing just under fifteen hands, he was purchased by the Earl of Godolphin after Coke's death in 1733 and, during a career of twenty years, covered some ninety mares. His most notable son was Cade (1733) and his most celebrated descendant was West Australian, sired in 1850. West Australian was the sire of Solon and Australian; from the latter descended the notable American sires Fairplay and Man o' War. Solon was the grandsire of Marco, by Barcaldine, who perpetuated the line in England through such legendary sires as Hurry On and Precipitation.

Going Used to describe the various states of the ground. Going can be soft, hard, holding (sticky mud) and so on.

Grand Pardubice A gruelling steeplechase in Czechoslovakia, founded in 1874 by Count Octavian Kinsky and held annually on the second Sunday in October. The course of $4\frac{1}{2}$ miles runs over ploughed fields and contains thirty-one fences, of which the most difficult is the Taxis ditch. This is 16 feet 5 inches wide and is fronted by a natural fence 5 feet high and 5 feet wide.

Hickstead Douglas Bunn started the All England Jumping Course in the fields of his home, Hickstead Place, in 1960 to provide a continental-style course with permanent obstacles for British horses and riders. His idea was to help them gain experience in order to accustom them to international conditions before they went abroad. The following year, Hickstead was sponsored by the British company W.D. & H.O. Wills, who have backed it ever since. It is now recognized as one of the greatest show jumping centres in the world.

Four meetings are held at Hickstead each year; the course is the home of the Prince of Wales (British Nations) Cup and of the

British Jumping Derby. In addition to the international arena, there are five secondary rings, while show classes, dressage tests and driving competitions have established Hickstead as an all-round show.

Hobdayed Horses with afflictions of their respiratory organs, or who are touched in the wind, can be cured by the Hobdaying operation – so-called because it was invented by Professor Frederick Hobday (1870–1939). The operation consists of removing the paralysed vocal cords, which inhibit breathing, from the larynx. The only side effect is that the horse can no longer whinney.

Interval training A system of conditioning horses to increase their speed and endurance. It is widely and successfully practised by the US Three-Day event team – the team and individual world champions in 1974 and the Olympic team and individual gold medallists in 1976.

Interval training improves respiration, circulation and removal of waste products by subjecting the horse alternately to the stress of curtailed effort and rest. Athletically efficient muscle can be developed by short gallops at speeds just below the maximum of which the horse is safely capable, with walking intervals between them. Each gallop is started after a period of walking, but before the horse has quite recovered from the previous gallop. This stimulates the heart and lungs to supply the oxygen shortfall in the blood.

During the first months, the trainer gradually increases the speed of each series of gallops until the horse reaches the speed required for the trial in view. At the same time, he improves the horse's stamina by galloping it over a constant distance, say 700 yards, a fixed number of times (not more than five in one day), with a constant $1\frac{1}{2}$ minute walking period, twice a week.

In the following weeks he prepares the horse to stay the whole distance required by progressively increasing the number of daily gallops from five to perhaps nine. To develop speed, he uses a few short gallops at increasing speeds; to develop stamina, he uses an increasing number of slightly longer gallops at slower speeds.

Kentucky Derby The most famous Thoroughbred race in the USA. It is held at Churchill Downs, Louisville, Kentucky, for three-year-olds carrying 57kg (126 1lbs) and run over $1\frac{1}{4}$ miles; the first race was in 1875, when the distance was $1\frac{1}{2}$ miles (this was shortened in 1896). The race attracts the best three-year-olds in the USA, as well as entrants from overseas. It is the inaugural race in the Triple Crown series, with Preakness and Belmont following it.

Long-distance Riding Major sport in the USA and, now, in other countries, such as Australia and the UK. In the USA, endurance riding started in 1919, when the US cavalry held a series of tests to compare the quality of Thoroughbreds with Arabs; each horse and rider had to cover 300 miles, averaging sixty a day, carrying weights from 200 to 245lbs. Following this, the annual Vermont One Hundred Mile Three-Day Competitive Trail Ride was founded, while, in the west, the North American Trail Ride Conference set up a similar series over shorter distances of twenty to thirty miles. The championship is the Tevis Cup ride, started in 1955, from Tahoe City in Nevada to Auburn, California. It follows the same steep trail over the Sierra Nevada mountains that the Wells Fargo express riders used to take, with conditions ranging from snow and icy winds at Squaw Pass to 100-degree heat in El Dorado Canyon. Of the 175 starters, forty per cent usually drop out.

Rules governing such rides are designed to protect the horses as much as possible. Riders finishing early are eliminated, for instance, and the horses are frequently examined for condition and soundness. Condition is judged on recovery of pulse and respiration after a climb, on the horse's willingness to eat, and by signs of dehydration and the quality of the sweat – profuse lathery sweat, as opposed to clear sweat, is an obvious sign of unfitness. Horses are penalised for sore backs, stiffness, filled legs, and nicks or cuts due to tiredness or faulty action.

Lungeing Rein A webbing rein, some forty feet long, which is attached to the bridle. It enables the horse to be schooled or exercised in circles around the user without actually being ridden.

Martingale A device designed to prevent a horse raising its head far enough to evade the bit. A standing martingale, which has a neck strap, goes from the noseband to the girth and is attached to both. A running martingale, which also has a neck strap, goes from the girth to a small ring around each rein – in the case of a double bridle, to the snaffle rein. The Irish martingale is simply two rings at either end of a short strip of leather which has the reins passed through it at the front of the horse's neck.

Maryland Hunt Cup One of the oldest and most celebrated steeplechases in the USA, the Maryland Hunt Cup has been run annually since 1896 at Glyndon, some ten miles from Baltimore, over a permanent course built in natural hunting country. The fences are solid timber up to 5ft 6in in height.

Until 1972, the only prize was a silver cup for the winner, though now there is a purse. One of the race's most famous winners was Jay Trump, who pulled off the unique treble of the Hunt Cup in 1963 and 1964 and the British Grand National in 1965.

Nap A nappy horse refuses to do as the rider wishes, usually failing to move in the desired direction. Instead, the horse stands still and may try to buck or rear.

Navicular Disease A chronic inflammation of the navicular bone in the foot, caused by concussion. Show jumpers are particularly prone to it and are often de-nerved (the nerves cut) in order to prolong their active life. In its early stages, the disease can be identified if the horse leaves the stable lame but becomes sound as work progresses.

Newcastle, William Cavendish, Duke of (1592–1676) Celebrated seventeenth-century British cavalryman and horse trainer, noted for his sympathetic treatment of the horse. His basic precept was to 'put as little iron in your horse's mouth as you can.'

Newmarket Centre of UK racing since the reign of Charles II and the headquarters of the Jockey Club, British racing's governing body. It is renowned both as a race course – the Two Thousand Guineas and the One Thousand Guineas are run there in the spring and the Cesarewitch and the Cambridgeshire in the autumn – and for its Thoroughbred sales. The National Stud has been there since 1967 and there are some fifty other Thoroughbred studs in the area, in addition to countless training establishments.

Numnah A pad, usually made of sheepskin, the same shape as the saddle. It is placed under the saddle to prevent it rubbing the horse's back.

One-Day Event A modified Three-Day event, it was first held in the UK in 1950 as a nursery for the higher level. It is now so popular that there is a spring and an autumn season at every level, from restricted novice through intermediate and open intermediate to advanced. The test consists of dressage, cross-country and show jumping, the missing elements being roads and tracks and steeplechase.

Pacer A harness horse who, instead of employing a true (trotting) pace, moves the near and the hind leg simultaneously on the same side. Such horses are frequently hobbled to encourage this type of movement.

Passage A High School movement consisting of a very rhythmic, collected, elevated, cadenced trot in which there is pronounced engagement of the quarters, an accentuated flexion of the knees and the hocks, and graceful elasticity of movement. Each diagonal pair of legs is raised and lowered alternately, gaining little ground, with an even cadence and a prolonged suspension.

Pelham A bit which combines SNAFFLE and CURB in one mouthpiece.

Piaffe A very collected trot on the spot asked for in dressage and High School work. The horse's back should be supple and vibrating, with the hocks well engaged, so giving great freedom and lightness to the action of the forehand.

Pirouette A High School movement in which the horse turns a full circle in its own length.

Polo A stick and ball game on horseback for teams of four players. Polo probably originated in Persia, though it was played all over the east, particularly in China and India. It came to Britain from India in the mid-nineteenth century and spread from there to the USA, the Commonwealth and Argentina. The Argentine is now the leading polo nation in the world, with some 3,000 players. The USA has 1,000 and the UK 500 active.

Polocrosse A game based on polo and lacrosse, particularly popular in Australia. It is less exclusive than polo because of its relative cheapness.

Rig A male horse with one or both testicles retained in the abdomen. An operation can enable them or it to descend; after this, the animal should be gelded, as the tendency can be hereditary.

Sickle Hocks A conformational fault. Seen broadside-on, the hocks are too concave – literally shaped like a sickle.

Sidebones Ossification of the lateral cartilages of the pedal bone, these are in the main confined to the forefeet of cart horses. Ringbone is an inflammatory growth of bone, or extosis, connected with the pastern, high ringbone involving the lower end of the first phalanges and low ringbone, involving the lower end of the pedal bone. Both cause lameness and can result in fusion of the pastern and pedal joints. The disease is found among show jumpers.

Side Reins Part of breaking equipment. They are attached to the horse from the bit to the roller or saddle.

Snaffle The simplest form of bit and the one in most frequent use. It consists of a straight or jointed mouthpiece and a ring at either end for the reins.

Spavin A bony enlargement on the lower inner aspect of the hock joint, caused by a periostitis.

Speedy Cut A wound inside the leg, around the knee or cannon bone, caused by the shoe of the opposite foot.

Splints Inflammatory bony outgrowths involving the small metacarpal or metatarsal or 'splint' bones. They seldom cause lameness when formed, or after six years of age.

Sprained Tendons Sprains usually affect

the flexor or back tendons of horses used for fast work, such as racehorses or hunters. When the sprain is really serious, the horse is said to have broken down. Sprain of the suspensory ligament comes under the same heading.

The degree of pain and swelling depends on the number of tendon fibres which are ruptured. In all cases, a long period of rest is necessary.

Strangles An acute infectious disease of the lymph glands in the intermandibular cavity. Symptoms are fever, nasal discharge and abscesses, which may also develop in other glands about the head.

Surcingle A webbing band with straps and buckles which passes round the horse's girth. It is used to hold rugs in place.

Temperature The normal temperature for a horse is 100.5°F (38°C). It is taken by inserting a thermometer into the rectum, taking care to position it to one side to obtain an accurate reading.

Tetanus One of the chief killers of unprotected horses. Infection usually comes from bacterial penetration of a puncture wound. In advanced cases, the horse stands rigid, with head and neck outstretched and tail extended. The limbs are fixed, while the jaws become locked, making normal eating and drinking virtually impossible. The protrusion of the third eyelid is an early and significant symptom

Prevention is all important, for cures are rare. Strict sanitary attention to all wounds, especially punctures and those in the region of the feet, is essential. So, too, are regular injections of anti-tetanus toxin and regular booster doses.

Thoroughpin This can be either articular (a chronic distension of the capsule of the hock joint, at the side and back, which usually is accompanied by bog spavin), or tendinous. This is made manifest by a fluctuating swelling on either side of the tendon just above the point of the hock.

Thrush A evil-smelling infection of the frog of the foot. It is caused by unhygenic stable conditions.

Treble Three fences in such close alignment that they are related and have to be jumped as a combination.

Triple bar One staircase-type fence of three bars of progressive height.

Turn on the forehand In the turn on the forehand, the hind legs move around the stationary forelegs. In the turn on the haunches, the forelegs move around the stationary hind legs. Both movements are required schooling for the horse.

Weaving A stable vice, caused by boredom. A weaving horse rocks from side to side and loses condition through not getting adequate rest.

Windgalls Synovial distensions in the region of the fetlock joint. They are usually caused by working young horses too much on hard going.

Windsucking A stable vice, usually connected with CRIB-BITING and caused by boredom. The horse grips the edge of the manger in its teeth, arches the neck, and gulps in great draughts of air.

Xenophon (born c. 430 BC) A Greek cavalry officer and historian, born in Athens. He achieved fame among horsemen for his essays on horsemanship and hunting, the first to have been written. He is still read on the former subject, a translation from the original Greek having been published as relatively recently as 1893 under the title *The Art of Horsemanship*.

Equestrian centres
Since the Second World War, the horse world has become extremely international, at least at the competitive level. This is partly due to the proliferation of international equestrian events at all levels and the increasing ease of travel – even with horses. it is also by no means unusual for riders and instructors to take and give courses in countries other than their own.

Australia and New Zealand
Though Australia and New Zealand are both major forces in the international horse world, they have been handicapped until fairly recently by the difficulties of distance and transport. Many riders from both nations, however, have gained international distinction. The Australian Three-Day Event team was led to victory in the Rome Olympics of 1960 by their Viennese trainer, Franz Maininger, while Australia's top eventer, Bill Roycroft, has also won at Badminton as well; his sons too, now represent Australia internationally.

In Australia, most state capitals hold shows, the most important of which are the Royal Shows at Sydney, Brisbane, Adelaide, Melbourne, Perth and Launceston. Dressage and eventing are both extremely popular – the Gawler Three-Day Event is considered to be one of the world's toughest.

Austria
The Spanish Riding School of Vienna – the home of Classical dressage – has always taken foreign pupils, most of whom stay for at least a year. The fees are high (in 1972, when the school celebrated its four hundredth anniversary, they were £2,400 a year) and the competition fierce. Only four candidates a year are accepted, one of the conditions being a recommendation from the national equestrian federation involved.

The basic principles of the school were laid down in the middle of the nineteenth century and are still adhered to today. They derive from the belief that the art of riding must never be confined to Haute Ecole alone, but must comprise all types. The routine is a tough one. The pupils, who enter the school at eighteen, come from every walk of life. They live in, start riding at 7 am, and continue until 12.30. After three or four years, they are given a young horse to train under supervision. Each fully-fledged rider has five horses under him.

The best working stallions – the famous Lipizzaners – go back to the stud at Piber when they are trained at the age of ten or twelve; the others go on working and may live to thirty. There are fifty-eight in the school and 120 at the stud, including forty mares. The daily training sessions are open to the public and the school gives bi-weekly performances on Sunday mornings and Wednesday evenings.

France
Saumur's Cadre Noir, so-called because of their black uniforms, can be likened a little to the Spanish School because they both wear old-fashioned costume, but there the similarity ends. Founded in 1814, Saumur is the French cavalry school, preserving the traditions of equitation and, at the same time, training would-be pupils. Ten-month courses are run for both officers and NCOs.

An *ecuyer*'s (riding master's) day is thus very full. He starts at dawn, training steeplechasers or show jumpers. He then spends two or four hours working with his human pupils, and the same period of time working with his liberty jumper, which he must train completely. In the evening, he attends a technical, non-equestrian conference with his colleagues. The Marquis d'Orgeix and Commandant Pierre Durand are the chief instructors.

France also has the *Centre National des Sports Equestres* at Fontainebleau as a training centre for international competitors. The personnel consists of ten officers, ten NCOs, ninety grooms and 150 horses.

West Germany
The chief centre for both show jumping and dressage in West Germany is the small market town of Warendorf, near Munster, in Westphalia. There, the equestrian facilities include a depot for more than 200 stallions and a riding school, where the quintuple Olympic gold medallist Hans Günther Winkler holds courses in show jumping and

Willi Schultheiss teaches dressage.

Perhaps the most popular dressage trainer at the moment, however, is Herbert Reibaum, who can count Britain's double European three-day event champion, Lucinda Prior-Palmer, among his pupils. Once a pupil of the famous Bubi Gunther, he now works with the Olympic rider Karen Schluter. Another prominent trainer is Herr Theoderescu, who defected from Romania to West Germany. He and his wife have their own school and ride internationally for their adopted country. In Karlsruhe in the south, at the *Reinstitut von Neindorff*, dressage is taught as an art, with classical music as a continuous background.

West Germany's only three-day event trainer of any repute is Ottomar Pohlman, who has a school near Munich. It is in the cross-country section of this sport that the West Germans are weakest, though they dominate world dressage and show jumping.

Great Britain

The National Equestrian Centre at Stoneleigh in Warwickshire imports trainers such as Ernst Bachinger of the Spanish Riding School to give courses, and Britain's standard of dressage riding has greatly improved since his first course in 1977. But for an all-round trainer it would be very hard to beat Bertie Hill, who trains at his North Devon home. His most distinguished pupil is Captain Mark Phillips.

Other notable British instructors include Sylvia Stanier and Richard Stillwell, who can number Richard Meade and Lucinda Prior-Palmer among his products. Swedish-born Lars Sederholm, the trainer of Chris Collins, attracts a great number of overseas pupils. Alison Oliver trains Princess Anne in Berkshire. Dressage is the speciality of her partner, David Hunt, of Robert Hall, of Franz Rochawansky, formerly at the Spanish School, and of John Lassiter, who also trained in Vienna. Captain Eddie Goldman, a Swiss, is old but brilliant.

Iran

Iran's riders are trained at home by Major Paul Weier, late of the Swiss Army and jumping team, who hold courses in Teheran six times a year. In Europe, they are trained in Ireland by Iris Kellett, the former Ladies European Champion who trained Eddie Macken.

Sweden

Pupils from the USA are regularly sent to the Cavalry School at Stromsholm, established in 1868. The system of training is basically German in concept, but also owes a good deal to Italian influence.

The United States

Two of the greatest trainers in the world teach in the USA. The Hungarian-born Bertalan de Nemethy has coached the US show-jumping team since 1955, turning it into a world-famous and extremely successful body, whose riders are distinguished for their style. He trains at Gladstone, New Jersey, where promising riders go as the result of nationwide screening trials.

Jack le Goff, the US event trainer, is a Frenchman. A member of the Cadre Noir, he rode with the French Olympic team in Rome and Tokyo and trained Guyon to win an Olympic gold medal in 1968. He went to the USA in 1972 to train at Hamilton, Massachusetts; two years later, the US team won the team and individual world championships at Burghley and in 1976 they won both titles at the Montreal Olympic Games.

Horse Societies Of The World

The International Equestrian Federation (Fédération Equestre Internationale) Avenue Hamoir 38, 1180 Brussels, Belgium.

National Equestrian Federations (affiliated to the F.E.I.)

Algerian Equestrian Federation *(Fédération Algerienne des Sports Equestres), Rue Didouche Mourad 21, Algiers*

American Horse Shows Assocciation, *527 Madison Avenue, New York, N.Y. 10022*

Argentine Equestrian Federation *(Federacion Ecuestre Argentina), Rodriquez Pena 1934, Planta Baja, Buenos Aires*

Austrian Equestrian Federation *(Osterreichische Campagnereiter Gesellschaft), Haus des Sports, Prinz Eugenstrasse 12, Vienna IV*

Belgian Equestrian Federation *(Federation Royale Belge des Sports Equestres), Avenue Hamoir 38, 1180 Brussels*

Bolivian Equestrian Federation *(Federacionliviana des Deportes Ecuestres), Casilla 329, La Paz*

Brazilian Equestrian Federation *(Confederacao Brasileira de Hipismo), Rua Sete de Setembre 81, Sala 302, Rio de Janeiro*

British Equestrian Federation, The, *(National Equestrian Federation), Stoneleigh, Kenilworth, Warwickshire*

Bulgarian Equestrian Federation *(Comite Supreme de Culture Physique et des Sports), Boulevard Tolbukhin 18, Sofia*

Canadian Equestrian Federation *57, Bloor Street West, Toronto, Ontario*

Chilean Equestrian Federation *(Federacion Nacional de Deportes Ecuestres), Calle compania 1630, Santiago de Chile*

Colombian Equestrian Federation *(Association Colombienne des Sports Equestres), Calle 13 no. 8–39, Oficina 609, Bogota*

Cuban Equestrian Federation *(Federacion Ecuestre Cubana), Comite Olimpico Cubana, Hotel Habana Libre, Havana*

Czechoslovak Equestrian Federation *(Fédération Equestre Tchecoslovaque), Na Porici 12, Prague 11*

Danish Equestrian Federation *(Dansk Rideforbund), Vestre Paradisvej 51, Holte*

Ecuadorian Equestrian Federation *(Federacion Ecuatoriana de Deportes Ecuestres), Apartado 410, Quito*

Equestrian Federation of Australia, *Royal Show Grounds, Epsom Road, Ascot Vale 2*

Finnish Equestrian Federation *(Suomen Ratsastajainliitto), Paasitie 9 B 2, Helsinki 83*

French Equestrian Federation *(Fédération Francaise des Sports Equestres), Faubourg St. Honore 164, 75 Paris VIIIe*

German Democratic Republican Federation *(Deutsche Pferdesport Verband der Deutschen Demokratischen Republik), Nationale Reiterliche Vereinigung, Storkowerstrasse 118, Berlin 1055*

German Federal Republican Federation *(Deutsche Reiterliche Vereinigung), Adenaurallee 174, 53 Bonn*

Greek Equestrian Federation *(Association Hellenique d'Athletisme Amateur), Avenue Panepistimioy 25, Athens*

Guatemalan Equestrian Federation *(Federacion de Ecuestre de Guatemala), Apartado Postal 1525, Guatemala C.A.*

Hungarian Equestrian Federation *(Fédération Hongroise d'Equitation), Holda Utca 1, Budapest V*

Iranian (Persian) Equestrian Federation, *Iranian Olympic Committee, Kakke Verzesh, Teheran*

Irish Equestrian Federation, *Ball's Bridge, Dublin*

The Israeli Horse Society, *P.O. Box 14111, Tel Aviv*

Italian Equestrian Federation *(Federazione Italiana Sport Equestri), Palazzo delle Federazioni, Viale Tiziano 70, Roma*

Japanese Equestrian Federation *(Fédération Equestre Japonaise), Kanda Surugadai 4–6, Chiyoda 6 ku, Tokyo*

Korean Equestrian Federation, *19 Mukyo-Dong, K.A.A.A. Building, Room 611, Seoul*

Lebanese Equestrian Federation *(Fédération Libanaise des Sports Equestres), B.P. 5035, Beirut*

Libyan Equestrian Federation *(Fédération Libyenne Equestre), Maidan Abi Setta, P.O. Box 4507, Tripoli*

Luxembourg Equestrian Federation

(Fédération Luxembourgeoise des Sports
Equestres), Route de Thionville, 90,
Luxembourg

Mexican Equestrian Federation (Federacion
Ecuestre Mexicana), Insurgentes Sur no. 222
Desp. 405, Mexico 7 D.F.

Moroccan Equestrian Federation (Fédération
Royale Marocaine des Sports Equestres, Garde
Royale, Rabat,

Dutch Equestrian Federation (Nederlandse
Hippische Sportbond, Waalsdorperlaan 29a,
Wassenaar (Post Den Haag)

New Zealand Horse Society, The, P.O. Box
13, Hastings

Norwegian Equestrian Federation (Norges
Rytterforbund), Postboks 204 L, Oslo

Peruvian Equestrian Federation (Federacion
Peruana de Deportes Ecuestres), Estadio
Nacional, Puerta 29, Lima

Polish Equestrian Federation (Polski Zwiazek
Jecdziecki), Sienkiewicza 12, Warsaw

Portuguese Equestrian Federation (Federacao
Equestre Portuguesa), Rua de San Pedro de
Alcantara 79, Lisbon 2

Puerto Rican Equestrian Federation
(Federacion Puertorriquena de Deportes
Ecuestres), Apartado de Correos 4959, San
Juan

Rhodesian Horse Society, The, P.O. Box
2415, Salisbury

Romanian Equestrian Federation (Federatia
Romina de Calarie), Vasile Conta 16,
Bucharest

Russian Equestrian Federation (Fédération
Equestre d'U.R.S.S.), Skaternyi Pereulok 4,
Moscow

Senegalese Equestrian Federation (Fédération
Senegalaise des Sports Equestres), Avenue
William Ponty 16, Dakar

South African National Equestrian
Federation, 17 Tulip Avenue, Sunridge Park,
Port Elizabeth

Spanish Equestrian Federation (Federacion
Nacional Hipica), Montesquinza 8, Madrid 4

Swedish Equestrian Federation (Svenska
Ridsportens Centralforbund), Ostermalmsgatan
80, Stockholm 0

Swiss Equestrian Federation (Fédération
Suisse des Sports Equestres), Comite Central:
Bahnhofstrasse 36, Zurich Section Concours
Hippiques: Blankweg 70 3072 Ostermundigen

Tunisian Equestrian Federation (Fédération
Tunisienne de Tir et d'Equitation), Stand
National de Tir El Ouardia, Sidi Belhassen,
Tunis

Turkish Equestrian Federation (Fédération
Equestre Turque), Ucyol-Mazlak, Istanbul

United Arab Republican Equestrian
Federation (Fédération Equestre de la
Republique Arabe Unie), 13 Sharia Kasr-el-
Nil, Cairo

Uruguayan Equestrian Federation (Federacion
Uruguaya de Deportes Ecuestres), Avenida

Agraciada 1546, Montevideo

Venezuelan Equestrian Federation
(Federacion Venezolana de Deportes Ecuestres),
Apartado 3588, Caracas

Yugoslavian Equestrian Federation
(Fédération Equestre Yougoslave), 27 General
Zdanov Street, Belgrade

SOCIETIES IN GREAT BRITAIN

Arab Horse Society, Lieutenant-Colonel J. A.
Denney, Sackville Lodge, Lye Green,
Crowborough, Sussex

British Driving Society, Mrs. P. Candler,
10 Marley Avenue, New Milton, Hampshire

British Field Sports Society, 26 Caxton Street,
London, S.W. 1

British Equine Veterinary Association,
Paddock House, Cold Overton, Oakham, Leics.

British Horse Society, National Equestrian
Centre, Stoneleigh, Kenilworth, Warwickshire

British Show Hack and Cob Society,
Stoneleigh, Kenilworth, Warwickshire

British Show Jumping Association,
Stoneleigh, Kenilworth, Warwickshire

British Show Pony Society, Captain R.
Grellis, Smale Farm, Wisborough Green,
Sussex

Cleveland Bay Horse Society, 20 Castlegate,
York

Hackney Horse Society, 35 Belgrave Square,
London, S.W. 1

Hunters' Improvement and National Light
Horse Breeding Society, 8 Market Square,
Westerham, Kent

Hurlingham Polo Association, Brig. J. R. C.
Gannon, C.B.E., M.V.O., 204 Idol Lane,
London EC3

Jockey Club, Newmarket, Suffolk, and
42 Portman Square, London, W. 1

Masters of Foxhounds Association and Hunt
Servants' Benefit Society, Col. J. E. S.
Chamberlayne, The Elms, Chipping Norton,
Oxfordshire

National Pony Society, B. A. Roberts,
7 Cross and Pillory Lane, Alton, Hampshire

Ponies of Britain, Mrs. Glenda Spooner,
Brookside Farm, Ascot, Berkshire

Racehorse Breeders Association, Col. F. M.
Beale, 26 Charing Cross Road, London

Thoroughbred Breeders' Association,
26 Bloomsbury Way, London, W.C. 1

Weatherby & Sons, 41 Portman Square,
London W. 1

THE U.S.A.

American Dressage Institue, Daniels Road,
Saratoga Springs, New York

American Hackney Horse Society,
527 Madison Avenue, New York, N.Y.

American Horse Council, 1776 K Street
NW, Washington, DC 20006

American Horse Shows Association, 527
Madison Avenue, New York, N.Y. 10022

American Masters of Foxhounds
Association, 112 Water Street, Boston,
Massachusetts

American Morgan Horse Association, P.O.
Box 17157, West Hartford, Connecticutt
06117

American Quarter Horse Association, P.O.
Box 200, Amarillo, Texas 79105

American Saddle Horse Breeders'
Association, 929 South Fourth Street,
Louisville, Kentucky

American Veterinary Medical Association,
600 South Michigan Avenue, Chicago, Illinois

Arabian Horse Registry of America,
1, Executive Park, 7801 Belleview Avenue,
Englewood, Colorado

The Jockey Club, 300 Park Avenue, New
York City, N.Y., 10022

Morven Park International Equestrian
Institute, Route 2, Box 8, Leeburg, Virginia,
22075

National Cutting Horse Association, 806
First National Bank Building, Midland, Texas
79701

National Steeplechase and Hunt
Association, 6407 Wilson Boulevard,
Arlington, Virginia 22205

U.S. Trotting Association (Standardbred),
750 Michigan Avenue, Columbus, Ohio 43215

SOUTH AFRICA

Thoroughbred Breeders' Association, P.O.
Box 7679, Johannesburg 2000

South African Veterinary Association, P.O.
Box 2460, Pretoria 0001

Jockey Club of South Africa, P.O. Box 3409,
Johannesburg 2000

South African National Equestrian
Federation, 17 Tulip Avenue, Sunridge Park,
Port Elizabeth

AUSTRALIA

Australian Stock Horse Society, P.O. Box
288, Scone, NSW 2337

South Australian Bloodhorse Breeders
Association, Morphettville, S.A. 5043

Light Horse Breeders Association, Mrs. M.
Potts, Revlis Park, Gawler Ricer, S.A. 5118

Equestrian Federation of Australia, Royal
Show Grounds, Epsom Road, Ascot Vale 2,
Victoria 3032

Adelaide Polo Club, 34 Pirie Street, Adelaide,
S.A. 5000

Adelaide Hunt Club, Main Road, Cherry
Gardens, S.A. 5157

Trail Riding Club, B. Virgo Esq., HQ., South
Australian Police Force

Horse Riding Clubs Association, Miss D.
Mansom, 5 Rose Terrace, Wayville, S.A. 5034

Index

Page numbers in italic
refer to illustrations

Acknowledgements

15 Bruce Macfadden. 16 Snark International, Paris. 17 Michael Holford (British Library). 18 Ronald Sheridan; Michael Holford. 19 Michael Holford (B.L.). 20 Ronald Sheridan. 21 Michael Holford. 22 Michael Holford (Victoria and Albert Museum, London). 23 Scala, Florence. 24 Snark International; Lady Butler, Leeds City Art Galleries. 25 National Army Museum, London. 26 The Mansell Collection, London; Walter Rawlings (West Point Museum). 27 Peter Newark's Western Americana, Brentwood. 28 Imperial War Museum, London; Novosti Press Agency. 29 The Mansell Collection. 30 Bodleian Library, Oxford (MS Bodley 264 f.44); Michael Holford (B.L.). 32 Mansell 33 Photograph by courtesy of British Waterways Board. 34 Punch Publications Ltd.; Western Americana. 37 Western Americana; National Coal Board. 38 Walter Rawlings; Colour Library International; U.S. Travel Service. 39 Elisabeth Weiland; Picturepoint Ltd., London; Colour Library International. 40 Roger Pring; Elisabeth Weiland. 41 Western Americana. 42 Michael Holford (B.L.); Scala (Taranto Museum). 44 Michael Holford (B.L.). 45 Historical Picture Service, Brentwood; Mander and Mitchenson. 46 Mary Evans Picture Library; Royal Borough of Kingston-upon-Thames Central Library, Museum and Art Gallery. 47 Western Americana. 48 Michael Holford (V & A); Snark (Sawebrück – Musie Saarland). 51 Walter Rawlings; National Film Archive, from the MGM release National Velvet © 1944 Loew's Incorporated. Copyright renewed 1971 by Metro-Goldwyn-Mayer Inc., California; City of Manchester Art Galleries. 94 John Wyand. 95 John Wyand. 99 Colin Maher. 100 Colin Maher. 101 Colin Maher. 102 Colour Library International; Bruce Coleman Ltd. 104 Picturepoint Ltd. 105 Picturepoint Ltd. 107 U.S. Travel Service. 108 Jay Swallow; Leslie Lane. 109 Leslie Lane. 110 Jay Swallow; Sally Anne Thompson. 111 Jay Swallow. 112 Jay Swallow. 113 Jay Swallow; E. D. Lacey. 114 Jay Swallow. 115 Jay Swallow. 116 Leslie Lane; Jay Swallow. 117 Jay Swallow. 127 Leslie Lane. 130 Elisabeth Weiland. 133 Ardea Photographics. 138 John Wyand. 139 John Wyand. 142 Michael Busselle. 144 Michael Busselle. 145 David Mallott. 148 Michael Busselle. 150 Sally Anne Thompson. 157 Michael Busselle. 161 John Wyand. 162 Sally Anne Thompson. 163 Sally Anne Thompson. 164 John Wyand; Gerry Cranham. 165 F. M. Bordis/Zefa. 168 Elisabeth Weiland. 169 Gerry Cranham; Elisabeth Weiland; Picturepoint Ltd.; Leo Mason. 170 Kit Houghton; Elisabeth Weiland; Homer Sykes. 171 Sally Anne Thompson; Paolo Koch; E. D. Lacey; Elisabeth Weiland. 172 Sally Anne Thompson; Kit Houghton; Gerry Cranham; Elisabeth Weiland. 173 Elisabeth Weiland; Gerry Cranham. 174 U.S. Travel Service. 175 Colour Library International; Sally Anne Thompson; U.S. Travel Service. 176 Elisabeth Weiland; Walter Rawlings; Picturepoint Ltd. 177 Roger B. Gilroy; Elisabeth Weiland. 178 Ronald Sheridan. 179 Mary Evans Picture Library. 180 John Wyand; Gerry Cranham. 181 John Wyand; Roger Pring. 184 Stockphotos International; Revers-Windauer/Zefa; Tony Duffy. 185 Picturepoint Ltd.; Elisabeth Weiland. 186 U.S. Travel Service. 187 Colour Library International; Elisabeth Weiland. 188 Keystone Press Agency Ltd.; Syndication International Ltd. 189 Sally Anne Thompson; Syndication International Ltd., Mary Evans (photo: J. F. Herring). 190 W. W. Rouch & Co.; Syndication International Ltd. 191 Paul Popper Ltd.; Keystone Press Agency Ltd. 192 Syndication International Ltd. 193 W. W. Rouch & Co.; Paul Popper Ltd.; S & G Press Agency. 194 Don Morley/All Sport; Keystone Press Agency Ltd.; W. W. Rouch & Co. 195 S & G Press Agency; W. W. Rouch & Co.; Keystone Press Agency Ltd. 196 Syndication International Ltd.; W. W. Rouch & Co. 197 Syndication International Ltd.; Paul Popper Ltd.; W. W. Rouch & Co.